THE LITERATURE

OF THE

FRENCH RENAISSANCE

T0370892

THE LITERATURE

OF THE

FRENCH RENAISSANCE

BY

ARTHUR TILLEY, M.A.

FELLOW AND LECTURER OF KING'S COLLEGE, CAMBRIDGE

VOLUME I

CAMBRIDGE:

AT THE UNIVERSITY PRESS

1904

CAMBRIDGE
UNIVERSITY PRESS

University Printing House, Cambridge CB2 8BS, United Kingdom

Cambridge University Press is part of the University of Cambridge.

It furthers the University's mission by disseminating knowledge in the pursuit of education, learning and research at the highest international levels of excellence.

www.cambridge.org
Information on this title: www.cambridge.org/9781107505513

© Cambridge University Press 1904

First published 1904
First paperback edition 2015

A catalogue record for this publication is available from the British Library

ISBN 978-1-107-50551-3 Paperback

PREFACE

IN 1885 I published as a prologue to a larger work an *Introductory Essay*[1], which purported to give a brief summary of the condition of learning and literature in France at the close of the Middle Ages, and to trace the first workings of the Renaissance spirit down to the opening of the reign of Francis I. The First Part of the main history was nearly completed by the beginning of 1890, when ill-health added to the claims of other work compelled me practically to lay it aside. It was not until five years ago that I was able to take it up again in more than a desultory fashion.

This enforced delay has been to my advantage, for it has enabled me to profit by numerous works which have appeared in the last fifteen years. When I first began to study the subject, the only complete account of it was the admirable summary by Darmesteter and Hatzfeld, first published in 1878[2]. I could not have wished for a better guide at the outset. There was also the well-known *Tableau* of Sainte-Beuve[3] dealing with the poetry and drama, and an excellent little book of extracts, with notices of all the principal writers, by E. Réaume[4]. In 1889 Professor Birch-Hirschfeld,

---

[1] *The Literature of the French Renaissance—an Introductory Essay.* Cambridge, 1885.

[2] A. Darmesteter and A. Hatzfeld, *Le seizième siècle en France*, 1878; 6th ed. 1895.

[3] C.-A. Sainte-Beuve, *Tableau historique et critique de la poésie française et du théâtre français au xvie siècle*, 2 vols. 1828; 2 vols. 1876.

[4] E. Réaume, *Morceaux choisis des prosateurs et poëtes français du xvie siècle*, 1876.

of Leipsic, published the first instalment of a history of modern French Literature[1] embracing the reigns of Louis XII and Francis I. It is characterised by thoroughness and sound judgment, and merits a more attractive form than the publisher has given to it. My own account of the reign of Francis I was almost finished when it appeared, but I owe something to its full and accurate bibliography. In 1897 appeared the sixteenth century volume (III) of the History of the French Language and Literature published under the direction of the late L. Petit de Julleville. It is on the whole disappointing. The high level of some of the chapters, such as those of M. Bonnefon on Montaigne and the other moralists, of M. Rigal on the Renaissance Drama, and of M. Brunot on the language is by no means maintained throughout. A common fault is the neglect of minor writers. For instance, in the late M. Marty-Laveaux's chapter on Rabelais and *Les Conteurs*, though Rabelais receives the adequate treatment that might be expected from a successful editor of his works, Margaret of Navarre is dismissed with three pages, and Des Periers with one. A year later, in 1898, Professor Morf published a small volume on the same period, the first part of a history of modern French Literature[2]. Its condensed treatment makes it a handbook rather than a short history, but the author has overcome the difficulty imposed upon him by his method as well as can be expected. There can be no question as to the thoroughness and accuracy of his knowledge. To the serious student the most valuable part of the book is its careful bibliography, in which special attention is paid to the most recent literature, and to which I cordially acknowledge my obligations. Other recent works of a more general character are M. Faguet's *Seizième siècle*, 1894, a collection of essays on the principal writers of the sixteenth century, and the

---

[1] A. Birch-Hirschfeld, *Geschichte der französischen Litteratur seit Anfang des xvi Jahrhunderts…Erstes Buch, Das Zeitalter Ludwig's XII und Franz's I.* Stuttgart, 1889.

[2] H. Morf, *Geschichte der neueren französischen Litteratur (xvi–xix Jahrhundert). Erstes Buch: das Zeitalter der Renaissance.* Strasburg, 1898.

newly appeared First Part, embracing the reign of Francis I,
of M. Brunetière's history of modern French Literature[1].
I cannot always accept M. Brunetière's views, but he has
often helped me to state my own more clearly. With his
evolutionist method I have the strongest sympathy.
But a work which pretends to independent treatment
naturally owes less to writers of general histories than to
those who have edited or elucidated particular authors.
Recent years have seen the completion of Marty-Laveaux's
edition of Rabelais, of MM. Courbet and Royer's edition of
Montaigne, and of MM. Réaume and de Caussade's edition of
D'Aubigné. An edition of the *Histoire Universelle*, omitted
by the last editors, has been completed by the late Baron de
Ruble, and one of Brantôme's works by M. Lalanne. Bertaut
has been edited by M. Chenevière, and Montchrestien by
L. Petit de Julleville. The publication of the *Dernières
poésies* of Margaret of Navarre by M. Abel Lefranc, if it has
not added to her literary reputation, has thrown new light
on her character and her religious opinions. M. Bonnefon's
Montaigne et ses amis, M. Hauser's *La Noue*, M. Vianey's
Regnier, and M. Chamard's *Joachim du Bellay* are all of the
highest importance. Special mention also must be made of
M. Laumonier's elaborate work on the text of Ronsard, of
M. Séché's services to Joachim du Bellay, and of M. Rigal's
noteworthy studies in the history of the Renaissance drama.
M. Picot and M. Vianey on the French side of the Alps and
Professor Flamini and Signor Toldo on the Italian have
carried on fruitful and important researches in the relations
between France and Italy. It will soon be possible to write
that history of Italianism in France for which M. Brunetière
has so long called in vain. Much of this special work, to
which I am under the highest obligation, has naturally
appeared in periodicals, especially in the *Revue d'histoire
littéraire de la France*, the more recently established *Revue
de la Renaissance*, and the *Revue des Études Rabelaisiennes*,
which made an excellent start in 1903 under the editorship

---

[1] F. Brunetière, *Histoire de la littérature française classique. Première partie:
Le Mouvement de la Renaissance.*

of M. Lefranc. All these are of the first importance for the study of the Renaissance period.

Besides editions, monographs, and special studies an important source of information for the historian of literature is bibliography. The chief guide in this department is Brunet, but Brunet, like all the older bibliographers, makes no attempt to supply the absence of a date on the title-page or in the imprint of a book, and the supplement to Brunet was published nearly a quarter of a century ago. Of more recent sources of bibliographical information by far the most important for the Renaissance literature is M. Picot's elaborate and scholarly catalogue of the library formed by the late Baron James de Rothschild. In acknowledging my debt to it I must renew my thanks to M. Picot personally for shewing me some of the treasures of the library. I have also consulted with profit some of the sale-catalogues of private libraries which have been dispersed since the publication of the supplement to Brunet, and I have learnt not a little from the periodical catalogues of the well-known bibliographer, M. Claudin. I have visited a good many European libraries —the chief omissions are, I think, Munich and Turin—and have examined for myself most of the early editions which raise any point of interest or difficulty, including of course all those of which I have given a collation. The Bibliographies which I have appended to the chapters and which are in part the result of these investigations will, I hope, prove useful to students and especially to any successor who may work in the same field. In the list of books "to be consulted" my object has been to include only those that have any real utility ; I have included none with which I am not personally acquainted. I shall be sincerely grateful for corrections from those who have made a special study of particular authors.

In this and in other respects I am fully conscious of the disadvantages under which a writer lies who treats of the literature of a country to which he is a stranger. He has to work at a distance from his natural base, he never acquires that intimate knowledge of the lie of the land which a native possesses almost instinctively, and above all he misses that living intercourse with other workers in the same field the place of which no amount of reading can supply. If in points of accurate scholarship my book is not more defective than it is, this is in a large measure due to the care with which my friends, Mr E. G. W. Braunholtz, University Reader in Romance, and the Rev. H. F. Stewart, Chaplain of Trinity College, have between them read the whole of the proofs. I here tender them my warmest thanks. My thanks are also due to Professor Bury for kindly reading the proof of chapter XXIV, to Mr Charles Sayle of St John's College for help readily given in bibliographical matters, to many librarians from M. Léopold Delisle downwards for most courteous assistance, and lastly but not least to the Syndics of the University Press for undertaking the publication of my book, and to the Reader and other members of the staff for the care with which they have executed the task.

A. T.

CHURCH STRETTON.
August 23, 1904.

PRINCIPAL PERIODICALS REFERRED TO

Archiv für neueren Spr. und Litt. or *Archiv = Archiv für das Studium der neueren Sprachen und Litteraturen,* edd. A. Tobler und A. Brandt, 1846 ff. Published quarterly.

Bull. du Bib. = Bulletin du Bibliophile, 1834 ff. Monthly.

Bull. prot. franç. = Bulletin de la Société de l'Histoire du protestantisme français, ed. N. Weiss, 1833 ff. Every two months.

Journal des Savants, 1816 ff. Monthly.

Rev. des deux mondes, 1829 ff. Twice a month.

Rev. des Études Rab. = Revue des Études Rabelaisiennes, 1903 ff. Quarterly.

Rev. d'hist. litt. = Revue d'histoire littéraire de la France. Quarterly.

Rev. de la Ren. = Revue de la Renaissance, ed. L. Séché, 1901 ff. At irregular intervals.

Rev. historique, 1876 ff. Every two months.

Zeitschr. für franz. Spr. = Zeitschrift für französische Sprache und Litteratur, ed. D. Behrens, Berlin, 1879 ff. Quarterly (twice a year for articles, and twice for reviews).

OTHER WORKS OF REFERENCE

Anc. poés. franç. = Anciennes poésies françaises or *Recueil de poés. franç. des xve et xvie siècles,* edd. A. de Montaiglon and J. de Rothschild, 13 vols. 1855–1878 (*Bib. Elzévir.*).

Birch-Hirschfeld = A. Birch-Hirschfeld, *Geschichte der französischen Litteratur seit Anfang des xvi Jahrhunderts.* I. *Das Zeitalter der Renaissance. Erstes Buch, Das Zeitalter Ludwig's XII und Franz's I.* Stuttgart, 1889.

Darmesteter and Hatzfeld = A. Darmesteter et A. Hatzfeld, *Le seizième Siècle en France,* 1878; 6th ed. 1895.

Herminjard, *Corr. des réformateurs* = A. L. Herminjard, *Correspondance des réformateurs dans les pays de langue française,* 9 vols., Geneva and Paris, 1866–1897.

Le Petit = J. le Petit, *Bibliographie des principales éditions originales d'écrivains français du xv⁰ au xviii⁰ siècle*, 1888.

Morf = H. Morf, *Geschichte der neueren französischen Litteratur (xvi–xix Jahrhundert). Erstes Buch: das Zeitalter der Renaissance.* Strasburg, 1898.

Niceron, *Mémoires* = J.-P. Niceron, *Mémoires pour servir à l'histoire des hommes illustres dans la république des lettres*, 43 vols. 1729–1745. (See vol. II, Appendix G.)

Pasquier, *Recherches* = Estienne Pasquier, *Les Recherches de la France*, ed. André Duchesne, 3 vols. 1619.

Petit de Julleville = *Histoire de la langue et de la littérature françaises des origines à* 1900, *publiée sous la direction de L. Petit de Julleville.* III. Seizième siècle, 1897.

Picot = E. Picot, *Catalogue des livres composant la bibliothèque de feu M. le baron James de Rothschild*, 3 vols. 1887–1893.

Sainte-Beuve, *Tableau historique et critique de la poésie française et du théâtre français au xvi⁰ siècle, suivi des œuvres choisies de P. de Ronsard*, 2 vols. 1828; 2nd ed. 1838; new ed. in one vol. 1843 with the selection from Ronsard omitted, and with the addition of a second part containing eight separate studies, of which seven relate to the 16th century; 2 vols. 1876.

N.B.—In the above lists and in the Bibliographies at the end of the chapters the place of publication is omitted in the case of English books published in London and of French books published at Paris.

SALE CATALOGUES

J.-L.-A. Coste	Paris and Lyons	1854
N. Yemeniz	Paris	1867
Sunderland Library	London	1881
Baron Seillière	,,	1887
R. S. Turner	,,	1888
Baron A. de Ruble	Paris	1899

CONTENTS

PART I (1525–1550)

MAROT AND RABELAIS

CHAPTER I

FRANCIS I AND HIS COURT

CHAPTER II

HUMANISM

CHAPTER III

THE MOULDING OF THE LANGUAGE

1. *Orthography and Grammar*

2. *Translations from the Greek and Latin*

3. *Translations from the Italian and Spanish*

CHAPTER V

THE SCHOOL OF MAROT

CHAPTER VI

MARGARET OF NAVARRE

1. *The Mediæval Story-books*

2. *The Heptameron*

CHAPTER VII

DES PERIERS

CHAPTER VIII

THE PRECURSORS OF THE PLEIAD

1. *The School of Lyons*

PART II (1550–1580)

THE PLEIAD

CHAPTER XIV

VALOIS AND MEDICI

CHAPTER XV

SCHOLARS AND ANTIQUARIES

1. *Amyot*

CHAPTER XVI

RONSARD AND DU BELLAY

CORRIGENDA

p. 7, l. 8.   *For* Baif *read* Baïf.

p. 17, l. 12.   *For* du Tartas *read* de Tartas.

p. 20, l. 14.   *For* Baif *read* Baïf.

p. 26, l. 6 from bottom.   *For* Saint-Marthe *read* Sainte-Marthe.

p. 45, l. 18.   *For* Vasquier *read* Vasquin.

p. 97, l. 16.   *For* 1482 *read* 1462.

p. 129, l. 7 from bottom.   *For* of Ausonius *read* formerly ascribed to Ausonius (see a letter to the *Spectator* of Jan. 23, 1903, by J. E. Sandys).

p. 150, l. 19.   *For* more than a quarter of a century *read* sixteen years.

p. 182, l. 6 from bottom.   *For* Boyssonne *read* Boyssone.

p. 183 n. 1.   *For* Claude *read* Charles de.

p. 296, l. 7.   For *language* read *langage*.

ADDENDA

p. 263.   Another facsimile of the Dresden *Pantagruel* has been published under the auspices of the *Soc. des Études Rab.*, edd. P. Babeau, J. Boulenger and H. Patry, 1904.

PART I

1525–1550

MAROT AND RABELAIS

CHAPTER I

FRANCIS I AND HIS COURT

ON the 1st of January, 1515, Francis, Count of Angoulême, succeeded his cousin, Louis XII, as king of France. He was in his twenty-first year[1]. For a people like the French, whose destinies have always been moulded in a large degree by the personal character of their ruler, this change of sovereign could not fail to have a marked effect upon their social and political development. The mere change from a comparatively old man[2] to a young one was in itself something, especially at a time when ideas were moving as rapidly as they were at the beginning of the sixteenth century. There was inevitably a wide difference between the intellectual outlook of a monarch who had reached manhood in the reign of Louis XI, and that of one who was born in the memorable month in which Charles VIII first set foot in Italy. In short while Louis XII was born in full Mediævalism, Francis I was a child of the Renaissance. And this difference was strongly accentuated by the characters of the two men. Louis was homely, thrifty, and averse to display ; and though under the influence of the Cardinal of Amboise he proved a fairly liberal patron of art and letters, and attracted to France not a few Italian artists and men of learning, he never became thoroughly imbued with the Renaissance spirit.

[1] He was born Sept. 12, 1494.

[2] Louis was in his fifty-sixth year at the time of his death. Louise of Savoy, though doubtless with the feelings of a mother whose son was heir-presumptive to the throne, speaks of him on the eve of his second marriage as *fort antique et débile.*

Even if he had been, he lacked the requisite qualities to enable him to give any serious impulse to the new movement.

Francis, on the other hand, of noble presence and winning manners, generous, open-handed, exuberant with youth and vitality, was just the man to call forth enthusiasm in those around him. The very defects of his character, which made his rule on the whole so harmful to his country; the egotism which led him to impose upon her a system of personal government from which even the convulsions of a revolution have hardly availed to liberate her; the vanity which stimulated by the victory of Marignano at the outset of his reign urged him on a senseless career of rivalry with Charles V; the love of display and extravagance which caused him to grind his people with taxes in order to minister to his own pleasures—all this helped to make him, as they made Louis XIV, a munificent patron of art and letters. But he had also a real taste for literary and artistic culture, and was thus not only a munificent but an appreciative patron. If we may judge from his relations with Benvenuto Cellini, his bearing towards artists and men of letters was marked by singular courtesy and *bonhomie*. He never presumed on his position either as purchaser or as monarch to dictate to them. He paid for their works royally, but he behaved to them as a gentleman to gentlemen. A king who could retain for five years in his dominions an artist so hot-tempered and so deeply sensible of his own merits as Cellini deserves high praise as a patron[1].

Francis himself was far from learned. At Amboise, where his boyhood from his seventh to the close of his fifteenth year was spent under the care of his mother Louise of Savoy, he shewed much less devotion to his lessons than to hunting, falconry, archery, tennis, and the other games in which he took part with his young companions, Anne de Montmorency, Fleuranges, and others. He was a bold rider and an excellent archer, but he especially excelled in the game of *pallone*,

---

[1] Cellini was in France for a short time in 1537 and then again from 1540—1545. See *Vita*, book III. cc. iv—ix.

introduced from Italy, which was played with a large foot-
ball and a tin gauntlet lined with felt, and which required
considerable skill and strength[1]. His tutor was François
de Rochefort, afterwards Bishop of Condom, who taught
him and his sister Margaret Latin and ancient history, while
their mother instructed them in Italian and Spanish. But
Francis learnt next to no Latin and apparently little Spanish[2].
We hear of him conversing in Italian with Benvenuto Cellini.
His governor Artus Gouffier, seigneur de Boisy, a brother
of Admiral Bonnivet, who had been with Charles VIII and
Louis XII in Italy, is said to have inspired him with an
interest in Italian culture and in art and literature generally.

Francis thus grew up to manhood without any great
burden of learning. But having much curiosity, considerable
quickness, and a retentive memory, he managed, by question-
ing judiciously the many learned men by whom he was
surrounded, to acquire a fair amount of superficial knowledge.
Hubert Thomas of Liège, the secretary of the Elector Palatine
Frederic II, says in his life of that prince that, though he had
often dined with kings and cardinals and bishops and even
with the Pope, he had nowhere heard such learned conversation
as at the table of the King of France, and that the king
took a leading part in it[3]. A similar report of his conversational powers is made by the Venetian ambassador, Marino
Cavalli[4], writing in 1546, and in the *Cortegiano* Giuliano
de' Medici, the third son of Lorenzo, who had spent some
time in France, is made to say that the young Count of
Angoulême's love of literature had excited great hopes that

[1] *Mémoires* de Fleuranges (Petitot XVI. 151; Michaud et Poujoulat, V. 7).
Paulin Paris in his *Études sur François premier*, 1885, has an interesting chapter
(c. i) on the childhood and education of Francis; see also R. de Maulde la Clavière,
*Louise de Savoye et François I*er, 1895.

[2] Brantome does not mention Francis among the princes and princesses who
spoke Spanish (*Œuvres* VII. 85).

[3] Leodius, *De Vita Frederici II*, Frankfort, 1624, lib. X. p. 202.

[4] *Il sapere è grandissimo: e si può giudicarlo, udendolo ragionare d' ogni cosa e
studio e professione che faccino gli uomini, delle quali ne parla e ne giudica prontis-
samente, e tanto bene quanto li professori proprii di quelle arte* (Albèri, *Relazioni,*
i. 239).

his accession to the throne would be signalised by a literary revival.

Nor were these hopes disappointed. Francis proved himself a generous friend to men of letters. The list of those who held appointments in the royal household and contributed to the learned atmosphere of the court is a long one. His diplomatists were generally scholars, who combined with their political duties that of collecting manuscripts, a pursuit in which they encountered a formidable rival in the great Spaniard, Hurtado de Mendoza. Most of these diplomatists were also bishops; for the Concordat in transferring to the king the patronage of some six hundred bishoprics and abbeys had furnished him with a convenient and inexpensive method of rewarding political and literary merit[1].

The king's patronage was not confined to his own subjects. Following the precedent of his two immediate predecessors, he freely invited Italian artists and men of letters to his court. Leonardo da Vinci spent the last three years of his life in France[2]. The visit of Andrea del Sarto, which after four years came to an abrupt termination, is equally well known. Other Italian artists who accepted the king's invitation were, besides Cellini, the architect Vignola, and the painters Paris Bordone, Rosso, and Primaticcio. The two latter, who were employed on the decorations of Fontainebleau, were rewarded with Church preferment. Scholars and men of letters found as ready a welcome as artists. The illustrious Greek Janus Lascaris, Alciati the reformer of jurisprudence, Guido Guidi the great anatomist, Matteo Bandello, and Luigi Alamanni were among those who shared in the French king's patronage[3].

This disposition of the king naturally reacted on the leading men of the kingdom. The great prelates amongst whom Francis so lavishly distributed the revenues of the

---

[1] See an amusing passage by Brantome in defence of this system (Œuvres, III. 105—110).

[2] See Vasari, Opere, IV. 49, n. 1 (ed. Milanesi, 8 vols. Florence, 1878—1885). The story told by Vasari of the painter dying in the king's arms is apocryphal.

[3] For Francis I as a patron of art and letters see Sainte-Beuve, Portraits littéraires, III. 59—61.

Church, some from a real interest in learning, others from a wish to stand well with their royal master, became in their turn patrons of struggling scholars. It was in the suite of some episcopal ambassador that many a poor scholar visited that country which, though the pride of place was fast passing from it, was still the happy land of scholarship, and where books and manuscripts were to be found in greater abundance than in France. Lazare de Baif, Georges de Selve and François de Dinteville, Georges d'Armagnac and the Cardinal de Tournon all gave a helping hand in this way to promising scholars.

But of all the noble patrons who helped on the cause of learning and letters during the reign of Francis I, the first place belongs to the brothers du Bellay. Of these, Martin, lieutenant-general of Normandy, was the principal author of the well-known memoirs ; René, bishop of Le Mans, was a horticulturist, and had a garden famous for its collection of rare plants ; Guillaume, the eldest, Seigneur de Langey, eminent both in war and peace, was one of the ablest men in the kingdom. He was a steady patron of Rabelais, who was attached to his household during the last years of his life, and who stood by his death-bed. The remaining brother, Jean, who was even more closely connected with Rabelais, was made Cardinal in 1535, and at one time enjoyed the revenues of five sees and fourteen abbeys, including the rich Benedictine abbey of St Maur des Fossés, of which he made Rabelais a canon. But he spent, and more than spent, his large revenues in the patronage of art, letters, and learning. No one was more constant in urging their claims upon his master. It was largely through his influence that the royal professorships were at last founded.

With a king so favourably disposed towards letters, it was no wonder that the group of men who formed the vanguard of Humanism in France allowed their hopes to run high. When at the beginning of the year 1516 Francis returned in triumph from Italy, they looked confidently forward to a return of the Augustan age. Montaigne speaks of his father as fired by the new ardour with which Francis the First

embraced letters and brought them into credit[1]. " How happy
is France under such a prince ! how happy are you with such
a patron ! " writes Erasmus to Cop in February, 1517[2].

Budé's letters to Erasmus at this time are full of enthusiastic praise of the king. The project, which Budé had
so greatly at heart, of founding at Paris a royal college for the
study of ancient languages seemed in a fair way towards
realisation[3]. But soon his note begins to change. Writing
at the end of April, 1518, to the Englishman Richard Pace,
after congratulating him with effusion on the devotion to
letters of the English king, he says regretfully that " the zeal
and good-will of the French king has been diverted to other
things by some sinister fate[4]." That indeed was one of the
weak places in Francis's character ; he was easily diverted.
In 1521 he was very seriously diverted from the patronage of
letters. For in that year his rivalry with Charles V, which
had been roused by the election of Charles to the Empire
in 1519, broke out into open war, which was only terminated
by the disaster of Pavia (1524). Then followed the captivity
of Francis, the Treaty of Madrid, and his consequent release
(1526), his violation of the Treaty and the renewal of
hostilities, down to the humiliating Treaty of Cambrai (1529).
It was not till then that Francis, sickened of unsuccessful
warfare, turned to recover in the arena of letters the glory
he had lost as a military captain. The part of the Victor of
Marignano had been played out ; it was time to resume that
of the Father of Letters.

But the scholars had now another obstacle to contend
against, and one which proved in the end even more disastrous to learning than the rivalry with Charles V. Two
months and a half before the Treaty of Cambrai was
signed a gentleman of Picardy, by name Louis Berquin, a
scholar and a correspondent of Erasmus, had been burnt for
heresy at Paris. For the next six years Francis's attitude

---

[1] *Essais*, II. c. xii.
[2] Erasmus, *Epp.* p. 186.
[3] Budé to Erasmus Feb. 5, 1517 (*Epp.* p. 170), and April 12, 1518 (*Epp.* p. 315).
[4] Budæus, *Opera*, I. 242.

towards the Reformers oscillated from persecution to favour, according as he was anxious to win the support of the Pope or that of the German princes. But after the winter of 1534—1535, when the breach between the two religious parties was enormously widened by the affair of the "Placards" and the terrible persecution which followed it, the king's face began to be set steadily towards Catholicism. From 1538, the year in which the second war with Charles V was terminated by the truce of Nice, followed by a meeting of the two monarchs at Aigues Mortes, he was irrevocably Catholic. Before the close of his reign another scholar was burnt in the person of Estienne Dolet (1546).

Thus, while those scholars and men of letters who had never strayed from the fold of orthodoxy, or who kept their religious opinions to themselves, might bask unmolested in the sunshine of the royal favour, those on the other hand who in any way openly favoured the new doctrines were in constant danger of their sunshine being turned into shade. The same king who used to visit the printing-house of Robert Estienne in the Rue St Jacques issued letters patent, though happily the Parliament refused to register them, forbidding any book to be printed, under pain of death, in his kingdom[1]. Learning had not saved Berquin or Dolet from the stake: for all the king's friendship the first poet of the age, Clément Marot, suffered imprisonment and exile.

But in spite of these somewhat numerous drawbacks, Francis on the whole fairly earned his title of Father of Letters. We shall see in the next chapter that three direct benefits to the cause of Humanism may be ascribed to him : the collection of manuscripts and the formation of a royal library ; the foundation of royal professorships ; and the creation of a royal press. But besides this, the general sympathy which he shewed for learning, however much it might be diverted at times by sinister influences, acted as an effectual stimulus throughout the kingdom.

[1] The text of the letters patent which were substituted for these, and which refer to them, is given in A. F. Didot's *Essai sur la typographie*, p. 760.

In this beneficent and useful work he was warmly seconded
by the two women to whom he was bound by close ties of
affection—his mother and his sister. We have seen how
carefully Louise of Savoy attended to the education of her
children : in her husband's château of Cognac there is the
simple inscription "*Libris et liberis.*" Several manuscripts in
the *Bibliothèque Nationale* shew signs of their having been
written for her. But it was the king's sister, Margaret, whose
influence was most constantly exercised on behalf of letters
and learning, who encouraged him to liberal measures for
their advancement, who recommended scholars and men of
letters to his favour, and who stood between them and his
wrath.

In the library of Francis's father were magnificent copies
of the romances of Lancelot and Tristram, printed on vellum
and bound in velvet[1]. It was possibly from these volumes
that he learned the love of chivalry, or at least of its outward
semblance, which distinguished him in after-life. The battle
of Marignano, in which he was knighted on the field by
Bayard, and in which the hitherto invincible Swiss footmen,
the *dompteurs des princes*, the representatives of democracy,
gave way before the onslaught of the French cavalry, did
much to spread the same feeling through the nation[2]. This
in turn brought, if possible, additional popularity to the old
romances, and caused new ones to be printed in which the
element of chivalry was largely introduced. *Perceforest*, for
instance, which was written in the fifteenth century but was
not printed till 1528, describes how Alexander the Great
introduced tournaments into England[3]; and in *Meliadus*,
published in the same year, jousting plays a conspicuous part.
The same sentiment accounts for the extraordinary popularity
of the French translation of *Amadis*, though the more licentious
tone which the translator gave to the work shews that it was

---

[1] See E. Sénemaud, *La bibliothèque de Charles d'Orléans, Comte d'Angoulême,
au château de Cognac, en 1496* (1861), nos. 17, 21, 72, 74.

[2] J. S. Brewer, *The reign of Henry VIII*, 1884, I. 103.

[3] i. 29—33. *Perceforest* is one of the chief sources used by Sainte-Palaye in his
Mémoires sur l'ancienne chevalerie.

the outward forms of chivalry, rather than its true spirit,
which appealed most strongly to the positive character of the
French nation. Bayard had no successor: French literature
produced no *Fairy Queen*.

Apart from *Amadis* it was in purely superficial ways that
the prevailing fashion influenced literature. Heraldry became
a popular study, and a handbook of the science, entitled *Le
Blason des Armes*, was one of the most frequently printed
books of the time. The wearing of arms and badges was
imitated by the non-noble classes. Even printers and publishers had their devices, which in many cases form a
beautiful feature on the title-pages of their books. Poets
had their mottoes. That of Marot was *La Mord n'y mort*;
of Herberay des Essars, *Acuerdo olvido*; of Maurice Sceve,
Souffrir non souffrir; of Peletier, *Moins et meilleur*. Others,
generally the more foolish, called themselves by names
borrowed from the language of disguised knight-errants.
Just as the knight Amadis was *Le beau ténébreux*, so the poet
Habert was *Le banni de liesse*, Jean Bouchet *Le traverseur des
voies périlleuses*, Michel d'Amboise *L'esclave fortuné*[1]. A still
more foolish literary fashion derived from heraldry was that
of writing poems called *blasons*, a practice which, having
received the countenance of Clément Marot, was carried to a
still greater height of absurdity by his followers.

The love of emblems may also be traced to the symbolism
inherent in heraldry. The popular emblem-writer of the day
was the Italian jurist, Alciati[2]; but a Frenchman, Guillaume
de la Perrière, of Toulouse, also produced a book of
emblems, which he called *Le théâtre des bons engins*, and
which had considerable success[3]. The same taste accounts

[1] Both this and the preceding fashion are attacked by J. du Bellay in a well-
known passage of the *Deffence et Illustration* (lib. II. c. xi).

[2] See H. Green, *Alciati and his Book of Emblems*, 1872. Alciati's book was
first published at Milan in 1522; it appeared in France in 1534, still in Latin, but
two years later it was translated into French. See *Cat. Yemeniz*, Paris, 1867,
nos. 2106—2113, for this and later French editions.

[3] The first edition with figures, which is printed at Paris, is probably of 1540,
the privilege being dated Jan. 31, 1539. The British Museum has a copy of an
earlier edition without figures, printed at Lyons about 1536.

for the popularity of the well-known *Hieroglyphica* of Horapollo[1].

But Francis I gave a tone to French literature that was of far greater importance than this fictitious taste for chivalry. By conferring places at court on men of letters he brought to bear on them the influence of a comparatively polished society, and thus did something to cure the provincialism which was paralysing French literature at the beginning of his reign. It was the court, as well as his own good sense, which taught Marot tact and urbanity; it was at the court that he learned to use a language which was purged of provincialism in its various forms, of the street-slang of a Coquillart, of the lumbering commonplaces of a Jean Bouchet, and of the pedantry of the *grands rhétoriqueurs*. There was of course some danger in this court influence. If Marot himself was too independent to suffer from it, his contemporary Mellin de Saint-Gelais became a typical court-poet, and in the days of the Pleiad the evil increased. But these are points which will become clearer in future chapters. At present it is only necessary to call attention to the fact that French literature more or less followed the course of French politics. In literature, as in politics, the centralising forces which culminated under Louis XIV began to make themselves felt in the reign of Francis I. Moreover, during his reign the centre of court-life shifted from Touraine to Paris. The Kings of France from Charles VII to Louis XII had resided chiefly in Touraine. Francis was too restless to remain long in any one place, but during the last twenty years of his reign his favourite place of residence on the whole was Fontainebleau, where he began to build a new château in 1528. In the same

---

[1] A Latin translation appeared in France in 1521, and a French one, by Jean Martin, in 1543. Horapollo wrote, either in ancient Egyptian or Coptic, in the 5th or at the end of the 4th century of our era; his work was translated into Greek by one Philip.

See for the fashionable taste for emblems Mary F. S. Hervey, *Holbein's Ambassadors*, pp. 219 ff. With reference to this book it may be convenient to mention here that Mr W. H. Dickes in his more recent book on the same subject has conclusively shewn that the so-called ambassadors are not Selve and Dinteville but the brothers Otto Henry and Philip, Counts Palatine of the Rhine.

year he also began the *château de Madrid* in the Bois de
Boulogne; in 1532 that of Villers-Cotterets, not fifty miles
from Paris; in 1539 that of Saint-Germain. Thus if the
court rather than any single town was the focus of the literary
and artistic, as well as of the political life of France, that
court now revolved more or less in an orbit of which the
centre was Paris.

CHAPTER II

HUMANISM

HUMANISM played too important a part in the developement of French literature in the time of Francis I for it to be possible to omit all notice of it in this history. It was to classical learning that the best intellect of the day was directed, and it was the scholars who took the first rank in the world of letters. Moreover those who, with the instinct of genius, wrote to be 'understanded of the people,' were all more or less imbued with the spirit of Humanism. Rabelais was steeped in it; Calvin was a considerable Latin scholar and a fair Greek one; Margaret of Navarre knew Latin, and had dabbled in Greek and Hebrew; Bonaventure Des Periers translated for her benefit, with the help of a Latin version, a dialogue of Plato; Mellin de Saint-Gelais was a man of some learning; even Clément Marot, who knew next to no Latin, appeared as a translator of Virgil and Ovid.

The leading humanist of the reign was Guillaume Budé. On the very eve of it, in 1514, he had published his first important treatise *De Asse et partibus ejus.* The popularity which it enjoyed, passing as it did through ten editions within twenty years, testifies to the widely spreading interest in everything that related to the ancient world. Budé was born in 1467, a year after his friend and rival Erasmus[1]. His

---

[1] *G. Budæi Vita*, per Ludovicum Regium (Louis le Roy), 154⅔ (a panegyric rather than a biography); Rebitté, *G. Budé, restaurateur des études grecques en France*, 1846; E. de Budé, *Vie de G. Budé*, 1884 (more laudatory than critical); M. Triwunatz, *G. Budé's De l'Institution du Prince. Münchener Beiträge*, no. 28, 1903.

Budæi opera, 4 vols. Basle, 1557; this does not include his French treatise, *De l'Institution du Prince*, which was published, after his death, in 1547, nor his

father was a rich man and had, for the time, a good library; he was, says his son, *librorum emacissimus.* Guillaume's early education was of a perfunctory character. He was a student in arts at Paris, and in law at Orleans, but in neither branch of study did he reap any profit. It was not till he had reached the age of twenty-four that he was seized with a passion for learning which never afterwards deserted him. The remainder of his life was dedicated to untiring industry, and it was a current story that even on his wedding-day he worked for three hours. In 1520 he published a collection of his letters, including several Greek ones, which definitely established his reputation as a Greek scholar. From this time he was recognised as sharing with Erasmus the primacy of European scholarship. In 1529 he gave a more convincing proof of his powers by the publication of his *Commentarii linguae graecae*[1], a species of Greek lexicon which Erasmus had once or twice urged him to write; and which like all his writings is a mass of erudition put together without any attempt at mèthod. Though now of little value its appearance was a notable event in the history of French scholarship.

In the dedicatory letter to the king Budé reminds him in very plain language of the promise he had long before made, to establish a royal college for the study of ancient languages. The project, which is said to have emanated from Francis himself, but which at any rate was suggested by the college for the study of the three languages founded by Jérôme Busleiden in 1515 at Louvain, had been formed as early as 1517, and one of the reasons for desiring to attract Erasmus to France was the wish that he might take some part in the direction of the new college. But before the scheme was sufficiently matured to be put into execution Francis's attention was diverted by the war with Charles V; and it was not till after the Treaty of Cambrai that weary of

---

correspondence with Erasmus, which, with several other of his letters, will be found in the Leyden edition of Erasmus's works.

[1] The first edition was published by Badius; the best is that of Robert Estienne (1548), a magnificent specimen of typography.

unsuccessful warfare he again turned his attention to the arts of peace. The moment chosen by Budé for his appeal was therefore an opportune one, and it was in part successful. Though the idea of building a college and endowing it with revenues for the maintenance of a large body of scholars was for the time abandoned, royal professorships were founded, and on the 24th of March, 1530, the new professors, four in number, entered on their duties. They were François Vatable and Agatho Guidacerio for Hebrew, Pierre Danès and Jacques Toussain, both pupils of Budé, for Greek, and Oronce Finé for Mathematics. Their annual stipend was 200 crowns[1].

The foundation of the professorships had from the first been hotly opposed by the obscurantist party of the University, under the leadership of Noel Beda, principal of the college of Montaigu. In January 1534 he presented to the Parliament of Paris in the name of the Faculty of Theology a formal complaint against the delivery of public lectures on the Holy Scriptures by 'simple Grammarians or Rhetoricians who had not studied in any Faculty.' A day having been fixed for hearing the contending parties, Beda, who appeared in person, said in the course of his speech that it was very far from his intention to object to the study of Greek or Hebrew, but that it was to be feared that the new professors, though excellent Humanists, were not sufficiently versed in theology to interpret the Holy Scriptures, and criticise, as they did, the Vulgate; and even if they were, there might be a danger of their inducing their hearers to doubt its fidelity. "Finally," he said, "the greater part of the Greek and Hebrew editions which they use as text-books have been made in Germany, a country infected with heresy either by Jews, or by Catholics who have turned Lutherans, who are therefore quite capable of tampering with the original text." The actual decision of the Parliament is not known, but it was no doubt favourable to the royal professors, for they continued to give their

---

[1] See A. Lefranc, *Histoire du Collège de France*, 1893, cc. ii—v. According to Goujet the first professor of mathematics was Jean Martin Poblacion, a Spaniard, but there is no other mention of this; Finé was certainly appointed in 1530.

lectures, and before the end of the year a Latin Professorship, to which Beda and his friends had especially objected, was established.

Though the followers of Beda were in the majority in the University they did not have it all their own way. There had always existed a feeling of considerable jealousy between the Faculty of Arts and that of Theology with regard to their respective rights and privileges, and this doubtless helped to dispose those colleges which had few or no theological professors in favour of the new studies. In some of the colleges there were Greek lectures, notably the college of Lisieux, which under the rule of Jean du Tartas (1525—1533), became distinguished for enlightened views. But the principal home of Humanism in the University was the college of Sainte-Barbe, of which the Portuguese Jacques de Gouvea and his nephew André were successively principals. Here from 1525 to 1528 lectured a man who perhaps more than any single individual helped to infuse the spirit of true Humanism into the University. This was Maturin Cordier, who for sixteen years (1514 to 1530) devoted himself to the work of reforming the education of the younger students of the Paris University[1]. He taught in various colleges besides Sainte-Barbe; at La Marche Calvin was one of his pupils. In 1530 he published a little treatise, *De corrupti sermonis apud Gallos et loquendi latine ratione libellus*, in which he waged war against the monkish jargon which passed for Latin among the students. In the same year he left Paris for Nevers, where he taught for four years, and in 1534 he joined the staff of the new college of Guienne at Bordeaux[2]. In 1537 he yielded to Calvin's pressing invitation to help him with the organisation of his new college at Geneva. The temporary defeat of Calvin and his friends by the opposite party in the

[1] 1479—1564. See Haag, *La France Protestante*, 2nd ed. 1884; F. Buisson, *Sébastien Castellion*, 1892, I. 124 ff.; E. Puech, *Maturin Cordier*, Montauban, 1896; N. Weiss, *Le collège de Nevers et M. Cordier* in *Rev. pédagogique, nouv. sér.* XVIII. 1890.

[2] He had become a Protestant, and in 1535 his name appeared on the list of those who were cited to appear before the Paris Parlement (*Cronique du roy Françoys premier*, p. 130).

following year caused him to migrate to Neuchâtel, where he became head of the college. It was not till 1559 that he returned to Geneva, and there he died in 1564, teaching to the end. It was at Geneva, a year before his death, that his famous Colloquies, a series of dialogues in Latin and French for the use of schoolboys, were published. They acquired an enormous popularity, which they retained till the last century[1].

In 1522 Budé had been appointed to the newly-created office of 'master of the king's library' at Fontainebleau, and not long afterwards the king began to form there a collection of Greek manuscripts[2]. His first acquisition was made in 1529; it consisted of fifty volumes purchased for him by Girolamo Fondulo, a native of Cremona and a man of considerable learning[3]. In 1542 he bought the collection of Georges de Selve, and in 1545 Cardinal d'Armagnac presented him with twenty-four volumes. The chief hunting-ground for Greek manuscripts at this time was Venice, and here the copying of manuscripts formed a regular industry among the exiled Greeks. About 1540 the most renowned of these copyists, Angelo Vergecio, was persuaded to enter the French king's service[4].

In 1544 Francis moved to Fontainebleau the library at Blois which he had inherited from his predecessor Louis XII. It contained 1891 volumes, including about forty manuscripts which Janus Lascaris had brought to France in 1508[5]. The great majority of these volumes consisted of manuscripts, there being only 109 printed volumes. In 1545 Vergecio made a

---

[1] The latest edition in the British Museum is of 1830 (London).

[2] L. Lelisle, *Cabinet des manuscrits de la Bibl. Imp.* I. 151—165; H. Omont, *Cat. des manuscrits grecs de Fontainebleau*, 1889, pp. iv—viii.

[3] Fondulo's extraordinary thinness was a constant joke (see *Joyeux Devis*, xlvii. ed. Lacour, II. 187).

[4] For Vergecio see the *Dict. historique* of Prosper Marchand; *Rev. critique d'hist. et de litt.* March 9, 1872, p. 159.

[5] It was composed of (1) the library which Louis XII had inherited from his father, the Duke of Orleans, (2) the library of Charles VIII, (3) the collection of the Dukes of Milan, (4) a collection of beautifully illuminated MSS. formed by Louis of Bruges, (5) additions made by Louis XII and his wife Anne of Brittany. See Delisle *Cabinet des manuscr.* 98—146; *Essai hist. sur la bibliothèque du roi* [by Leprince], 1782.

list of the Greek manuscripts, which amounted to about 190[1]. In a library like this which had a quasi-public character manuscripts were of more service to learning at this stage of its development than printed books, for they were freely lent to various Paris publishers, and books were thus rapidly multiplied. Before 1528 hardly any Greek books were printed in France, but in that year a real start was made, and four Greek books, all of some importance, were printed. In 1530 the work received an impulse from an unexpected quarter, for no less than eleven Greek books were printed in that year by Gerardus Morrhius in the Sorbonne itself. One of them was a Greek-Latin lexicon. Still greater encouragement came from the appointment of a king's printer for Greek in 1539. The first holder of the post, Conrad Néobar, died a year after his appointment, and he was succeeded in 1540 by the well-known Robert Estienne, who already held the office of king's printer for Hebrew and Latin.

In August of the same year Budé died, four years after Erasmus. The following words of Calvin give a just estimate of his services to his country. *Gulielmus Budaeus primum rei literariae decus et columen, cuius beneficio palmam eruditionis hodie sibi vindicat nostra Gallia!* The first place in the world of scholarship had in fact passed from Italy to France, and it was mainly the work of Budé. Out of the many verses, French and Latin, that were written in his honour the following by Mellin de Saint-Gelais give a good idea of the estimation in which he was held by his countrymen.

> Qui est ce corps que si grand peuple suit?
> Las, c'est Budé au cercueil estendu.
> Que ne font donc les cloches plus grand bruit?
> Son nom sans cloche est assez espandu.
> Que n'a l'on plus en torches despendu
> Suivant la mode accoustumée et sainte?
> Afin qu'il soit par l'obscur entendu
> Que des François la lumière est esteinte![2]

---

[1] Printed by Omont. *op. cit.* pp. 355 ff.

[2] Saint-Gelais, *Œuvres*, I. 120. Budé's will contained a clause that he should be buried by night without any ceremony.

Among the small band who worked with Budé in the cause of Humanism at Paris the most noteworthy were Germain de Brie (better known as Germanus Brixius) and Nicolas Berauld, who at the beginning of the reign of Francis I ranked next to Budé as Greek scholars. Brixius had learnt Greek from Janus Lascaris at Venice and from Marcus Musurus at Padua. He was famous as a Latin poet, and in that capacity had a notable passage of arms with Sir Thomas More[1]. Berauld was at one time tutor to the three Châtillon brothers; he had a great reputation as a speaker. Of the younger generation, the pupils who reaped the harvest which their teachers had sown, the foremost were the two Greek professors, Danès and Toussain, and the diplomatist Lazare de Baif, father of the poet Jean Antoine de Baif, who ranked high as a writer of Latin prose and translated two Greek plays into indifferent French verse.

Budé was succeeded both in his official post of royal librarian and in his still more important unofficial position of chief adviser to Francis I in literary matters by Pierre du Chastel. The early career of this man is so typical of that of many self-taught and wandering scholars of the period that it is worth briefly relating here[2]. The son of a Walloon gentleman who lived in Burgundy his earliest schooling was at Dijon. At the age of thirteen he began to teach himself Greek, and at sixteen he was appointed to a lectureship at Dijon. Having travelled through Germany to Basle, attracted by the fame of Erasmus, he became corrector to Froben's press and was of some service to Erasmus in his translations from the Greek. About 1530 he went to Bourges to study law under Alciati, and not long afterwards accompanied François de Dinteville, the bishop of Auxerre, to Rome and Venice. At Venice he accepted a professorial chair in Cyprus, holding it for two years. But the passion for travel had seized him.

---

[1] He is mentioned by Rabelais in *Pant.* iv. 21, a passage which seems to prove that his name was De Brie and not Brice.

[2] There is an excellent Latin life of P. du Chastel (*circ.* 1508—1531) by Pierre Galland. It remained in manuscript till 1674 when it was published by Étienne Baluze.

He went to Egypt, going up the Nile as far as Memphis, where he was stripped by robbers. From Egypt he made his way through Arabia, Palestine, and Asia Minor (where he nearly died of fever at Iconium) to Constantinople. Here he impressed the French ambassador, La Forest, so favourably that he sent him to France with despatches and a letter of recommendation to the king. Francis was equally impressed, and henceforth Du Chastel's career was one of uninterrupted prosperity. In 1537 he.became the king's reader and successively archdeacon of Avignon and bishop of Mâcon, Tulle, and Orleans. Scholars and men of letters found in him a sure and constant support. The king declared that he was the only man whose learning he had not exhausted in two years.

So far we have been concerned with the various forces of Humanism which had their centre in Paris. But in the reign of Francis I, when the unity of the French kingdom was but of recent date, Paris had nothing like the monopoly of learning and literature which she afterwards enjoyed. She had as rivals flourishing provincial towns, of which some until more or less recent times had been capitals of practically independent kingdoms. Moreover the provincial Universities were on the whole far more favourably disposed towards the new studies than their Paris sister. At Bordeaux, where the University was at a very low ebb, an important step was taken by the transformation of the College of Arts into the College of Guienne (1533)[1]. The first principal was Jean de Tartas, but it was his successor, André de Gouvea (1534), who made it into one of the most enlightened and flourishing places of education in the kingdom. Such already was its reputation in the year 1539 when Montaigne became a scholar there.

Closely analogous to the College of Guienne was the new University of Nismes, which was founded in 1539 with a single Faculty, that of Arts. The first rector was Claude Baduel, a native of Nismes, who had got his religious opinions from Melanchthon at Wittenberg, and his educational views

---

[1] E. Gaullieur, *Hist. du Collège de Guienne*, 1874.

from John Sturm at Strassburg. The method of study which
he inaugurated and which was closely modelled on that of
Sturm proved very successful[1]. The new University owed
much to the energetic patronage of Margaret of Navarre, as
did that of Bourges, the capital of her duchy of Berry. It
was for Bourges that she secured the services of the great
Italian jurist Alciati, the founder of the new jurisprudence
in France. He came to Bourges in the first half of 1528,
and in the following year was appointed a Professor with
a regular salary[2]. *Ainsi vint à Bourges où · estudia bien
longtemps et profita beaucoup en la faculté des loix*[3], says
Rabelais of his hero Pantagruel, and it is almost certain that
Pantagruel here spells Rabelais.

The other universities that were celebrated for their law
schools were Orleans, where Calvin attended the lectures of
Pierre de l'Estoile, Poitiers, and especially Toulouse. The
latter, however, was the stronghold of mediaeval jurisprudence,
and Jean de Boissone, who introduced the new methods there,
found serious difficulties in his path. In 1532 he was accused
of heresy, but being like his friend Rabelais a martyr *jusqu'au
feu exclusivement* recanted, while his colleague Jean de Caturce
was burnt. The most important medical school was that of
Montpelier. Here Vesalius began his studies and Rabelais
took his degrees.

Several of these provincial capitals profited by the residence
of a humanist bishop, who after employment on diplomatic
missions in Italy returned home to diffuse the light of Humanism in the neighbourhood of his see. Thus Guillaume
Pellicier, the friend and correspondent of Rabelais, was bishop
of Montpelier. He had a particularly fine library, the Greek
manuscripts alone being 1104 in number, and filling over two
hundred volumes[4]. At Toulouse the learned and accomplished

---

[1] See M. J. Gaufrés, *C. Baduel et la réforme des études au xvie siècle*, 1880;
Ménard, *Hist. de la ville de Nismes*, 1750—1755, IV. 148 ff.

[2] For the dates see Mazzuchelli, *Gli scrittori d' Italia.*

[3] *Pant.* ii. c. 5.

[4] H. Omont, *Cat. des manuscrits grecs de G. Pellicier*, 1886. There are, or
were, nearly a hundred of Pellicier's MSS. in the Middlehill Collection, and there
are some in the Bodleian.

bishop of Rieux, Jean de Pins, generally resided, and extended
a ready patronage to any promising scholar who was brought
to his notice[1]. Another friend of Rabelais, Geoffroy d'Estissac,
bishop of Maillezais, became the centre of the literary society
of Poitiers, as he spent much of his time at his priory of
Ligugé in the neighbourhood.

We hear little or nothing of the University of Caen during
the first half of the sixteenth century, and it was not till the
next century that the town became an important literary
centre and called itself the 'Norman Athens.' The Norman
capital, Rouen, one of the largest and most important towns
of France, was as conservative in its literary fashions as
Toulouse. It possessed a local school of poets, who, like the
German Meistersingers, competed for an annual prize with
compositions written according to the strict rules of a highly
elaborate code.

Of all the provincial towns of France none equalled Lyons
as a centre of learning and literature[2]. In the activity of its
intellectual life, in the number of scholars and men of letters
that congregated there, in the books which issued from its
presses, it fell little, if at all, short of Paris. In some respects
it was a more desirable place of residence for scholars, for it
breathed an air of greater intellectual freedom, untainted
by the blighting influence of the Sorbonne. It was half
Italian in character. Already in the fifteenth century Italian
merchants had begun to settle there; in 1528 Andrea Navagero
wrote that more than half the inhabitants were foreigners, and
that nearly all of these were Italians[3]. In the first thirty years
of the sixteenth century the governorship of the city was held
by members of the Milanese family of Trivulzi, all of whom
warmly sympathised with every form of intellectual progress.

---

[1] See R. C. Christie, *E. Dolet*, pp. 60—73.

[2] There is an excellent account of Lyons in Christie, *ib.* c. ix. See also
Colonia, *Hist. litt. de la ville de Lyon*, 2 vols. 1728—30, II. 459—517; Pernetti,
Recherches pour servir à l'hist. de L. 2 vols. Lyons, 1757; Breghot du Lut,
Mélanges Biog. et Litt. pour servir à l'hist. de L. 2 vols. Lyons, 1828—31 ; Mon-
falcon, *Hist. de la ville de L.* 2 vols. 1847, I. c. 6; Buisson, *S. Castellion*, c. ii.

[3] Tommaseo, *Récits des ambassadeurs vénitiens*, I. 36.

In 1535 Pompone de Trivulce was succeeded by Cardinal de Tournon, who seems to have shewn less severity here than elsewhere towards heterodox opinions, and whose patronage of men of letters was as liberal as that of his predecessors.

Among the distinguished men who inhabited Lyons during the reign of Francis I were Symphorien Champier, a bad poet but a good physician and writer on medical subjects, an eager antiquary and editor of ancient chronicles and records of chivalry, and a warm sympathiser with the new studies[1]; the three brothers, Matthieu, Georges, and Jean de Vauzelles, and their friend Jacques de Vintimille, the translator of the *Cyropaedia*; Sanctes Pagnini, the Hebraist; Guillaume du Choul, the archaeologist; Benoist Court, the witty commentator of the *Aresta Amorum*; the physicians, Pierre Tolet and Jean de Canappe; Maurice Sceve and his brother Guillaume; Jean Grolier, the prince of bibliophils; and the architect Philibert de l'Orme, who however seems to have done little work in his native town. Among the occasional residents were Rabelais, Marot, and Des Periers. Nor must we forget that remarkable man Cornelius Agrippa, who practised medicine there and wrote there his *De incertitudine et vanitate scientiarum*. In 1529, partly through the exertions of Symphorien Champier, a college was founded at Lyons of the same character as that of Guienne at Bordeaux. It was called Trinity College, and had a great influence on the development of humanistic studies.

The chief printer and publisher of Lyons was Sebastien Gryphius, whose services to Humanism were inferior to no other French printer. Himself a good Latin scholar he especially devoted himself to the printing of Latin classics, especially in pocket editions[2]. Rabelais and Estienne Dolet both found employment as correctors to his press, and

---

[1] For S. Champier (1472—*circa* 1538) see P. Allut, *Étude sur S. Champier, biographique et bibliographique*, Lyons 1859, and for a list of his works *Cat. Yemeniz*, nos. 2427—2452.

[2]   Inter tot nôrunt Libros qui cudere, tres sunt
                   Insignes: languet caetera Turba fame.
              Castigat Stephanus, sculpit Colinaeus, utrumque
              Gryphius edocta mente manuque facit.

in 1538 Dolet set up a press of his own. The life of this interesting man has been told by Christie[1] with such a rare combination of accurate learning, searching criticism, and generous sympathy, that there is no French humanist about whom we have such complete information. If his tragic fate has given him an interest somewhat greater than either his character or his attainments deserve, if his vanity, egotism, and quarrelsome temper make it difficult to accord him un-reserved sympathy, his high enthusiasm for learning and sincere devotion to its interests must at any rate command our admiration. His *Commentaries on the Latin tongue* (1536—1538) is a solid piece of work, and, in Christie's words, "one of the most important contributions to Latin scholarship which the sixteenth century produced[2]."

In one of his Latin poems Dolet describes a banquet which was held in his honour at Paris in February 1537 to celebrate the royal pardon which had been granted him for a homicide committed in self-defence at Lyons. "There were assembled," he says, "those whom we justly call the luminaries of France; Budé, the first in every branch of learning; Bérauld, fortunate in his natural endowments and in his flowing eloquence; Danès, distinguished in all arts; Toussain, deservedly entitled the living library; Macrin, to whom Apollo has given empire over every kind of poetry; Bourbon, likewise rich in verse; Dampierre; Voulté, who inspires the learned world with high hopes; Marot, that French Maro, who shews a divine force in his poems; François Rabelais, the honour and sure glory of the healing art, who even from the threshold of Pluto can recall the dead and restore them to the light[3]."

We learn from the account of this little dinner-party, held in honour of a scholar who in his enthusiasm for Latin

---

[1] *Etienne Dolet*, 1880; new and revised edition, 1899. I know no single book which gives so graphic and so faithful a picture of French Humanism. See pp. 175—178 for S. Gryphius. For Dolet see also Prof. Saintsbury in *Macmillan's Magazine*, XLIII. 273 ff.

[2] For a full account and estimate see Christie, *op. cit.* 242—288.

[3] *Doleti poemata*, Lyons, 1538, p. 62.

did not neglect his own language, how close was the alliance in those days between scholarship and literature, between those who wrote in Latin and those who wrote in French. Rabelais indeed would naturally have taken his place in any gathering of learned men, but Marot had no learning. and his presence in the midst of these ardent humanists is noteworthy. The four names mentioned before his are those of the most distinguished Latin poets of their day in France; Jean Salmon, whose nickname Maigret was latinised into Macrinus; Nicolas Bourbon, who was tutor to Lord Hunsdon and the Dudleys, and a friend of Bishop Latimer and Dean Boston; Jean Dampierre; and Jean Visagier, called Vulteius, and generally known in French as Voulté[1]. The poems of all these writers, especially Voulté's, are full of biographical details and throw much light on the humanist society of the period.

It was on the 3rd of August, 1546, that Dolet was burnt in the *place Maubert* for his religious opinions. What these opinions were, whether he was a sceptic, or whether, without being exactly a Protestant, he was a biblical Christian, has long been a matter of discussion, which need not be continued here. But his fate suggests a short inquiry into the general attitude of the French humanists towards the Reformation[2]. In the first place in speaking of a general attitude it must be borne in mind that all the humanists did not think by any means alike on the subject. Not to mention Calvin and Farel, who gave up profane studies to become the leaders of the religious movement, there were Robert Estienne, Maturin Cordier, Charles de Saint-Marthe, Claude Baduel, Clement Marot and others who, while they continued to devote themselves to secular learning or polite letters, definitely embraced the reformed doctrines. A few, like Pierre Danès, may be described as ultra-Catholics, while possibly Dolet and almost certainly Des Periers were avowed sceptics. Putting aside

---

[1] For the real name of Vulteius see *Rev. d'hist. litt. de la France*, I. 530.

[2] See M. Henri Hauser's admirable article, *De l'humanisme et de la réforme en France* in the *Rev. hist.* LXIV. 258 ff., 1897. Our conclusions have been arrived at independently.

then those humanists who definitely joined one camp or
another, what was the attitude of the rest, of those who may
be described as the moderates, or the middle party?
At first there is no doubt that "the whole band of the
learned," as a contemporary writer puts it, looked with a
favourable eye on the reformed doctrines, on the preaching
of Lefèvre d'Étaples and his friends, and the writings of
Luther. As statesmen and patriots they welcomed the
prospect of a reform of the national Church; as humanists
they welcomed the extension of liberty of thought to the
domain of theology. In their eyes the Reformation was
a logical sequel of the Renaissance[1]. The king himself was
at first disposed to take a similar view. But political complications, the result of his struggle with Charles V, interfered
with the natural bent of his mind. In the very year in which
he was most active in the support of Humanism, in the year
of the foundation of the Royal Professorships, he had, as we
have seen, allowed the distinguished scholar and friend of
Erasmus, Louis Berquin, to be burnt at the stake (1529).
Was it a tacit compromise, was it the price he paid to the
Sorbonne for the withdrawal of their opposition to the
professorships? For the next five years and a half he veered
round from persecution to toleration, according as the political
wind blew, according as supposed political necessity dictated
the alliance of the Pope or that of the German Protestant
princes. During the whole of Lent 1533 the evangelical
preacher Gérard Roussel preached daily in the Louvre to
large congregations. In the following Lent a Sorbonnist
preacher complained from his pulpit that he saw no one
round him but old women; "all the men go to the Louvre."
The chief supporter of this evangelical preaching was the
king's sister, now Queen of Navarre; but the Bishop of
Paris, Jean du Bellay, was said to favour it, and so did
Budé and the humanist circle, many of whom attended the
sermons[2].

[1] See Hauser, *Rev. hist. ib.* 264 ff.
[2] See A. L. Herminjard, *Correspondance des Réformateurs dans les pays de la
langue française,* 9 vols. Geneva and Paris, 1866—1897, III. 161, 239.

Then there came a thunderclap which scattered the hopes of the moderate Reformers to the wind. On the morning of October 18, 1534, the inhabitants of Paris awoke to find the walls of all the principal thoroughfares placarded with a broadside in which the Mass and its celebrants were attacked in the coarsest and most offensive terms. A copy was even affixed to the door of the royal bedchamber at Amboise, where the king was residing at the time. This outrageous act on the part of some of the more fanatical Reformers and the rigorous persecution which ensued made a breach between the two religions too wide to be repaired. The year 1535 therefore marks the parting of the ways. From this time it became necessary to choose definitely between Catholicism and Protestantism. The majority of the humanists chose the religion of their fathers; some from unworthy motives, fear[1], or interest; many because they were moderate men and hated fanaticism, because they were patriots and were attached to their national Church, because they were humanists and not theologians. When a contemporary says of Guillaume du Bellay, "that he desired the ancient and apostolic form of religion to be restored by moderate means[2]," he is describing the attitude of the majority of the humanists.

But there was another reason, and one which strongly influenced the greatest humanist of all, François Rabelais. If in 1535 the French Catholics began seriously to organise their forces, so did the Protestants. In 1535 they had a Protestant Bible, in 1536 they had a theological system. But the 'Christian Institution,' which gave them this system, at the same time helped to repel those humanists who remained true to the spirit of the Renaissance. This spirit had taught them to prize beyond everything, to prize even unduly, two principles, that of free enquiry and that of individualism. But Calvinism closed the door to free enquiry, and sacrificed the individual to the community. Can we wonder if the humanists would have none of it, or if

---

[1] A typical instance is the Latin poet Nicolas Bourbon (see Buisson, *Séb. Castellion*, I. 80 ff.; Hauser, *op. cit.* 282).

[2] Herminjard, *op. cit.* III. 183.

Rabelais classed Calvin with the bigots and papists and the
other children of *Antiphysie*? He would have used even
stronger expressions had he lived to see the burning of
Servetus[1].

---

[1] Some portions of this chapter have appeared in the *English Historical Review*,
xv. 456 ff. (1900), where the subject is treated at greater length.

CHAPTER III

THE MOULDING OF THE LANGUAGE

1. *Orthography and Grammar.*

IN his treatise, *De l'Institution du Prince*, written during the last five years of his life (1535—1540) Budé tells us that "he is little practised in writing French, for he had been occupied entirely with the study and practice of good literature (*bonnes lettres*)," meaning thereby classical literature[1]. Similarly Olivetan in the preface to his translation of the Bible published in 1532 speaks of the French language as a barbarous jargon in comparison with Greek and Hebrew[2]. But it was Latin that was the most formidable rival of French. Latin was in exclusive possession of the Church, the University, and the Law-courts. The first breach was made on the side of law, when Francis I ordained in the famous edict of Villers-Cotterets (August, 1539) that thenceforth the judgments, orders, and other official acts of every court of justice should be pronounced in French[3]. But if the king could control the Law-courts, the Church was too strong for him. Though the translation of the New Testament by Lefèvre d'Étaples was made with his approval, the Sorbonne and the dignitaries of the Church set their faces against all attempts to bring the divine text within the comprehension of the unlettered. The Sorbonne found a firm ally in the Parlement

---

[1] *Inst. du Prince*, 1547, 3v⁰ ; and cf. 192v⁰.

[2] *Il est autant difficile de pouvoir bien faire parler a léloquence Ebraiique et Grecque le languaige Francoys (lequel n'est que barbarie au regard dicelles) si que lon vouloit enseigner le doux rossignol a chanter le chant du corbeau enroué.*

[3] Clause III (Isambert, *Anc. lois franc.* XII. 622).

of Paris, which by an edict of August 28, 1525, forbad the circulation of Lefèvre's translations. Equal resistance was naturally offered to the later and confessedly Protestant translation of Olivetan.

In the Universities and the schools the ban on the mother tongue was maintained with almost equal rigour throughout the first half of the sixteenth century. It was obligatory on the students to speak Latin, and all lectures were delivered in that language. It was not till the year 1559 that we find Jean Bodin, the founder of modern political science, but at that time only a young teacher of law at Toulouse, venturing to declare in a Latin address on education, delivered before the consuls of the town, that he believed it would be a great thing if the arts and sciences were taught in the vernacular[1].

Certainly the condition of the French language at the beginning of the reign of Francis I was far from encouraging, and it required a robust and discerning faith to foresee its future glories. The language itself was disfigured by the pedantry of the *grands rhétoriqueurs*, while as for the literature, not a single work of genius, except *Patelin*, and hardly one of merit had been published for half a century[2]. The reading of the ordinary educated classes, of those who without any pretence to scholarship were not wholly unlettered, was confined to a few standard books such as the *Roman de la Rose*, the prose versions of the Romances of Chivalry, the *Légende dorée*, and some of the works of Alan Chartier. Nor during the first half of the reign of Francis I was there any visible change. It was not till the year 1532 that the first collected edition of Marot's poems was published, and the first instalment of Rabelais's great work appeared.

The first man who seems seriously to have been moved by the unsatisfactory condition of his native language and

---

[1] *De instituenda in republica iuventute actio*, Toulouse, 1539, cited by F. Brunot in Petit de Julleville, III. 649, in a chapter which is of great importance for the history of the development of the French language in the sixteenth century. Even towards the close of the century we find Montaigne saying that he would have written in Latin *si c'eust este une matière de durée* (*Essais*, III. ix.).

[2] It must be remembered that Comines's *Memoirs* were not published till 1523, and *Jehan de Paris* not till 1530.

literature was Geoffroy Tory[1], one of those remarkable many-sided men produced by the Renaissance, who passed through the various phases of professor, miniaturist, engraver, wood-cutter, bookseller, grammarian, translator, and painter, and attained in the majority of them considerable success[2]. Born at Bourges about the year 1480 he studied in Italy under Philippo Beroaldo in 1504, then settled at Paris and was for some years professor in various colleges of the University, his last appointment being that of Professor of Philosophy at the College of Burgundy. About the year 1516 he threw up his appointment in order to travel in Italy, and on his return to Paris set up as a bookseller, practising at the same time the art of woodcutting, in which he soon became extremely proficient. It was now that he began to turn his attention to his native language. He saw around him, he says, "men who wished to write Greek and Latin before they could speak their own language correctly, and it seemed to him that it would be more glorious for a Frenchman to write in French than in any other language, as well for the preservation of his language as for the honour of his nation and the enrichment of his native tongue, which is as beautiful and good as any other, when it is well written[3]." One morning as he lay in bed, *pensant a milles petites fantaisies tant serieuses que joyeuses*, there came into his mind a passage of Cicero's *De officiis,— Non nobis solum nati sumus, ortusque nostri partem patria vindicat partem amici*—and he thereupon determined to write a book on the subject he had so much at heart[4]. Though this was at the beginning of 1524, the book did not appear till 1529. It bore the curious title of *Champ fleury*.

There are three classes of men, says Tory, in an interesting preface, who try to corrupt the language, *Escumeurs de Latin*, *Plaisanteurs*, and *Jargonneurs*, and then he gives a specimen

---

[1] b. *circ.* 1480—d. 1533. See A. Bernard's admirable monograph, *G. Tory*, 2nd ed. 1865, and Didot, *Essai sur l'histoire de la gravure sur bois*, 1863, pp. 134—151.

[2] See his epitaph quoted by Bernard (p. 68) from La Caille.

[3] *Champ fleury*, 12 r°.

[4] *ib.* 1 r°. The passage of Cicero is a translation from the spurious letter of Plato to Archytas of Tarentum.

of the style of the *Escumeurs* which is no unfair caricature of that of the *grands rhétoriqueurs: Despumon la verbocination latiale et transfreton la Sequane au diluctule et crepuscule, puis deambulon par les Quadrivies et Platees de Lutece et comme verisimiles amorabundes captivon la benivolence de l'omnigene et omniforme sexe feminin*[1]. The work itself, which is divided into three books, is highly digressive and unmethodical, but the third book contains some practical suggestions for the improvement of orthography which before long were generally adopted. These are the use of the cedilla, of the apostrophe to mark the place of an elided letter, and of the acute accent to mark a final close *e*. These signs first appeared in Tory's fourth edition of Marot's *Adolescence Clementine*, the printing of which was finished on June 7, 1533.

Another characteristic figure of the French Renaissance, who, like Tory, was enthusiastic for the improvement of his native language, was Estienne Dolet. He planned a work to be entitled the *Orateur Francois*, which was to consist of nine parts, and three of these, dealing with punctuation, accents and the method of translating, were published in 1540[2]. These little treatises had a great success and were frequently reprinted, but the remaining ones, which were to include a grammar, an art of rhetoric and an art of poetry, were never written.

The first regular French grammar was the work of an Englishman, John Palsgrave, and was published in London under the title of *L'esclarcissement de la langue francoyse* in the year 1530, with a dedication to the author of *Champ fleury*[3]. In the following year a Frenchman, the celebrated

---

[1] Readers of Rabelais will recognise that this is almost word for word the same as the speech put by him into the mouth of the Limousin scholar (*Pant.* II. c. vi.). Probably it was a stock joke among the University students.

[2] *La maniere de bien traduire d'une langue en autre. D'advantage de la punctuation de la langue Francoyse. Plus Des Accents à ycelle.* Lyon, 1540. There is a modern reprint by Techener. A reform proposed by Dolet, which became established, was the substitution of *és* for *ez* in the plural of substantives ending in a masculine *e*. (See Christie, *E. Dolet*, pp. 353 ff.)

[3] *Compose par maistre Jehan Palsgrave, Angloys natyf de Londres et gradue de Paris.* Johan Haukyns 1530. There is a modern edition by Génin in the *Documents inédits* (1852).

T.   3

physician and medical writer, Jacques Dubois, better known as Sylvius, published his *In linguam gallicam Isagωge, una cum eiusdem Grammatica Latino-gallica*[1]. Though the treatise was written in Latin, it was something that a man who was saturated in classical studies, and who always lectured and wrote in Latin, should have occupied himself with the foundations of his native language.

A difficulty which presented itself at the outset to the champions of their native language was the lawless condition of its orthography. *Pource que la matiere pend encore au clou ung chascun estime son orthographe estre la plus seure*, says Olivetan. But it was not only that different persons followed different systems; the majority had no system at all and would spell the same word in two or three different fashions in the course of a few pages. Thus above all things there was need of uniformity. But there were two diametrically opposite theories as to how this was to be attained. The conservative school was for developing the theory of etymological spelling which had been more or less in favour during the fifteenth century. Opposed to them were the radical reformers who advocated phonetic spelling. Sylvius expressed views in this direction, but the first person to construct a regular system of phonetic spelling was Louis Meigret, a native of Lyons, who in 1542 published his *Traité touchant le commun usage de l'escriture francoise*[2]. He put his system into practice in a translation of Lucian (1548), and in a grammar which he entitled *Le tretté de la grammẹre françoẹze, fẹt par Louis Meigret Lionnẹs* (1550)[3]. Unfortunately it is difficult to construct a system of phonetic spelling which will satisfy everybody, especially in an age when there is no fixed standard of pronunciation. Meigret's treatise soon elicited some friendly criticisms from his disciple and admirer, Jacques Peletier, who after a short controversial warfare produced a rival system

---

[1] The printing was finished on Jan. 7, 1531. This is probably 153⅔ as Dubois does not call himself a bachelor of medicine, which he became in June, 1531.

[2] For Meigret's system see F. Brunot, *loc. cit.* pp. 752 ff. There is a long article on him in the *Nouv. biog. gén.*

[3] Reprinted by Wendelin Foerster, Heilbronn, 1888.

under the title of *Dialogué de l'Ortografé e Prononciacion françoęsé départi an deus liurés* (1550)[1]. But to follow the course of the long controversy to which these attempts to reform French spelling gave rise would take us beyond the limits of the period and the subject. It need only be added that the etymological theory, in spite of successive attacks, kept the field throughout the sixteenth century. This led to the introduction of a good many letters which not only did not count in pronunciation but shewed ignorance of the first principles of etymology. These however were gradually got rid of, though a few survive to the present day[2].

2. *Translations from the Greek and Latin.*

Another means employed by those few scholars who had at heart the improvement of their native language and literature was the translation of the classical masterpieces. They saw that if these masterpieces were to have any real influence upon the literature and thought of the nation, they must be made known to a wider circle of readers. Thus we find the same men who wrote treatises on language and orthography, Tory, Dolet, Meigret, Peletier, all taking part in the work of translation. Fellow-workers were Antoine Macault, secretary and *valet de chambre* to Francis I, Jean Colin, bailie of the county of Beaufort, and Estienne Le Blanc, one of the controllers-general.

But the merit of being the first to foresee the importance of this work belongs to Claude de Seyssel, bishop of Marseilles and afterwards archbishop of Turin, where he died in 1520. He had made early in the century, with the help of Latin versions and his friend Janus Lascaris, for he was not much of a Greek scholar himself, translations of various Greek his-

---

[1] See Brunot, *loc. cit.* 765 ff. Peletier accepted Meigret's *e crochu* (ę) to denote open *e*, but devised a barred *e* for *e* mute.

[2] There is a good sketch of the spelling controversy in Darmesteter and Hatzfeld, 1878, pp. 194—200. See on the whole subject of grammar and orthography, Stengel, *Chronologisches Verzeichniss französischer Grammatiken* etc., Oppeln, 1890; Livet, *La grammaire française et les grammairiens du xvie siècle*, 1859; Loiseau, *Étude historique et philologique sur Jean Pillot*, 1866.

torians. These were now printed by the king's orders; they
included Thucydides (1527), Xenophon's *Anabasis* (1529),
books XVIII.—XX. of Diodorus (1530), Eusebius (1532), and
Appian (1544)[1]. To these were added the first three books
of Diodorus translated by Macault (1535), Herodian by Jean
Colin (1541), the first five books of Polybius by Meigret
(1542)[2], Dio Cassius by Claude Desrosiers from an Italian
version (1542), Xenophon's *Cyropaedia* by Jacques de Vintimille and, some years later, Herodotus by Pierre Saliat (1556).

The Eusebius and Macault's translation of Diodorus[3] were
printed by Tory, who also worked as a translator, contributing
the *Table* of Cebes and thirty dialogues of Lucian (1529)[4],
Xenophon's *Oeconomicus* (1531), and some of Plutarch's
political treatises (1532). Other treatises of Plutarch were
translated during the reign of Francis I, including the treatise
on Marriage, which became very popular, and five others
translated by Estienne Pasquier, rector of the schools of
Louhans. Moreover George de Selve, the bishop of Lavaur,
translated, with the help of Pierre Danès, eight of the Lives
(1543). The work of Amyot, the man who was to make
Plutarch almost a Frenchman, belongs to the next reign[5].

Estienne Dolet gave a practical illustration of his *Manière
de bien traduire* by translating the *Hipparchus* of Plato and
the spurious *Axiochus* (1544). Part of the *Symposium* was
done into verse by Antoine Heroet, under the title of *Androgyne* (1542), the *Ion* was translated by Richard le Blanc
(1546), the *Crito* by Pierre Duval[6], bishop of Séez (1547),

[1] His translation of Justin, not published till 1559, contains a remarkable
preface written in 1509, in which he advocates the claims of the French language.
See Brunot in *Rev. d'hist. litt.* I. (1894) 27—37.

[2] Two fragments of book VI. and one of XVI. were added by Meigret in 1545
(Seillière, *Cat.* no. 870).

[3] The title-page has a beautiful woodcut of Macault presenting his book to
Francis I: the portrait of the king is excellent.

[4] In the same year Simon Bourgoin translated the *Vera Historia* and the
dialogue on Calumny.

[5] For early translations of Plutarch see A. de Blignières, *Essai sur Amyot et
les traducteurs français au xvie siècle*, 1851, pp. 167 ff.

[6] Sometimes confused with his son Philibert. It is doubtful whether the
translation of the *Crito* ascribed to Simon Vallambert (1542) ever existed.

and the *Lysis* by Des Periers (before 1541). Little was
done at this time for Aristotle. The old translations by
Nicolas Oresme of the *Politics* and the *Ethics* still kept
the field.

It must be borne in mind that all these translations
were made either entirely from Latin versions or at most
with occasional reference to the original Greek[1]. The few
scholars who at this time were really competent to translate Greek had, like Budé, little or no practice in writing
French. They wrote in Latin for the learned of all countries ;
rarely, if ever, for their unlearned countrymen. The one
exception was Rabelais, and he was employed on a greater
work than that of translating. Towards the close of Francis's
reign, however, a new generation was growing up which
profited by the greatly increased facilities for studying Greek
in France. In the year 1544, the year of Marot's death,
Pierre Ronsard began to learn Greek under Daurat. It marks
the dawn of a new era in French literature, of an era in which
French men of letters were to penetrate some of the secrets of
Greek style and to infuse into their own literature something
of the true classical spirit. The movement began with some
attempts to translate the masterpieces of Greek poetry. To
Lazare de Baïf's indifferent renderings of the *Electra* of
Sophocles (1537) and the *Hecuba* of Euripides (1544) were
now added verse-translations of the first ten books of the
Iliad by Hugues Salel (1545)[2] and of the first two books of
the *Odyssey* by Jacques Peletier (1547). But it was not till
the next reign that Greek poetry began to exercise a real
influence upon French literature.

Of the Latin poets the most popular in France in the
fourteenth and fifteenth centuries was Ovid. He was however
chiefly known through a paraphrase of the *Metamorphoses*,
with a moral commentary, made in the fourteenth century by

---

[1] Christie has shewn conclusively that this was the case with Dolet's
translations.

[2] This edition is remarkable for its beautiful woodcuts, attributed to Jean
Cousin. The 11th book was published after Salel's death. The remaining books
were translated by Amadis Jamyn.

Pierre Bersuire, the translator of Livy[1]. A French version of this, in which the stories were told at greater length and much of the commentary was omitted, was compiled and printed by Colard Mansion in 1484 and was several times reprinted in France under the title of *La bible des poëtes*. There was also a prose translation known as *Le grand Olympe*. But in 1532 Marot re-introduced the *Metamorphoses* to French readers in a verse-translation of the first two books, to which Barthélemi Aneau afterwards added a third. The dispute between Ajax and Ulysses from the thirteenth book was rendered by Marot's friend, Jacques Colin (1547), and the story of Byblis and Caunus from the sixth by Bochetel[2]. The translation of the *Epistles* by Octovien de St Gelais, first published in 1500, still continued to be in great demand. An anonymous version of the *Remedium amoris*, which appeared in 1509 after his death, has also been attributed to him. The same poet also made a very indifferent translation of the *Æneid*, and of the same quality were those of the *Eclogues* and *Georgics* by Guillaume Michel of Tours. In 1541 a lady named Helisenne de Crenne published a new translation of four books of the *Æneid* and in 1547 Louis des Mazures, a poet of the Pléiad school, began a new verse translation which he completed in 1560. The first book of the *Georgics*, by Jacques Peletier, also appeared in 1547. We shall see that Marot's first poetic attempt was a translation of the first *Eclogue*, and that he wrote Eclogues which were either free imitations of Virgil's or closely modelled on them. A translation of Horace's *Ars Poetica* by Peletier (1544), who also rendered a few of the *Odes*, marks the beginning of his influence on French poetical theory; it took shape in Sibilet's *Art Poétique*, published four years later, which shews a close study of him. The influence of Seneca, which was to become so marked, on French tragedy dates from a somewhat later period. Pierre

---

[1] B. Hauréau, *Mem. Acad. Inscr.* XXX. pt 2, pp. 45—55, has shewn that the real author is Bersuire and not Thomas Waleys (of Wales) as supposed by Colard Mansion.

[2] Both these are printed in a collection of poetry published at Lyons in 1548 and entitled *Le livre de plusieurs pièces c'est a dire, faict et recueilly de divers Autheurs, comme de Clement Marot et autres.*

Grosnet's so-called translation of the Tragedies was merely a paraphrase of some portions of them. The only complete and competent version of a Latin drama made in the reign of Francis I was that of the *Andria* of Terence by Charles Estienne (1542)[1].

The most successful translator of Latin prose at this time was Estienne Dolet, whose versions of Cicero's Letters (*Epistolae ad Familiares*) and the first three books of the *Tusculan Disputations*, first published in 1542 and 1543 respectively, were reprinted no less than fourteen times before the middle of the century[2]. Various other works of Cicero found translators. Meigret rendered the *De officiis* (1547) and Jean Colin the *De legibus*, the *De amicitia*, the *De senectute* and the *Dream of Scipio* (1537—1539), while the *Philippics* were translated by Estienne Le Blanc and ten other speeches, including the *Pro Milone*, by Macault (1548)[3]. In 1545 Antoine du Moulin brought out revised versions of Gaguin's translation of Caesar's *De bello Gallico*, and of Estienne de Laigue's translation of the *De bello civili*. Meigret translated the second, seventh, and eighth books of Pliny's *Natural History* (1540—1543) and the *Catiline* and *Jugurtha* of Sallust (1547). The old version of Livy by Pierre Bersuire kept the field till 1582, but a new one was begun by Jacques Gohorry in 1548, and in the same year Estienne de la Planche translated the first five books of the *Annals* of Tacitus[4]. The translation of Vitruvius by Jean Martin (1547) may also be mentioned, for it testifies to the influence of Vitruvius on the architecture of the French Renaissance. Martin also translated architectural works by Serlio and Alberti.

Special mention must be made of the versions of " Æsop,"

---

[1] Goujet's *Bibliothèque française*, IV.—VIII., may be consulted for translations from Greek and Latin poets and also for those from Italian poets. For translations from Latin and Italian generally see J. Blanc, *Bibliographie italico-française*, 2 vols., Milan, 1886, vol. II.

[2] See Christie, *E. Dolet*, p. 541.

[3] For a more complete list of translations from Cicero see Blanc, *op. cit.* II. 1054 ff. For Macault and Le Blanc see L. Delisle in *Journal des Savants* 1900, 476 ff., 520 ff.

[4] The translation of Tacitus was completed by Claude Fauchet in 1582.

which had been introduced to French readers at the close of
the fifteenth century through two channels[1]. The principal
one was a translation of Steinhöwel's Latin *Æsop*, made by
Julien Macho, an Augustine friar, and printed rather before
1480. The other was a free version made between 1491 and
1498 by Guillaume Tardif, reader to Charles VIII and a
professor of the college of Navarre, of Valla's *Facetiae morales*,
which is a Latin translation of thirty-three fables taken from
the Greek prose *Æsop*. Tardif's version has the charm and
freshness of original work, and the fables are told with the
verve and liveliness of a practised *conteur*[2]. Towards the
close of the reign of Francis I two versions of *Æsop* in
French verse were produced. The first was by the Paris
bookseller, Gilles Corrozet, and appeared in 1542[3]. It consists
of a hundred fables, which are rendered in a somewhat tame
and uninteresting fashion. The second is of far greater
merit; it was the work of Guillaume Haudent, master of the
choristers of Rouen Cathedral, and was published at Rouen in
1547[4]. Many of the fables, which number 366, are told with
considerable liveliness and dramatic power. Both of these
versions must have been known to La Fontaine. There was
also a prose version, which appeared at Lyons in the same
year as Haudent's work[5].

The two translations of the Bible that were made in the
reign of Francis I belong to the domain of theology rather
than of literature. It is only an extreme enthusiast that
could say of Olivetan that " by the excellence of his modes of
" expression he exerted an influence upon the French lan-
" guage perhaps not inferior to that of Calvin or Montaigne[6]."

[1] See for the whole question of "Æsop" Joseph Jacobs, *The fables of
Æsop*, 2 vols., 1889.

[2] Charles Rocher has edited a re-impression of Verard's edition (Le Puy,
1877).

[3] *Les Fables du tres ancien Esope*, Paris, D. Janot, 1542, with full-page
woodcuts (*Bib. Nationale*); Lyons, Jean de Tournes, 1547 (*Cat. Yemeniz*, no. 2080).

[4] *Trois centz soixante et six Apologues d'Esope* (*Bib. de l'Arsenal*, the only
known copy). Reprinted by Ch. Lormier for the Soc. des Bibliophiles Normands,
Rouen, 1877.

[5] *Cat. Yemeniz*, no. 2078.

[6] Baird, *Rise of the Huguenots*, I. 233.

Nor was his predecessor, Lefèvre d'Étaples, a man of any literary power. It may however be useful to point out here how these two translations were related to each other and to the Bible of Jean de Rely, which reproduced, with very little alteration, the old thirteenth century version[1]. For the greater part of the Bible Lefèvre merely revised Jean de Rely's text, and it was only for the Pentateuch and the historical books from Joshua to Kings that he had to make a new translation from the Vulgate, this part being represented in the earlier Bible only by a narrative based on the famous *Historia Scholastica* of Peter Comestor. Lefèvre thus gave to his countrymen the first complete Bible in their own tongue, and in a version which reproduced the Vulgate with considerable fidelity and was written in the language of the day. It was published by instalments from 1523 to 1528, and finally the complete Bible appeared at Antwerp in 1530—for it was under the ban of the Sorbonne and the Parliament of Paris—from the press of Martin de Keyser (Martin Lempereur) the printer of the second complete edition of Tindall's New Testament[2]. It thus got the name of the Bible of Antwerp. After undergoing revision at the hands of the doctors of the University of Louvain, it appeared in 1550 as the Bible of Louvain, the recognised French Bible of the Catholic Church.

The Protestant Bible was the work of Pierre Robert Olivetan, a cousin of Calvin, and like him a native of Noyon in Picardy. It was printed at Neuchâtel by Pierre de Wingle in 1535, the Vaudois of Piedmont having contributed five hundred gold crowns to the expense[3]. Olivetan used throughout Lefèvre's version as a basis to work on, but he revised it by the light of the original text, being, what Lefèvre was not, a competent Greek and Hebrew scholar. As however he only spent a year upon his work, it could not have been done

---

[1] For the mediæval French Bible see S. Berger, *La Bible française au moyen âge*, 1884, and E. Reuss in *Revue de Théologie*, XIV. 1 ff., 73 ff., 129 ff.

[2] Luther's New Testament was published in 1523 and his Old Testament in 1534; Tindall's New Testament in 1525 and 1526. For Lefèvre's translation of the O.T. see A. Laune in *Bull. Prot. franç.* 1901, pp. 595 ff.

[3] See Herminjard, *op. cit.* II. 452 ff., III. 290 n.[20]; Reuss in *Rev. de Théologie*, 3me série, III. 217 ff.

with any great thoroughness or accuracy[1]. The following passage from the respective versions of Jean de Rely, Lefèvre and Olivetan will enable readers to judge of the relation between them and also of their respective merits.

1 Cor. xiii. 1—7.

JEAN DE RELY.

Se je parle de bouche dhomme et de bouche dange et je nay charite je suis fait comme arain sonnant : ou comme cloche. Et se jay esperit de prophetiser et de cognoistre tous misteres et toutes sciences. Et se jay toute foy si que je remue les montagnes et je nay charite je ne suis rien. Et se je donne en viande des poures toutes mes richesses et donne mon corps a ardoir et je nay charite ce ne me prouffite riens. Charite est souffrant et debonnaire charite na pas envie et ne fait pas destourbier : et nest pas orgueilleuse ne convoiteuse, et ne quiert pas ce que est sien. Elle ne fait pas vanite : elle ne pense pas mal : elle na pas joye de peche, elle a joye de verite. Elle seuffre tout et croit tout et espere tout, charite ne creut oncques.

LEFÈVRE.

Sy je parle langages des hommes et des anges et que je naye point charite, je suis faict comme laerain qui resonne, ou la cimbale qui tinte. Et si jay le don de prophetie et congnois tous misteres et toute science : sy jay aussi toute foy, tant que je transmue les montagnes, et que je naye point charite je ne suis riens. Et sy je distribue tous mes biens en viandes des poures : et sy je baille mon corps en telle maniere que je soie brusle, et que je naye point charite : il ne me proffite riens. Charite est patiente, elle est benigne. Charite nest pas envieuse, elle ne fait riens p(er)versement, elle ne se enorgueillist point. Elle nest pas ambicieuse, et ne se cerche point ses profitz : elle ne se courrouce point, elle ne pense point mal, elle ne sesjouist pas de liniquite, mais elle se esjouist de la verite : elle seuffre toutes choses, elle croit toutes choses : elle espere toutes chose(s) : elle attend toutes choses.

OLIVETAN.

Si je parle languages des hommes et des anges, et que je naye point charite, je suis faict comme laerain qui resonne, ou la cymbale qui tinte. Et si jay la prophetie et cognoy tous secretz et toute science : et si jay toute foy, tellement que je transmue les montaignes, et que je naye point charite, je ne suis rien. Et si je distribue tous mes biens en viandes[2], et

---

[1] See Reuss's estimate of his work, *loc. cit.* IV. 1 ff., 281 ff.

[2] ἐὰν ψωμίσω. Si insumam in alimoniam, *Erasmus.* Si distribuero in cibos pauperum, *Vulgate.*

si je livre mon corps pour estre brusle, et que je naye point charite: il ne me proffite rien.

Charite est patiente, elle est benigne: charite nest pas envieuse, charite ne faict rien perversement, elle ne se enorgueillist point, elle ne faict point deshonnestement[1], elle ne cerche point ses proffitz, elle ne se esmeut point a courroux, elle ne pense point a mal, elle ne sesjouyst point de linjustice, mais elle sesjouyst de la verite: elle soubstient toutes choses, elle croit toutes choses, elle espere toutes choses, elle endure[2] toutes choses.

3. *Translations from the Italian and Spanish.*

In the libraries of the Abbey of Thelema six languages were represented, Greek, Latin, Hebrew, French, Italian, and Spanish. These were at that time accounted the six literary languages of Europe. Arabic had fallen out of favour; English and German were as yet of little or no account. It was natural that there should be considerable literary intercourse between France and the two Romance-speaking countries that were her neighbours. With Italy there had been a reciprocity of influence ever since the thirteenth century, and with the expedition of Charles VIII the current had set strongly from Italy to France. We have seen that Lyons, so important as a literary centre, was a half Italian town. Several Italian books were printed both there and at Paris. The fall of Florence (1530) and the marriage of the French king's second son with Catharine de' Medici (1533) brought a considerable number of Italians, for the most part Florentines, to the French Court. Her *maître d'hôtel* was the Florentine exile, Luigi Alamanni, who had recently published an edition of his poems in France[3]. He rose high in the royal favour, and his didactic poem *La Coltivazione* was also published in France[4]. Another Italian poet, Bernardo Tasso,

---

[1] οὐκ ἀσχημονεῖ. Non est fastidiosa, *Erasmus.* Non est ambitiosa, *Vulgate.*

[2] ὑπομένει. Sustinet, *Erasmus, Vulgate.*

[3] *Opere Toscane*, 2 vols., Lyons, Gryphius, 1532, 3; they were dedicated to Francis I who paid for the printing.

[4] Paris, 1546.

who in his earlier life had visited France on diplomatic missions, found there a refuge from 1550 to 1554. But with these two exceptions the Italian men of letters to whom Francis I gave so cordial a welcome were, in the words of Professor Flamini, all charlatans[1].

This intercourse between France and Italy naturally led to Italian being studied, and there were not a few persons of distinction in France who could write as well as speak Italian. Chief among these was the king's sister, Margaret of Navarre, who not only corresponded with Vittoria Colonna in her own language but also wrote Italian verse. Other Italian scholars of note were Jean de Monluc, Bishop of Valence, and the Cardinal de Tournon[2]. Of the great masterpieces of the fourteenth century the most popular in France at this time was the *Decameron*. For the greater part of Francis's reign readers were content with the old translation of Laurent du Premierfait, which was however more a paraphrase than a real translation[3]. It was not till 1545 that it was superseded by a new version made by Antoine le Maçon, treasurer of the finances for Burgundy, and secretary to Margaret of Navarre, by whose command the translation was made[4]. He undertook the task, he tells us in his ingenuous and modest preface, with some reluctance, feeling doubtful whether his powers or those of the French language were equal to producing an adequate representation of the original. The encouragement however which he received from those persons, Frenchmen and Italians, to whom he submitted part of his work, induced him to complete it, and his publisher, Estienne Roffet, in his advertisement to the reader, confidently appeals to the translation as a " strong proof and sure testimony of the richness and copiousness of our French vernacular." It is in fact a thoroughly good piece of work. If it misses

[1] F. Flamini, *Studi di storia letteraria, Le lettere italiane alla corte di Francesco I*, Leghorn, 1895, pp. 197—237.

[2] See E. Picot, *Des français qui ont écrit en italien au xvie siècle* in the *Rev. des bibliothèques*, 1898 (four articles).

[3] See *post* c. VI.

[4] See *ibid.* Le Maçon's translation has been often reprinted of late years; ed. Bonneau, 6 vols. 1878; ed. Dillaye, 5 vols. 1882—4.

the exquisite grace and harmony of Boccaccio, in other respects it catches much of his spirit, and it reads like an original work. The French is racy, forcible, and wholly free from affectation. Estienne Pasquier is right in naming Le Maçon, with other translators, as one to whom the French language was not a little indebted[1]. The only other works of Boccaccio's that were translated in this reign were the *Fiammetta* (1532)[2] and the *Filocopo* (1542), the latter by Adrien Sevin, a gentleman in the household of the Maréchal de Gié.

The influence of Petrarch, or rather of Petrarchism, had, as we shall see, a marked effect on the poetry of the second half of the sixteenth century. But this influence was not exercised through translations, the poets who imitated him being Italian scholars. Six, however, of the sonnets were translated by Clement Marot, and twelve by Peletier, while Jean Meynier, Baron d'Oppède, the butcher of the Waldenses, published in 1538 a verse translation of the *Trionfi*. Finally Vasquier Philieul of Carpentras published in 1548 a translation of 196 sonnets and 24 *canzoni*, and in 1555 a complete translation of Petrarch's Italian works[3].

No translation of the works of the greatest member of the Triumvirate found its way into print till quite the close of the sixteenth century. The only student of Dante among the writers of the reign of Francis I was his sister Margaret. It was a current story that Francis, to whom Alamanni used to read and explain the great Florentine, on hearing the line about Hugh Capet:

Figliuol fui d' un beccaio di Parigi[4],

was moved to such wrath that he threatened to forbid his being read in his kingdom[5]. In the early part of his reign (between 1517 and 1524) François Bergaigne dedicated to

---

[1] Pasquier, *Recherches*, vii. c. 5.

[2] *Complainte des tristes amours de Flammette à son ami Pamphile*, Lyons, Nourry, 1532; *La complainte tres piteuse de F.* etc., [Lyons] Juste, 1532 (*Cat. Coste*, nos. 975, 6).

[3] See H. Chamard, *Joachim du Bellay*, p. 169.

[4] *Purg.* xx. 52.

[5] Pasquier, *Recherches*, vi. 1.

Queen Claude, the Chancellor Du Prat, and Admiral Bonnivet respectively[1], three copies of a manuscript translation of the *Paradiso* written in *terza rima*. Only fragments of two of the copies are now in existence[2]. The version, which is so literal as to be in parts unintelligible, has no literary merit. Nor can much higher praise be given to a complete translation of the whole poem, partly in Alexandrines and partly in ten-syllable couplets, made about the close of the reign, of which the manuscript is in the imperial library of Vienna[3].

The period of Italian Renaissance literature may be said to extend from the accession of Lorenzo de' Medici to power in 1469 to the treaty of Cateau-Cambrésis in 1559. Of this the first five-and-twenty years, down to the death of Poliziano and the expedition of Charles VIII, represent the fresh dawn, the opening bud. It is the age of Poliziano and Lorenzo de' Medici, of Pulci and Boiardo. Of these Pulci is represented by a prose paraphrase of his poem entitled *Morgant le Geant*, which appeared in 1519, while a translation of Boiardo by Jacques Vincent was published in 1549—50. That many-sided genius, Leon Battista Alberti, found a translator of his *Ecatonfila* in 1534[4] and of his *Deifira* in 1547. The subject of both these works is the philosophy of love; it was one which exercised a peculiar fascination at this time, and two other Italian works of a similar tendency, which belong to the same period, had a considerable vogue in France. These are the curious *Hypnerotomachia Poliphili* of Francesco Colonna, written in 1467 and published in 1499, and Caviceo's *Libro del peregrino*, a prolix and not very edifying love story. In the case of both, Jean Martin[5], the most active translator of Italian

---

[1] Bonnivet was made Admiral in 1517; Queen Claude died in 1524.

[2] In the *Bib. Nationale*; the copy dedicated to Queen Claude is lost. See L. Auvray, *Les manuscrits de Dante des bibliothèques de France*, 1892.

[3] The Vienna MS. and the fragments of Bergaigne's translation, together with a 15th century translation of the *Inferno* from the library of the University of Turin, have been published by C. Morel, *Les plus anciennes traductions françaises de la Divine Comédie*, 1897. See also H. Oelsner, *Dante in Frankreich bis zum Ende des xviii Jahrhunderts*, 1898, where the subject is treated with great completeness.

[4] See *Mélanges tirés d'une grande bibliothèque*, x. 278—391.

[5] For J. Martin (died before 1553) see La Croix du Maine, I. 539 ff.; Nicéron,

literature at this time, revised an existing version. His revision of the *Hypnerotomachia* which, like the original work, is far more celebrated for the woodcuts than for the text, was published in 1546, that of the *Libro del peregrino* in 1528[1]. The first half of the sixteenth century is called by Italian writers the golden age of their literature, but by the year 1515, the year of the accession of Francis I, nearly all the works which render this period illustrious had already been written. The first complete edition of the *Arcadia* appeared in 1504, the *Prince* was written in 1513, the *Cortegiano* was probably completed in 1513. Trissino's *Sofonisba*, the first regular Italian tragedy, was finished in 1515, and in the same year Ariosto sent to the press the great poem upon which he had been at work for ten years, the *Orlando Furioso*[2]. A few years later the dictatorship of Italian literature passed into the hands of Pietro Bembo, a man of great industry and literary enthusiasm, but little genius or originality. His influence on literature was twofold. He was a jealous guardian of the purity of the language and a devoted admirer of Petrarch. It was largely owing to him that for some years to come Italian literature at any rate by its style made good the claim of the age to be one of gold. It was also through his example that a mass of poets devoted themselves to imitations of Petrarch, copying and exaggerating his faults and utterly missing his great qualities. Thus the characteristics which French men of letters, when they journeyed across the Alps, found dominant in Italy were a strong feeling for purity of style and a Petrarchist revival. If the former exercised on them a beneficial influence, the latter was an almost unmixed misfortune.

Of the great Italian writers who produced their masterpieces about the time that Francis I ascended the throne, the

---

XLII. 330. ff.; C. Popelin in *Le songe de Poliphile*, traduit par C. P., 2 vols., 1880, I. 201. He was secretary first to Maximilian Sforza and then to the Cardinal de Lenoncourt.

[1] For the earlier translation by François Dassy, see Picot, II. no. 1744; Lakelands Cat. no. 651.

[2] It was published in 1516, the *Sofonisba* in 1524, the *Cortegiano* in 1528, the *Prince* in 1532.

one who exercised the greatest influence in France was beyond all question Ariosto. A complete prose translation of the *Orlando Furioso* appeared in 1543, possibly by the hand of Jean Martin[1], and before long it was followed by numerous verse translations of particular episodes. Among the translators were Mellin de Saint-Gelais, La Boétie, Baïf, and Desportes. The same poem furnished Garnier with the plot of his tragi-comedy *Bradamante*. Ariosto's comedies, especially the *Suppositi*, which was translated in 1545 and again by Jean Pierre de Mesmes in 1552, had also a considerable influence, and in fact, as we shall see later, helped to determine the character of French comedy. Of Machiavelli's writings the *Art of War* was translated by Jean Charrier in 1546, the first book of the *Discourses on the first decade of Livy* by Jacques Gohorry in 1544, followed by the other books in 1548. There were two translations of the *Prince*, both published in 1553. It was supposed to be the favourite reading of Catharine de' Medici, to whose father it was dedicated, and consequently after the massacre of St Bartholomew there sprang up a fine crop of anti-Machiavellian treatises.

Another work which exercised great influence in France was the *Cortegiano*. It appealed alike to the prevailing taste for chivalry and to the growing feeling for literary culture. It helped to imbue the French Court with a love of literature and still more with a love of art, especially of those branches of it which ministered to individual vanity, such as architecture and portrait-painting and sculpture. A French translation, the work of Jacques Colin, the king's reader, was published in 1537, and in the following year there appeared a revised version by Mellin de Saint-Gelais and Estienne Dolet[2]. It also inspired the production of original treatises on the same subject, such as Claude Chappuys's *Discours de la Court* (1543) and Philibert de Vienne's *Philo-*

[1] La Croix du Maine and Du Verdier assign it to Jean des Goutes, but Niceron (XLII. 333) points out that he was only the editor.

[2] Lyons, 1538, printed by Juste, who, in his dedicatory preface, apparently written by Dolet, speaks of the numerous errors of the earlier edition. But Christie, who had compared the two editions, says that very few changes have been made (*Dolet*, p. 280).

sophe de Court (1547)[1]. The influence of the *Arcadia* was purely literary; it gave an impulse to the production of pastoral poetry, and its influence can be traced in at any rate one of Marot's Eclogues. But a translation of it did not appear till the year of Marot's death (1544). It was by Jean Martin, who also translated Bembo's *Gli Asolani* (1545), another work which, treating as it did of the popular theme of spiritual love, found appreciative readers in France.

Nor must we forget the two masters of burlesque, Berni and Folengo, among the Italian writers who helped to shape the forces of French literature, though neither of them did so by means of a translation. But to Folengo, as we shall see, Rabelais was indebted, not only for certain incidents in his immortal work, but in some measure for his greatest creation, the character of Panurge, while Berni was, with Ariosto, the influence which led Joachim du Bellay to abandon the Petrarchian sonnet for the personal note and the realistic satire of the *Regrets*.

The influence of Spain upon French literature, which became so pronounced in the reign of Louis XIII, did not begin to make itself generally felt till nearly the close of the sixteenth century. In the reign of Francis I Spanish literature was not sufficiently mature to serve as a model to other nations. Still some of its productions were very popular in France, and one at least had a wide-spread influence. This was the famous *Amadis de Gaula* which will have special treatment in a subsequent chapter. It is enough to say here that the French translation of the first book appeared in 1540. Another Spanish work of European reputation assumed rather earlier a French dress, namely the *Marco Aurelio con el Relox de principes* of Antonio de Guevara, bishop of Mondoñedo. In the original form in which it appeared in 1529 it bore the title of *Libro aureo de Marco Aurelio*, and consisted of an imaginary life of the Emperor followed by his letters. But this having been printed from a surreptitious copy of the author's manuscript, he published in the same year a greatly enlarged edition and added to the title the words *El relox de principes*. A French

---

[1] See P. Toldo in *Archiv*, CIV. (1900), 75 ff.

translation of the earlier edition by René Bertaut de la Grise
was published in 1531 under the title of *Livre d'or de Marc
Aurele*[1], and of the enlarged edition under that of *L'horloge
des princes* in 1540[2]. Herberay des Essarts began a new
translation, but after translating two-thirds of the first book,
contented himself with a mere revision of the remainder. The
only part of this once famous book that has survived is the story
of the Peasant of the Danube, which La Fontaine developed
into one of his finest fables. Guevara's *Epistolas familiares*,
which obtained almost as high a reputation as *Marco Aurelio*,
were not translated till 1558. But his *Menosprecio de la Corte*,
published in 1539, appeared in 1542 in a French translation by
Antoine Alaigre with the title of *Du Mepris de la Cour*[3] and
became very popular.

Another Spanish book which, like those of Guevara, was
popular in its day, and even more than his has fallen into
oblivion, is the *Silva de varia leccion* of Pedro Mexia, historiographer to Charles V and a friend of Erasmus. First published
at Seville in 1548 it was translated into French under the title
of *Les diverses leçons* by Claude Gruget in 1552. It is, as the
title implies, a compilation from various sources ; the subjects
are equally various, and there is a fair proportion of anecdote,
historical and otherwise[4]. Of very different character and
merit is the famous tragi-comedy of *Calisto y Melibea*, better
known by the name of *Celestina* which its French translator

---

[1] By Galliot du Pré, who in 1529 had published it in Spanish. This unauthorised edition consists of only a single book of 48 chapters, followed by
19 letters. In the enlarged form there are three books and the letters are worked
in with the life. A correct account of the difference between the two editions is
given by Hallam in his *Literature of Europe*.

[2] Lord Berners's English translation (1534) was made from the earlier edition;
that of Sir T. North (1557) from the enlarged edition.

[3] Two editions were printed at Lyons in 1542, one by Dolet and the other by
P. de Tours (Christie, *E. Dolet*, p. 544). The companion treatise to the *Menosprecio de la Corte, Aviso de privados y doctrina de cortesanos*, was translated in
1556 under the title of *Le favori de court*. See on the influence of Guevara in
France L. Clement in *Rev. d'hist. litt.* VII. (1900) 590 ff. and for Montaigne's debt
to him, *ib.* VIII. (1901) 214 ff.

[4] An Italian translation was published at Lyons in 1552. T. Fortescue translated it into English in 1571.

gave to it[1]. This translation appeared in 1527, and was three
times reprinted before the end of Francis's reign[2]. If in the
Celestina Spain furnished Europe with the earliest example of
realistic drama, she may be said to have done the same for
the sentimental love story with Diego de San Pedro's *Arnalte
y Lucenda* and *Carcel de Amor*, which were published in 1491
and 1492 respectively. Both became popular in France. The
latter was the first to appear there, a translation of it being
published by the enterprising Galliot du Pré in 1526[3]. The
former found a translator in Herberay des Essarts, whose
version appeared in 1539 under the title of *Lamant mal
traicte de sa mye*. The later editions, of which there were
several from 1540 to 1560, bore the proper title of *Arnalte et
Lucinde*[4].

Another Spanish writer whose works were very popular in
France at this time, relating as they did to the favourite topic
of love, was Juan de Flores. A French translation of his
Grisel y Mirabella was published in 1527 under the title of
Jugement d'Amour[5]. It was afterwards called (after the name
given to it by its Italian translator) *Aurelio et Isabelle*, and
a translation with this title was made by the printer Gilles
Corrozet, who printed it side by side with the Italian version
from which he had made it (1546)[6]. Another love-treatise by
Juan de Flores takes the form of a discussion on Boccaccio's
Fiammetta, and bears the title of *Grimalte y Gradissa*[7]. It was
translated by Maurice Scève under the title of *La deplourable
fin de Flamete* (1535).

[1] First published, it appears, at Burgos in 1499. It is now generally agreed
that it is wholly the work of Fernando de Rojas (see Mr Fitzmaurice-Kelly's
admirable *History of Spanish Literature*, p. 125).

[2] Twice in 1529 and again in 1542.

[3] See Picot, II. no. 1747.

[4] *ib.* no. 1746.

[5] H. Harrisse, *Excerpta Colombiniana*, 1887, p. 119.

[6] A copy is in the British Museum, 8vo, collation A[8]—Q[8], pp. 128.   Brunet
does not mention any edition earlier than 1547.

[7] A reproduction has been published at Madrid (1883) of an old edition in
Gothic characters of this very rare work, which Gayangos, who contributes an
introduction, believes to be of the 15th century and to come from the same press
as the first edition of *Grisel y Mirabella*.

Finally it may be noticed that not only some of the works above mentioned, such as those of Guevara and the *Celestina*, but other Spanish writings were published in France in their original language.   In 1543 the piety of Boscan's widow had given to the world her husband's poems together with those of his greater friend, the brave, the noble, the brilliant Garcilaso de la Vega.   Three years later an edition of the two poets was published at Lyons[1].

---

[1] Boscan and Garcilaso were contemporaries of Clément Marot, Boscan (1490—1542) being rather older and Garcilaso (1503—1536) six years younger.

CHAPTER IV

MAROT

AT the beginning of the reign of Francis I the fashionable school of poetry was that of the *grands rhétoriqueurs*. Their most glaring faults were, firstly, the abuse of allegory; secondly, the adoption of a language full of latinised words and idioms; thirdly, the cultivation of highly artificial and even puerile forms of verse. They exaggerated in fact to the pitch of grotesqueness the respective tendencies of the *Roman de la Rose*, Alain Chartier and Eustache Deschamps. The head of the school was now Guillaume Cretin, *souverain poëte françois*, the pupil and successor of Jean Molinet, who had died in 1507. It was Molinet who had taught him the abomination of the *rime équivoque* or punning rhyme[1]. Another distinguished member of the school was Jean d'Auton, historiographer to Louis XII and the author of a tolerable prose chronicle of his reign. His pupil, Jean Bouchet[2], had also acquired fame at the court of Louis XII and Anne of Brittany, but in the next reign he retired to

---

[1] Marot calls him *le bon Cretin au vers équivoqué*. He could write simply sometimes, as in his pastoral poem on the birth of the Dauphin. For Cretin and the other poets who preceded Marot see Goujet, x.; Viollet Le Duc, *Bibliothèque poétique*, 1843; E. Crépet, *Les poëtes français*, I. 1861; Birch-Hirschfeld, pp. 87—108; Petit de Julleville, III. 84—97; Morf, pp. 9—28.

[2] 1476—c. 1558. See for contemporary editions of his writings Picot, I. nos. 504—511.

Poitiers, where he became the centre of an admiring circle, and during the intervals of his business as a hard-working lawyer continued to pour out reams of absolutely prosaic verse. He called himself *le Traverseur des voies périlleuses* and gave equally absurd names to his poems.

Another favourite poet of Anne of Brittany was Jean Marot. Besides a considerable number of minor pieces, he wrote *Le Voyage de Gênes* and *Le Voyage de Venise*, describing in great detail the Italian expeditions of Louis XII in 1507 and 1509, of which he was an eye-witness. They are considerably superior to the other rhymed chronicles of the period. Written in a great variety of metres they show some power of lively description, and on the whole, considering their subject, maintain a fairly high level of poetic language and harmony[1].

All the above mentioned poets were still living at the accession of Francis I. Another poet who had a high reputation was Octovien de Saint-Gelais, the scion of a noble family of Angoumois, who had died, as bishop of Angoulême, in 1502, at the early age of thirty-six. Though he had been trained in the *rhétoriqueur* school, his poetry bears more resemblance to that of Charles d'Orléans, whose work, though it was unprinted and apparently unknown at the beginning of the sixteenth century, he has been accused of plagiarising. But while Charles d'Orléans, at any rate in his later and better work, handles his allegorical machinery with taste and delicacy, Saint-Gelais works it to excess and crowds his canvas with all the cold and faded abstractions of the *Roman de la Rose*. However, in *Le Séjour d'honneur*[2], a poem interspersed with prose in which he gives in the form of an allegory an account of his own life, together with some

---

[1] The *Voyages* were first printed in 1533 in a volume edited by Clément Marot. The victories of the French in Italy were also celebrated by the Italian Alione, of Asti in Piedmont, but in indifferent French and still more indifferent verse. His later pieces are better, and the *Chanson d'une bergère*, if it still betrays the hand of a foreigner, has the merit of being fresh and natural (*Poësies françaises*, ed. J. C. Brunet, 1836, from the only known copy of Alione's *Opera iocunda*, 1521½).

[2] The earliest edition with a date is of 1519 (Picot, I. no. 478). It is analysed at length in Viollet Le Duc's *Bibliothèque poétique*, pp. 108—128.

interesting details of contemporary events and society, he frequently drops into a natural and graceful, if not highly poetical, style.

At the opposite pole to the courtly *rhétoriqueurs* were the poets who wrote, not for a noble or learned public, but for the *bourgeoisie*, and who may be conveniently described as the school of Villon. Not that Villon left any real inheritor of his genius, of his deep soul-stirring pathos and splendid harmony; but Guillaume Coquillart, an ecclesiastical lawyer, who held important offices in his native town of Reims, may by virtue of his knowledge of life, his faculty of observation, his power of realistic description, his dramatic touches, his copious vocabulary drawn largely from the speech of common life, his skilful use of picturesque epithets, be said to represent the more transmissible and accidental qualities of Villon[1]. On the other hand it must be admitted that his power of observation is confined to the external world, that his science of words becomes at times a mere trick, and that his use of the language of the streets often degenerates into an unintelligible jargon. Moreover, he writes in a jerky disconnected style and a slip-shod octosyllabic metre which, though giving the idea of careless ease, soon becomes intolerably wearisome.

His only professed disciple was Roger de Collerye, a native of Paris, who passed the greater part of his days at Auxerre in obscurity and poverty, unknown to all but a very few of his fellow-poets. The name, Roger Bontemps, by which he called himself in his joyous moods, has made him a familiar figure in French literature, and his poems are interesting on account of their strong personal element, but in spite of D'Héricault's warm eulogies it is difficult to regard

---

[1] Coquillart was born in 1421 and died (according to D'Héricault) in 1510, but, though he was thus ten years older than Villon, his literary work did not begin much before Villon's death. His poems, of which the principal are *Les droits nouveaux*, *Le Playdoyer d'entre la Simple et la Rusée*, *L'Enqueste d'entre la Simple et la Rusée*, *Le Blason des Armes et des Dames* and *Le Monologue Coquillart*, were first collected in an edition printed about 1512-15. The best modern edition is that of D'Héricault in the *Bib. Elzévirienne*, 2 vols., 1857.

him as other than an indifferent and belated mediæval poet, upon whom the breath of the Renaissance never blew[1].

There is more resemblance to Coquillart in the work of the two popular Paris playwrights and managers of dramatic companies, Pierre Gringore and Jehan du Pontalais, both of whom were satirists of contemporary vices and follies. Gringore's chief interest lies in his dramatic work[2]. Though he lived till near the end of the reign of Francis I, the repressive measures which that king put in force against the Basoche and the *Enfans sans souci* led him to retire to the court of Lorraine, where, as the herald of Duke Antoine, he spent his remaining days partly in organising plays for the court and partly in translating Hours and writing religious and didactic poems. Jehan de l'Espine du Pontalais, who was also an important figure at the court of Lorraine between 1517 and 1525, and whose name frequently occurs in the literature of the time[3], was till recently only known as the chief of a troupe of actors, but it has been shewn on documentary evidence that a satirical poem, remarkable for the boldness of its satire and the racy vigour of its expression, entitled *Les Contreditz de Songecreux*[4], which was formerly attributed to Gringore, is really the work of Jehan du Pontalais, who was known by the soubriquet of Songecreux[5].

---

[1] Roger de Collerye was born about 1470 and died probably soon after 1536, the year in which the first and only edition of his poems, until the modern one of D'Héricault, was published by P. Roffet, of which only two perfect copies and one imperfect one are known to exist. (See *Œuvres*, ed. D'Héricault, 1885. Picot, I. no. 517.)

[2] See *Introductory Essay*, pp. 176 ff.

[3] See Marot, *Epître du coq à l'asne* (*Œuvres*, I. 187); Des Periers, *Nouvelles* XXX.

[4] Paris, 1529.

[5] This identification was first suggested by E. Fournier in *Variétés hist. et litt.* X. 356. See *Anc. poésies franç.* XII. 170; L. Petit de Julleville, *Les comédiens en France au moyen âge*, 1885, pp. 167—179; *Œuvres de Marot*, ed. Guiffrey, III. 235 n. 4 and 254 nn. 1 and 2; Picot, I. no. 502. Jehan du Pontalais was one of the actors arrested in December 1516 by order of Francis I for having insulted Louise of Savoy (*Anc. poésies franç.* XI. 250, n. 1). Pontalais or Pontalletz is a corruption of Pont des Allez, a bridge over the sewer near Saint-Eustache (Fournier, *ib.* III. 146).

Finally there is another poet who, like Jehan du Pontalais, has been more or less discovered in quite modern times, and to whom undoubted resemblances are to be found in Marot. This is Henri Baude, a native of Moulins, who may be said to derive partly from Charles d'Orléans, to whose poetical circle he at one time belonged, and partly from Villon; he resembles the former in his occasional touches of elegance and tendency to allegory, the latter in his simple and direct style of writing and considerable power of expression. He is, however, by no means free from the prosaic malady from which, as we have seen, the age was suffering[1].

Such were the poets who were most in repute in France in the year 1515 when Francis I ascended the throne. In that year a new aspirant to poetical fame printed and dedicated to the king a poem called *Le Temple de Cupidon*. The young poet was Clément Marot, the only son of Jean Marot. He was now in his nineteenth year, having been born in the winter of 1496–97 at Cahors on the Lot, the capital of the province of Quercy, which still retains its striking fourteenth-century bridge with its three towers. His father's family, the name of which was variously written as Mares, Marais, Des Mares and Desmarets, was Norman by origin, and certainly Clément had far more of the Norman than the southerner in his temperament. But some time before his birth his father had settled at Cahors, where he acquired some property and married. Clément's mother was his second wife. In 1506 the boy, to use his own expression, was taken to France[2] and matriculated at the University of Paris. After

---

[1] Baude seems to have lived from *circ.* 1430 to *circ.* 1495. An edition of some of his poems, edited by his discoverer Quicherat in 1856, forms one of the volumes of the *Trésor des pièces rares ou inédites.* Another poem, *Le debat de la Dame et de l'Escuyer,* is printed in the *Anc. poésies franç.* IV. 151 ff. See Crepet, I. 469 ff. (notice by A. de Montaiglon). Marot's *Epigram* 168 (*Œuvres* III. 68) is founded on Baude's *Lamentations Bourrien,* the last two lines of which are borrowed without any alteration.

[2]
    Car une matinée,
N'ayant dix ans en France fuz mené
Là ou depuis me suis tant pourmené
Que j'oubliay ma langue maternelle
Et grossement apprins la paternelle
Langue françoyse.   *L'Enfer* (*Œuvres,* I. 60).

completing his course in arts, during which he seems to have
made little progress in learning, and in particular to have
acquired but a smattering of Latin[1], he became a law student,
but occupied himself more with the plays of the Basochiens
than with legal business. In 1513 he abandoned the law and
became page to Nicholas de Neufville, Seignéur de Villeroy,
whom he accompanied to the wars in Italy.   The poem
which he dedicated to Francis I was not his first attempt.
In 1512 he had made a translation, with the help doubtless of
some friend more learned than himself, of Virgil's first Eclogue.
Though wanting in polish and vigour, it has the merit, which
is a great one considering the time of its production, of being
written simply and naturally, without affectation or pedantry.
    It was from his father that he had his first poetical lessons:

> Il me souloit une leçon donner
> Pour doulcement la musette entonner,
> Ou à dicter quelque chanson ruralle
> Pour la chanter en mode pastoralle.
> Aussi le soir, que les trouppeaux espars
> Estoient serrez et remis en leurs parcs,
> Le bon vieillard après moy travailloit,
> Et à la lampe assez tard me veilloit[2].

But two early pieces, the *Ballade des enfans sans soucy*[3] and
the *Cry du jeu de l'Empire d'Orléans*[4], are evidently inspired
by Villon and Coquillart, while two translations, written about
1515, the *Jugement de Minos*[5] and *Les tristes vers de Beroalde
sur le jour du vendredy sainct*[6], shew traces of *rhétoriqueur*
influence. Then in *Le Temple de Cupidon*[7], the poem dedicated
to Francis I in 1515, we come upon a full burst of allegory :

> C'est Beau Parler, Bien Celer, Bon Rapport,
> Grace, Mercy, Bien Servir, Bien Aymer,
> Qui les amans font venir à bon port,

and *Bel Acueil* and *Faulx Danger* and *Ferme Amour*. But,
the allegorical machinery apart, the poem lacks neither grace
nor simplicity, as for instance in the following lines :

---

[1] See a letter of Jean de Boysonne quoted by Guiffrey, II. 20 n. 1.
[2] *Œuvres*, I. 40.   [3] II. 61.   [4] II. 62.
[5] III. 126.   [6] III. 138.   [7] I. 5.

Car d'amourettes les services
Sont faictz en termes si tresclairs,
Que les apprentifz et novices
En sçaivent plus que les grans clercs.

The title of the poem was evidently suggested by Jean le
Maire's *Temple de Venus* and *Temple d'Honneur et de Vertus*.
Of this poet I have already spoken in my *Introductory Essay*,
where I pointed out that real poetical sentiment underlay his
respectful adherence to the traditions of the *rhétoriqueur*
school, and that it occasionally found its way to the surface[1].
It was Le Maire who called Marot's attention to his faulty
use of the *coupe féminine* after the caesura in his juvenile
poems[2], and the young poet speaks of him in one of his poems
with the greatest admiration as

Jean Le Maire Belgeois,
Qui l'ame avoit d'Homere le Gregeois[3].

During the next eight or nine years Marot made little
progress in the development of his poetical talent. The
epistles, songs, *ballades* and *rondeaux* which date from this
period are seldom entirely free from one or other of the
fashionable follies of allegory and rhythmical trifling[4]. But
about the year 1524 he began to throw off the baneful
influences of his predecessors and to write in a really natural
vein. To this and the following year belongs some of his
most graceful work, such as the exquisite *chanson* beginning
Qui veult avoir liesse[5], the charming early elegies[6], and the
ballade of *Frère Lubin*[7]. Some of the elegies, which are
probably addressed to the lady who soon afterwards became

[1] Pp. 167–9. Le Maire's works have been edited by J. Stecher, 3 vols.
Louvain, 1882–5, and see A. Becker, *Jean Lemaire Der erste humanistische
Dichter Frankreichs*, Strasburg, 1893.

[2] In the ed. of 1534 *O Melibée mon bon amy parfaict* is corrected to *O Melibée,
amy cher et parfaict*.

[3] *Œuvres*, I. 258 (*Epistre* 55).

[4] In the *chanson*, *Dieu gard ma Maistresse et regente* (II. 176) we have instances
of the *rime annexée, couronnée* and *enchaînée*. For the *rime batelée* see the *ballade*
on the birth of the Dauphin (1517), II. 68, and for the *rime équivoque* the *Epistre
au Roy* (I. 149).

[5] II. 181.   [6] II. 5 ff.   [7] II. 63.

his wife, were written during the disastrous campaign which ended in the defeat of Pavia (1525). Marot was wounded in the arm and taken prisoner, but after a short time recovered his liberty and returned in safety to France.

The end of the first quarter of the sixteenth century marks not only the rise of the new school of poetry, but the fall of the old. By the year 1525, Guillaume Cretin, and almost certainly Jean le Maire, were dead; Jean Marot died the year after; Jean d'Auton in the first month of 1527. The popularity of the *rhétoriqueur* poetry survived for a few years, but the new poet had no longer any older rivals to overshadow his growing fame.

Meanwhile he had secured for himself the favour of the king, and in the year 1526 he succeeded his father as one of the *valets de chambre* of the royal household[1] with a salary of 240 *livres* a year. Before this he had been for some years attached to the household of Margaret of Angoulême, then Duchess of Alençon. The time had come when powerful protection was very necessary to him. In 1525 stringent measures had been set on foot for the suppression of heresy, and as a consequence the observance of Church ordinances was enforced with rigour. Apparently owing to the spite of some fair enemy Marot was arrested in February 1526 for eating meat in Lent[2] and thrown into the Châtelet. Through the efforts of his friend, Lyon Jamet, and the friendly interposition of the Bishop of Chartres, he was transferred to a nominal prison at Chartres, till on the king's return from captivity he was released altogether[3].

---

[1] For the evidence as to the date of Jean Marot's death and his son's succession to his office see Harrisse, *Excerpta Colombiniana*, 153 ff., where the subject is fully discussed. Chaucer, like Marot, was a *valet du roi* and, like Marot, was taken prisoner in his first campaign.

[2] The simple explanation of the cause of Marot's arrest is undoubtedly the correct one (see Guiffrey, III. 76, n. 2). M. Douen has rashly adopted an "important discovery" of Henry Morley, that the Isabeau of *rondeau* lxvi, the *amie* of *ballade* xiv, and the Luna of *L'Enfer* denote the Catholic Church.

[3]   *J'euz à Paris prison fort inhumaine;*
         A Chartres fuz doulcement encloué.   II. 166.

He was released in Easter week, *Le premier jour de la verte semaine.*

There is some doubt as to when Marot's conversion to Protestantism took place, but on the whole there seems no reason to doubt his own statement in the Epistle to Bouchart, by whose orders he had been imprisoned :

> Point ne suis lutheriste
> Ne zuinglien, et moins anabaptiste[1].

The treatment, however, which he received no doubt helped to draw him more closely to the reformers. From this time the tone of his poems becomes much more hostile and impertinent to the Catholic Church.

His actual conversion seems to have taken place while he was on a visit to Blois, probably in the year 1527[2]. Certainly the *Complainte de Robertet*, written at the close of that year on the death of Florimond Robertet, finance minister to Francis I and his two predecessors[3], in which the doctrine of justification by faith is put prominently forward, purgatory is carefully omitted from the economy of the other world, and the ministers of the Catholic religion are treated with scant respect, could only have been written by a thorough Lutheran[4].

---

[1] *Epistre* x (I. 153). In the editions of Roffet and Bonnemère (both of 1536) *encoire moins Papiste* was substituted for *moins anabaptiste*, but it was subsequently altered again.

[2] In *Le Balladin* (I. 107 ff.), an allegorical account, unfortunately unfinished, of Marot's conversion to Protestantism, he speaks of Christine, who represents the Reformed Faith, as meeting him on the banks of the Loire and awakening his heart, and Malingre, in a rhyming epistle to him written December 2, 1542, says :

> ...Il y a desia quinze ans passez
> Que ces abus tu congnoissois assez....
> Comme tu m'as ouy prescher à Bloys.

Lefèvre d'Etaples had been residing at Blois in the capacity of keeper of the royal library since the beginning of July, 1526.

[3] He died November 29, 1527 (*Journal d'un bourgeois*, pp. 330, 1). In spite of this exact statement the *Nouv. Biog. Gén.* and M. Lalanne in his *Dictionnaire historique* give 1522 as the year of his death.

[4]
> Prie à Dieu seul que par grace te donne
> La vive foy, dont sainct Paul tant escript.
>
> Le bon chrestien au ciel ira grand'erre.
>
> Messes sans nombres et force anniversaires,
> C'est belle chose, et la façon j'en prise ;
> Si sont les chants, cloches et luminaires ;
> Mais le mal est en l'avare prebstrise :

Soon after this he gave another proof of his sympathy with
the reformers by writing an epistle on the occasion of Berquin's
execution (April 17, 1529), in which he gives an account of
his last moments[1]. Another Epistle, written in the autumn
of this year when he was leaving Paris in attendance on the
Court, shews what his feelings then were towards the Catholic
Church:

> L'oysiveté des prebstres et cagotz,
> Je la dirois, mais garde les fagotz!
> Et des abuz dont l'Eglise est fourrée,
> J'en parlerois, mais gare la bourrée![2]

In September 1531 Louise of Savoy died, and Marot
lamented her death in a pastoral Eclogue of considerable
beauty[3]. In the same year he presented Duke Antoine of
Lorraine with a translation (probably in manuscript) of the
first book of Ovid's *Metamorphoses*[4]. In March 1532, just
after he had recovered from a long and severe illness, he was
again in trouble for having eaten meat in Lent, but the queen
of Navarre interposed and saved him from the prosecution
with which he was threatened[5].

Since the year 1524 Marot's poetical powers had been
steadily maturing; he had been gaining in ease and vigour
and certainty of touch. We see this especially in the Epistles
written during this period. His first attempts in this direction
(Epistles i—ix) are marked by the stiffness and affectation of
the *rhétoriqueur* school, qualities which are particularly out of
place in a kind of poetry which demands above all things ease

> Car si tu n'as vaillant que ta chemise,
> Tien toy certain qu'après le tien trespas
> Il n'y aura ne convent ne eglise
> Qui pour toy sonne ou chante ou face un pas.
>
> *Œuvres*, II. 244 ff.

[1] Found by Guiffrey with other pieces by Marot in a MS. at Soissons (Guiffrey,
III. 107).

[2] *Aux Dames de Paris* (*Œuvres*, I. 161).

[3] First published separately in 1531 (Brunet). In the editions of Marot's
works it appears among the *Complaintes* (*Œuvres*, II. 260 ff.). See *post*, p. 78.

[4] See *Epistre* xv, *A Mons. de Lorraine*. This translation was not printed, so
far as is known, till 1534. See Guiffrey, II. 302.

[5] Guiffrey, III. 206, n. 1; 226, n. 1.

and directness. The first Epistle in which Marot shewed his peculiar aptitude for this branch of poetry is the well-known one addressed from the prison of the Châtelet to his friend Lyon Jamet, containing the Fable of the Lion and the Rat, which he relates with a liveliness and dramatic power worthy of La Fontaine[1]. Equally good are two Epistles to the king, the one written towards the end of 1526 in which he begs him to see that his name is duly inserted in the place of his father's on the roll of the royal household[2], and the other written in 1527, in which he asks Francis to order his release from prison, where he had been thrown for having tried to rescue a prisoner from the archers of the watch[3]. Both these are no less remarkable for the tone of respectful familiarity with which the poet addresses his royal master than for their literary merit. But the masterpiece among his Epistles, the one which is quoted in every anthology of French poetry, is the *Epistre au Roy pour avoir esté derobé*, written in 1532, just after he had recovered from a long and severe illness, and containing the famous lines:

> J'avois un jour un vallet de Gascongne,
> Gourmand, ivrongne, et asseuré menteur,
> Pipeur, larron, jureur, blasphemateur,
> Sentant la hart de cent pas à la ronde,
> Au demourant, le meilleur filz du monde[4].

The same narrative power which is displayed in these Epistles, the same vigour, directness and dramatic liveliness which such a power implies, are found in his poem *L'Enfer*, written at Chartres and giving under the guise of a trial in Hades before Minos an account of his imprisonment in the Châtelet and his examination before his judges[5]. The Elegy on behalf of Jacques de Samblançay[6], the superintendent of the finances, who was hanged in August 1527, and which takes

---

[1] *Ep.* xi (I. 154).

[2] *Ep.* xxxv, *Au Roy pour succeder en l'estat de son pere.* (I. 202.)

[3] *Ep.* xxvii, *Au Roy pour le delivrer de prison.* (I. 190.)

[4] *Ep.* xxxix (I. 195). See the *dixain* addressed to Marot by Saint-Gelais (Saint Gelais, *Œuvres*, II. 131).

[5] *Œuvres*, I. 47; first published at Antwerp in 1539, and then by Dolet in 1542.

[6] *Elegie* xxii (II. 51).

the form of a dying speech by the condemned man after his
death, though necessarily written in a different vein, shews
the same ease and directness that we find in the narrative
poems, the same use of the *mot propre* instead of some
grandiloquent or subtle periphrasis. It is interesting, too,
to find in this Elegy a reminiscence of Villon, for the line

> Lavé de pluye et du soleil seché,

must surely have been suggested by

> La pluye nous a debuez et lavez,
> Et le soleil dessechez et noirciz.

There are other less obvious reminiscences in the same poem.
Marot was a great admirer of Villon; he speaks of the
" beautiful and heroic vein" of his ballads, says that his
works are " full of good doctrine and painted with a thousand
colours," and acknowledges his own indebtedness to him[1].
Villon's poems had been frequently printed since the invention
of printing, but all the editions since that of Trepperel in 1497
were ill-arranged and carelessly printed with great injury to
the sense and the rhyme, and they contained various pieces
not written by Villon. Marot, therefore, partly from his
admiration for his poetry and partly as a pious recognition
of what he had learnt from him, undertook to prepare for
Galliot du Pré, for whom he had already edited the *Roman
de la Rose* (1527), a new and carefully revised edition of his
works, which appeared at the end of 1533, with an admirable
appreciation by way of preface[2].

It is interesting to notice that Galliot du Pré, who in 1526
had brought out a volume containing works of the three
successive chiefs of the *rhétoriqueurs*, Chastelain, Molinet and
Cretin[3], was now busy publishing poems of the opposite
school. Thus in 1530 he published *Les Contreditz de Songecreux*,
and in 1532 Villon, Coquillart, Gringore[4], and *Pathelin* in

---

[1] Marot's Preface to Villon's works (*Œuvres*, IV. 190). See H. Rose, *Der
Einfluss Villon's auf Marot*, Glückstadt, 1877.

[2] See Longnon's ed. of Villon (1892), p. ciii, no. 21. It is sometimes incorrectly stated that Marot's edition was published in 1532.

[3] See Picot, I. no. 487.

[4] *Le Chasteau de Labour* and *Les faintises du monde*, the latter possibly not by
Gringore (*ib.* no. 493).

a uniform series. When we consider that, in spite of his bold motto of *Vogue la gallée*, he was as prudent as a Scotchman and confined his publications to works which were likely to be remunerative, and when we see that in the two years 1532 and 1533 *Pathelin* and *Les Contreditz de Songecreux* were published once and Coquillart twice by other publishers, we may reasonably infer that the fashion in poetry had entirely changed, and that the literary public had at last grown tired of the cold and wearisome abstractions of the *rhétoriqueurs* and welcomed as a relief the racier and more national flavour of poets who had not had the advantage of " being brought up in the courts of kings and princes[1]."

At any rate the year 1532 is an important date, not only in Marot's poetical career, but in the history of French poetry, for it marks the publication of the first collected edition of Marot's poems. It must be remembered that in these days poets were not in so great a hurry to see themselves in print as they are in modern times. They passed their poems about in manuscript among their friends and patrons long before they ever thought of a collected edition. So Marot's poems had hitherto only circulated in manuscript, or at most had been published like the *Temple de Cupidon* as simple broadsides[2]. But, at last, partly urged thereto by his admiring friends and partly in order to rid himself of the annoyance of hearing incorrect and badly-printed versions of his poems hawked about the streets, he entered into an agreement with the enterprising publisher, Pierre Roffet, for a collected edition. The printing of it was entrusted to Geoffroy Tory, the king's printer, and was finished on the 12th of August[3]. It was entitled *Adolescence Clementine*. A second, third, and fourth edition, which followed at short intervals, testified to its popularity[4].

The first nine months of the year 1533 were a period of considerable promise for the French Reformers. Gérard Roussel preached daily during Lent in the Louvre, and Noel

[1] Marot's preface to Villon.
[2] See Guiffrey, II. 14, n. 1.   [3] See Appendix A.
[4] The printing of the 4th edition was finished June 4, 1433.

Beda, having accused the King and Queen of Navarre of
heresy and tried to create a commotion, was banished from
the city. In consequence of this the walls were placarded
with rival verses and lampoons. To a Catholic poster which
appeared on May 27, beginning with

> Au feu, au feu ceste heresie,

Marot replied with the following *rondeau* :

> En l'eau, en l'eau ces folz seditieux,
> Lesquelz en lieu des divines paroles
> Preschent au peuple un tas de monopoles
> Pour esmouvoir debatz contentieux.
>
> Le Roy leur est un peu trop gratieux :
> Que n'a-il mis à bas ces testes folles
> En l'eau.
>
> Ilz ayment tant les vins delicieux
> Qu'on peult nommer cabaretz leurs escoles :
> Mais refroidir fauldroit leurs chauldes colles
> Par le rebours de ce qu'ilz ayment mieulx
> En l'eau[1].

It is to this period that we must assign the publication of
his translation of the sixth Psalm[2]. In 1534 he published
a fresh collection of poems under the title of *Suite de
l'Adolescence*[3], and then came the affair of the placards[4]
(October 18) which made danger and exile his portion for the
rest of his days. His name figured high on the list of the
fugitive Lutherans who were summoned to return to Paris
within three days under pain of attainder and banishment.
He was at Blois at the time and fled forthwith to the Court
of the Queen of Navarre. But even this shelter was not considered sufficient to protect him, and he was sent by Margaret,
who provided for the expenses of the journey, to Renée,
Duchess of Ferrara, the daughter of Louis XII, a woman of

---

[1] *Rondeau* lxxii (*Œuvres*, II. 169).

[2] It first appeared by itself, printed in Gothic letter, without name of place or
printer. It was republished later in the same year with Margaret of Navarre's
Le Miroir de l'âme pecheresse. See *Excerpta Colombiniana*, pp. 153 ff., where
M. Harrisse shews that the separate issue of Psalm vi must have preceded the
1533 edition of the *Miroir*.

[3] See Appendix A.   [4] See *ante* p. 28.

deep piety and high mental culture, whose court vied with
that of Nérac as a centre for men of letters and artists, and as
an asylum for the persecuted. Here Marot arrived about the
middle of 1535, and before long was appointed poet and
secretary to the Duchess with a salary of 200 *livres*. But the
Duke of Ferrara, Ercole d'Este, was no friend to the new
doctrines, and in the following summer (1536), having joined
the alliance of Charles V and the Pope, he found it necessary
to expel the French refugees from his court. Marot retired
to Venice, where he remained till the winter, pining, like a
true Frenchman, for his native land[1]. At last the king gave
him permission to return. In spite of the winter season he
set out at once and made his way to Lyons, where he was
warmly received by the literary coterie of that city[2]. But a
less pleasant reception was in store for him. He was compelled by the Cardinal de Tournon, now governor of Lyons,
to make a public recantation of heresy. The ceremony was an
impressive one, and it included the application at intervals
of a rod to the penitent's shoulders[3]. Marot was glad to
leave Lyons and return to Paris, where he was reinstated
in his post in the royal household.

> Va, Lyon, que Dieu te gouverne ;
> Assez long temps s'est esbatu
> Le petit chien en ta caverne,
> Que devant toy on a batu.
> Finablement, pour sa vertu,
> Adieu des foys un million ·
> A Tournon, de rouge vestu,
> Gouverneur de ce grand Lyon.
>
> *Adieux à la ville de Lyon*[4].

He celebrated his return to favour in an epistle of considerable
dignity and elevation of tone, entitled *Le Dieu gard à la court*[5].

---

[1] See Vulteius, *Epigrammata* (1536), pp. 120—123.

[2] *Epistre* xlviii, *à Mons. le Cardinal de Tournon* (I. 234). Marot arrived at
Lyons about Dec. 10, 1536.

[3] In spite of Marot's apologists there is no doubt that this recantation took
place. See J. Bonnet in *Bull. prot. franç.* XXXIV. 300, 1885.

[4] I. 237.

[5] *Ep.* 1 (I. 138) ; published first as a separate piece in May 1537 (Brunet).
Marot reached Paris in the middle of January of that year.

During his absence at Ferrara a Norman priest named
François Sagon, who had won seven prizes for poetry at local
contests, including four at the Puy of Rouen, moved partly by
professional jealousy, partly by orthodox zeal, published under
the title of *Coup d'Essay* a poem in which Marot's poetry,
religion and morals were attacked in the most offensive terms.
Marot at first made no reply, but his friends and disciples,
Des Periers, Charles Fontaine, Borderie and Brodeau, took up
the cudgels on his behalf, while Sagon was backed by an
obscure poet, Charles Huet, who was known as La Hueterie[1].
Then Marot, on his return to Paris, flayed his opponents, to
use his own expression, in an Epistle purporting to be written
by his valet, Fripelipes :

> L'un est un vieux resveur Normand,
> Si goulu, friand et gourmand
> De la peau du povre Latin,
> Qu'il l'escorche comme un mastin.
> L'autre un Huet de sotte grace,
> Lequel voulut voler la place
> De l'absent : mais le demandeur
> Eust affaire à un entendeur.
> O le Huet en bel arroy
> Pour entrer en chambre de Roy[2] !

One poet tried to pour oil on the waters by addressing a
poetical epistle to both the combatants in which he adjured
them as Christians to put an end to their quarrel.   This was
Germain Colin Bucher, a native of Angers, whose poems have
been disinterred in quite recent times[3].   His attitude to the
two representatives of the old and the new school of poetry
corresponds pretty closely to his own poetical achievement.

---

[1] The poems of Marot's supporters were collected and published under the title
of *Les disciples et amys de Marot contre Sagon, le Huet et leurs adherents*, Jehan
Morin, Paris, 1537 ; and two editions without a date.   See Picot, III. no. 2594.

[2] *Ep.* li (*Œuvres*, I. 240) ; printed separately by Morin in 1537.

[3] The manuscript of his poems was discovered in the *Bibliothèque nationale* by
M. Joseph Denais and published in 1890.   To this M. Picot added a supplement,
Supplément aux poësies de Germain Colin, 1890, consisting of the epistle to
Marot and Sagon and one addressed to Francis I appealing from a sentence
of banishment passed on him for heretical opinions.   M. Picot thinks that he was
about Marot's age, which is probable : we hear nothing of him after 1545.

For though he is in the main a provincial poet of the type of Bouchet or Grosnet, he shews occasional gleams of Marot's grace and *naïveté* and tact.

There is little to interest us in this literary battle beyond the fact that Sagon was a representative of the pedantry and provincialism against which Marot's poetry was a perpetual protest[1]. Rouen, Sagon's native town, was in fact one of the two remaining strongholds from which the older poetry had not been completely dislodged. The annual poetical contests which the *Confrères de l'Immaculée Conception* had established in 1486 under the name of the *Puy de l'Immaculée Conception* and the *Puy du Palinod* had no doubt helped to keep alive the old traditions[2]. It was at Rouen, too, that was published, in 1522, the "art of poetry" of another Rouen ecclesiastic, Pierre Fabri, which was based entirely on the practice of the *rhétoriqueur* school[3]. It was reprinted at Paris alone no less than five times between 1532 and 1544. The other stronghold of the old poetry was Toulouse, where the "master-singers" also had their contests under the name of *Jeux Floraux*, dating from 1324, but re-organised towards the close of the fifteenth century. Toulouse, too, produced an "art of poetry" written by Gracien du Pont, seigneur de Drusac, in which he explained every conceivable form of rhythmical puerility[4]. He also kept up the mediæval tradition of abusing women in *Les controverses des Sexes Masculin et Femenin*[5], a

[1] There is an excellent account of the whole affair by M. Bonnefon in the *Rev. d'hist. litt.* I. (1894), 103 ff.; 259 ff. See also E. Voizard, *Œuvres choisies de M.*, pp. xxxiv—xlvi, and a Latin thesis by the same writer.

[2] Corneille gained the prize at the Rouen Puy in 1633, and Jacqueline Pascal, then a girl of fifteen, in 1640. There were Puys in other Norman towns such as Evreux and Dieppe; they flourished also in Picardy. See Petit de Julleville, *Les comédiens en France au moyen âge*, pp. 42 ff. He derives *puy* from *podium*—the platform from which the poems were recited, which seems the natural derivation. Gaston Paris derives it from Le Puy, the place where, according to him, the contests were first instituted (*Litt. franç. au moyen âge*, p. 185).

[3] *Le grand et vray art de pleine Rhetorique*, Rouen, 152½; reprinted at Rouen, 2 vols. 1889-90, with notes by A. Heron for the *Société des bibliophiles normands.*

[4] *Art et Science de Rhetoricque metrifiee.* Toulouse, 1539. For this and for Fabri's treatise see H. Zschalig, *Die Verslehren von Fabri, Du Pont et Sibilet.* Leipsic, 1884.

[5] Toulouse, 153⅔ (Picot, III. 2596).

work which had considerable success, and he had a violent feud with Dolet, the ardent supporter of the new order of things[1].

At Lyons Marot had made the acquaintance of Dolet, and we have seen that he was present at the dinner given to him at Paris in February 1537. In the following year he transferred to Dolet's press, recently established at Lyons, the new and revised edition of his poems which Gryphius had just published[2]. He tells us in an interesting preface that numerous pirated editions of his poems had appeared, especially at Lyons, which contained pieces not by his hand, and which either from being 'ill-composed' had 'touched his honour,' or from being 'full of scandal and sedition' had endangered his person[3]. It was one of the dangers which writers tainted with heresy incurred in those days of imperfect copyright. No author likes to see himself in an unauthorised edition; he likes it still less when it exposes him to the risk of being burnt. We shall see that a few years later Dolet played the same trick on Rabelais, thereby forfeiting his friendship.

In the year 1539 Marot presented to the king an Eclogue, in which in proper pastoral language he gives an interesting sketch of his poetical career, and concludes by asking him for the grant of a small estate as a provision for the approaching winter of his life[4]. As he was only forty-two he was making provision in good time. Never was a poet's begging appeal couched in more graceful language, and it obtained the success it deserved. The king gave him "a house, grange and garden, all enclosed by walls, and situated in the *faubourg* Saint-Germain."

But in this year the poet must have been chiefly occupied with his translation of the Psalms. We have seen that he had translated one Psalm in 1533. In the following year appeared

---

[1] Christie, *E. Dolet*, 109 ff.; and for Du Pont generally see Goujet, XI. 184.
[2] See Appendix A. [3] *Œuvres*, IV. 194.
[4] *Œuvres*, I. 39. It first appeared in an edition of Marot's works published at Paris by Bignon in 1540, but with a separate pagination. There is a copy in the British Museum.

Vatable's Latin translation which Marot doubtless used for the rest of his work[1]. But it was not till the close of 1539 that thirty Psalms were completed and circulated. The king was greatly pleased with them, and they became the fashion at the Court. The Dauphin was especially enthusiastic and set one to music[2]. In spite, however, of their success, the Psalms were not printed at Paris till the winter of 1541-42[3]. The reason is not difficult to find. However much Francis and his Court might take pleasure in Marot's harmonious verses, the theologians had come to the conclusion that translations of the Scriptures into the vernacular were highly heretical, and Francis since his reconciliation with Charles V being in a thoroughly orthodox mood, it was impossible for any publisher to obtain a privilege to print the Psalms. But by the autumn of 1541 Francis had quarrelled again with the Emperor and was making active preparations for war. His orthodoxy began once more to decline, and as a consequence, on the last day of November, 1541, the necessary privilege was granted to Estienne Roffet.

But before long fresh political complications arose which resulted in a new edict against Protestantism being issued at Lyons on August 30, 1542. Marot fled with the intention of going to Cahors, but hearing on the road that an order for his arrest was abroad he changed his mind and crossed the frontier. From November 1542 to the winter of 1543-44 he resided at Geneva[4], ill at ease in the austere atmosphere of that city. But he found a suitable occupation in working at his translation of the Psalms, of which a new edition, with nineteen additional Psalms and the song of

[1] In the *Epistre de Fripelipes* written, as we have seen, soon after Marot's return to Paris in 1537, there is a quotation from the ninth Psalm almost in the words of his translation as it was afterwards printed. It is not unlikely that it was in the Protestant atmosphere of Ferrara that he determined to make a complete translation of the Psalms and proceeded to carry his design into execution.

[2] See the testimony of an eye-witness cited by O. Douen in *C. Marot et le psautier huguenot*, 1878, p. 284.

[3] Twelve Psalms were printed with five of Calvin's in the Strasburg Psalter, the primitive Psalter of the French Protestants, in 1539, and the whole thirty were published at Antwerp in 1541.

[4] Calvin to Viret in Calvin's *Opera*, XI. 468.

Simeon, was published in August or September 1543. However, a game of backgammon which he played with Bonivard,
a congenial spirit, for five sous caused a scandal. Bonivard
was cited before the Consistory, and Marot retreated to
Savoy[1]. Then hearing of the French victory at Cérisoles he
again crossed the Alps and joined the French camp. On his
return he was taken ill at Turin, and died somewhere about
the month of August, aged forty-seven years. Shortly before
his death a new edition of his poems had been published at
Lyons, in which, for the first time, they appeared in the order
which has been more or less adhered to in all subsequent
editions[2].

Of all the French poets who have from time to time given
a new direction to the course of French poetry Marot is the
only one who effected this change modestly and peacefully.
He made no warfare on his predecessors, he issued no
manifestos; but he gradually emancipated himself from the
poetical traditions with which he was surrounded in his youth,
and when by the age of twenty-seven he had found an
independent style of his own it was seen that French poetry
had undergone a remarkable transformation. This was most
visible in the matter of language. In place of the pseudo-
classical pedantry of the *rhétoriqueurs* and the scarcely less
affected jargon of the would-be followers of Villon it now
spoke a language which, without being vulgar or commonplace, had the true savour of the soil of France. It was clear,
firm, easy, lending itself alike to tenderness and pathos, to wit
and humour. Here at last was a true Frenchman. This
transformation was in a large measure due to Marot's native
tact and good sense. But he was helped by two external
influences, the Court and classical models. In the preface to
his edition of Villon he says "that he has no doubt that
Villon would have surpassed all the poets of his time had he
been bred at the court of kings and princes, where judgment
becomes finer and language more polished." This implies
that he recognised his own debt to the Court. At a time

[1] Douen, *op. cit.* pp. 413, 414.
[2] See Appendix A.

when the crying need of French poetry was for a natural language, the conversation of polite society could not fail to have a beneficial influence upon a young poet.

The other influence, that of classical models, has been sometimes exaggerated, sometimes unduly neglected. We have seen that Marot was very slightly equipped with classical learning, that he knew no Greek, and very little Latin. But nevertheless his poetry shews decided traces of classical influence. He translated two books of Ovid's *Metamorphoses*, an Eclogue of Virgil, and a few epigrams of Martial; and, through Latin versions, the *Hero and Leander* of Musæus and the *Fugitive Eros* of Moschus[1]. His translations are such as one might expect from a man who knew little Latin; they are free and inaccurate. There are also obvious reminiscences of Virgil and Ovid in some of his original poems[2]. But the most important feature is that the form of no inconsiderable portion of his poetry is moulded on classical models. He wrote epigrams on the model of Martial, he followed Ovid in his elegies, and Virgil in his eclogues. Moreover, in the species of poetry in which he attained perhaps the most marked success, namely the Epistle, he was largely influenced by Horace. The ease, the good-humour, the personal confidences, the introduction of a story or a fable, and, above all, the perfect tact of his bearing towards the great men to whom his epistles are addressed—these are all true Horatian characteristics[3].

Marot was on the whole, like most French writers, a conscientious artist. Like La Fontaine, who owed not a little to him, he combined perfection with apparent ease. In his best songs and *ballades* and *rondeaux* he attains the simplicity which is the highest achievement of art. Though there is not a word that seems out of place, there is no sense of painful elaboration. The following *chanson* is at once perfectly artistic and perfectly natural:

---

[1] See Guiffrey, II. 129. Marot ascribes the original to Lucian.

[2] Marot's literary sources are fully discussed in a Latin thesis by A. Guy, *De fontibus C. M. poetae.* Foix, 1898.

[3] This is well brought out by Birch-Hirschfeld, pp. 136, 137.

Qui veult avoir liesse,
Seulement d'un regard
Vienne veoir ma maistresse,
Que Dieu maintienne et gard :
Elle a si bonne grace,
Que celluy qui la veoit
Mille douleurs efface,
Et plus s'il en avoit.

Les vertus de la belle
Me font esmerveiller ;
La souvenance d'elle
Faict mon cueur esveiller ;
Sa beauté tant exquise
Me faict la mort sentir ;
Mais sa grace requise
M'en peult bien garantir[1].

And the same may be said of the *rondeau, De sa grande amye,*
which must have suggested to Alfred de Musset his *Chanson
de Fortunio.*

Dedans Paris, ville jolie,
Un jour, passant melancolie,
Je prins alliance nouvelle
A la plus gaye damoyselle
Qui soit d'icy en Italie.

D'honnesteté elle est saisie,
Et croy (selon ma fantasie)
Qu'il n'en est gueres de plus belle
        Dedans Paris.

Je ne la vous nommeray mye,
Si non que c'est ma grand'amye ;
Car l'alliance se feit telle
Par un doulx baiser que j'eus d'elle,
Sans penser aucune infamie,
        Dedans Paris[2].

Marot's epigrams have generally received high praise, but
on the whole they are less successful than his songs or his
rondeaux. The best are those in which he makes least
pretence to wit and a point, as for instance the following,
which is full of charm and grace:

---

[1] *Œuvres,* II. 181.   [2] II. 149.

> Bouche de coral precieux,
> Qui à baiser semblez semondre ;
> Bouche qui d'un cueur gracieux
> Sçavez tant bien dire et respondre,
> Respondez-moy : doit mon cueur fondre
> Devant vous, comme au feu la cyre?
> Voulez vous bien celuy occire
> Qui crainct vous estre desplaisant?
> Ha ! bouche que tant je desire,
> Dictes Nenny en me baisant[1].

Probably the best known is the one on the death of Samblançay, which appears in nearly every selection of Marot's poetry[2]. A great many appeared in the edition of 1596, which are attributed to Marot without any authority. Most of these are licentious in thought and coarse in tone ; the genuine ones which are of this character form only a small proportion of the whole.

The Epistles are perhaps Marot's most characteristic work. Other poets have written songs as natural, as tender, and as graceful, but in these familiar Epistles, with their rapid movement, their picturesque and yet concentrated language, their liveliness and wit and humour, he has certainly never been surpassed, and has probably never been equalled, in modern times. The one addressed to Lyon Jamet (xi)[3], and the one to the king, *pour avoir esté derobé* (xxix)[4], are among his best-known pieces. Equally good is the one, *Au roi pour le delivrer de prison* (xxvii), which begins as follows :

> Roy des Françoys, plein de toutes bontez,
> Quinze jours a (je les ay bien contez)
> Et dès demain seront justement seize,
> Que je fuz faict confrere au diocese
> De Sainct Marry, en l'eglise Sainct Pris :
> Si vous diray comment je fuz surpris,
> Et me desplaist qu'il fault que je le die ;

and ends with the inimitable lines :

> Trèshumblement requerrant vostre grace
> De pardonner à ma trop grand' audace

---

[1] *Œuvres*, III. 43.   [2] III. 19.   [3] I. 154.   [4] I. 195.

D'avoir emprins ce sot escript vous faire,
Et m'excusez si pour le mien affaire
Je ne suis point vers vous allé parler :
Je n'ay pas eu le loysir d'y aller[1].

Among them are four pieces called *du coq à l'âne*, in which satirical allusions to contemporary events and persons are strung together without any apparent connexion, the writer jumping from one subject to another as from a cock to an ass. They are written in octosyllabic couplets, the metre invariably used by Coquillart, and they are in fact merely an exaggerated form of his jerky and disconnected verse. But having been patronised by Marot they soon became fashionable with his school. The Pleiad regarded them with not unmerited contempt[2]; yet the first two, at any rate, of Marot's are undeniably clever. The following lines, which refer to his imprisonment in 1526, will serve to give an idea of their style :

Ma dame ne m'a pas vendu,
C'est une chanson gringotée ;
La musique en est bien notée,
Ou l'assiette de la clef ment :
Par la morbieu, voyla Clement ;
Prenez le, il a mengé le lard.
Il faict bon estre papelard,
Et ne courroucer point les fées.
Toutes choses qui sont coiffées,
Ont moult de lunes en la teste.
Escrivez moy s'on faict plus feste
De la lingere du Palais,
Car maistre Jehan du Pont Alays
Ne sera pas si oultrageux,
Quand viendra à jouer ses jeux,
Qu'il ne vous face trestous rire[3].

Marot's success in the lighter and secondary kinds of poetry has been so complete that critics are apt to overlook

[1] *Œuvres*, I. 190—192.

[2] See Du Bellay's *Deffence*, books ii and iv, and the remarks of *Le Quintil Horatian* thereon.

[3] *Œuvres*, I. 187. *Le Grup*, a coarse and bitter satire first printed by Guiffrey (II. 439 ff.) is a sort of *coq à l'âne*.

his partial success in the higher and graver kinds. If his poetry lacks deep emotion or passion, it wants neither for tenderness nor pathos, and it is in the Elegies that we naturally find these qualities best represented. The following lines from the third Elegy, written to his lady-love probably on the eve of his departure for the campaign which ended in the battle of Pavia, are a good example of his tender strain :

> Et puis j'ay peur, quand de vous je suis loing
> Que ce pendant Amour ne prenne soing
> De desbander ses deux aveuglez yeulx,
> Pour contempler les vostres gracieux,
> Si qu'en voyant chose tant singuliere
> Ne prenne en vous amytié familiere,
> Et qu'il ne m'oste à l'ayse et en un jour
> Ce que j'ai eu en peine et long sejour.
>   Certainement, si bien ferme vous n'estes,
> Amour vaincra vos responses honnestes.
> Amour est fin, et sa parolle farde
> Pour mieulx tromper : donnez vous en donc garde,
> Car en sa bouche il n'y a rien que miel,
> Mais en son cueur il n'y a rien que fiel[1].

The seventh and eighth Elegies, and especially the fifteenth, which begins with

> Ton gentil cueur, si haultement assis,
> Ton sens discret à merveille rassis,
> Ton noble port, ton maintien asseuré,
> Ton chant si doulx, ton parler mesuré,

and contains the charming lines,

> Tous deux aymons gens pleins d'honnesteté,
> Tous deux aymons honneur et netteté,
> Tous deux aymons à d'aucun ne mesdire,
> Tous deux aymons un meilleur propos dire ;
> Tous deux aymons à nous trouver en lieux
> Où ne sont point gens melancolieux ;
> Tous deux aymons la musique chanter,
> Tous deux aymons les livres frequenter[2],

are all admirable specimens of tender pathos, and shew that Marot, coarse and rough though he could be when he

---

[1] *Œuvres*, II. 14.   [2] II. 34, 35.

pleased, had some notes in his song of great delicacy and sweetness.

Without the pathos of the Elegies, but resembling them in grace and urbanity, are the pastoral Eclogues, the *Eglogue au Roy* (from which I have already quoted), the *Complaincte de Loyse*, the Eclogue on the birth of Francis II, and the *Complaincte d'un Pastoreau Chrestien*[1]. The following lines are from the *Complaincte de Loyse*:

> Dès que la mort ce grand coup eut donné,
> Tous les plaisirs champestres s'assoupirent ;
> Les petis ventz alors n'ont allené,
> Mais les forts ventz encores en souspirent.
> Fueilles et fruictz des arbres abbatirent ;
> Le cler soleil chaleur plus ne rendit ;
> Du manteau vert les prez se devestirent ;
> Le ciel obscur larmes en respandit.
> Le grand pasteur sa musette fendit,
> Ne voulant plus que de pleurs se mesler,
> Dont son trouppeau, qui plaindre l'entendit,
> Laissa le paistre et se print à besler[2].

It is a mistake to suppose that this kind of poetry was purely a Renaissance revival. There are plenty of examples of it in French mediæval literature. The thirteenth century opera of Adam de la Halle, *Li Gieus de Robin et de Marion*, is pastoral in character, and a short poem of the fourteenth century called *Les dits de Franc Gontier*, written by Philippe de Vitry, bishop of Meaux, gave rise to a mass of pastoral literature about *Franc Gontier* and his *compagne Hélène* which provoked Villon's well-known *ballade* of *Contredictz de Franc Gontier*[3]. But of the two characteristics which distinguish the Eclogues of Virgil from the Idylls of his model Theocritus, and which have been reproduced in nearly all the modern examples of pastoral poetry, namely, the identification of pastoral life with the golden age, and the reference to contemporary events and persons, the second was entirely absent from mediæval pastoral

---

[1] I. 39; II. 260; I. 64; I. 97. The *Complaincte de Loyse* and the *Eglogue au Roy* are imitated by Spenser in the *Shepherd's Calendar* (Eclogues xi and xii).
[2] II. 263.   [3] See *Anc. poësies franç.* X. 193 ff.

poetry. The revival of the Virgilian Eclogue began, as might have been expected, in Italy. Dante and Petrarch both wrote Latin Eclogues in direct imitation of Virgil. But the popular pastoral poet at the beginning of the sixteenth century was Baptista Mantuanus, Shakespeare's 'good old Mantuan[1],' who conformed even in the number of his Eclogues to the example of his great fellow-townsman. He found great favour with the humanists of all countries, and nowhere more so than in France. His Eclogues were printed at Poitiers in 1498, and were frequently reprinted during the first few years of the sixteenth century. In 1530 the industrious Michel d'Amboise translated them into French.

The first Virgilian Eclogue written in France in the vernacular, which was not a translation, was one by Cretin on the birth of the Dauphin (1517). In this mediæval and classical influences are curiously blended, and Franc Gontier and Hélène appear side by side with Galatea and Gallus and Damon and Menalcas. In Italy vernacular pastoral poetry was represented by two works of considerable importance, Poliziano's tragedy of *Orfeo*, written in 1472, though not printed till 1494, the first act of which is pastoral in character, and the poetical parts of Sannazaro's *Arcadia*, the first complete and authorised edition of which appeared in 1534[2]. In the *Orfeo* there is no reference to contemporary life, but in the *Arcadia* all the Virgilian characteristics are represented. Alamanni's Eclogues, published at Lyons in 1532, are also Virgilian in character.

In Marot's Eclogues, the first of which he wrote in the year 1531, the influence of mediæval models goes little beyond the name of Robin, the regular name for a shepherd in mediæval pastorals[3], and perhaps those of Colin and Thenot. He mainly wrote under the influence of Virgil, of whose first eclogue his earliest work was as we have seen

[1] *Love's Labour's Lost*, Act IV. Sc. 2, where Holofernes quotes the first line of his first eclogue.
[2] Printed at Naples. Before this some very imperfect editions had appeared without the authority of the author.
[3] As in Adam de la Halle's *Robin et Marion*, and Henryson's *Robyne and Makyne*.

a translation. His first original eclogue, that on the death
of Louise of Savoy, is full of Virgilian reminiscences, such
as the concluding lines:

> Sus, grans toreaux, et vous, brebis petites,
> Allez au tect, assez avez brousté ;
> Puis le soleil tombe en ces bas limites,
> Et la nuict vient devers l'autre costé[1].

So the Eclogue on the birth of the prince who was afterwards
Francis II is a close and beautiful adaptation of the famous
Pollio[2].

As a metrist Marot was not, like Ronsard, a bold
experimenter in new rhythms. He generally contented
himself with some old established metre like the ten-syllable
couplet, or with such fixed forms of verse as the *rondeau*, the
ballade, or the *chant-royal*. In the two latter he has won the
admiration of so competent and exacting a judge as Théodore
de Banville. Non-professional readers will rather note that
his best pieces fall on the ear with a most harmonious cadence[3].
It is principally in the translations of the Psalms that he
indulged in metrical experiments. Here we find several new
forms of strophe, in which the rhymes are interlaced with
considerable ingenuity, and some of which are fairly successful.
Unfortunately French critics have for the most part too
hastily decided that the sublime thoughts and elevated diction
of the grand Hebrew melodies were so entirely alien to the
levity of Marot's character that his renderings of them are not
worth serious consideration. In so doing they have left out
of account an interesting development of his Muse, which
from the historical, if not from the purely literary point of view,
is of some importance. His version of the 24th Psalm, which
is short enough for quotation in full, and is one of the most
successful, will enable the reader to judge for himself.

---

[1] *Œuvres*, II. 268. Signor Torraca is, I think, right in pointing out that some
lines in this eclogue are imitated from the fifth eclogue of the *Arcadia* (*Gli
imitatori stranieri di J. Sannazaro*, 2nd ed., 1882, pp. 66, 67).

[2] I. 64.

[3] See a good account of his versification by E. Faguet, *Seizième Siècle*,
pp. 68—73 ; he is mistaken in thinking that Marot wrote only one sonnet.

La terre au Seigneur appartient,
Tout ce qu'en sa rondeur contient,
Et ceulx qui habitent en elle ;
Sur mer fondemens luy donna,
L'enrichit et l'environna
De mainte riviere trèsbelle.

Mais sa montaigne est un sainct lieu ;
Qui viendra donc au mont de Dieu,
Qui est ce qui là tiendra place ?
L'homme de mains et cueur lavé,
En vanitez non eslevé,
Et qui n'a juré en fallace.

L'homme tel, Dieu le benira :
Dieu son sauveur le munira
De misericorde et clemence.
Telle est la generation
Cherchant, cherchant d'affection
Du Dieu de Jacob la presence.

Haulsez voz testes, grans portaulx,
Huys eternelz, tenez vous haultz,
Si entrera le Roy de gloire.
Qui est ce Roy tant glorieux ?
C'est le fort Dieu victorieux,
Le plus fort qu'en guerre on peult croire.

Haulsez voz testes, grans portaulx,
Huys eternelz, tenez vous haultz,
Si entrera le Roy de gloire.
Qui est ce Roy tant glorieux ?
Le Dieu d'armes victorieux,
C'est luy qui est le Roy de gloire[1].

It is unnecessary to point out that the great popularity which the Psalms attained is no test of their literary merits. The religious enthusiasts who sang them, often on their road to the stake, were not likely to be close critics. They only needed plain language and simple harmony. Judged strictly as literary performances Marot's Psalms have obvious shortcomings. It is evident at once that he is not at home in this style of composition. If he begins with a lofty flight, it is rarely sustained. He either drops into colloquialism, or he disfigures his style either by harsh inversions or by what the French call *chevilles*, words put in merely for the sake of the

[1] IV. 102.

metre or the rhyme, the common refuge of poets when their inspiration fails them[1]. But if he fails to rise to the sublimity of the Psalms, as we know them in our English prose version, it must be admitted that he has done his work on the whole with considerable spirit and a fair measure of success. Moreover, in thus attempting to introduce a more elevated tone and a more varied harmony into French lyric poetry, he was to some extent a forerunner of Ronsard. Had not the members of the Pleiad been too closely identified with the Catholic party to take any notice of such heretical literature as the Protestant Psalter, they would probably have entertained a greater respect for Marot's poetical powers. In fact Marot did a great deal more for French poetry than his successors gave him credit. It is true that he had drunk too sparingly of the classical streams of inspiration to do the work that was done. by them. Indeed, had he been better equipped as a classical student, it is probable that in an age when no humanist altogether escaped a touch of pedantry he would not have emancipated French poetry from the pedantry of his predecessors. But he possessed by nature a considerable measure of the self-restraint and concentration which are such distinguishing features of the classical masterpieces, and which had been so painfully lacking in French poetry for more than two centuries. Even the higher attributes of the classical spirit, elevation of thought and language, rigorous self-criticism, constant striving after perfection, were not altogether wanting to him. But it was by tact and good sense rather than by depth of feeling or brilliancy of execution that he saved French poetry, that he undermined the pretentious shams of the *rhétoriqueur* school, and laid a solid foundation for future workers to build on. It has been well said that 'he had more than anybody else of his time the literary characteristics of the ordinary Frenchman[2].' Because this was so, his poetry has obtained a lasting place in the affections of his countrymen.

[1] It is interesting to compare Marot's Psalms with Sidney's. Sidney's, as might be expected, are far more poetical. Both are more diffuse than the English prose version, but, while Marot fills up his lines with mere tags or repetitions, Sidney introduces new poetical ideas.

[2] Prof. Saintsbury.

BIBLIOGRAPHY.

EDITIONS.

Ladolescence Clementine, Paris, 1532; *La Suite de l'Adolescence Clementine*, Paris [early in 1534]; *Œuvres*, Lyons, 1538 (printed by Gryphius, but published by Dolet); Lyons, 1544. For a full bibliographical description of these editions published in Marot's life-time, see Appendix A.

Œuvres, Niort, 1596. (Edited by François Mizière, a physician of Niort, with several additions. See Picot, I. no. 614.)

6 vols., The Hague, 1731. (Edited by Lenglet du Fresnoy, under the pseudonym of Gordon de Percel, on the basis of the Niort edition; it contains the poems of Jean and Michel Marot, and also those which belong to the controversy with Sagon.)

4 vols., ed. Pierre Jannet, 1868—1872; 2nd ed. 1873—1876.

Ed. G. Guiffrey, vols. II and III, 1875—1881. The completion of this sumptuous and elaborate edition, which was to have been in 6 vols., the first containing Marot's life, was prevented by the editor's death.

A manuscript in the library at Chantilly, which was presented by Marot to the Constable de Montmorency in March, 153⅚, contains some unpublished matter, including an epistle to Francis I and one to Margaret of Navarre. (See G. Macon in *Bull. du Bibl.* 1898, pp. 157 ff.; 233 ff.)

Good selections of Marot's poems have been edited by Ch. d'Héricault, 1867 (out of print), and E. Voizard, 1888.

LIFE.

There is no really good life of Marot. The fullest is that by O. Douen in *Clément Marot et le Psautier Huguenot*, 1878; but unfortunately the author in his anxiety to prove that Marot was a pillar of the Reformed Church has been led to adopt hypotheses which are either not proved or are absolutely disproved. The same line had been previously taken, though with far less knowledge at his command, by Henry Morley in *Clement Marot and other Studies*, 1871. On the other hand, Ch. d'Héricault in his introduction to the *Œuvres choisies* maintains that Marot was never a Protestant at all. On the whole the most accurate and serviceable accounts of his life are those in Haag, *La France Protestante*, and in the *Encyclopædia Britannica* (by Prof. Saintsbury), and that by E. Voizard prefixed to the *Œuvres choisies*. There are valuable gleanings in the notes of Guiffrey's edition. In Colletet's lives of the three Marots (ed. Guiffrey, 1871) there is nothing of any value or interest except the description of Clément's personal appearance.

CRITICISM.

C.-A. Sainte-Beuve, *Tableau historique*, 1828; E. Faguet in *Seizième Siècle*, 1894.

CHAPTER V

THE SCHOOL OF MAROT

Schools of poetry have been more common in France than in this country, and at certain periods have played a prominent part in her literary history. Just as the nineteenth century produced in succession the Romanticists, the Parnassians, and the Symbolists, so during the sixteenth century the *rhétoriqueurs* were followed by the school of Marot, and the school of Marot by the Pleiad. It is characteristic of most of these schools, firstly, that their names indicate very obscurely the nature of their distinctive doctrines, and secondly, that while the disciples of the school pay an exaggerated respect to the letter of these doctrines, the masters are contented with a general observance of their spirit. It is the folly of the disciples which generally leads to the downfall of the school. As the founder of a new school Marot is honourably distinguished in two ways. He never attacked his predecessors and he gave his own name to his school, which was called the *Ecole Marotique*. We have seen how his admiring disciples rallied round him when he was attacked by Sagon. They consisted of a group of young men some ten to twenty years his juniors, the youngest having been born about the beginning of the reign of Francis I. Among them were Charles Fontaine, Victor Brodeau, La Borderie and Almanaque Papillon[1]. Charles

---

[1] The first three are mentioned in the *Epistre de Fripelipes*:

> Venez, mon mignon Borderie,
> Grand espoir des muses haultaines;
> Rochers, faictes saillir Fontaines.
>
> .   .   .   .
>
> Vien, Brodeau, le puisné, son filz.
>
> Marot, *Œuvres* I. 244.

See also Picot, I. no. 621. Marot's last Epistle is addressed to Papillon (*Œuvres*

Fontaine[1] is known by a single poem, the beautiful lines on the birth of his son Jean, of which the following are the first two stanzas :

> Mon petit fils qui n'as encor rien vu,
> A ce matin ton père te salue ;
> Vien-t-en, vien voir ce monde bien pourvu
> D'honneurs et biens qui sont de grant value ;
> Vien voir la paix en France descendue,
> Vien voir François, nostre roy et le tien,
> Qui a la France ornée et desfendue ;
> Vien voir le monde où y a tant de bien.
>
> Jan, petit Jan, vien voir ce tant beau monde,
> Ce ciel d'azur, ces estoiles luisantes,
> Ce soleil d'or, ceste grant terre ronde,
> Ceste ample mer, ces rivières bruyantes,
> Ce bel air vague et ces nues courantes,
> Ces beaux oyseaux qui chantent à plaisir,
> Ces poissons frais et ces bestes paissantes ;
> Vien voir le tout à souhait et desir[2].

The volume of poems in which this piece appeared was entitled *S'ensuivent Les Ruisseaux de Fontaine,* while to an earlier volume he gave the name of *La Fontaine d'Amours,* graceful and harmless conceits such as the fashion of the day delighted in, but which greatly moved the wrath of Joachim du Bellay. *Combien je desire voir secher ces printemps, chastier ces petites jeunesses, rabbattre ces coups d'essay, tarir ces fontaines.*

Victor Brodeau, a younger brother of the distinguished scholar Jean Brodeau, after being *valet de chambre* to Francis I became secretary and controller-general to the Queen of Navarre and died comparatively young in 1540[3], leaving some religious poems which were published in that year under the title of *Les Louanges de Jesus nostre Sauveur* with a dedication

---

i. 287) and see Ep. lix, *Au Roy, pour lui recommander Papillon, poëte françois, estant malade.*

[1] b. 1515, d. *circ.* 1587.

[2] Printed by Prof. Saintsbury in *Specimens of French Literature,* and by L. Becq de Fouquières in *Œuvres choisies des poètes français du xvie siècle.*

[3] Ferrière-Percy, *Marguerite d'Angoulême, son livre de dépenses,* p. 26. Jean Brodeau is sometimes said to be the son of Victor, but he was no doubt his elder brother, the Brodeau *aisné* mentioned in the preface to the translation of Dolet's *Genethliacum* (Christie, *E. Dolet,* p. 347).

to Margaret[1]. There is some ingenuity displayed in the arrangement of the rhymes, but the poems have no real poetic value. Of his lighter poetry very little has been preserved. Voiture in his well-known *rondeau, Ma foi c'est fait,* invokes him as an acknowledged proficient in this form of poem, but only one specimen of his art has come down to us, an answer to Marot's *De l'amour du siècle antique*[2].

Jean Boiceau, seigneur de La Borderie, published in 1542 first a tame and uninteresting account in verse of a journey to Constantinople which he had made in 1537 in pursuance of a diplomatic mission[3], and secondly a poem entitled *L'Amie de Court* in which a coquette gives her views on the subject of matrimony. Better, she says, a rich fool than a poor man of intelligence, but until she has found this desirable husband she likes to have round her a crowd of admirers. This chaste but passionless lady provoked a rejoinder from Charles Fontaine, who in his *Contr' Amye de Court* proclaimed the rights of love. He was followed by an obscure poet, Paul Angier, who in his *L'Expérience contenant une briefve deffense en la personne de l'honneste amant pour l'Amye de Court contre la Contr' Amye* took the part of La Borderie and attacked Fontaine with some asperity[4]. Finally Almanaque

---

[1] There is a copy in the *Bib. Mazarine* bound up in the same volume with a poem of Margaret's; it was apparently printed at Lyons.

[2] Marot, *Œuvres* II. 163. A translation by Brodeau of a couplet of Meleager will be found in Blanchemain's edition of Saint-Gelais II. 12 and an *Elégie du semi-dieu Faunus par* V. B. (of no merit) among the *Rimes* of Pernette du Guillet, 1547, reprint of 1856, p. 128.

[3] *Discours du voyage de Constantinople,* Lyons, 1542; printed in *Les poëtes françois* III. 291 ff. Goujet XI. 148 and 156 makes two distinct persons of the authors of the *Discours* and *L'Amie de Court.*

[4] The whole series was published at Paris in 1544 in a volume with *Le Mespris de la Court.* There are two editions of this year, by Thiboust and by Galliot du Pré. The series was republished with other pieces at Lyons in 1547 under the title of *Opuscules d'Amour* (Brit. Mus.). See Picot, I. no. 806; Cary, *The early French poets,* pp. 29—34. It is generally considered that a poem by Heroet, *La Parfaicte amye,* printed by Dolet in 1542 and afterwards included in the collected series, was the first occasion of the controversy (see Viollet Le Duc, pp. 25, 26). But in the first place there is nothing to shew that *L'Amie de Court* was meant to be an answer to this poem, which by reason of its philosophical character stands apart from the others; and secondly, Dolet's preface to Heroet's volume is dated June 1, while that to *L'Amie de Court* is dated May 5, which makes it probable

Papillon contributed in *Le nouvel amour*, under the guise of a mythological narrative, another apology for honourable love. The poetry of this controversy is not of a high order, but it is for the most part characterised by an ease of style and clearness of expression which testify to the progress that French poetry had made since the beginning of Francis's reign. Fontaine's verses are perhaps the most poetical, while La Borderie's have the most point and interest.

Gilles d'Aurigny, a native of Beauvais, is on the whole a better poet than any of the foregoing. His *Tuteur d'Amour*, which tells how he captured Cupid and shut him up in a tower and how Mercury was sent by Jupiter to help guard him, and how he escaped with the help of Venus and finally turned his tutor into his scholar, is the best piece of work produced by any of the minor disciples of Marot. It is an excellent specimen of the lighter narrative style, graceful, direct, concise. There is the same kind of merit in the epistles published in the same volume[1]. The other contents of the volume, elegies, complaints, epitaphs, *chants royaux*, *rondeaux*, epigrams, mark Aurigny as a true disciple of Marot. Like his master he had a motto—*un pour tout*—and a *nom de guerre*—sometimes *le Pamphile*, sometimes *l'innocent esgaré*. *Je ne souhaite moins*, cries Du Bellay, *que ces Despourveuz, ces humbles Esperans, ces Bannis de lyesse, ces Esclaves, ces Traverseurs soient renvoyes à la Table ronde: et ces belles petites devises aux Gentilshommes, et Damoiselles, d'ou on les a empruntées.*

Le Banni de Lyesse was the name adopted by a young Toulouse student, François Habert, who under the shadow of that orthodox University strove humbly to walk in Marot's footsteps and produced in great abundance[2] poetry which is quite pathetic in its badness and its servility. The concluding lines of an epistle addressed to Marot are worth quoting as

that the latter appeared first. Moreover Dolet's edition of this is very likely posterior to one printed at Paris by Corrozet the privilege for which is dated March 9, 154½ (see Christie, *op. cit.* p. 543).

[1] Paris, 1546. D'Aurigny died in 1553.
[2] *J'ai sous les yeux deux douzaines de volumes de sa composition.* Paulmy, *Mélanges tirés d'une grande bibliothèque* VII. 247.

a specimen of the adoring attitude which the disciples
adopted towards the master:

> Quant est de moy, je suis le plus petit
> Qui eut jamais de rimer appetit ;
> Mais tel qu'il est ton humble serf se tient,
> Et des Francoys le plus grand te maintient,
> Comme Virgile entre Latins, Homere
> Entre les Grecz a louenge premiere.
> Si te supply la presente escriture
> Daigner du don de ta seule lecture,
> L'epistre est rude, helas je le confesse :
> Car elle vient du Banny de liesse[1]:

Estienne Forcadel, another Toulouse student, who achieved
a somewhat unenviable notoriety as the successful rival of
Cujas for the professorship of law in that University in 1556[2],
is a no better poet than Habert, but there is a third representative of the Toulouse University who deserves honourable
mention. This is Jean Rus, a prize-winner at the famous
Jeux Floraux, whose poems were recently disentombed by
Tamizey de Larroque. Though of little originality they
sometimes catch Marot's spirit happily enough, as for instance
in the following:

> Madame avoit une rose en sa main,
> Fresche et vermeille, oultre tout aultre rose,
> Tant que chascung qui la voyoit, soubdain
> S'esbahissoit de veoir si belle chose.
> L'ung dict qu'elle est paincte ; l'autre suppose
> Que Venus l'a de rechief enrougie :
> Je leur diz lors : "Amys, ne soyez mye
> Tant esbahiz de ceste nouveaulté :
> Elle a touché aux lebvres de mamye
> D'où elle a prins sa frescheur et beaulté."

---

[1] Habert wrote *La jeunesse du Banny de Lyesse*, Paris, 1541; *La suite du B.
de L. ib.* 1541 and numerous other works, including translations of Latin poets,
of which a list is given in Niceron XXXIII. 184 ff. and some account will be found
in Paulmy *op. cit.* See also Picot, I. nos. 643—8. Hardly anything is known of
his life; he was born at Issoudun about 1520 and the date of his last published
work is 1561.

[2] "They preferred Forcadel to Cujas," says Gravina writing in the eighteenth
century, "a monkey to a man."

And in the *Blason de la Rose* there is some graceful and picturesque writing[1].

The fashion of writing *blasons*—another imitation of heraldry—was one of the characteristics of Marot's school. To borrow the definition of Sibilet in his *Art Poétique*, a blazon is " a perpetual praise or continuous vituperation of that which one has set oneself to blazon." A sort of development of the mediæval *dit*, it had come into fashion like so many literary puerilities, at the close of the fifteenth century, the most notable examples of this time being Coquillart's *Blasons des armes et des dames* and the *Grand Blason des Faulces amours* of Guillaume Alexis. In the next generation Roger de Collerye wrote a *Blason des dames* in the form of a dialogue, and Pierre Gringore a *Blason des heretiques*[2]. Marot wrote two blazons which had considerable vogue, *Le beau tetin* and *Le laid tetin*, and straightway all his followers set to work to write blazons till there was not a part of the human body that was left unblazoned[3].

Other writers of blazons were Lancelot de Carle, Claude Chappuys, and Eustorg de Beaulieu, all ecclesiastics. Carle, who became a figure of some importance in the literary world as a patron of letters, will be mentioned again in connexion with the Pleiad. Chappuys, who held a canonry at Rouen, was at one time attached to the royal household as *Sommelier de chapelle*. In 1534 he was at Rome with Rabelais in the suite of Jean du Bellay, and later he had a post in the royal library at Fontainebleau. Besides blazons he wrote a poem

---

[1] *Œuvres de Jean Rus*, 1875, p. 39. The original volume, of which Tamizey de Larroque believes there is only one copy extant, was published at Toulouse about 1540. M. Picot (I. no. 649) on the authority of a contemporary reader attributes to Rus a poem entitled *Description poétique de l'Histoire du beau Narcisse* (Lyons, 1550), which Brunet, following Du Verdier, attributes to Habert.

[2] See M. d'Héricault's account in his edition of Coquillart, II. 147–160.

[3] See Marot, *Epistre* xli (*Œuvres* I. 210). Several of these blazons were published in 1537 at the end of an edition of the *Hecatomphile*, and they were finally collected under the title of *Blasons anatomiques du corps feminin, &c.*, the earliest known edition of which is of 1543 (Turner Catalogue, no. 375), though probably there was an earlier edition. In 1807 Méon published a collection of these and other *Blasons*.

on the French Court called *Discours de la Court*[1]. Eustorg
de Beaulieu, who was born in the Limousin, about 25 miles
from Cahors, wrote poems of the usual Marotic type and
collected them in volumes to which he gave fanciful titles,
such as *Divers Rapports* and *Les Gestes des Solliciteurs*. After
a somewhat dissipated youth he embraced the new religious
doctrines, left France for Geneva, became a minister in the
Reformed Church, and with Calvin's permission published a
collection of religious songs set to music of his own composition under the title of *Chrestienne rejouissance*[2]. Several
of them are printed in the *Chansonnier Huguenot*[3], but they
are of little merit.

The reformers had a better though less popular poet in
Matthieu Malingre, who for thirty-six years was pastor of
Yverdon on the lake of Neuchâtel. His best piece is a
chanson addressed to Henry II at the beginning of his reign,
but it is hardly worth quoting[4].

The indecency by which the blazons of Eustorg de
Beaulieu and his fellow-blazoners were often disfigured was
attacked by the worthy Paris bookseller, Gilles Corrozet[5], in

[1] Paris, 1543 (*ante* p. 48). He was born *circ.* 1505 and died soon after 1572.
He appears as *sommelier de chapelle* in 1523 (*Heptaméron*, ed. Le Roux de Lincy
III. 240). In *Gargantua* (cviii) he figures as *le capitaine Chappuys*. Guiffrey,
Œuvres de Marot, II. 493 ff. prints an Eclogue on the battle of Pavia which he
attributes to him. (See also Rabelais's preface to Marliani, *Topographia antiquae
Romae*; Niceron, XXXIX. 85 ff.; Bernard, *G. Tory* 395, 6).

[2] For E. de Beaulieu (*circ.* 1505—1552) see G. Becker, *E. de B.* 1880; *La France
Prot.* II. 31 ff. (2nd ed.) a good article with an excellent bibliography borrowed from
the late Baron James de Rothschild. Colletet's life has been published with notes
and appendix by P. Tamizey de Larroque (no. 1 of the *Plaquettes Gontaudaises*,
1878). His principal works are: *Les Gestes des Solliciteurs*, Bordeaux, 1529 (Picot,
I. nos. 518, 519); *Divers Rapports*, Lyons, 1537, Paris, 1544; *Chrestienne rejouissance* (prob. Geneva), 1546. They are all very rare, only one or two copies of each
being known to exist. An epistle in verse from E. de B. to Marot from the
Chrest. rejouissance is printed by Guiffrey III. 746.

[3] *Le Chansonnier Huguenot du xvie siècle*, ed. H. Bordier, I. 165.

[4] Printed in the *Chansonnier Huguenot* II. 199, which see for his other *chansons*
(pp. 418—426). He also wrote an epistle in verse to Marot, which has been
reprinted (Haarlem, 1868). He was born *circ.* 1500 and died 1572. See an
article by H. A. Junod in the *Musée neuchâtelois* XXVI. 101 ff. and Herminjard,
Corr. des réformateurs IV. 46, n. 12.

[5] b. 1509 or 1510, d. 1568.

some spirited verses entitled *Contre les blasonneurs des membres*, but his own blazons, *Les blasons domestiques*[1], in which every conceivable article of household furniture was blazoned, must have done more than his direct attack to bring the fashion into discredit. He also wrote, besides a good deal of indifferent poetry on contemporary events[2], and a verse-translation of Æsop which has been already noticed[3], a narrative poem of considerable charm called *Le conte du Rossignol*[4]. He is further interesting as the author of the first guide-book to Paris, which he published in 1532 under the title of *La Fleur des Antiquitez de Paris*[5].

Jacques Gohorry[6] was a man of various attainments, in spite of which he lived in poverty and solitude. He wrote scientific treatises on tobacco and the vine, and, as royal historiographer, a continuation of the Latin history of Paulus Emilius, copying the work of Arnoul le Ferron without acknowledgment. He also translated part of Livy, Machiavelli's *Discourses on the first decade of Livy*, and three books of *Amadis* (x, xi, xiii). But his chief merit is that he wrote a poem of considerable beauty, a free version of Catullus's *Ut flos in septis*.

> La jeune fille est semblable à la rose,
> Au beau jardin, sur l'espine naïve,
> Tandis que seure et seulette repose,
> Sans que troupeau ni berger y arrive.
> L'air doux l'eschauffe et l'aurore l'arrose ;
> La terre, l'eau par sa faveur l'avive.
> Mais jeunes gens et dames amoureuses
> De la cueillir ont les mains envieuses.

---

[1] Both printed in the *Anc. poésies franç.* VI. 223 ff.

[2] Originally published as broadsides; some of them have been reprinted in the *Anc. poésies franç.* (vols. I. V. VI.).

[3] *Ante*, p. 40.

[4] *Anc. poésies franç.* VIII. 49 ff.; *Les poètes françois* III. 392 ff. It was originally published in 1546 by the author himself, and there is a Lyons edition of the same year from the press of Jean de Tournes.

[5] Reprinted, with an introduction by Le Bibliophile Jacob (P. Lacroix), 1874. After it had gone through several editions Corrozet brought out what was practically a new work, *Les Antiquitez, histoire, et singularitez de Paris*, which formed the basis of Dubreul's well-known *Théâtre des Antiquités de Paris*, 1610.

[6] *circ.* 1500—1576. He called himself *Le Solitaire* and *Leo Suavius*. See *Nouv. Biog. Gén.* (by L. Lacour).

La terre et l'air qui la souloient nourrir,
La quittent lors et la laissent flestrir[1].

Charles de Sainte-Marthe, a native of Poitou, the first
literary representative of a distinguished literary family, was
a scholar and religious reformer of some note[2]. He was
one of the original professors of the College of Guyenne at
Bordeaux, and one of the first preachers of the new doctrines
in Poitou. His opinions caused him to be imprisoned at
Grenoble for two years and a half, after which he became a
professor at Trinity College, Lyons. He was a bad poet and
a tiresome prose-writer. In poetry he was a faithful disciple
of Marot, whom he calls his *père d'alliance*. He found a
mother in the Queen of Navarre, to whom he dedicated his
poems[3] and who conferred on him various posts. His friend
Dolet had more capacity for handling his native language,
but scarcely a larger measure of poetical genius. Dolet's *Le
Second Enfer*[4], the title of a thin volume of verse, which
in imitation of Marot he published on the subject of his
second imprisonment, is essentially prosaic. The *Epistre
au Roy*[5] is interesting for its biographical details, and shows
in parts considerable liveliness and power of expression, but
on the whole it is very inferior to Marot's work in this line.
It has not the condensation or the picturesqueness which even
this pedestrian kind of poetry requires to lift it above the level
of mere prose. But the measure of Dolet's capacity for poetry
may be best judged by a poem which, had he been a true
poet, would have called forth his fullest powers, the *Cantique*
written just before his death. It breathes a spirit of strong

[1] Becq de Fouquières, p. 314. Originally published in Gohorry's translation of
book x. of Amadis. Sainte-Beuve, *Port. litt.* III. 84, supposed that it was translated
from the Spanish, but he could not have consulted the Spanish Amadis. It is also
printed in *Les poètes françois*, III. 259 with other poems by Gohorry not without
merit, especially a *chanson* beginning *O combien est heureux* (p. 263).

[2] 1512–1555. See Haag, *La France Prot.*; P. J. Odolant-Desnos, *Mémoires
historiques sur la ville d'Alençon*, I. 545.

[3] *Poésie françoise*, Lyons, 1540. Some of his poems will be found in *Les
poètes franç.* III. 418 ff.

[4] Lyons, 1544; reprinted by Techener in 1830. Only two copies of the original
edition are known to exist (Christie, *E. Dolet*, p. 549).

[5] Printed in *Les poètes françois*, III. 364.

emotion and noble thought, true sources of poetical inspiration, but the divine *afflatus* is wanting.   The first three stanzas are on the whole the best, especially the third, after which the inspiration dies away.

> Si au besoing le monde m'abandonne,
> Et si de Dieu la volunte n'ordonne
> Que liberté encores on me donne
>   Selon mon vueil :
> Doibs je en mon cueur pour cela mener dueil,
> Et de regretz faire amas et recueil?
> Non pour certain, mais au ciel lever l'œil
>   Sans autre esgard.
> Sus donc, esprit, laissés la chair à part,
> Et devers Dieu qui tout bien nous despart
> Retirez vous comme à vostre rempart,
>   Vostre fortresse[1].

A similar incapacity for poetry is shewn by a far greater prose-writer than Dolet, namely Rabelais.   His *Epistre à Bouchet* has nothing but rhyme to distinguish it from prose. Prefixed to the first book of *Pantagruel* is a *dizain* by Hugues Salel, who enjoyed a considerable reputation amongst his contemporaries, chiefly as a translator of several books of the *Iliad.*   He was a native of Cazals in Quercy, and like his fellow-provincial, Clément Marot, was *valet de chambre* to Francis I, who made him abbot of Saint-Chéron near Chartres. His poetry is of little value ; the best of his pieces is perhaps a marine eclogue on the death of the Dauphin, in which Mellin de Saint-Gelais and Victor Brodeau are the speakers. It contains at any rate two pretty refrains, *Chantez, mes vers, chantez melencolie* and *Chantez, mes vers, chantez deuil et tristesse.*   Towards the close of his life he rallied to the new school[2].

---

[1] From Techener's edition of 1830, which professes to be a reprint of an original edition of 1546.   No such edition however ever existed; the *Cantique* was first printed by Née de la Rochelle in his *Life of Dolet*. (See Christie, *op. cit.* p. 552.)   It is also printed in *Les poètes françois* III. 376.

[2] Born 1503 or 4, died 1553.   His works were published at Paris 15⅓⅓, the year being fixed by a reference in the piece entitled *Chasse Royale* to the visit of Charles V to Francis I.   See Niceron, XXXVI. 166 ff.; Goujet, XII. 1 ff.; Cary,

It must be confessed that in all this poetry produced by Marot's disciples there is little that is really interesting or distinctive. It is all more or less a pale reflexion of their master's work. But as a whole it is instructive, for it is an evidence of the change which had come over French poetry since the accession of Francis I. We have only to compare the minor poetry of the last ten years of his reign with that of the first ten to see what an advance had been made. In place of the rough and garrulous outpourings of the older poetry with its allegorical frippery and rhythmical puerilities we find a language which is at once correct and natural, an easy and flowing style, and a pleasing harmony. And this change was due to Marot. It was not his fault if his followers were mere imitators. He had provided them with an excellent instrument and they played on it correctly; but he could not make them produce original music. There were, however, some poets writing in the reign of Francis I who, while they regarded themselves as belonging to the school of Marot, possessed a considerable amount of individuality, and in various ways carried French poetry a step further in advance, thus forming various connecting links between Marot and the Pleiad.

These are firstly Margaret of Navarre, whose poems have a strong spiritual element of which there is little or no trace in Marot; secondly a small group of writers more or less under the influence of Margaret, who are generally spoken of as the school of Lyons; and lastly Mellin de Saint-Gelais, who had strong Italian leanings, and thus paved the way for that sympathy with the Italian Renaissance which characterises the Pleiad. But before we consider Margaret of Navarre as a poet we must deal with a more important side of her talent, her work as a *conteuse*. In her wake will naturally follow her *valet de chambre* Bonaventure des Periers, who is not only her rival in the story-telling art, though in a totally different style, but in two or three poems breathes a spiritual note, equal to hers in feeling and far superior in expression.

pp. 40 ff.; C. Calmeilles, *Hugues Salel*, Tours, 1899. His translation of the *Iliad* will find mention later.

BIBLIOGRAPHY.

EDITIONS.

CHARLES FONTAINE, *La Fontaine d'Amours*, Lyons, 1545 (Brit. Mus.);
Les Ruisseaux d'Amour, Lyons, 1555; *Les Ruisseaux de Fontaine*,
Lyons, 1555. VICTOR BRODEAU, *Les Louanges de Jesus nostre Sauveur*
[Lyons?], 1540 (*Bib. Mazarine*). LA BORDERIE, *L'Amie de Court*,
Lyons, 1542 (Christie library, Victoria University, Manchester). *Le
Mespris de la Court, L'Amie de Court*, &c., 1544. *Opuscules d'Amour*,
Lyons, 1547 (Brit. Mus.).
GILLES D'AURIGNY, *Le Tuteur d'Amour*, 1546. FRANÇOIS HABERT,
La jeunesse du Banny de Lyesse, 1541, and numerous other works. JEAN
RUS, *Œuvres*, Toulouse [*circ.* 1540]; reprinted by P. Tamizey de Larroque,
1875. EUSTORG DE BEAULIEU, *Chrestienne rejouissance* [Geneva?],
1546 (Imperial Library, Vienna). [GILLES CORROZET], *Le conte du
Rossignol*, 1546. CHARLES DE SAINTE-MARTHE, *Poésie françoise*,
Lyons, 1540. ESTIENNE DOLET, *Le Second Enfer*, Lyons, 1544 (*Bib.
Mazarine*, see Christie, *op. cit.* p. 449); reprinted 1830 (Techener) and
1868. HUGUES SALEL, *Œuvres*, 15⁴⁰⁄₄₆.

The fullest selection will be found in vol. III. of *Les poètes françois
depuis le xii⁵ siècle jusqu'à Malherbe* [ed. P. R. Auguis], 6 vols. 1824.
Most of the writers are included in vol. XI. of Goujet. See also Viollet
Le Duc, *Bibliothèque poétique*, 1843; H. F. Cary, *The early French
poets*, 1846 (Papillon, La Borderie, Salel).

CHAPTER VI

MARGARET OF NAVARRE

1. *The Mediæval story-books.*

THE two works which form the principal subjects of this and the following chapter, namely, the *Heptameron* and the *Joyeux Devis*, belong to a branch of literature in which the French have always excelled—the short prose tale of ordinary life. The first important collection of such tales which appeared in France was that of the *Cent Nouvelles Nouvelles* completed in 1462. It was the direct though not immediate descendant of the *fableau* or verse-tale, which flourished from the middle of the twelfth to the beginning of the fourteenth century, and which whether it was derived from personal experience or through various intermediate agencies from Indian literary sources was always a tale of real life. The practise of introducing stories into sermons, which began with Jacques de Vitry, Bishop of Acre in 1217, and was carried on by the Dominican and Franciscan preachers, led to the publication of collections of *exempla*, as they were called, specially designed for the use of preachers. Though the stories were told in the dialect or patois of the district where the sermons were preached, they were published in Latin, so as to give them a wider circulation not only throughout France but also in other countries[1]. We have however one interesting collection

---

[1] Among the best known and most popular collections were those of Robert Holcot, an Oxford professor (d. 1349), John Bromyard, a Cambridge professor (d. 1418), and Johann Herolt a native of Basle and a contemporary of Bromyard's. They were all Dominicans. See for the whole subject, A. Lecoy de la Marche, *La*

of *exempla* in the vernacular in the *Contes moralisés* of Nicole Bozon, an English Franciscan who wrote in Anglo-French in the first quarter of the fourteenth century[1].

The *fableau* began to die out early in the fourteenth century. Its immediate successor in Western Europe was the prose-tale of Italy, which was largely indebted to France for its materials[2]. Its oldest representative is generally considered to be the *Novellino*, which in its original form probably dates from the close of the thirteenth century[3]. It was followed by the *Cento novelle antiche*, probably first collected between 1325 and 1350, the *Decameron* written about the middle of the fourteenth century, the *Novelle* of Sacchetti and the *Pecorone* of Ser Giovanni, both written during the last quarter of it. Poggio's Latin *Facetiae* belong to the early part of the next century.

It was not, as we have seen, till the year 1482 that the *fableau* reappeared in France in the form of the prose-tale, as we have it in the *Cent Nouvelles Nouvelles*. The caustic but good-natured humour of these stories and the licence alike of subject-matter and expression leave us no doubt as to their ancestry, nor must their uniform coarseness blind us to their undeniable merits as specimens of the story-telling art. The work was first printed in 1486. Shortly before this Masuccio's *Novellino* (1476) and Sabbadino degli Arienti's *Novelle Porretane* (1483) had been added to the Italian story-books, and the *Decameron* had been published in a French version by Verard (1485). This was a translation, or rather paraphrase, made from a Latin version by Laurent du Premierfait for Jean Duc de Berry at the beginning of the fifteenth century. It was not badly written and it enjoyed considerable popularity, going through numerous

---

chaire française au moyen âge, 2nd ed. 1866, and an admirable article by F. T. Crane in the *Proceedings of the American Philosophical Society* XXI. (1883–4) pp. 49–78.

[1] Edited for the *Société des anciens textes français* by Lucy Toulmin Smith and P. Meyer (1889).

[2] See M. Landau, *Die Quellen des Dekameron*, 2nd ed. Stuttgart, 1884.

[3] See A. d'Ancona in *Romania* II. 385 ff.

editions until, as we have seen, it was superseded in 1545 by the translation of Le Maçon.

About the same time as the publication of the *Cent Nouvelles Nouvelles* and the French *Decameron* some of Poggio's *Facetiae* were rendered into French by Guillaume Tardif, who has already been mentioned as the translator of Valla's *Facetiae morales*[1]. His work is an expansion rather than a translation, the dry and concise statements of the original being transformed into lively and dramatic pictures. Subsequent writers of prose-tales could hardly have found a better or more suggestive model[2].

The only other French collection of stories that appeared in print before the opening of the reign of Francis I was that completed in 1372 by the Chevalier de la Tour Landry for the instruction of his three daughters, and first printed in 1514. The stories are taken from the Bible, the *Gesta Romanorum*, chronicles, and other sources, and, like those of the *Gesta*, have a 'morality' appended to them[3].

The popularity of the short tale at this period is again shewn by its use in the pulpit. As in the thirteenth century, the popular preachers Menot, Maillard and others won the attention of their hearers by the liberal use of stories[4]. Moreover, the old collections of *exempla* were printed and reprinted, especially Herolt's *Promptuarium*, which was trans-

---

[1] *Ante*, p. 40.

[2] Brunet mentions an edition by Jean Trepperel who printed from 1491 to 1511, but his description is only at second hand and no copy of it is known to exist. In the Rothschild library there is an edition printed by Trepperel's widow, who printed from 1522 to 1527 (Harrisse, *op. cit.* XLVIII.). There is also an edition in the *Bib. de l'Arsenal*, apparently later, which has been reprinted by Montaiglon (1878). The edition of the *veuve* Trepperel contains 115 *facetiae* out of the 273 of the printed editions of the Latin text. The MSS generally have 330, and one has as many as 381. For a detailed account of Tardif's translation see *Vierteljahrs-schrift für Kultur und Litteratur der Renaissance*, ed. L. Geiger, I. 309 ff.

[3] There is a modern edition by A. de Montaiglon in the *Bib. Elzévirienne*, 1854. There are two English versions of it, one made by Caxton (see Blades's *Caxton*, 2nd ed. pp. 274 ff.), and another, of superior merit, made some half a century later, which has been edited by Wright for the Early English Text Society, 1868. There is a good article on the work in the *Retrospective Review*, 2nd Ser. I. 177 ff., 1827.

[4] See *Introductory Essay*, pp. 178–181.

lated into French under the title of *Fleur des Commandements de Dieu*. The same preacher's *Sermones Discipuli* attained an even greater popularity. Thus, when the reign of Francis I opened, a teller of short stories relating to ordinary life was sure of an audience, and there were open to him many storehouses which he could plunder at will.

The first additions to the French story-books that were made during the reign of Francis I were translations. First came a version of 149 tales from the *Gesta*, printed in 1521 under the title of *Le Violier des histoires romaines* and thrice reprinted in the course of the next few years[1]. Ten years later appeared a small collection taken principally from Boccaccio and Poggio under the title of *Le Parangon des nouvelles honnestes et delectables*[2]. For Poggio the translation of Macho was used, but for Boccaccio, whose beautiful story of *The Falcon* opens the volume, the compiler had recourse to a translation by some unknown writer. The collection also included some of Valla's Apologues or *Facetiae morales*, and five taken from the famous *Ulenspiegel*. In the following year (1532) *Ulenspiegel* was published in French in a more complete form, the translation being made from the Flemish version, which contains forty-six stories out of the ninety-six of the earlier German versions[3].

It was not till the year 1535 that a Frenchman followed in the footsteps of the author of the *Cent Nouvelles Nouvelles* by writing original tales. His name was Nicolas of Troyes, and he called his collection, which was completed on March 1, 1537, *Le grand Parangon des nouvelles nouvelles*[4]. The manuscript, which, so far as is known, was never printed until recent

---

[1] There is a modern edition by G. Brunet, 1858.

[2] Lyons, 1531; reprinted 1532 and 1533. There is a modern edition by E. Mabille.

[3] *Nouvellement translate et corrige de Flamant en francoys*, 1532. The original version was in Low-Saxon, but the earliest known version is a High-German one printed at Strasburg in 1521. The Flemish version was printed at Antwerp between 1520 and 1530 (C. H. Herford, *Literary relations between England and Germany*, Cambridge, 1886, pp. 283 ff.).

[4] The author says March 1, 1536, but this must be 153⅞, as one of the stories relates to an event which happened in May, 1536.

years, was in two volumes, but only one has come down to
us[1]. It contains 180 stories, of which about fifty are original.
Of the rest sixty are taken from the *Cent Nouvelles Nouvelles*,
fifty-five from Boccaccio, the same translation being used as
in the older *Parangon*, and ten from the *Violier*. The longest
is an arrangement of some of the least edifying scenes of the
Celestina, of which, as we have seen, a French translation had
appeared in 1527. Of the tales written by Nicolas himself
some, he says, had been told him by *bons compagnons*, while
others related to events which he had witnessed, or in which
he had actually taken part. He was a saddler by trade, and
possibly, as Mabille has suggested, saddler to the Court. At
the time when he wrote his book he was living at Tours, and
several of the stories relate to that place. The scene of others
is laid at Amboise, of others in Poitou, while several have to
do with the writer's birthplace, Troyes, or with other places
in Champagne.

In the general character of his stories and in his manner
of relating them Nicolas of Troyes comes nearest to the
author of the *Cent Nouvelles Nouvelles*. He has the same
direct and natural style, without the caustic humour, but with
more point and incision, the same love of his story for the
story's sake, the same moral indifference and the same coarseness. This very indifference makes his picture of social life
all the more faithful. We more readily believe in his stories
of the cruelty and oppression of great lords, of the injustice
of judges, of the ignorance and licentiousness of monks,
because he writes as a pure *conteur* without any bias, either
religious, or moral, or political, and because he does not exclude
stories which give the other side of the picture. But all this
shews that he and his work belong rather to the old than the
new order of things[2].

[1] In the *Bib. Nationale*. E. Mabille has edited from it a selection of fifty-five
stories, 1869.

[2] There is still unprinted a collection of stories by Philippe de Vigneulles, a
hosier of Metz, which was completed in 1515, and which appears also to have
been modelled on *Les Cent Nouvelles Nouvelles*. I only know it from the account
of it by H. Michelant, *Gedenkbuch des Metzer Bürgers P. von Vigneulles* in the
Bibliothek des Litt. Vereins, Stuttgart, 1852, pp. xxvi—xxviii.

2. *The Heptameron.*

Margaret of Angoulême, as she was called before her marriage, was older than her brother Francis by nearly two and a half years[1]. Her girlhood was passed with him in the castle of Amboise, where she applied herself to study with much greater diligence than he did, acquiring Latin, Italian, and Spanish[2]. In 1509 she was married to Charles, Duke of Alençon, for whom she seems to have had little affection. In 1517 she received from her brother the Duchy of Berry as an appanage; we have seen how much the University of Bourges owed to her fostering care. During the king's captivity she took an active part in the government of the kingdom[3], her name having been inserted in the patent of regency. She was now a widow, her husband having died of pleurisy (1525)[4], but in January, 1527, she married Henri d'Albret, king of Navarre, to whom on the whole she seems, at any rate until near the end of her life, to have been sincerely attached. The two were united in their efforts to promote the welfare of their tiny kingdom. The courts of justice were reformed, agricultural labourers were brought from Brittany and Saintonge, and a cloth-manufactory was set up[5]. There were two royal residences, Pau and Nérac, but we hear most of Margaret in connexion with Nérac, where men of letters and artists found a ready welcome. Guillaume du Maine, a pupil of Budé's, and afterwards tutor to his children, was her reader. Other men of note in the literary world held posts in her household—Charles de Sainte-Marthe, Bonaventure des Periers, Victor Brodeau, Antoine du Moulin, Jacques Symon de la Haye, and above all Clément Marot[6]. It was to Nérac that Marot betook himself in times of persecution; and

---

[1] Born April 11, 1492.　　　　[2] Brantôme, *Œuvres*, VII. 75.

[3] *ib.* VIII. 121.

[4] Leroux de Lincy in *Heptaméron* I. cxlvi. The common account is that he died of shame at his misconduct at the battle of Pavia.

[5] Olhagaray, *Hist. des Comptés de Foix Béarn et Navarre*, 1609, pp. 562, 563; Hilarion de Coste, *Éloges des Dames illustres* II. 272, 273.

[6] See La Ferrière-Percy, *op. cit.*

there the aged Lefèvre d'Etaples spent his last years in peace. Another of the Meaux preachers, Michel d'Arande, was Margaret's almoner, and a third, Gérard Roussel, was her spiritual adviser, and was through her influence made bishop of Oloron.

It has often been discussed to what extent she herself embraced the new doctrines. The thorough-going Reformers of her own day, men like Calvin and Beza, spoke of her as one whose early zeal for the truth had been tainted by superstition in later years[1]. Among modern writers she is generally claimed as a Catholic by Catholics and as a Protestant by Protestants, each party being anxious to claim as their own so illustrious an example of Christian piety and charity. The latter point to the undoubted fact that she accepted some of the cardinal doctrines of the reformed faith, the former to the equally undoubted fact that she lived and died a professed Catholic. The truth would seem to be that while she warmly embraced some of the Protestant doctrines, especially that of justification by faith, she yet clung to the Church in which she had been brought up, and never altogether renounced practices such as the worship of the Saints and the Virgin Mary and the adoration of the Host in the Mass, which to Calvin and his followers seemed grossly superstitious, but to which she attached no importance.

In fact her religious attitude was very similar to that of the mass of the English people at the beginning of the reign of Elizabeth, and to that of Elizabeth herself. Moreover Margaret's views, like those of many others who at first strongly sympathised with the doctrines of the Reformers, were modified by circumstances. On the one hand the uncompromising hostility which her brother began to show to Protestantism after the affair of the Placards must have had great weight with her[2]. On the other the narrow dogmatism of Calvin was doubtless as distasteful to her as it was to

[1] Beza, *Icones*, fo. i. iii.

[2] This was Brantôme's view. Pour ce la soubçonnait-on de la relligion de Luther. Mais pour le respect et l'amour qu'elle portoit au roy son frère, qui l'aymoit unicquement et l'appelloit tousjours sa mignonne, elle n'en fist jamais aucune profession ni semblant; et si elle la croyoit, elle la tenoit dans son âme fort secrette, d'autant que le roi la haïssoit fort (VIII. 116).

Rabelais and other humanists. For tolerance was one of the key-notes of her religion, and towards the end of her life she gave shelter at her Court to the two leaders of the sect known as the "Spiritual libertines," Poque and Quantin, and paid no regard to Calvin's remonstrances on the subject[1]. Her religion also had a strongly mystical side, which appears in her correspondence with Bishop Briçonnet, and, in a more intelligible form, in much of her poetry. In her later years it was greatly influenced by the study of Plato and Christian Neo-Platonism. Finally, her whole life was spent in acts of practical charity and kindness[2]. It was this religion, at once mystical and practical, which formed her chief consolation during the three sad years of life which remained to her after her brother's death. Her last work, left unfinished, was a poem on the Passion of our Saviour; her last word was His Name[3].

Margaret's contemporaries were as unanimous in their praises of her intellectual qualities as they were of her moral ones. "I believe her to be the wisest, not only among the women, but among the men of France," wrote Matteo Dandolo in 1542; "on questions of state policy you could not wish for sounder remarks than hers[4]." The Venetian ambassadors, however, were in the habit of painting in flattering colours the princes of friendly states, and Dandolo's opinion must not be taken too seriously[5]. The confidence which Francis placed

[1] See Calvin's treatise against the *Libertins spirituels* (*Op.* VII. 149 ff.) and his letter to Margaret dated April 28, 1545 (*ib.* XII. 64). In 1548 Poque figures on the list of Margaret's household as her almoner (La Ferrière-Percy, p. 178).

[2] *Elle estoit très-bonne, douce, gratieuse, charitable, grand' ausmonière et ne desdaignant personne* (Brantôme, VIII. 122).

[3] She died Dec. 21, 1549. The discovery and publication of Margaret's *Dernières poésies* by M. Abel Lefranc gave rise to some discussion on the subject of her religious views. See Lefranc, *Les idées religieuses de Marguerite de Navarre d'après son œuvre poétique*, 1898; E. Faguet in *Cosmopolis* for April, 1896; H. Hauser in *Revue Critique d'hist. et de litt.* I. 510 ff. 1896. See also an earlier article in the same review by Paul Desjardins, *ib.* I. 474, 1886. Capito's preface to his Commentary on Hosea (Strasburg, 1528) addressed to Margaret—the most important part is translated in Herminjard II. 119 ff.—shews how the hopes of the Reformers were centred on her at that time.

[4] Albèri, *Relazione*, Series I. vol. IV. p. 48.

[5] Though down to 1589 the *Relazioni* were theoretically secret, copies of them used to get abroad.

in his sister arose, as we can see plainly from her letters to
him, rather from her intense unquestioning devotion to his
plans than to any statesmanlike qualities of a high order.
She had in fact more sympathy than originality, more quickness than depth, more sweetness than strength.   Add to these
qualities her frankness, her impulsiveness, her genial enjoyment of life, her noble pity for the afflicted, and you have the
picture of a charming and loveable woman.

> Une doulceur assise en belle face
> Qui la beauté des plus belles efface,
> D'un regard chaste où n'habite nul vice,
> Ung rond parler sans fard, sans artiffice,
> Si beau, si bon, que qui cent ans l'ourroit
> Jà de cent ans fascher ne s'en pourroit;
> Ung vif esprit, ung sçavoir qui m'estonne,
> Et, par sus tout, une grace tant bonne,
> Soit à se taire ou soit en devisant,
> Que je vouldrois estre assez souffisant
> Pour en pappier escripre son merite
> Ainsi qu'elle est dedans mon cœur escripte[1].

Whatever Margaret's character, her influence upon the
thought and literature of the French Renaissance was of
the first importance.   Michelet's happy phrase, "the amiable
mother of the Renaissance," expresses a literal truth.   Her
encouragement of various schemes for the promotion of learning, her patronage of men of letters have been frequently
noted in former chapters.   There were few writers who did
not dedicate some work to her; there was hardly a poet who
did not compose in her honour a *dizain* or a Latin ode.   But
we must now consider her not as a patroness of letters, but as
an actual combatant in the literary arena.

If the *Grand Parangon* belongs in character to the Middle
Ages, there is no single book which is more inspired by the
spirit of the Renaissance in the form which it assumed in
France than the *Heptameron* of Margaret of Navarre.   The
idea of her book came to her from the *Decameron*, of which,

---

[1] Marot, IV. 171—2.   The epistle of which these lines form part was first
printed by Génin at the head of his edition of Margaret's letters.   Though it
does not bear Marot's name, it is evidently by his hand.

as we have seen, Antoine le Maçon made a new translation by her orders. This was just after his return from a year's visit to Italy, probably in the latter part of 1537[1]. His work, though not printed till 1545, must have been finished before November, 1540, and while still in manuscript was read to his patroness in the presence of the King and the Dauphin and his wife. They all expressed so much delight with it, says Margaret, "that if Boccaccio could have heard them he must have come to life again."

In May, 1541 Margaret, being with her husband the King of Navarre at the baths of Cauterets in the Pyrenees for the benefit partly of his health and partly of her own, conceived the idea of composing a new *Decameron*. This must not be taken to imply that none of the stories were written before this date, but merely that she then formed the intention of making them up to Boccaccio's number of a hundred and setting them in a similar frame-work to his. But various events, political and otherwise, intervened, and it was not till the summer of 1546 that she found the necessary leisure to put her project into execution[2]. How much Margaret added to her work after her brother's death (March 31, 1547) it is impossible to say, but there is, so far as I know, only one distinct reference to any later event, namely to the marriage of Antoine de Bourbon with her daughter, Jeanne d'Albret (October 20, 1548). At any rate the original idea was never completed. When Margaret died, only seventy-two stories had been written. These remained in manuscript till 1558, when Pierre Boaisteau, the author of the *Théâtre du Monde* and the translator of Bandello, published them under the title of *Histoires des Amans Fortunez*. But he altered the order of the stories, and suppressed five of them, as well as passages in others which seemed to have too strong an heretical flavour.

---

[1] Le Maçon says in his dedicatory address to Margaret, *S'il vous souvient du temps que vous feistes séjour de quatre ou cinq mois à Paris, durant lequel me commandastes etc.*; Margaret was at Fontainebleau, Paris and the neighbourhood from September 1537 till the end of the year.

[2] The above account of the genesis of the work is a fair deduction from the statements in Margaret's Prologue. Compare M. Frank's Introduction, pp. xlvi—lv.

He also omitted the prologues. In the following year a busy translator named Claude Gruget, secretary to Louis de Bourbon, Prince de Condé, published a new edition, which contained seventy-two tales arranged in their proper order with the prologues. But while he restored the 63rd and 66th stories, in which there is no question of heretical doctrine, he substituted three of his own invention for the 11th, 44th and 46th, which the former editor had also omitted. He also invented the title of *Heptameron* to suit the number of the novels, Margaret herself having apparently intended to call her work the *Decameron*[1].

Gruget's text was followed more or less faithfully down to the close of the seventeenth century, when there was published with the imprint of Amsterdam an illustrated edition under the title of *Contes et Nouvelles de Margaret de Valois, Reine de Navarre, mis en bĕau langage* (1698). This version, so characteristic of the literary tastes of the eighteenth century, held its own till 1841, when Paul Lacroix published a reproduction of Gruget's text. Finally in 1853—4 Le Roux de Lincy edited for the *Société des Bibliophiles françois* from a manuscript in the *Bibliothèque Nationale* an edition of the *Heptameron*, in which for the first time Margaret's work was given to the world as she left it[2].

There was one feature, Margaret tells us, in which she intended that her *Decameron* should differ from Boccaccio's. It was to contain nothing that was not a true history[3]. This of course does not mean that she inquired closely into the truth of every story that was told her, but with one exception which she expressly mentions, namely the 70th story, she adhered to her rule of taking nothing from books. It is true that some seven or eight of the stories appear in a similar

---

[1] It bears this title in a MS. of the *Bib. Nat.* copied by Adrian de Thou, uncle of the historian, in 1553 (see Le Roux de Lincy I. p. clx.).

[2] The text and notes of this edition were republished in 4 vols. in 1880, edited by Le Roux de Lincy and De Montaiglon. In vol. I. will be found Charles de Sainte-Marthe's *Oraison funèbre* (of little value or interest) and the passages from Brantôme which relate to Margaret or the *Heptameron*.

[3] *Nulle nouvelle qui se soit véritable histoire.*

form in earlier collections, such as the *Cent Nouvelles Nouvelles*, Poggio's *Facetiae*, the book of the Chevalier de la Tour Landry (no. 37) and the novels of Sacchetti and Masuccio; but this does not preclude their having been derived by Margaret from independent and oral sources[1]. The great majority of the stories relate to events which happened within the memory of the actual narrator[2]. Of those for which a date is either expressly given or clearly indicated only nine relate to a period earlier than the sixteenth century, only four to a period before 1490, when Louise of Savoy, the oldest of the narrators, was thirteen, and only one to as early a date as the middle of the fifteenth century[3].

Le Roux de Lincy was the first person to insist on the historical character of the *Heptameron*, but it was left to M. Frank to work out the subject more in detail. One point made by Le Roux de Lincy was that the speakers all stood for real persons, but he only identified a few of them. It is this part of the subject that has been investigated by M. Frank with great patience and acuteness, and with the result that he has found a representative for each of the ten *devisants*. Some of his identifications may be considered as reasonably certain, while there is not one that has not a fair amount of probability in its favour. Having established that three of the characters, Osile, Parlamente, and Hircan stand respectively for Louise of Savoy, Margaret herself, and her second husband Henry of Navarre, he perceived that the period between her second marriage (January 24, 1527) and the death of her mother (September 22, 1531) was the only time which would suit the combined presence of her husband and mother among the company. He therefore infers that it is during this period, and not at the date of Margaret's visit to the baths of Cauterets in 1541, that the meeting of the ten personages of Margaret's drama is supposed to take place. The period may be narrowed

---

[1] See G. Paris in *Jour. des Savants*, 1895, p. 344.

[2] Brantôme refers to several of the stories as having actually happened (IX. 211, 236 ff., 388, 489, 678).

[3] The King Alfonso to whose time the third tale is referred appears to be Alfonso V, king of Aragon and Sicily from 1443 to 1458.

still further with the help of some of the other identifications which M. Frank may be considered to have made certain ; for it was not till 1529 that two of the *devisants*, François de Bourdeille and his wife, were appointed to the household of the King and Queen of Navarre. The whole tone of the work suits this date. Margaret could then speak of herself as free from melancholy, and the speakers could then be represented as expressing opinions strongly flavoured with evangelical doctrines with a frankness and openness which, after the affair of the Placards, would have been impossible to persons closely connected with the Court. But though 1530 or thereabouts may be taken as the time at which the scene is laid, several of the stories refer to events of a later date. The rule however is strictly maintained that no story is assigned to any narrator of events which took place after his or her death[1].

The identification of Ennasuicte with Anne de Vivonne, the wife of François de Bourdeille, is one of the strongest links in the theory that all the characters stand for real persons, for Brantôme expressly tells us that his mother was one of the *devisantes* of the *Heptameron*[2], and to suppose that *Enna* is an anagram of Anne and *suicte* an abbreviation of *suivante* is reasonably simple. Further Simontault's age, coarse speech, and rough good-natured humour accord well with Brantôme's description of his father as *homme scabreux, haut à la main*, and of the amusing stories of his relations with Pope Julius II.[3] It also seems probable that Geburon, who hates monks and expresses himself on religious topics in distinctly Protestant language, represents M. de Burye, who, according to Brantôme, was suspected of being 'of the religion'; that Longarine, *la jeune demoiselle-veuve*, is Mme de Silly, the *châtelaine* of Longrai, and that Dagoucin, the Platonic

---

[1] It is just possible that Margaret may have paid a visit to the baths of Cauterets in September 1530. At any rate if we had to select a particular date this is the year that would suit best, for it was in the autumn of that year that Henry and Margaret went to live in their own country of Béarn, having up till then spent most of their time since their marriage in France (see Génin, *Nouvelles Lettres*, p. 107, n. 2).

[2] IX. 238.   [3] X. 42.

lover, is Nicolas Dangu, Abbot of Juilly, an illegitimate son of
Cardinal du Prat, who afterwards became successively bishop
of Séez and Mende[1]. The identification of Saffredent and
Nomerfide with Jean de Montpezat and his wife is of a more
conjectural character. It may be noted however in its favour
that Mme de Montpezat joined the reformed religion before
her death, and that Nomerfide speaks of monks and indulgences in terms of the most lively abhorrence. Saffredent,
like Simontault, is a representative of the *esprit gaulois*, but
he is of a more refined and more profoundly sceptical type ;
he has the spirit in fact of the *Roman de la Rose* rather than
that of the *fableaux*.

Whether the characters of the *Heptameron* be real or not,
there can be no doubt that they are admirably selected as
representatives of the society of Margaret's day. It is the
devisants themselves and their conversation, in a word the
setting of the *Heptameron*, which constitute its greatest charm
and merit. It is this that makes it with *Pantagruel* the most
characteristic book of the early French Renaissance, the book
which gives us the best picture of its social and intellectual
atmosphere, of that curious mixture of coarseness and refinement, of cynicism and enthusiasm, of irreverence and piety,
of delight in living and love of meditation on death, which
characterised that period of transition between the mediæval
and the modern world.

The idea of appending a discussion by way of epilogue to
each story seems to be Margaret's own. It is a happy substitute for the formal moral of the *Gesta Romanorum* and the
Chevalier de La Tour Landry, or the dry comments of Masuccio, and in Margaret's hands it is managed with great
artistic skill. The individuality of each speaker is clearly
defined, and the part he bears in the conversation is always
in perfect keeping with his character. The lively touches,
the asides, the good-humoured banter, give the conversation
a dramatic flavour which is in the highest degree attractive.
As M. Frank well points out the only *Conteur* whom Margaret

---

[1] See *Gallia Christiana*, XI. 702.

resembles in this dramatic character of her setting is Chaucer[1].

A noticeable feature of the setting is its strong bias in favour of the new religious doctrines. The day was begun with an hour's reading of the Scriptures and they are constantly quoted by all the company, even by the cynical Saffredent. The hatred of monks is very conspicuous. Three of the stories relate to the evil-doings of the secular clergy, but no less than ten are told against monks, the Franciscans being specially marked out for reprobation. We have seen that the chief exponent of this feeling is Geburon. But the good lady Osile is hardly less strong in her condemnation, which reminds one of the often-quoted entry in Louise of Savoy's diary, where she says that "her son and she had begun to understand the hypocrites white, gray, smoky, and of all colours." At last Osile exclaims, "Shall we never have done with those tiresome Franciscans?" The whole epilogue to the 55th story is a severe attack on the monks, so severe that the first editor thought it prudent to substitute for it one of his own invention. We also find distinctively Protestant doctrines enunciated, such as justification by faith and not by works (23), grace (epilogues to 23, 26 and 67), election (epilogue to 2), and the sinfulness of human nature (21)[2].

A great deal of the discussion in the epilogues naturally turns on the absorbing question of the relations between men and women. It was one in which Margaret evidently took great interest and it forms the subject of two of her longest poems, *Les quatre dames et les quatre gentilshommes* and *La Coche*, which seems to have been also called *Le Débat d'Amour*[3]. It was indeed only natural that a woman of her active and inquiring mind and strong religious feelings should occupy herself with an important social question in which she saw the law of God and the law of man so diametrically

---

[1] Introduction, lxiii—lxvii.

[2] The Protestantism of the *Heptameron* is well brought out in an article of the *Edinburgh Review* for July 1888, pp. 115, 116.

[3] For the connexion between Margaret's poems and the *Heptameron*, see Frank, *Heptaméron* III. 466 ff.

opposed. We have seen how many translations of Italian and Spanish works relating to the subject of love found favour at this period; it was in fact one of the most popular of the various moral and intellectual questions which were perpetually being discussed in this restless and critical age of the Renaissance, when thoughtful minds were no longer content to accept the old traditional standards. The morality of the *Heptameron* on this point may seem inadequate if judged by a modern standard, but compared with French mediæval literature, with *Les Cent Nouvelles Nouvelles*, with *Jehan de Saintré*, with the Romances of Chivalry, even with *Amadis of Gaul*, it shews a considerable advance. This is especially the case with Margaret's own views, as represented by Parlamente and Osile, as opposed to those of the male *devisants*[1]. Even with regard to the story of the young prince (Francis I) and the advocate's wife (25), which as being told by a virtuous woman like Longarine without any sign of disapproval is most open to the charge of immorality, Parlamente herself distinctly speaks of the prince's act as a sin.

Of coarseness of language there is very little in the *Heptameron*; of indelicacy of thought there is decidedly more, but not more than may fairly be accounted for by the different standard of a different age. Of deliberate appeal to the grosser passions, such as we find in many modern novels, there is nothing at all, and anybody who takes up the *Heptameron* with the expectation of gratifying these instincts will be grievously disappointed.

From the *Heptameron* too we learn not only what the people of that day thought, but how they dressed and generally managed their social life. The delicate touches by means of which these features are brought before us, so utterly unlike the laboured inventories of the naturalist school, testify to Margaret's womanlike power of observation[2].

Apart from the light that they throw on the thought and life of the age, it must be confessed that the stories in them-

---

[1] See especially the epilogue to no. 26.

[2] See A. Mary F. Robinson (Mme Duclaux), *M. of Angoulême*, 1886, pp. 158, 159, and 175, 176.

selves are, for the most part, not very entertaining. The majority are neither exciting nor humorous nor pathetic; nor are they well told. Margaret is conspicuously wanting in the artistic sense of proportion, the firm concentration and the dramatic power necessary for a narrator of short stories. As might be expected from the diffuse character of her workmanship it is in the longer stories that she shews to the best advantage, as in *The gentleman and the princess* (4), in *Floride* (10)[1], in the tragic story of Sister Marie Heroet (22) and in the story about a Duchess of Burgundy (70), which she borrowed from a prose version of the thirteenth century poem of the *Châtelaine de Vergy*. On the other hand the long story of *Rolandine and the Bastard* (21) is decidedly dull. Among the shorter stories the best of the pathetic class are the 21st, the 32nd and the 67th, while the 54th, 55th, 69th and 72nd are good specimens of fun and humour. But that which on the whole shews the highest narrative power is the 61st, the story of a lady who deserted her husband for a Canon of Autun. It is a strange and affecting story, told with great impressiveness and within moderate compass. Two stories of no particular merit, but which are worth noting for the events which they relate, are the 12th, which tells of the assassination of Alessandro de' Medici by his cousin Lorenzino, and the 36th, about the President of Grenoble[2], of which another version is told by Des Periers (xc.) and another by Bandello (I. 11), and which is used by Shirley in his play of *Love's cruelty*.

Though, however, only about a third of the stories can be praised as examples of the story-teller's art, they are all distinguished by the same charm of style. It is neither brilliant nor forcible nor imaginative, but it is clear, easy, unaffected, graceful and well-bred, a true reflexion of the candour, the good-humour, the charm of the writer. Perhaps its chief fault is that it is lacking in variety. Here are two specimens, the first from the opening of the story of

[1] In *The gentleman and the princess* she is almost certainly relating her own experiences, and very possibly also in *Floride*.

[2] Geoffroy Charles or de' Caroli. See G. Paris, *loc. cit.* p. 349.

Floride (10) and the second from the epilogue to the 8th story :

En la Comté d'Arande en Arragon, y avoit une Dame, qui, en sa grande jeunesse, demeura vefve du Comte d'Arande avecq un fils et une fille, laquelle fille se nommoit Floride. La dicte Dame meyt peine de nourrir ses enfans en toutes les vertuz et honestetez qui appartiennent à seigneurs et gentilz hommes ; en sorte que sa maison eut le bruict d'une des honnorables qui fust point en toutes les Espaignes. Elle alloyt souvent à Tollette, où se tenoit le Roy d'Espaigne ; et quand elle venoyt à Sarragosse, qui estoit près de sa maison, demoroit longuement avecq la Royne et à la cour, où elle estoit autant estimée que Dame pourroit estre. Une fois, allant devers le Roy, selon sa coustume, lequel estoit à Sarragosse, en son chasteau de la Jasserye, ceste Dame passa par un villaige qui estoit au viceroy de Cathaloigne, lequel ne bougeoyt point de dessus la frontière de Parpignan, à cause des grandes guerres qui estoient entre les Roys de France et d'Espaigne ; mais, à ceste heure-là, y estoit la paix, en sorte que le viceroy avec tous les cappitaines estoient venuz faire la révérence au Roy. Sçachant ce viceroy que la Comtesse d'Arande passoit par sa terre, alla au devant d'elle, tant pour l'amitié ancienne qu'il luy portoit que pour l'honorer comme parente du Roy. Or, il avoit en sa compaignie plusieurs honnestes gentilz hommes qui, par la fréquentation des longues guerres, avoient acquis tant d'honneur et bon bruict, que chascun qui les pouvoit veoir et hanter se tenoit heureux. Et, entre les autres, y en avoit un nommé Amadour, lequel combien qu'il n'eust que dix-huict ou dix-neuf ans, si avoit-il la grace tant asseurée et le sens si bon, que on l'eust jugé entre mil digne de gouverner une chose publique. Il est vray que ce bon sens-là estoit accompaigné d'une si grande et naïfve beaulté, qu'il n'y avoyt œil qui ne se tinst content de le regarder ; et si la beaulté estoit tant exquise, la parolle la suyvoit de si près que l'on ne sçavoit à qui donner l'honneur, ou à la grace, ou à la beaulté, ou au bien parler. Mais ce qui le faisoit encores plus estimer, c'estoit sa grande hardiesse, dont le bruict n'estoit empesché pour sa jeunesse ; car en tant de lieux avoit déjà monstré ce qu'il sçavoit faire, que non seulement les Espaignes, mais la France et l'Italie estimoient grandement ses vertuz, pource que, à toutes les guerres qui avoyent esté, il ne se estoit point espargné ; et, quand son païs estoit en repos, il alloit chercher la guerre aux lieux estranges, où il estoit aymé et estimé d'amis et d'ennemis[1].

The following passage is interesting as relating to the doctrine of spiritual love :

"Dagoucin," dist Hircan, "vous voulez tomber en une faulse opinion ; comme si nous devions aymer les femmes sans estre aymés ! "—" Hircan,"

[1] The Comtesse d'Arande possibly stands for Margaret, and Amadour for Bonnivet.

T.   8

dist Dagoucin, "je veulx dire que, si nostre amour est fondé sur la beaulté, bonne grace, amour et faveur d'une femme, et nostre fin soit plaisir, honneur ou proffict, l'amour ne peult longuement durer ; car, si la chose sur quoy nous la fondons défault, nostre amour s'envolle hors de nous. Mais je suis ferme à mon opinion, que celluy qui ayme, n'ayant aultre fin ne désir que bien aymer, laissera plus tost son ame par la mort, que ceste forte amour saille de son cueur.—"Par ma foy," dist Simontault, "je ne croys pas que jamais vous ayez esté amoureux ; car, si vous aviez senty le feu comme les aultres, vous ne nous peindriez icy la chose publicque de Platon, qui s'escript et ne s'expérimente poinct."—"Si j'ay aymé," dist Dagoucin, "j'ayme encores, et aymeray tant que vivray. Mais j'ay si grand paour que la démonstration face tort à la perfection de mon amour, que je crains que celle de qui je debvrois désirer l'amityé semblable, l'entende : et mesmes je n'ose penser ma pensée, de paour que mes œils en révèlent quelque chose ; car, tant plus je tiens ce feu celé et couvert, et plus en moy croist le plaisir de sçavoir que j'ayme perfaictement."

Note. Margaret's authorship of the *Heptameron* is not altogether uncontested. In 1839 Charles Nodier in an article in the *Revue des deux mondes* expressed an opinion that she only wrote a few of the stories, and that the greater part are the work of Des Periers. This view Professor Saintsbury regards as having at any rate probability in its favour[1]. There are however it seems to me essential differences between the prevailing style of the *Joyeux Devis* (assuming these to be by Des Periers) and that of the *Heptameron*. Madame Duclaux has well said of the latter that it is a woman's style. Moreover there is a high-bred flavour about it which is altogether wanting in Des Periers, whether in the *Joyeux Devis* or elsewhere. Professor Saintsbury's disbelief in Margaret's authorship seems to be based chiefly on the ground that there is nothing in her undoubted work to shew that she was capable of writing the *Heptameron*. But though her letters are greatly inferior to the tales in point of style, the sentences being long and cumbrous, and the thought often obscure, they at any rate reveal a certain capacity for style. They shew some command of vocabulary and expression, but more especially they are marked by that close sympathy between the writer and the subject, which is one of the charms of the *Heptameron*. So too Margaret's poems, whatever their defects as poetry, shew that she could write simply, clearly, and expressively, that she had in fact a decided literary faculty. There seems then no good reason for rejecting Margaret's authorship on the ground that the tales are beyond her powers. Further the theory held by some critics, which Professor Saintsbury accepts,

[1] *A short history of French Literature*, 5th ed. 1897, p. 164, and essay prefixed to the English translation of the *Heptameron* published in 1894, I. cxxxi, ii.

that the *Heptameron* is the joint production of Margaret and various men of letters who belonged to her court, seems disproved by the similarity of style which characterises the tales. They vary no doubt greatly in merit, but the style of the great majority is the same. Nor is there any noticeable difference between the style of the tales, and that of the setting, Margaret's authorship of which is not in dispute. We may therefore on the evidence of style conclude in favour of a single author, and of that author being Margaret. A few tales however are probably spurious, notably the 63rd and the 66th, which were omitted by Boaisteau, and which shew a coarseness of touch indicative of a man's hand. Finally to go to external evidence we have Brantôme's express statement, *Elle composa toutes ses nouvelles.*

3. *Margaret's Poems.*

The only collected edition of Margaret's poems which appeared in her life-time bore the poetical title of *Les Marguerites de la Marguerite des princesses.* It was published in 1547 under the care of one of her *valets de chambre*, whose name seems to have been Jacques Symon de la Haye, but who was also called Symon Silvius. The first and larger part of the volume is composed of religious poetry, and the second part of secular poetry[1]. Between the publication of this volume and her death Margaret wrote a good deal of poetry, but nothing was known of it till quite recently, when M. Abel Lefranc discovered in the *Bibliothèque Nationale* a manuscript which had hitherto escaped notice, and which was entitled *Les dernières œuvres de la Reine de Navarre*[2].

It cannot be said that these newly discovered poems, interesting though they are in many ways, and especially for the light they throw on Margaret's religious opinions, add anything to her reputation as a poet. The fact is she had not in her the making of a real poet. She had neither the imagination and the divine frenzy of an inspired poet, nor the technical skill, the sense of form, the power of concentration,

---

[1] The first part fills vols. I. and II. and the greater part of vol. III. of Frank's edition in 4 vols.

[2] Some of these pieces, viz. *Epistres* ii.—vi. and viii. had been published previously from another MS. by E. Frémy in 1883. He however assigned them to Catharine de' Medici.

the patient workmanship, and the critical judgment which go
to make an artistic poet. She wrote for

> Le plaisir de la douce escriture,
> Ou tant je fus enclinée de nature.

She was never weary of writing or dictating. Even while
travelling she used to dictate from her litter. Des Periers,
who was one of her secretaries, speaks of 'the facility with
which she abounded in verse and prose[1].' The result is that
she produced a large amount of dull and prosaic verse, which
is as difficult to read as it was easy to write.

The *Miroir de l'ame pecheresse*[2], which from its evangelical
character created much excitement on its appearance, is feeble
and prolix; equally so is the *Triomphe de l'Agneau*[3], an account
of the Redemption. The two longest poems of the *Dernières
poésies*, *Les prisons*[4] and *Le navire*[5], are interesting as shewing
the influence of Dante. It is especially noticeable in *Le navire*,
which is written in *terza rima*, and, as Gaston Paris points
out, probably when Margaret was fresh from reading the *Divina
Commedia*[6]. In the long poem in three books entitled *Les
prisons de la Reine de Navarre*, the influence is less marked,
but it contains a direct reference to the three beasts of the
first canto of the *Inferno*[7]. Of the longer poems in *Les
Marguerites de la Marguerite* the most interesting are the
secular ones. *Les Quatre Dames et les Quatre Gentilzhommes*[8],
though very unequal, is really good in parts; there is pathos
in *La Coche*[9] and grace in *L'Histoire des Satyres et des
Nymphes de Diane*[10], but they are both much too long. The
latter is founded on one of Sannazaro's Latin eclogues—the
sixth—and the fact that it is about ten times as long as its

[1] Des Periers, *Œuvres* (ed. Lacour), I. 139.
[2] *Les Marguerites de la M.* ed. Frank, I. 15—68. The oldest known edition
with a date was printed at Alençon in 1531. It was translated by Queen Elizabeth
in 1544 when she was eleven.
[3] III. 1—61.   [4] pp. 121—297.   [5] pp. 385—439.
[6] *Journal des Savants*, 1896, pp. 173 ff. (a review of Lefranc's edition).
[7] According to the printed edition (p. 182) Margaret speaks of *l'ourse, lyonne
et louve*. Is '*ourse*' for *once* her mistake or the scribe's?
[8] IV. 1—101.
[9] Written about 1532 and also called *Le Debat d'amour*.
[10] III. 167—200, first published in 1543.

model is a measure of Margaret's prolixity. It is a measure too of Margaret's poetical faculty that she is at her best when she is most simple and matter-of-fact, while the moment she attempts a higher flight and tries to express a really poetical idea, she becomes involved and obscure.

Her dramatic work consists of four mysteries[1], four so-called comedies[2] and three farces[3], but, as one might expect at this period, there is little attempt at dramatisation in any of them. The farces are nothing more than moralities, in which the characters are mere abstractions. Even in the comedies the characters, though human beings, bear no names. However, in these, which treat of love, and in the farces, which treat of religion and are strongly Protestant in tone, Margaret discusses her favourite topics with considerable skill and liveliness. One of these comedies is printed in the *Dernières poésies*, and is about the most interesting piece in the collection. We learn from the title that it was played on Shrove Tuesday, 1547[4], and there is no doubt that all Margaret's plays were written for representation. The other 'comedy' in the *Dernières poésies*, entitled *Comedie sur le trespas du Roy*, is in reality a pastoral elegy. It shews how vaguely the term 'comedy' was used at this period.

It is in the *Chansons spirituelles* that Margaret is most successful. In these her two sources of inspiration are the two subjects upon which she felt most deeply, the love of her God and the love of her brother. Hence, though they consist of simple words written for well-known airs[5], they sometimes rise to a note of true poetic fervour. The following will enable the reader to judge of Margaret's capacity for the poetry of mysticism :

[1] *Marguerites de la M.* II.

[2] One in vol. IV. of *Marguerites de la M.* and two in *Dernières poésies*, and one unpublished.

[3] One in vol. IV. of *Marguerites de la M.* and two in vol. I. of the *Heptameron* (1853), pp. cxcvii—ccliv.

[4] This must be 154⅞, for it could hardly have been played on Shrove Tuesday (Feb. 22) of 1547, when Francis I was already seriously ill.

[5] This was a common practice among the Protestants; they often borrowed the opening words of the profane song for which the air was written.

> Penser en la passion
> De Jesuchrist,
> C'est la consolation
> De mon esprit.

Seigneur, quand viendra le jour
  Tant desiré,
Que je seray par amour
  A vous tiré,
Et que l'union sera
  Telle entre nous
Que l'espouse on nommera
  Comme l'espoux?

Penser etc.

Ce jour des nopces, Seigneur,
  Me tarde tant,
Que de nul bien ny honneur
  Ne suis content ;
Du monde ne puys avoir
  Plaisir ny bien :
Si je ne vous y puys voir,
  Las ! je n'ay rien.

Penser etc.

Si de vostre bouche puys
  Estre baisé,
Je seray de tous ennuys
  Bien appaisé.
Baisez moy, accolez moy,
  Mon Tout en tous,
Unissez moy par la Foy
  Du tout à vous.

Penser etc.

Essuyez des tristes yeux
  Le long gemir,
Et me donnez pour le mieux
  Un doux dormir.
Car d'ouyr incessamment
  Voz saints propos,
C'est parfait contentement,
  Et seur repos.

Penser etc.[1]

There are sixteen *Chansons spirituelles* in the manuscript of the *Dernières poésies*[2] (though M. Lefranc only prints twelve), the best perhaps being no. xxviii, of which the following is the first stanza :

> Seigneur, je suis la mignonne
> D'un que je ne puis nommer,
> Mais par sa grace tant bonne
> Se peut cognoistre et aymer :
> Seulement n'est beau de face,
> Mais est la seule Beauté,
> Et vault mieulx sa bonne grace
> Qu'empire ny royaulté ;
> Sa doulceur est si très grande
> Et sa liberalite[3].

There is another characteristic of the *Chansons spirituelles* which is deserving of attention, and that is the great variety

---

[1] *Les Marguerites de la Marguerite*, III. 131—133.
[2] G. Paris, *Journal des Savants*, 1895.
[3] *Dernières poésies*, p. 325.

of metres employed in them. Lines of various length from
the line of four syllables to the Alexandrine, and stanzas of
from four to ten lines with a great variety in the arrangement
of the rhymes make up a considerable assortment. In fact,
out of the thirty-three *chansons* of the *Marguerites de la
Marguerite* it would be difficult to find two written in precisely
the same metre. It should be noticed that one of some length
(ninety-four lines) is written in feminine Alexandrines throughout[1], and that the series concludes with the only sonnet that
(so far as I know) Margaret wrote[2]. One of the purely lyric
metres also calls for attention, for in it she has to some extent
anticipated the classical stanza of French lyric poetry finally
developed by Malherbe. Marot in his Psalms had used a
stanza of ten lines with the rhymes arranged in the order of
Malherbe's stanza, but while his quatrain is composed of octo-
syllables, the remaining six lines are all of five syllables[3].
Margaret uses a line of six syllables throughout:

> Changeons tristesse en joye
> Et en chant nostre dueil;
> Afin que mieux on croye,
> Ouvrons de l'esprit l'œil.
> Laissons ceste chaire morte,
> Qui tant nous desconforte
> Avec son vieil Adam:
> De vive voix et forte,
> Chantons à chasque porte
> Noël pour fin de l'an[4].

For this Ronsard substituted a line of seven syllables and
Malherbe one of eight.

Thus it will be seen that in one important service which
Ronsard rendered to French lyric poetry, namely the invention
of new metrical effects, Margaret forms a connecting link
between him and Marot. Nor is it merely a question of
ingenious contrivance; both the combination of the sounds
and the arrangement of the rhymes shew that Margaret had
a really poetical ear. On the other hand she often mars her

---

[1] III. 105, *Sur l'arbre de la Croix d'une voix clere et belle*, modelled on the song
Sur le pont d'Avignon, j'ouys chanter la belle.

[2] III. 163.   [3] Ps. xxxiii. (*Œuvres* IV. 107).   [4] III. 159.

effects by carelessness, nor has she learnt any more than
Marot the art of choosing a metre suitable to the theme. A
dancing metre ill accords with words of passionate spiritual
adoration.

BIBLIOGRAPHY.

EDITIONS.

Le Violier des histoires romaines, 1521; ed. G. Brunet, 1858.
Le Parangon des nouvelles honnestes et delectables, Lyons, 1531; ed.
E. Mabille, 1865.
NICOLAS DE TROYES, *Le grand Parangon des nouvelles nouvelles*, ed.
E. Mabille, 1859.
MARGARET OF NAVARRE, *Histoires des Amans fortunez*, 1558 (see for
a reproduction of the title-page, Le Petit, p. 59); *L'Heptameron des
Nouvelles*, 1559 (*ib.* p. 61): *Contes et nouvelles, mis en beau language,*
1698; *L'Heptaméron des Nouvelles*, ed. A. J. V. Le Roux de Lincy,
3 vols. 1853, 4; ed. F. Frank, 3 vols. 1879; ed. Le Roux de Lincy and
A. de Montaiglon, 4 vols. 1880 (a republication of the text and notes of
the edition of 1853); ed. B. Pifteau in the *nouv. collection Jannet*, 1875
(the best cheap edition).
Les Marguerites de la Marguerite des princesses, Lyons, 1547 (a copy
in the library of Trinity College, Cambridge: Le Petit, p. 57); ed.
F. Frank, 4 vols. 1873.
Les dernières poésies, ed. A. Lefranc, 1896.
To these volumes must be added to complete Margaret's printed
poetical work, (1) 30 poems, chiefly *rondeaux*, printed by Champollion-
Figeac in his *Poésies de Francois Ier*; (2) two farces, five epistles and ten
short pieces printed by Le Roux de Lincy in his edition of the *Heptameron*
(I. pp. cxcvii—ccliv); (3) *Dialogue en forme de vision nocturne* printed
with *Miroir de l'ame pecheresse*, Alençon, 1533, and never re-printed;
(4) *L'Art et usage du souverain Mirouer du Chrestien* or *La Passion de
Jésus-Christ*, a poem left unfinished by Margaret at her death and published with considerable alterations by Pierre Olivier in 1556 (Paris,
G. le Noir).
The unpublished matter includes *Quatre epistres escriptes par quatre
damoyselles*, and a species of comedy or morality (*Bib. Nat. fonds franç.*
no. 883), besides various short poems in MSS. of the *Bib. Nat.* or the
library of the Arsenal. See Le Roux de Lincy, *op. cit.* I. clxxxiv ff.
Lettres de la Reine de Navarre and *Nouvelles Lettres*, ed. F. Génin
for the *Soc. de l'histoire de France*, 1841 and 1842.

TRANSLATIONS.

Sixteen of the tales of the *Heptameron* were translated by William Painter for his *Palace of Pleasure*, 1566, and the whole work by Robert Codrington, 1654. There are two modern translations, one in 5 vols. 1894, published for the Society of English Bibliophilists, with a prefatory essay by George Saintsbury, and the other made by A. Machen, and published in 1886.

LIFE.

Brantôme, *Œuvres*, ed. Lalanne, VIII. 114—126 (disappointingly meagre, considering Brantôme's opportunities); Bayle, *Dict. critique*, s. v. *Navarre*. The best modern life is that of Le Roux de Lincy in the introduction to his edition of 1853 ; on this is based the account prefixed to the English Translation of 1894. See also F. Frank's introduction to *Les Marguerites de la Marguerite des princesses*, 1873 ; and the same writer's *Dernier voyage de la Reine de Navarre aux bains de Cauterets* (1549), Toulouse and Paris, 1897 ; H. de la Ferrière-Percy, *Marguerite d'Angoulême, son livre de dépenses* (1540—1549), *étude sur ses dernières années*, 1862 ; A. Mary F. Robinson (Madame Duclaux), *M. of Angoulême*, 1886. Lotheissen's *Margarethe von Navarre*, Berlin, 2nd ed. 1885, is of no importance for her life, and Miss Freer's gushing and garrulous volume should be avoided.

TO BE CONSULTED.

For the whole chapter: P. Toldo, *Contributo allo studio della novella francese del* XV *e* XVI *secolo*, Rome, 1895 ; Gaston Paris in *Journal des Savants*, 1895, pp. 289 ff. and 342 ff. (a review of Toldo's book).

For Margaret of Navarre : C. A. Sainte-Beuve, *Causeries du Lundi* VII. 434 ff. 1853 (of great charm and delicacy) ; G. Saintsbury in vol. I. of the English Translation of 1894 ; René Doumic in the *Revue des deux mondes* for June 15, 1896.

CHAPTER VII

DES PERIERS

THE influence of Margaret of Navarre on the literature of the Renaissance was not confined to the patronage and protection of men of letters. Not a few of those who held posts in her household owed their literary career to her encouragement, or even her commands. Jacques de la Haye, the editor of her poems, prefixed to them an epistle in verse, celebrating her virtues and commending himself to her favour, which is at any rate as good as that of his mistress.

We have seen that it was at her bidding that Antoine le Maçon translated the *Decameron.* He too was something of a poet, as is shown by his translations of the poems in the *Decameron.* In these, especially in the one at the end of the ninth day, he almost rivals Marot in grace. Here are the first two stanzas :

> Moy jeune fille volontaire,
> Chante sur la saison nouvelle :
> Pensant au bien que ne puis taire.
>
> Par les vers prez vois m'esgarant,
> Entre fleurs blanches et vermeilles,
> Comme liz, roses et pareilles :
> Puis les voyant tous, comparant
> Au tainct de l'amy apparent,
> Qui m'a prise et tient, comme celle
> Qui n'a desir fors de luy plaire :
> Moy jeune fille volontaire.
>
> Et quand je trouve quelque fleur
> Qui me semble à luy bien semblable,
> Je la baise et cueil, comme aymable,

> Parlant à elle par douceur,
> Et luy descouvre tout mon cueur :
> Puys l'attache à ma girlandelle,
> Sous mes blonds crins que j'en vueil traire :
> Moy jeune fille volontaire[1].

But of all these literary members of the Queen of Navarre's household, by far the most remarkable was Bonaventure des Periers. Of his early life very little is known[2]. He was a Burgundian, born about the year 1510, and, according to a well-supported tradition, at Arnay-le-Duc, near Beaune[3]. Having become a teacher in a school attached to one of the numerous abbeys in France dedicated to St Martin, the abbot, who is probably to be identified with Robert Hurault, abbot of St Martin of Autun and formerly tutor to the Queen of Navarre, took a special interest in him and taught him Latin and Greek[4]. He also seems to have awakened in him a sympathy for the new religious doctrines. At any rate, we find him during the winter of 1534–35 taking part in Olivetan's translation of the Bible, and helping to draw up a table of Hebrew, Chaldee, Greek and Latin proper names. He was probably at Neuchâtel in May 1535, when this table was passing through the press[5]. After this he came to Lyons, where he helped Dolet to copy out and correct the manuscript of the first volume of his *Commentarii Linguae Latinae*[6]. It was in the latter half of the year 1536 that he entered the service of the Queen of Navarre, at first without a fixed salary, and then with an annual salary of 110 crowns[7]. He had the title of *valet de chambre*, but practically he was her secretary,

[1] *Heptaméron*, ed. Frank, III. 457.

[2] Des Periers's poems are almost the only source of information for his life.

[3] The best evidence is a manuscript note made in a copy of the *Recueil* by Jean Lacurne, *lieutenant-criminel* of Arnay-le-Duc, who died, an old man, in 1631.

[4] *Œuvres*, ed. Lacour, I. 150.

[5] See Herminjard, *Corr. des réformateurs*, III. 289 n.[12], 290 n.[21].

[6] *Joannes Eutychus Deperius Heduus cuius opera fideli ea quidem et accurata in primo Commentariorum nostrorum tomo describendo usi sumus. Comm. Ling. Lat.* II. 335.

[7] Des Periers, *Œuvres*, I. 139, 140, 166. He saw Margaret for the first time when she came to Lyons in July 1536 (*ib.* I. 130).

travelling about with her and either writing at her dictation or copying her manuscripts—*escrivant ses immortalitez,* as he expresses it[1].

Up to this time his Protestant sympathies seem to have continued; the *Prognostication des Prognostications,* a poem which he wrote in the latter half of 1536, is strongly Protestant in tone[2]. But whether under the influence of Dolet or because he was repelled by the dogmatism of Calvin's recently published *Christian Institution,* his opinions now underwent a complete change[3]. He became more or less of a disbeliever in all revealed religion, and gave expression to his new opinions in a little pamphlet of sixty-four pages, entitled *Cymbalum Mundi en francoys contenant quatre Dialogues Poetiques, fort antiques, joyeux et facetieux*[4]. It was printed at Paris in February 1538 for a young publisher named Jean Morin[5]. A work of this nature was not likely to escape the notice of the Paris Parliament, and so effectually were steps taken to repress it that at this day only one copy is known to exist, while of a new edition published at Lyons in 1538 there are not more than three or four examples.

In the first of the four Dialogues into which the *Cymbalum* is divided, Mercury is represented as arriving at Athens (Lyons) with various commissions from the gods and goddesses and particularly with one from Jupiter to have an old book, which was falling to pieces, rebound. It contains three Latin

[1] *ib.* I. 130.

[2] To this period must also belong his translations of the Canticles.

[3] M. Frank points out that the poem entitled *Prophétie* (I. 80) belongs to a period of transition between his Protestant and free-thinking phases. Of the *trois compagnons de Basle* there mentioned two no doubt are Calvin and Farel; this helps to make it probable that dislike of Calvin's doctrines was a strong motive in determining his change of opinions.

[4] *Cymbalum Mundi* was the nickname given by the Emperor Tiberius to a Greek rhetorician named Apion (Plin. *n. h. præf.*). He headed the anti-Jewish deputation sent by the Alexandrians to the Emperor Gaius (Mommsen, *Röm. Gesch.* V. 517) and he wrote a treatise against the Jews.

[5] The original edition, of which the only known copy is in the library of Versailles, is dated 1537 without any mention of the month, but as the matter came before Parliament only on March 7, 153⅞, it is probable that the book had only recently appeared. See a letter from P. Lizet to the Chancellor Du Bourg (Herminjard, *op. cit.* IV. 418).

VII]   DES PERIERS   125

treatises, a chronicle of the memorable acts performed by Jupiter before he was born, a record of future events, and a list of those heroes who are predestined to immortal life. At a hostelry where he stops to refresh himself Mercury encounters two Athenians named Byrphanes and Curtalius[1], who steal his book and substitute for it one of similar size and appearance containing a history of Jupiter's love-affairs.

The second Dialogue opens with a conversation between Mercury and Trigabus, who probably represents Des Periers himself. Mercury, it appears, had told the philosophers of the place that he was in possession of the Philosopher's stone, but, while he was apparently doubting to whom he should give it, he had let it drop and ground it to powder, which he had scattered among the sand of the amphitheatre. Accordingly Mercury and Trigabus adjourn there, and find three philosophers, Rhetulus (Luther), Cubercus (Martin Bucer) and Drarig (probably Erasmus) disputing as to which had found pieces of the true stone. Mercury and Trigabus laugh at them all alike, and Trigabus speaks in very plain terms of the folly of searching for stones like children. "A man," he says in conclusion, "is a great fool who expects to get any good from that which does not exist, and still more unhappy is he who hopes for an impossibility."

In the third Dialogue Mercury, who has in the meantime returned to Olympus and discovered the loss of Jupiter's book, again appears at Athens, with fresh commissions and with orders to find the book. He encounters Cupid, a young woman named Celia who has dismissed her lover and is now sighing for his return, and a horse named Phlegon, which he endows with the power of speech. The horse thereupon upbraids his groom Statius for the treatment he had received from him, while a bystander named Ardelio expresses sympathy with so novel a phenomenon as a speaking horse. The meaning of this Dialogue is not so clear as that of the others. Apparently the characters of Cupid, who, having told Mercury

---

[1] La Monnoye suggested that they represent Claude Rousselet, the Latin poet, and Benoist Court, the commentator of the *Aresta Amorum* (Breghot du Lut, *Mélanges* ii. 353).

that he has heard of a book that might be Jupiter's, says in answer to a further inquiry that he takes no interest in *ces matières-la*, and of Celia, who has learnt that "creatures cannot do without their fellows," are introduced to shew that love is more important than religion[1]. The horse seems to represent the inferior monks, who had long been oppressed by their superiors and condemned to celibacy, while Ardelio, who rejoices in the horse's newly acquired freedom of speech and promises to provide him with a wife, stands no doubt for Luther.

The fourth Dialogue has no connexion, so far as the story goes, with the others. We hear no more of Mercury and his adventures. It is a dialogue between two dogs, Hylactor and Pamphagus, who like the horse Phlegon have acquired the faculty of speech. They had once belonged to Acteon, and when Diana changed him into a stag they had taken part in his slaughter. On the whole, this is the most interesting of the four dialogues. Acteon is surely the Catholic Church, and the faculty of speech evidently signifies, as it did in the last Dialogue, freedom of thought, emancipation from the gag of authority and tradition. Hylactor is represented as rash and vainglorious, anxious to shew off his new accomplishment. "What?" he says to his companion, "have you not yet made known to people that you can speak?" "No," replies Pamphagus. "And why?" "Because I don't care to: I prefer to keep silence." But in spite of the prudent Pamphagus's remonstrances Hylactor leaves him, saying that he cannot restrain himself any longer. "That silly Hylactor," says Pamphagus, "cannot refrain from talking, that all the world may talk also of him."

M. Frank conjectures that Hylactor, the 'barker,' with his cut ear and the scar on his forehead, stands for the rash and quarrelsome Dolet, who had already had a foretaste of prison,

---

[1] R. Harmand in *Rev. d'hist. litt.* IX. 100 (1902) conjectures that Celia represents Claude Bectone or de Bectoz, Abbess of Saint-Honorat at Tarascon, with whom Des Periers interchanged some songs of an amatory character, though on her side they do not go beyond the limits of Platonic coquetry. (See Chenevière, pp. 73—89.)

and that Pamphagus, the 'all-devourer,' that is to say the devourer of all knowledge, represents the prudent Rabelais. This is decidedly ingenious, and is not without probability.

The style of the Dialogues is designedly popular, full of colloquialisms, with occasional comic touches. Its liveliness is unfailing, and though the general tone is that of mocking persiflage, it often shews considerable force and energy, especially in the third and fourth Dialogues. The following specimen is from the second:

TRIGABVS. Voy tu cestuy la qui se promene si brusquement? Ie vouldrois que tu louysses vng petit raisonner, tu ne vis oncques en ta vie le plus plaisant badin de philosophe. Il monstre ie ne scay quel petit grain dareine, & dict par ses bons dieux que cest de la vraye pierre philosophale, voire & du fin cueur dicelle. Tien la, comment il torne les yeulx en la teste? est il content de sa personne? voy tu comment il nestime rien le monde au prix de soy?

MERCVRE. En voyla vng aultre qui nest pas moins rebarbatif que luy, approchons nous vng petit, & voions les mines quilz feront entre eulx, & oyons les propos quilz tiendront.

TRIGABVS. Cest bien dict.

RHETVLVS. Vous auez beau chercher messieurs, car cest moy qui ay trouue la feue du gasteau.

CVBERCVS. Mon amy, ne vous glorifiez ia tant. La pierre philoso-phale est de telle propriete, quelle pert sa vertu si lhomme presume trop de soy apres quil en a trouue des pieces. ie pense bien que vous en auez: mais souffrez que les autres en cherchent, & en aient aussi bien que vous, si leur est possible. Mercure qui la nous a baillee, nentend point que nous vsions de ces reprouches entre nous, mais veult que nous nous en-traymions lung laultre comme freres. Car il ne nous a pas mis a la queste dune si noble & diuine chose pour dissension: mais plus tost pour dilection. Toutesfoys (a ce que ie voy) nous faisons tout le contraire.

RHETVLVS. Or vous auez beau dire, ce nest que sable tout ce que vous autres auez amasse.

DRARIG. Vous mentez par la gorge, en voyla vne piece, qui est de la vraye pierre philosophale, mieulx que la vostre.

RHETVLVS. Nas tu point de honte de presenter cela pour pierre philosophale? Est il pas bon a veoir que ce nest que sable? Phy phy, oste cela[1].

Regarded as an attack on Christianity the *Cymbalum* is not a very formidable or powerful production. But it is in-

---

[1] Ed. Frank, p. 17.

teresting as an expression of the opinions of one of the few men of letters in France at this period whose scepticism was directed against the whole scheme of Christianity. But even Des Periers's scepticism is not so thorough as some of his admirers have made out. In the fourth Dialogue, if my interpretation of *le bon maistre Acteon* is correct, he speaks with respect and affection of the primitive Catholic Church, and his conclusion seems to be that it is better, like Pamphagus, to keep your scepticism to yourself than to proclaim it on the housetops, like Hylactor.

The scandal caused by the publication of the *Cymbalum Mundi* cost the author his post in the Queen of Navarre's household, and though in 1539 he was for a short time taken back into favour, in deference to public opinion she had again to dismiss him. She seems however to have given him help secretly, and in October 1541 he received his pay for the year, though without being actually restored to his post[1]. In the year 1544, some time before the end of August, the unfortunate man, who had begun to shew symptoms of violent insanity, died by his own hand[2].

Not long after his death a collected edition of his works, without of course the *Cymbalum Mundi*, was published by his fellow Burgundian, Antoine du Moulin, who had recently left the service of the Queen of Navarre to act as reader, editor, and general adviser on literary matters to the celebrated Lyons printer, Jean de Tournes[3]. The book, which is dedicated to Margaret, opens with a translation of the *Lysis* of Plato which Des Periers had sent to her accompanied by a poem entitled, with reference to the subject of the dialogue, *Queste d'Amitié*. The translation, which was made with the help of Ficino's Latin version, is fairly correct and is rendered with a good deal of life and spirit. But the style is somewhat

---

[1] La Ferrière-Percy, *op. cit.* p. 45.

[2] The story of his suicide rests on the authority of Henri Estienne, who mentions it twice, saying that he threw himself upon his sword with such violence that he was found with the point sticking out of his back (*Apologie pour Hérodote*, cc. xviii. and xxvi. ed. Ristelhuber, I. 403 and II. 105).

[3] For Du Moulin see *Rev. d'hist. litt.* II. 469 ff.; III. 90 ff. His dedicatory letter to the Queen of Navarre is dated August 31, 1544.

rough and inharmonious, and is somewhat too colloquial for Plato. The poems are composed entirely of occasional pieces, many of them being addressed to the Queen of Navarre. Des Periers apparently took a very modest view of his poetical powers, being content to count himself a humble disciple of Marot. He speaks of him as his father, and he took an active part in defending him against Sagon. But both in form and in substance he has more than once made a distinct advance upon his master's work. The very poem addressed to Marot, *pere des poetes francoys*, is remarkable for the bold experiment of its rhythm, which in its rapid tripping harmony faintly presages *Le pas d'armes du roi Jean*. A paraphrase of "Who can find a virtuous woman? For her price is far above rubies," addressed to the Queen of Navarre, is written in the metre of *Bel aubespin florissant*, which had already been introduced by Marot :

> Qui est ce qui trouvera
>   Ou sçaura
> Femme bonne ou vertueuse?
> Le guerdon qu'il en aura
>   Passera
> Toute perle precieuse[1].

In another poem, which describes the annual *fête* held on May 15 at the abbey of St Martin on the Ile-Barbe in the Saône[2], this rhythm is constantly varied by altering the length of the lines, while in the *Chant de Vendanges*[3], the six-line stanza is expanded into one of ten lines.

Apart from the rhythm, these poems are marked by considerable grace and spirit. But in one poem of the *Receuil*, Des Periers rises to a higher flight. In *Des Roses*[4], an imitation of the *Collige, virgo, rosas* of Ausonius, and an extremely graceful piece of work, we come here and there upon a passage of a really high order of poetry. There is exquisite fancy in

> *Là où je veis la rosée espandue,*
> *Et sur les choulx ses rondelettes gouttes*
> *Courir, couler, pour s'entrebaiser toutes,*

---

[1] *Œuvres*, I. 103.   [2] *ib.* 54 ff.
[3] *ib.* 92 ff.   [4] *ib.* 68 ff.

and in the following lines we have the well-worn idea of the
transitoriness of human things treated with considerable novelty
of thought and great beauty of expression :

> Tant de joyaux, tant de nouveautez belles,
> Tant de presens, tant de beautez nouvelles,
> Brief, tant de biens que nous voyons florir,
> Un mesme jour les faict naistre et mourir!
> Dont nous, humains, à vous, dame Nature,
> Plaincte faisons de ce que si peu dure
> Le port des fleurs, et que, de tous les dons
> Que de vos mainz longuement attendons
> Pour en gouster la jouissance deue,
> A peine (las!) en avons-nous la veue.

> Des roses l'aage est d'autant de durée
> Comme d'un jour la longueur mesurée,
> Dont fault penser les heures de ce jour
> Estre les ans de leur tant brief sejour,
> Qu'elles sont jà de vieillesse coulées
> Ains qu'elles soient de jeunesse accollées.

> Celle qu'hyer le soleil regardoit
> De si bon cueur, que son cours retardoit
> Pour la choisir parmy l'espaisse nue,
> Du soleil mesme a esté mescongnue
> A ce matin, quand plus n'a veu en elle
> Sa grand' beauté, qui sembloit éternelle.

And the concluding lines are perfection :

> Vous donc, jeunes fillettes,
> Cueillez bientost les roses vermeillettes
> A la rosée, ains que le temps les vienne
> A desseicher; et, tandis, vous souvienne
> Que ceste vie, à la mort exposée,
> Se passe ainsi que roses ou rosée.

In the year 1558, fourteen years after Des Periers's death,
a Lyons publisher, named Jean Granjon, brought out a
collection of ninety tales under the title of *Les Nouvelles
Recreations et Joyeux Devis de feu Bonaventure Des Periers.*
The world, he says in his address to the reader, would have
been deprived of the volume but for the diligence of a certain

virtuous person. This 'virtuous person' was almost certainly Jacques Peletier. The *au lecteur* is followed by a sonnet which in its intensity of feeling, firmness of execution, and general modernity of tone is most remarkable. If, as there is no sufficient reason to doubt, it is by the hand of Des Periers and therefore written before the year 1544, it is all the more remarkable, for nothing like it had yet appeared in the whole of French poetry. But readers must judge of its merits for themselves:

> Hommes pensifz, je ne vous donne à lire
> Ces miens devis si vous ne contraignez
> Le fier maintien de voz frons rechignez:
> Icy n'y ha seulement que pour rire.
>
> Laissez à part vostre chagrin, vostre ire
> Et vos discours de trop loing desseignez.
> Une autre fois vous serez enseignez.
> Je me suis bien contrainct pour les escrire.
>
> J'ay oublié mes tristes passions,
> J'ay intermis mes occupations.
> Donnons, donnons quelque lieu à folie,
>
> Que maugré nous ne nous vienne saisir,
> Et en un jour plein de melancholie
> Meslons au moins une heure de plaisir.

Then comes the first story *en forme de preambule*, which is almost certainly inspired by the prologue to *Gargantua* and which was probably written just after the Treaty of Nice (June 18, 1538). Though in scope and character it reminds one of Rabelais, it is not a mere copy of his style; it is rather Rabelais pruned and purified. In fact as a specimen of that half-bantering, half-serious style which has the charm of meaning more than it says and of pre-supposing a friendly and intelligent understanding between the writer and the reader, a style in which Frenchmen at all times have shewn themselves masters, this prologue is of the very highest merit. "I have not," says the writer, "been to look for my stories at Constantinople or Florence or Venice." In fact the scene of all the stories, except a few in which no place is specified, is laid in France. But, as the writer hints, it does not follow that the stories all happened in the places with which he connects them. "Perhaps they are not all facts. What do I care, provided it is a fact that they give you pleasure."

Some five or six are borrowed from Poggio's *Facetiae*, a few possibly from the *Cent Nouvelles Nouvelles*; others form part of the common heritage of story-tellers; but more than three-fourths of the stories are apparently quite new[1]. The scene of a considerable number, twenty-five, is laid in the contiguous provinces of the Orléanais, Maine, Anjou and Poitou, eight of these being assigned to Maine and as many to Poitou. A dozen or so are located in the south of France, at Lyons, Toulouse, Avignon, Montpellier, while about twenty-five are represented as happening at Paris or the Court.

Naturally some stories are told better than others, but on the whole the writer must rank very high as a *raconteur*. He is extremely brief, the average length of his tales being about three pages and the longest not exceeding ten; but in this short space he contrives to pack a great deal of matter. He goes straight to his story at once; there are no digressions; every word tells; the conversations are short but extremely characteristic. Directly the point is reached the story ends, sometimes with a sly hit, after the manner of La Fontaine, by way of moral. But there is no moralising; the story is told for the story's sake, and the sole object of the writer is to amuse. *Il y en ha de tous boys, de toutes tailles, de tous estocz, à tous pris et à toutes mesures, fors que pour plorer.* Some readers may find this constant appeal to their laughter monotonous. *Ne les lisez donc pas.*

A story which gives a good idea of the writer's method is the one taken from the *Legende joyeuse Maistre Pierre Fai-feu* of Charles de Bourdigné[2], which tells how Pierre Fai-feu provided himself with a pair of boots at the expense of two bootmakers of La Flèche in Anjou, where the inhabitants took a particular pleasure in making fun of strangers. The following passage will serve as a specimen:

[1] See P. Toldo, *op. cit.* and Gaston Paris, *op. cit.*

[2] Angers, 1531; reprinted, 1883.

Il se trouva une foys entre toutes si pressé de partir de la ville d'Angiers qu'il n'eut pas loisir de prendre des botes. Comment ! des botes ? il n'eut pas le loysir de faire seller son cheval, car on le suyvoit un peu de près. Mais il estoit si accort et si inventif qu'incontinent qu'il fut à deux jectz d'arc de la ville, trouva façon d'avoir une jument d'un povre homme qui s'en retournoit dessus en son village, luy disant qu'il s'en alloit par là et qu'il la lasseroit à sa femme en passant ; et parce qu'il faisoit un peu maulvais temps, il entra en une grange, et, en grande diligence, fit de belles botes de foin toutes neufves, et monte sus sa jument, et pique, au moins talonne tant qu'il arriva à la Flèche tout mouillé et tout mal en point, qui n'estoit pas ce qu'il aymoit, dont il se trouvoit tout peneux. Encores, pour amender son marché, en passant tout le long de la ville, où il estoit cogneu comme un loup gris, et ailleurs avec, les copieux (ainsi ont-ilz esté nommez pour leurs gaudisseries) commencèrent à le vous railler de bonne sorte. Maistre Pierre, disoient-ils, il feroit bon à ceste heure parler à vous ! Vous estes bien attrempé. L'autre : Vous estes monté comme un sainct George, à cheval sus une jument. Mais, par sus tous, les cordouaniers se mocquoyent de ses botes. Ah ! vrayement, disoyent-ils, il fera bon temps pour nous : les chevaulx mangeront les botes de leurs maistres[1].

Note the *Comment ! des botes ? il n'eut pas le loisir de faire seller son cheval,* a favourite turn of language with the writer, the graphic *à deux jectz d'arc de la ville* and *cogneu comme un loup gris*, the colloquialisms, *et ailleurs avec* and *à le vous railler.* And one has only to turn to the *Legende de Pierre Fai-feu* to see how the story owes everything to the manner in which it is told.

Other stories of special merit are that of the advocate who talked in Latin to his maid-servant (xiv), that of the almoner of Bishop René du Bellay and the Bishop's donkey (xxvii), a group of four stories about the *curé* of Brou in the Orléanais (xxxiii—xxxvi), and one of a cobbler named Blondeau, who was only twice in his life melancholy (xix). There are three which treat of the manners and customs of the peasants of Poitou and in which the Poitevin dialect is imitated (lxix—lxxi), and a delightful one of the 'good drunkard Janicot and Jeannette his wife' (lxxvii). Des Periers's authorship of the *Joyeux Devis* has been

---

[1] *Nouv.* xxiii.

seriously challenged, but though some circumstances throw
suspicion on the publisher's statement, there is nothing that
compels us to discredit it[1].   But even if he be not the author,
he is still a remarkable figure in the literature of the French
Renaissance.   Though his attitude to his leading contemporaries, to Rabelais and Marot and Margaret of Navarre,
was one of respectful admiration, though we find him writing
under the influence now of the one and now of the other, he
managed to preserve his independence and originality.   The
Cymbalum Mundi owes nothing to any one except Lucian;
in one or two of his poems he has touched a note which
had not been heard before in French poetry.   His receptive
and versatile intellect and his restless spirit mark him as a
true child of the Renaissance; but the main source of his
inspiration was the artistic temperament, and this he had
in a larger measure than any of his contemporaries.

BIBLIOGRAPHY.

EDITIONS.

Cymbalum Mundi [Paris], 153⅜ (Versailles Library; Le Petit, p. 65);
ed. F. Frank, 1873.

Recueil des Œuvres, Lyons, 1544 (Brit. Mus.; Le Petit, p. 71).

Les Nouvelles Recreations et Joyeux Devis, Lyons, 1558 (printed in
lettres de civilité or court hand); Lyons, 1561; Paris, 1568 (with thirty-
one additional stories, all evidently spurious); Paris, without a date (with
eight more spurious stories); 3 vols. Amsterdam [Paris], 1735, with notes
by B. de la Monnoye, printed from his MS. notes in the margin of a
copy of an edition of 1572, now in the *Bib. Nat.*; ed. L. Lacour, forming
vol. II. of *Œuvres françoises*, 2 vols. 1856 (vol. I. contains the *Recueil*
and the *Cymbalum Mundi*).

[1] See Appendix B.

A. Chenevière with much plausibility attributes to Des Periers three *chansons* contained in the 1547 edition of Saint-Gelais's poems, supposing them to be addressed to Claude Bectone or de Bectoz.

LIFE.

A. Chenevière, *Bonaventure des Periers, sa vie et ses poésies*, 1885 (see pp. 78—87 for the three *chansons* in questions with the lady's answers).

TO BE CONSULTED.

P. Toldo and Gaston Paris, as cited in the bibliography of the preceding chapter.

CHAPTER VIII

THE PRECURSORS OF THE PLEIAD

1. *The School of Lyons.*

AMONG the poets of the school of Marot were three men whom the Pleiad more or less exempted from the contempt with which they spoke of the school generally. These were Maurice Scève, Antoine Heroet, and Mellin de Saint-Gelais[1]. They all three had a considerable share of that learning with the lack of which Du Bellay charged Marot[2]. Saint-Gelais was widely read in contemporary Italian literature, and in the Neo-Latin poets of Italy. His poetry in consequence shews a strong Italian influence. He is also essentially a court poet. Scève and Heroet are coupled by Estienne Pasquier in a well-known passage as the *avant-coureurs* of the Pleiad, " as the advance-guard of the army which at that time began to wage war against ignorance[3]." They both owed much to the friendship and guidance of Margaret of Navarre, and they were both closely connected with Lyons.

The importance of Lyons as a literary and intellectual centre has been noticed in an earlier chapter[4]. Of the society which helped to give it that distinction Maurice Scève, a member

---

[1] *J'excepte tousjours Heroet et Sceve et Sainct-Gelais*, says Ronsard in the preface to his *Odes*.

[2] *L'un* (Marot) *default ce qui est le commencement de bien escrire, c'est le sçavoir* (*Deffence* book II. c. 2), a mistranslation of Horace's *Scribendi recte sapere est et principium et fons*.

[3] *Recherches de la France*, VII. c. 6.

[4] *Ante*, pp. 23, 24.

of a Piedmontese family, was one of the principal figures[1]. Poet, musician, painter, and architect, proficient in many branches of learning, he attracted round him a crowd of admirers. He began his poetical career as a faithful follower of Marot, writing blazons and a pastoral poem called *Arion* on the death of the Dauphin (1536). He also published, as we have seen, in 1535, under the title of *La deplourable fin de Flamete*, a translation of Juan de Flores's *Grimalte y Gradissa*, a love-treatise which takes the form of a discussion of Boccaccio's *Fiammetta*, that long-drawn illustration of "When lovely woman stoops to folly[2]." From the psychology of love he passed to its philosophy, apparently under the influence of Margaret of Navarre.

It was about the year 1540 that Margaret's attention was drawn to the Neo-Platonic theory of spiritual love[3], and it was doubtless owing to her influence that during the next seven years a considerable number of works bearing more or less on this subject issued from the Lyons presses. Starting from Ficino's Latin commentary on the *Symposium* and the discussions of the Florentine Academy the topic had become very popular in Italy. It formed the staple subject of Bembo's *Gli Asolani*, and accordingly it is Bembo who is selected by Castiglione as the exponent of the Neo-Platonic doctrine in the fourth book of the *Cortegiano*. It is one of the finest parts of the whole work; Bembo himself could never have attained to such eloquence and passion[4]. Then in 1535, two years before the *Cortegiano* was translated into French, there appeared another Italian work based on the *Symposium* and dealing with the subject of spiritual love. It was entitled *Dialoghi di amore* and was the work of a Spanish Jew, Judah Abarbanel, who, having been banished from Spain in 1492, had gone to reside at Naples where his name was Italianised into Leone

---

[1] c. 1510—1564. We have very little information about his life. See *Recherches pour servir à l'histoire de Lyon, ou les Lyonnois dignes de mémoire* (by Pernetti), 2 vols., Lyons, 1757, I. 264 ff.; Breghot du Lut et Pericaud aîné, *Biographie Lyonnaise*, Lyons, 1839.

[2] See *ante*, p. 51.   [3] See *ante*, pp. 110, 111.

[4] See Professor Raleigh's admirable introduction to Hoby's *Courtier*, pp. lxviii–lxxvii, 1900.

Hebreo.   His book had been written as far back as 1502 and he was already dead when it appeared in print[1].

The first person in the immediate circle of the Queen of Navarre to respond to her impulse in the direction of Platonic study seems to have been Des Periers, whose translation of the *Lysis* was probably made in 1541.   The poem *Queste d'amitié* with which he accompanied it is an attempt, however unsuccessful, to expound in verse the doctrine of spiritual love[2].   In 1542 Antoine Heroet, who was also in the service of the Queen of Navarre, published a volume which contained, together with two other poems, a paraphrase in verse of part of the *Symposium*, entitled *Androgyne*, and a poem in three books called *La parfaite amye*, in which he set forth the philosophy of spiritual love with much greater clearness than Des Periers[3].   His work had a great success and was very highly thought of by his contémporaries.   It was followed in 1544 by Maurice Scève's *Delie, objet de la plus haute vertu*, in which he sang the praises of the ideal mistress of the Neo-Platonists, *Delie* being an anagram of *l'idée*.   In 1545 appeared Jean Martin's translation of *Gli Asolani*[4], from which Heroet had taken the story of the Fortunate Island for his *Parfaicte amye*.   In 1546 Symon Silvius published a translation of Ficino's commentary on the *Symposium*, and in 1547 appeared Gilles Corrozet's poem *Le conte du rossignol*, in which in graceful and natural language he tells how a lover was converted by his mistress to a belief in spiritual love[5].   Meanwhile Margaret

[1] For *Leo Hebræus*, as he is generally called, see B. Zimmels, *Leo Hebræus, ein jüdischer Philosoph der Renaissance*, Breslau, 1886.   Two French translations of his book were published in 1551, one by Pontus de Thyard and the other by Dionysius Sauvage.   One of Ronsard's *Odes* (v. 7) is addressed to Charles IX *en lui donnant un Leon Hebrieu*.   Ronsard also mentions Hebræus in a sonnet (*Œuvres*, ed. Blanchemain, I. 419).

[2] It is a probable conjecture of A. Lefranc that the translation of the *Lysis* was the cause of the payment made to Des Periers in October, 1541 (see *ante*, p. 128).

[3] Three editions were published in 1542 (by Dolet and by P. de Tours at Lyons, and by Nicole Paris at Troyes), and one in 1543 (by Dolet).   See Christie, *E. Dolet*, pp. 543 and 549.   There is a copy of the Troyes edition in the Brit. Mus. All the four poems in this volume were published in the *Opuscules d'Amour*, 1547.

[4] There is a copy of this in the Brit. Mus. ; Brunet only mentions one of 1547.

[5] *Anciennes poésies françoises*, VIII. 49 ff.

herself had been giving expression to similar doctrines in the epilogues of the *Heptameron*, choosing as their exponent the young bachelor, Dagoucin[1]. In the poems written after her brother's death the Neo-Platonism is still more marked, finally reaching the point at which love for the creature is sublimated into an absorbing passion for the Creator[2].

We may now return to Maurice Scève. According to the verdict of the poets of the next generation, his *Delie* marked the dawn of the new era, when poets, to use Pasquier's words, " began to aim at pleasing their own minds rather than the opinion of the multitude[3]." *Esprit divin* and *cygne nouveau* were the terms in which Du Bellay addressed him in verse[4], though in prose he alluded to him as one " who, in his desire to avoid the commonplace, has fallen into an obscurity which is as difficult for the most learned to explain as for the most ignorant[5]." Pasquier expresses a similar opinion[6]. There is no controverting it ; *Delie* is for the most part unintelligible. But it contains some intelligible passages, and the following *dizain* is one:

> Aumoins toy clere et heureuse fontaine
> Et vous o eaux fraisches et argentines,
> Quand celle en vous (de tout vice loingtaine)
> Se vient laver ses deux mains yvorines,
> Ses deux Soleils, ses levres corallines
> De Dieu créez pour ce Monde honnorer,
> Debvriez garder pour plus vous decorer
> L'image d'elle en vos liqueurs profondes.
> Car plus souvent je viendroys adorer
> Le sainct miroir de vos sacrées undes[7].

---

[1] See esp. the Epilogue to the 8th novel (from which a passage is cited, *ante*, pp. 113, 114), and also that to the 53rd.

[2] See esp. *Les prisons* in *Les dernières poésies*. In 1545 there appeared at Rouen, under the editorship of Pierre Du Val (not the Bishop of Séez of that name), a collection of pieces in praise of spiritual love under the title of *Le Puy du souverain Amour tenu par la Deesse Pallas* (Picot, I. no. 804 ; Viollet le Duc, *Bib. poét.* p. 239). See for much of what precedes an interesting article by M. Abel Lefranc, *Le platonisme et la littérature en France* in *Rev. d'hist. litt.* III. 1–44.

[3] *Recherches*, VII. c. 6. There is a modern reprint of *Delie* (1862).

[4] *Olive*, Sonnet cv.

[5] *Deffence*, II. c. 2. There can be no doubt that he is alluding to Scève.

[6] *Recherches*, *ib.*   [7] No. ccxxxv.

It will be seen from these lines that Scève's merit consists, not in his learning, as his admirers declared, but i.. his feeling for the elevated style of poetry, in his ability to express, however rarely, a serious poetical idea in stately verse.

Delie is also noteworthy for its form.   It is a series of 449 *dizains*, and is thus the forerunner of those sonnet-sequences addressed to real or imaginary mistresses which, beginning with Du Bellay's *Olive*, were produced in such numbers in France during the latter half of the sixteenth century and in England during its last decade[1].   Had *Delie* been written three years later it might have been written in sonnets, for in 1547 we find Scève writing two sonnets for the *Marguerites de la Marguerite*.   Moreover as became the descendant, as he professed to be, of an Italian family, he was a great admirer of Petrarch, and in 1533 had helped to discover at Avignon the supposed tomb of Laura[2].

In *Delie* however the influence of Petrarch is less marked than that of a third-rate Italian poet, Serafino of Aquila, who died in the year 1500, and whose poems, first printed in 1502, had a great vogue throughout the first half of the sixteenth century.   They consist chiefly of *strambotti*, written in *ottava rima*, and stuffed with conceits and extravagance[3].

Three years after the publication of *Delie* appeared *Saulsaye, Eglogue de la vie solitaire*, without the author's name, but with Scève's motto, *Souffrir non souffrir*[4].   Like *Delie* it is better in conception than in execution, such imaginative feeling for nature as it shews being hampered by obscure language and rough versification.   Scève also wrote a poem of an encyclopædic character called *Microcosme*, which in two ways shews his affinity to the Pleiad[5].   It is a long poem, and it is written in alexandrines.   But it did not appear till 1562, when the new school was well established.

---

[1] In England the great period for the production of sonnets was from 1591 to 1597.

[2] See Saint-Gelais, *Œuvres* (ed. Blanchemain), II. 165.

[3] See J. Vianey, *L'influence italienne chez les précurseurs de la Pléiade*.

[4] Lyons, J. de Tournes, 1547 (see Picot, I. no. 636); reprinted at Aix, 1829.

[5] Lyons, 1562.   The *Bib. Nat.* has a copy which belonged to Desportes and to Colletet.

Among Scève's adoring disciples at Lyons was Pernette du Guillet whose poems have been reprinted no less than three times during the present century. Chivalry rather than critical taste must have prompted the editors, for her poems are little more than mere echoes of her master's, less obscure but more feeble[1].

The merits and defects of Antoine Heroet, the other leading poet of the Lyons school, are precisely the opposite of Scève's. He writes clearly and without any trace of affectation or pedantry, but apart from the ease with which he handles his metre he can be hardly said to have a single quality which distinguishes a poet from a writer of prose. Du Bellay exactly hits the mark when he alludes to him as one "who is so destitute of poetical charm and ornament that he deserves the name of Philosopher rather than of Poet[2]."

We have as little information about his life as about Scève's[3]. M. Lefranc has pointed out that he was already in the Queen of Navarre's service in 1524[4]. He must therefore have been born early in the century. He became bishop of Digne, a small place high up in the Alps of Provence, in 1552, and he is said to have died in 1568[5]. His published work consists only of the little volume already mentioned, and of a poem entitled *Douleur et Volupté* which is printed in the editions of Marot's works[6]. Whatever be the merit of his chief poem, *La parfaicte amye*, as an exposition of the Neo-Platonic philosophy[7] of love, or as an expression of noble and virtuous sentiments, it is only in occasional passages that it rises to real poetry. One of these is the description of the Fortunate Island, but the inspiration only lasts for some twenty lines :

[1] She died in 1545 and her poems were edited after her death by Antoine Dumoulin (Lyons, J. de Tournes, 1545). There are also editions of 1547 and 1552, but all those are very rare. The best modern edition is that of 1864 ; to that of 1830 Colletet's life is prefixed.

[2] *Deffence*, II. c. 2.

[3] See Gouget, XI. 141 ff.

[4] *loc. cit.* p. 13.

[5] *Gallia Christiana*, III. 1132.

[6] Marot, I. 117 ff.

[7] See esp. pp. 23—25 (end of book I.) and pp. 35—38 of the Troyes edition.

On dit que pleine est une isle de biens,
D'arbres, de fruits, de plaisante verdure,
Qu'en elle ha faict son chef-d'œuvre Nature.
Et qu'immortelz les hommes y vivans
Sont, tous plaisirs, et delices suyvans.
Là ne se rend, ny jamais n'ha esté
Froideur d'yver, ny la chaleur d'esté.
La saison est un gracieux printemps,
Ou tous les plus malheureux sont contens.
De son bon gré terre produit le bien,
On ne dit point entre eux ny tien, ny mien.
Tout est commun, sans peine, et jalousie,
Raison domine, et non pas fantaisie.
Chascun sçait bien ce, qu'il veult demander,
Chascun sçait bien ce, qu'il fault commander;
Ainsi chascun ha tout ce, qu'il demande,
Chascun sçait bien ce, qu'ha faire commande.
  Cette ysle là se nomme fortunee,
Et comme on dit, par Royne est gouvernee,
Si bien parlant, si sçavante et si belle,
Que d'un rayon de la grand' beauté d'elle
Tous les païs voisins sont reluisans[1].

Jacques Peletier[2] had more natural capacity for poetry than either Scève or Heroet, and had he not been so many other things besides a poet—a physician, mathematician, a spelling-reformer—regarding, as he tells us, poetry merely as a relaxation from more serious pursuits, he might perhaps have anticipated Ronsard and Du Bellay. Born at Le Mans in 1517, he was sent, at the age of five, to the College of Navarre at Paris, of which his elder brother was Principal, and here he seems to have remained, except for a short interval which he spent in a lawyer's office, for fifteen years or more. He was a receptive and enthusiastic student. It was during his residence at Paris that he was introduced by his fellow-townsman, Nicolas Denisot, to Margaret of Navarre, and became attached to her circle. It was probably in the year 1540 that he

---

[1] From the second book ; translated by Cary, pp. 29 ff. This part is not in Bembo ; see *Gli Asolani*, Venice, 1553, 108 v° and 106 r°.

[2] For Peletier (b. 1517—d. 1582) see B. Hauréau, *Bibliothèque du Maine*, IX. 35 ff. ; M. de Clinchamp in *Bull. du Bibl.* 1847, 233 ff. ; 439 ff. ; C. Pagès in a notice prefixed to his reprint of *La Savoie*.

became secretary to René du Bellay, the horticultural bishop of Le Mans, with whom he resided till his death in 1546. His duties left him plenty of leisure, and in 1544 (apparently) he took the degree of Doctor of Medicine at Montpellier. In the same year he published a verse-translation of the *Ars Poetica* of Horace[1], prefixing to it a noteworthy dedication in which he anticipates many of the ideas to which five years later Joachim du Bellay gave such eloquent expression in his *Deffence*. He complains of the general neglect by French writers of their own language, declares that it is a mistake to write only in a foreign language in which it is impossible to equal your models, and points out that this was not the practice of the great Italian writers who were men of learning. In conclusion he prophesies that before long the French language will be a match for the Italian and the Spanish.

In the year 1547 he was made Principal of the College of Bayeux at Paris, and published a volume of poems. It contains, besides translations of the first two books of the *Odyssey* and the first book of the *Georgics*, which have been already mentioned, twelve sonnets translated from Petrarch, an original sonnet addressed to Cardinal du Bellay, some epigrams and a small number of *vers lyriques*. Here also is to be found the first printed poem of Ronsard's, an ode addressed to Peletier[2], whose acquaintance he had made at Le Mans in 1543 on the occasion of Guillaume du Bellay's funeral, when they compared together the result of their studies in Horace. The best of Peletier's own lyrical poems are those on the four seasons, which, in spite of much carelessness and awkwardness, and some bad taste, contain snatches of real poetry, and that in a style which anticipates the Pleiad. For Peletier's treatment of natural scenery is very different to Marot's perfunctory and unsympathetic handling ; it is serious, emotional, imaginative :

Les fresches nuitz croist la rousee tendre,
Qui peut encor' l'aube vermeille attendre :

[1] La Croix du Maine, I. 426. The earliest known edition *recongnu par l'auteur depuis la première impression* is of 1545. (See H. Chamard, *J. du Bellay*, p. 33 n. 3.)

[2] *Œuvres de Ronsard*, ed. Blanchemain, II. 402.

Mais ce luy est force d'evanouir
Aux premiers raiz que Phebus vient estendre,
Qui fait du chaud temperé qu'il vient rendre
A son lever la rose épanouir
Pour Venus resjouir.

   O quel plaisir en ce temps si heureux
Gouster la fleur et le fruit savoureux
De ses amours sus la gaye verdure!
O quel malheur n'estre point amoureux,
Encore plus grand, de vivre langoureux
Par la rigeur de sa maistresse dure
Tant que ce beau temps dure.

The faults in this are obvious, but it is poetry. Peletier's next volume of poetry, *L'amour des amours* and *Vers Liriques*, was published at Lyons in 1555 when the poetry of several of the members of the Pleiad was already before the world. It therefore naturally shews a further approximation to their methods; notably it contains ninety-six sonnets. The phonetic style of spelling which the author had now adopted makes the poems troublesome to decipher[1], and on the whole they are too indifferent to repay one for the trouble. There are however some pieces among the *Vers Liriques*, such as *Le Rossignol* and some new odes on the seasons, which have the same merits as his earlier volume[2].

In the same year, 1555, he also published at Lyons an *Art poëtique*. Its strange orthography prevented its having a wide circulation, but it was not without influence on Peletier's friends, especially on Ronsard, whose admiration for Virgil it doubtless helped to stimulate. Peletier goes much more into technical details than Du Bellay and is more moderate in his views. Thus, although by this time he had completely rallied to the Pleiad, he can find praise for Marot and Des Periers. The praise would be better worth having if he had not previously expressed the view that in his opinion no French poem was superior to Heroet's *La parfaicte amye*[3].

[1] See *ante*, p. 35.

[2] *L'Amour des Amours. Vers Liriques*, Lyons, 1555, a beautifully printed volume from the press of Jean de Tournes.

[3] See T. Rucktäschel, *Einige Arts poétiques aus der Zeit Ronsard's und*

Between the publication of his two volumes of poetry, Peletier, who had resigned his Principalship after a short tenure, had been living at Paris, Poitiers, Bordeaux (where he practised as a physician) and finally at Lyons, where he offered incense at the shrine of *La belle cordière*, Louise Labé, and burnt his fingers in the operation. In 1557 he returned to Paris where, except for a journey to Rome, he seems to have resided till about 1570, when the religious troubles compelled him to take refuge at Annecy. Here in 1572 he published a poem called *La Savoye*, and in the same year he was made Principal of the College of Guyenne at Bordeaux[1]. In the following year he was compelled to resign and was appointed Principal of the College of Le Mans at Paris, in which post he found rest till his death in 1582. The year before he had published his last work, entitled *Euvres poetiques*. He is one more example of the many-sidedness, the passion for learning, the restlessness of mind and body which characterised the Renaissance.

His compatriot Nicolas Denisot, who called himself Comte d'Alsinois (the anagram of his name) and who was a painter as well as a poet, is interesting to Englishmen as having lived for three years in this country as tutor to the three elder daughters of the Protector Somerset[2]. Like Peletier he rallied to the new school and we find him enrolled as a member of the Brigade, but his own poetry, which is chiefly religious, is poor stuff[3].

Malherbe's, Leipsic, 1889, pp. 12—20 ; H. Chamard, *De J. Peletarii Arte poetica*, Lille, 1900 ; P. Laumonier, *L'Art poétique de J. Peletier* in *Rev. de la Ren.* I. 248 ff. (a review of the preceding).

[1] M. Gaullieur conjectures that it was on his first arrival at Bordeaux that Montaigne shewed him hospitality. See *Essais*, I. c. 20.

[2] 1515—1559. See Hauréau, *op. cit.* III. 251—282. He edited the Latin verses which the Seymour ladies wrote on the death of Margaret of Navarre (Picot, I. no. 266).

[3] His collection of *Noelz* (1545) has been reprinted at Le Mans, 1847. Ronsard mentions him in *Les Bacchanales* (*Œuvres*, VI. 266).

2.   *Saint-Gelais.*

When Marot in his *Eglogue au Roy* writes

> *Et ce jour là à grand' peine on sçavoit*
> *Lequel des deux gaigné le prix avoit,*
> *Merlin ou moi,*

he is expressing in a courteous and modest fashion the general verdict of his contemporaries that Merlin or Mellin de Saint-Gelais[1] was second only to himself among living French poets. This contemporary verdict has been more or less confirmed by posterity, for however inferior Saint-Gelais may be in depth and sincerity of feeling to Margaret of Navarre or to Des Periers, there is no doubt that, next to Marot, he is the most competent craftsman of the time.

He was nine years older than Marot, having been born in November 1487, so that it was only natural that he should assume a more independent poetical attitude than the younger members of the new school.   His education was a brilliant one, as befitted the reputed son of the poet and bishop, Octovien de Saint-Gelais, in whose palace at Angoulême he resided from his seventh year till the Bishop's death, which took place when he was sixteen[2].   In 1507 we find him studying law at Poitiers, and soon afterwards he went to Italy to complete his studies, first to Padua, and then, on the temporary closing of that University in 1509, to Bologna, where he apparently remained till after the beginning of Francis I's reign.   But, in the words of his biographer, he soon deserted Ulpian and Papinian for Demosthenes and Virgil, or in other words the study of law for that of literature.

The condition of Italian literature at this time has been noticed in an earlier chapter.   But in considering its effect on Saint-Gelais's poetical developement, we must take into account not only the vernacular literature, but the Latin verse of the Italian humanists.   Among the chief living

---

[1] His name is variously written Mellin, Melin, or Merlin.   The form Merlin is used, not only by Marot, but by Rabelais, Peletier, and Salel.

[2] He was born three years before Octovien, who had led a very irregular life in his youth, took orders.

masters of this art when Saint-Gelais came to Italy were Sannazaro and Navagero, and on a somewhat lower level Bembo, Castiglione, Molza and Marcantonio Flaminio; of the older generation Pontanus, Marullus and the elder Strozzi had recently died, and still more recently the younger Strozzi. All of these, not excluding Sannazaro in spite of his celebrated epic on the birth of Christ, chiefly cultivated or at any rate excelled in the lighter kinds of verse, such as idylls, elegies and epigrams, and would therefore naturally commend themselves to a man like Saint-Gelais whose tastes lay in a similar direction.

Of his interest in the vernacular Italian poetry there is abundant evidence. He made a free version of part of the *Orlando Furioso*[1]; he revised Jacques Colin's translation of the *Cortegiano*; he collaborated with François Habert in a prose adaptation of Trissino's *Sofonisba* for the French stage[2]; he wrote *capitoli* (or *chapitres*, as he calls them) in *terza rima*[3]; and at one time, like Scève, was largely influenced by Serafino of Aquila[4]. But the chief novelty in poetical composition which he is credited with having introduced from Italy is the sonnet. Though the statement that he did so only rests upon an expression of opinion by Du Bellay, there is nothing to contradict it, and considering his residence in Italy and fondness for Italian models, it has probability in its favour[5]. One of the best known of his sonnets is imitated from one of Sannazaro's[6], first printed in 1531[7]:

> Voyant ces monts de veue ainsi lointaine,
> Je les compare à mon long desplaisir:
> Haut est leur chef, et haut est mon désir,
> Leur pied est ferme, et ma foy est certaine.

---

[1] Canto IV., stanzas 51 to the end, and v. 5—11.

[2] It was represented at Blois in 1554 and 1556, and was printed in 1559 (*Œuvres*, III. 159 ff.).

[3] *Œuvres*, I. 61; II. 182; II. 185.

[4] See J. Vianey, *loc. cit.* pp. 105—107.

[5] See note at the end of this chapter.

[6] F. Torraca, *Gli imitatori stranieri di J. Sannazaro*, 2nd ed., 1882, p. 31.

[7] It is the 3rd sonnet of the Third Part of the *Rime*.

D'eux maint ruisseau coule, et mainte fontaine :
De mes deux yeux sortent pleurs à loisir ;
De forts souspirs ne me puis dessaisir,
Et de grands vents leur cime est toute plaine,
   Mille troupeaux s'y promènent et paissent,
Autant d'Amours se couvent et renaissent
Dedans mon cœur, qui seul est leur pasture.
   Ils sont sans fruict, mon bien n'est qu'aparence,
Et d'eux à moy n'a qu'une différence,
Qu'en eux la neige, en moy la flamme dure[1].

The following witty imitation of an epigram by the
barber-poet, Burchiello, serves to explain Sibilet's theory of
the sonnet that it is nothing but a perfect epigram:

Il n'est point tant de barques à Venise,
   D'huistres à Bourg, de lievres en Champaigne,
   D'ours en Savoye, et de veaux en Bretaigne,
   De cygnes blancs le long de la Tamise,
Ne tant d'Amours se traitant en l'eglise,
   De differents aux peuples d'Alemaigne,
   Ne tant de gloire à un seigneur d'Espaigne,
   Ne tant se trouve à la Cour de feintise,
Ne tant y a de monstres en Afrique,
   D'opinions en une republique,
   Ne de pardons à Romme aux jours de feste,
Ne d'avarice aux hommes de pratique,
   Ne d'argumens en une Sorbonique,
   Que m'amie a de lunes en la teste[2].

In fact Saint-Gelais never realised the true character of
the sonnet. His examples lack the nervous concentrated
energy, the passion controlled by intellectual and artistic
force, of the true sonnet. Moreover he quite missed the
distinction between the two parts, between the octave and
the sestine.

When Saint-Gelais returned to France, he found his former
neighbour, the young Count of Angoulême, on the throne.
From him he received the ready welcome which Francis

---

[1] *Œuvres*, I. 78. This is the only sonnet in the 1547 edition. A translation
by Mr Austin Dobson, much superior to the original, will be found in S. Waddington,
Sonnets of Europe, 1886, p. 115. Sir Thomas Wyatt's "Like unto these un-
measurable mountains" is translated direct from Sannazaro.

[2] I. 288 ; admirably translated by Cary, *op. cit.* p. 36.

always extended to men of good family—the bar sinister made no difference—who were distinguished for learning or literary attainments. Endowed with all the qualities of a first-rate courtier, good looks, easy temper and easier morals, he rose quickly in the King's favour. After a short-lived flirtation with Protestantism he carefully avoided that stumbling-block in the way of advancement, and about the year 1524 assumed the habit, though by no means the character, of an ecclesiastic. He became royal almoner, custodian of the royal library at Fontainebleau, and abbot of Reclus, a Cistercian abbey in the diocese of Troyes. But his chief occupation seems to have consisted in directing the literary and dramatic entertainments of the Court. "Were there any brave orations to be made," says André Thevet, "whether in prose or verse, French or Latin, the whole business was intrusted to Saint-Gelais, to whom they had recourse as if to an Apollo." He arranged the masquerades, wrote the verses for them, and set them to music, for he was a good musician and had an agreeable voice, which he accompanied on the lute.

His poetical talents were considerable, but they were devoted chiefly to frivolous objects, to writing verses in ladies' albums or declarations of love in their Books of Hours, to inditing passionless sonnets and *dizains* to the numerous objects of his inconstant flame, to pointing an epigram of the grossest indecency, or to polishing the halting lines of his royal master. He carried to excess the fashion of his time in shunning the publicity of print; and this was attributed by his enemies to prudence rather than modesty. There is a manifest allusion to him in the concluding lines of Du Bellay's *Le Poete courtisan*, where it is said that a certain courtier-poet, the most esteemed poet of his time, would have lost his reputation if he had ever printed anything, and he is advised to rest content with the verdict of those who can give him a snug post or a rich benefice, and not to court the *popularis aura* with its noisy but fruitless applause[1]. Estienne Pasquier

---

[1] I have no doubt that Du Bellay is also alluding to Saint-Gelais in the *Deffence*, II. c. 2, when he says, "*Un autre, pour n'avoir encore rien mis en lumière soubz son nom, ne merite qu'on luy donne le premier lieu.*"

too speaks of Saint-Gelais's prudence in avoiding print, "for after his death a collected edition of his works was published which died almost as soon as it saw the light[1]."

As a matter of fact some of Saint-Gelais's poems were published in his life-time. Seven of them appeared in a small selection of poems published in 1534 under the title of *Les fleurs de poesie françoise* in the same volume with the anonymous translation of Alberti's *Ecatomfila*[2]. The *Deploration de Venus* and six others formed the chief part of another small volume, edited in 1545 by Antoine du Moulin[3]. Finally in 1547 a collected edition appeared in the form of a thin octavo volume of seventy-nine pages. But owing either to the heretical flavour of two of the pieces or to the indiscretion of a third, in which the love-affairs of the ladies of the court were celebrated under transparent disguises, it was speedily suppressed, and so effectually that not only are there now only two copies in existence, but neither Pasquier nor apparently Du Bellay had ever heard of its publication[4]. It was not till 1574, more than a quarter of a century after Saint-Gelais's death, that another and much fuller edition of his poems was published.

Though Estienne Pasquier dismisses Saint-Gelais too briefly and contemptuously, there is considerable propriety in the term *mignardises*, or pretty affectations, which he applies to his poetry[5]. A good instance is the following *huitain*, written with characteristic irreverence in a Book of Hours:

Tout ainsi que ces Heures blanches
Ont peu obscures devenir,
Et comme les feuilles des branches
Tombent quand l'hiver veut venir,

[1] *Recherches*, VII. c. 5.

[2] See Picot, I. no. 803 ; none of these pieces were included in the 1547 edition.

[3] *Cat. Coste*, no. 796. MM. Cartier and Chenevière (*ante*, p. 128 n. 3) have not seen this edition, but they reasonably conjecture that it contained the ten pieces (including three not by Saint-Gelais) which form pp. 1—40 of the enlarged edition of 1547. This later edition has twenty-one pieces by Saint-Gelais.

[4] See *Œuvres*, I. 70 (a piece entitled *Enigme*, much in the style of a *coq à l'asne*, relating to Marot's imprisonment) ; I. 108, a *dizain* in which the initial letters of the lines form the words *La Papalité*; I. 121, *Chanson des astres*.

[5] *loc. cit.*

Ainsi vous doit-il souvenir
Que le temps finit la beauté,
Mais chose qui puisse advenir
Ne finira ma loyauté[1].

Or the following *dizain*, inspired by the first two stanzas
of Horace's *Sic te diva potens Cypri* :

Heureuse nef flottant en mer profonde,
Dans laquelle est marchandise si chere
Qu'encore assez n'est cogneue du monde,
Las ! garde toy de la coste rochère ;
Maine à bon port, à saine et bonne chere
Les deux qui sont eslongnez de leur tiers !
Toy, Eolus, enferme tes vents fiers,
Fors que le Nord, qui bientost les rameine
Avec le flot ; car aultre bien ne quiers,
Que reveoir ceulx sans qui ma vie est vaine[2].

Saint-Gelais, as a rule, is happier in imitation or translation
than in purely original work. The *Deploration de Venus*[3], one
of the pieces most admired by his contemporaries, is an
imitation of an idyll of Bion, and the lively, witty and grace-
fully expressed *Description d'amour*[4] is inspired by Bembo's
Amor è, donne care, un vano e fello.

Saint-Gelais not only introduced into French poetry the
imitation of Italian models, and with it the Neo-Petrarchism
at this time so fashionable in Italy, but he is also the first
representative of that element in French poetry which found
so much favour throughout the seventeenth and eighteenth
centuries, of an element into which the intellect enters largely,
the fancy a little, and the heart not at all, the element in
short of pure *esprit*.   He is thus the forerunner of Desportes
and Voiture and Voltaire.   Indeed in his Italian sympathies,
his conceits and his wit, Desportes is Saint-Gelais over again.
But the earlier poet is a more slovenly workman than his
successor.   Writing as he did chiefly for an uncritical circle of
courtiers and court-ladies, and without any view to publication,
he was seldom at the pains to work his verses up to perfection.

[1] *Œuvres*, II. 64.   [2] *ib.* III. 59.
[3] *ib.* I. 127 ff.   [4] *ib.* I. 82.

In the year which intervened between the publication of Saint-Gelais's poems in 1547 and the appearance of Du Bellay's manifesto in 1549, there was published a work which may be regarded as the epilogue to the whole Marotic school. This was the *Art poëtique François* of Thomas Sibilet, a Paris lawyer, who, like Saint-Gelais, preferred literature to law[1]. The very title of his work as contrasted with that of the *Art de rhetorique* of Pierre Fabri[2] points to the nature of the change which Marot had wrought. Poetry was no longer a branch of rhetoric. Writing when he did, Sibilet inevitably takes the work of Marot and his school as the basis of his poetical doctrines. His chosen models are Marot, Saint-Gelais, Scève, Heroet and Salel. But he looks forward as well as backward, and he shows considerable knowledge of the *Ars poetica*, while his classical learning generally is somewhat in advance of Marot's. He speaks of the *rondeau* and the *virelai* and the *coq à l'asne* as out of date, and he recommends the sonnet (which he says is much in vogue), the ode, the eclogue and the elegy. It is in the somewhat timid conservatism of its tone rather than in any vital difference in its theory and precepts, that his treatise differs from the confident and thorough-going manifesto which appeared a year later. There was no such breach as Du Bellay would have us believe between Marot and the Pleiad.

Note on the introduction of the sonnet into France. The earliest French sonnets to appear in print are, so far as I know, two of Marot's in the 1538 edition of his works, being printed, as in all subsequent editions, among the epigrams (nos. 144 and 152). Next comes one by Saint-Gelais. It was printed in 1540 at the beginning of Herberay des Essarts's translation of *Amadis*. The 1544 edition of Marot's poems contains six fresh sonnets, all translated from Petrarch. In the 1547 edition of Saint-Gelais's poems there is only one sonnet, the one quoted on pp. 147, 148; in *Les Marguerites de la Marguerite*, also published in 1547, there are three sonnets, one by Margaret herself and two by Maurice

---

[1] According to Pierre L'Estoile, who was his intimate friend, he died in 1589 at the age of 77, *un des plus verts vieillards de Paris* (*Journal*, v. 13). See La Croix du Maine, II. 434, and Goujet, III. 92—95.

[2] See H. Zschalig, *Die Verslehren von Fabri, Du Pont and Sibilet*, Leipsic, 1884; G. Pellissier, *L'Art poëtique de Vauquelin de la Fresnaye*, pp. ix–xix.

Scève; and in Peletier's poems of 1547 there are thirteen, twelve translated from Petrarch and one original. Thus so far as print goes Saint-Gelais's claim cannot be sustained. But as I have pointed out, poems in those days were often circulated in manuscript long before they were printed. Can we then determine when Saint-Gelais's sonnets were written? Of the nineteen of his which have been published nine were certainly not written before 1544; one is at any rate later than 1533; one, as we have seen, was written in 1540; one may have been written in 1531, but cannot well be earlier; the remaining eight cannot be dated. Of Marot's two earliest sonnets, the one entitled *Pour le May planté par les imprimeurs de Lyon devant le logis du seigneur Trivulse* must have been written not later than May 1, 1532, for Trivulce, the governor of Lyons, died in October of that year. It is however quite possible that one or more of Saint-Gelais's sonnets to which no date can be assigned were written before this, though there is nothing to prove it.

BIBLIOGRAPHY.

EDITIONS.

MAURICE SCÈVE, *La deplorable fin de Flamete*, Lyons, 1535. *Arion*, *ib.* 1536. *Delie, object de plus haulte vertu, ib.* 1544; reprinted *ib.* 1862. *Saulssaye, Eglogue de la vie solitaire, ib.* 1547; reprinted, Aix, 1829. *Microcosme*, Lyons, 1562.

ANTOINE HEROET, *La parfaicte amye, avec plusieurs aultres compositions*, Lyons, Dolet, 1542 (Christie library, Victoria University, Manchester).

JACQUES PELETIER, *L'Art Poëtique d'Horace*, Paris, 1545 (the earliest known edition, but not the first). *Les Œuvres Poëtiques, ib.* 1547; reprinted *ib.* 1904. *L'amour des amours, Vers liriques*, Lyons, 1555. *L'art poëtique, ib.* 1555. *La Savoye*, Annecy, 1572; ed. Dessaix, Chambéry, 1856; ed. Pagès, Moûtiers-en-Tarantaise, 1897. *Euvres poëtiques*, Paris, 1581.—See Picot, I. nos. 699—671.

MELLIN DE SAINT-GELAIS, *Œuvres de luy tant en composition que translation, ou allusion aux auteurs Grecs et Latins. Lyon, Pierre de Tours*, 1547. Of this edition only two copies are known, one (in bad condition) in the *Bib. Nationale*, and the other, from the Hamilton library, in the Rothschild collection (Picot, I. no. 629). *Œuvres poëtiques*, Lyons, Antoine de Harsy, 1574, a new and much enlarged edition, omitting however 16 pieces which had appeared in the 1547 edition; printed by Frellon (Le Petit, p. 84; Picot, I. no. 630); Paris, 1719 (this contains several additional pieces, both Latin and French); ed. P. Blanchemain, 3 vols. 1873 (*Bib. Elzévirienne*). This latter contains twenty new pieces, and La Monnoye's commentary, which he wrote in the margins of his copy of the 1574 edition.

[Thomas Sibilet,] *Art poëtique François*, Paris, 1548 (*Bib. Nat.*; Picot, I. 427); *Reveu et augmenté*, Lyons, 1556 (Brit. Mus.). A modern edition is in preparation by Prof. L. E. Kastner, who also proposes to edit *La parfaicte amye*.

LIVES.

For Scève, Heroet and Peletier, see the notes to the text. Colletet's life of Saint-Gelais, published in the *Poètes Angoumoisins*, ed. E. Gellibert des Seguins and E. Castaigne, 1863, has little of interest except the account of his personal appearance, which is copied from Thevet's *Portraits et Vies des hommes illustres*, 1584. The portrait in Thevet, which is a remarkably fine one, represents a handsome man with a full beard.

To be consulted.

Estienne Pasquier, *Recherches de la France*, VII. cc. 5, 6, 15; H. F. Cary, *The early French poets* (Scève, Heroet, Saint-Gelais), 1846; E. Crépet, *Les poëtes français*, I. 1861; F. Brunetière, *Un précurseur de la Pléiade, Maurice Scève*, in *Études critiques sur l'histoire de la littérature française*, VI. 1899; J. Vianey, *L'influence Italienne chez les précurseurs de la Pléiade* in *Bull. ital.* III. 85 ff. 1903.

CHAPTER IX

THE ROMANCES OF CHIVALRY

THE popularity of the prose romances of chivalry continued unabated throughout the reign of Francis I. In their ultimate origin they were neither romance nor written in prose. Even the *Chanson de Roland*, the oldest form in which the *chansons de geste* have come down to us, relates exclusively to events of national history, and while admitting the usual poetical license in the treatment of facts, never strays beyond the bounds of sober probability. But before the middle of the twelfth century French narrative poetry began to occupy itself with fresh subject matter. To the *chansons de geste* were added the romances of Antiquity, and, a little later, the Arthurian romances. Largely substituting fiction for fact, and the interest of love or of the portrayal of contemporary society for that of the warlike deeds of national heroes, Odysseys, as they have been happily called, instead of Iliads, they were true romances. The romances of Antiquity were derived mainly from Byzantine sources, the Arthurian from Celtic, and both these sources supplied an element which became more and more conspicuous—that of magic. The beginning of the thirteenth century saw the introduction of a new class, that of the *romans d'aventures*, which are either pure fiction or grotesque violations of history, and in which the magical element is largely represented.

These new forms of narrative poetry reacted in several ways on the *chansons de geste*. New ones were written, and old ones were re-fashioned under their influence. Novel and wholly fictitious adventures, the scene of which was frequently laid in the East to suit the crusading spirit, were liberally provided for the heroes. Moreover, whereas in the old *chansons de geste* Charlemagne is portrayed as a great and wise ruler, as a king of heroic mould, in those of the twelfth century his barons are glorified at his expense, and their rebellions against his authority take the place of national wars under his standard. Then in the thirteenth century under the influence of the *romans d'aventures* we have the introduction of the magical element, dwarfs, fairies and enchanters, and all the fantastic machinery of oriental origin. Finally, in the fourteenth century, when the power of original creation is wholly exhausted, the *chansons de geste* grow to an inordinate length by long and feeble additions of heterogeneous elements.

One of the best instances of these successive transformations is *Huon de Bordeaux*. Beginning its existence as a quasi-historical poem, of which there are distinct traces, it is in the oldest form known to us, that of a Tours manuscript of ten thousand verses, largely concerned with the doings of the fairy-king Oberon. The next stage is represented by a Turin manuscript, in which numerous additions from various sources swell its length to thirty thousand verses[1].

The principal Arthurian romances had already been done into prose by the middle of the thirteenth century. The others in turn underwent the same change, the great age of the compilation of prose romances being from the latter part of the fourteenth to the end of the fifteenth century. By the time of the accession of Francis I about thirty-five prose romances had been printed, while nearly thirty more were added during his and the succeeding reign.

In their relation to the reading public there was a marked distinction between the Arthurian prose romances and the rest. The Arthurian romances, composed as they were in the aristocratic age of the first half of the thirteenth century, were read chiefly by high-born lords and ladies. Even the two favourites, *Lancelot* and *Tristan*, never descended from their

---

[1] See Gautier, *Les épopées françaises*, II. pp. 732 ff.; *Huon of Bordeaux*, edited or the Early English Text Society with an introduction by S. L. Lee, 1882.

stately folios to seek a wider circulation in a less magnificent and expensive form. The only one that seems to have reached a more popular audience was *Le petit Artus*, the connexion of which with the Arthurian cycle is extremely slight. It was the prose romances of the fifteenth century, the representatives of the *chansons de geste* in their last decadence, or of the *romans d'aventures*, which were read by the middle classes in the sixteenth century, which were printed again and again, and which finally in the form of chap-books penetrated to the lowest stratum of French readers. Of these the most popular (judging by the number of times they were reprinted) were *Pierre de Provence, Valentin et Orson, Paris et Vienne, Fierabras, Ogier le Danois* and *Les quatre fils Aymon*. Somewhat less popular were *Baudouin de Flandres, Huon de Bordeaux, Godefroy de Bouillon, Galien rhétoré, La belle Hélène, Ponthus et la belle Sidoine, Robert le Diable, Richard sans peur, Mélusine* with its continuation *Geoffroy à la gran dent,* and *Maugis* and *Mabrian,* the continuations of *Les quatre fils Aymon*[1]. Of these *Valentin et Orson, Les quatre fils Aymon, Huon de Bordeaux, Galien, La belle Hélène, Robert le Diable* and *Richard sans peur* kept their place in the ranks of the *Bibliothèque bleue* till its final extinction in 1863[2].

Again taking the number of times that they were printed as a test, it would appear that none of the prose romances from the old sources which were printed for the first time in the reign of Francis I had much success, except *Maugis, Mabrian* and *Richard sans peur*. The latter was a prose version made by Gilles Corrozet about the year 1535 from a

[1] It is interesting to compare with this list the names of the heroes of romances who figure in Rabelais's picture of the infernal regions, *Pant.* II. 30. He mentions the following: Lancelot, Valentin and Orson, Giglan and Gawain, Geoffrey with the great tooth, Godfrey of Boulogne, Huon of Bordeaux, Jason, Arthur of Britain, Perceforest, Ogier le Danois, Galien *restauré,* the four sons of Aymon, Mélusine and Matabrune (a character in the *Chevalier au cygne*). In the *ballade* prefixed to the *Légende de Pierre Faifeu,* which was published in 1532, mention is made of *Artus, Lancelot, Merlin, Tristan, Aymon, Robert le Diable, Fierabras, Orson* and *Pontus.*

[2] A. Assier, *La bibliothèque bleue,* 1874.

fifteenth century poem. Not long before this the prose
romance of *Turpin* had been made by order of Francis I
from the Latin chronicle of Pseudo-Turpin. But towards the
close of the reign a new source was tapped, which proved far
more successful, for it produced a romance which among the
aristocratic class of readers eclipsed all others, even *Lancelot*,
in popularity. This was a translation of the Spanish *Amadis
de Gaula*. The origin of this famous work belongs to the
history of Spanish literature, and need not be discussed here.
The following is a brief statement of the facts. The first four
books of the Spanish *Amadis* were the work of Garci-Ordoñez
de Montalvo, who completed it about the year 1470. He tells
us in his preface that he had "corrected those three books of
Amadis which, from the fault of bad copyists and writers
(*componedores*), were in a very corrupt and faulty state," thus
implying that he had an older version of these books to work
upon. Now a Portuguese chronicler of the middle of the
fifteenth century, by name Zurara, says that *Amadis* "was
made at the pleasure of a man named Vasco de Lobeira in the
time of King Dom Fernando (1367—1383), everything in the
book being the product of the author's fancy." In reliance
upon this statement the existence of an original Portuguese
version was formerly maintained by Southey and others, and
is still upheld by Portuguese historians of literature[1]. There
was at any rate a Spanish version in existence and well
known before 1360[2].

There is no external evidence to help us to trace the origin
of *Amadis* further back than the old Spanish version, but
Baret's view, which is supported by Dr Braunfels, that the
work itself shews traces of a Celtic origin, either Breton or

[1] *e.g.* T. Braga, *Hist. da litteratura Portugueza*, 1885, pp. 103—107; C.
Michaëlis de Vasconcellos in Gröber, *Grundriss der romanischen Philologie*, II. ii.
216—226, 1897, and in *Revista Lusitana*, VI. 26 ff. 1900.

[2] The Spanish origin is maintained by Gayangos in his translation of Ticknor's
History of Spanish Literature, 1851 (I. 520—522), and at greater length in his
Discurso preliminar to *Libros de Caballerias*, pp. xxi—xxvi; by E. Baret in *De
l'Amadis de Gaule*; by Dr L. Braunfels in *Amadis von Gallien*; and by G. Baist
in Gröber, *op. cit.* pp. 440, 441.

English, has much to recommend it. The countries mentioned are Great Britain, Wales (Gaula), Scotland, Ireland and little Britain (Brittany); the towns are London, Windsor and Bristol. Moreover, as Ormsby points out, the character of Urganda *la Desconocida*, who reminds one strongly of Morgan the Fay, is also suggestive of a Celtic origin, for in the indigenous Spanish romances the supernatural element is conspicuously absent. This Celtic origin was also maintained by Sir Walter Scott.

Montalvo's *Amadis* originally consisted of four books, three books which he had worked up from the old version, and a fourth which he had "translated and emended," a statement which in the opinion of Gayangos implies that it was his own composition. Of these four books the earliest known edition was printed at Saragossa in 1508, and is represented by a single copy which was discovered at Ferrara in 1872 by M. Tross[1]. In 1492 Montalvo completed a fifth book, confessedly his own composition, relating to the history of Esplandian, son of Amadis. Other books were added from time to time by other hands, till by the middle of the sixteenth century the Spanish *Amadis*, with its continuations, had expanded to twelve books.

In the year 1540 there appeared a French translation of Montalvo's first book from the pen of Nicolas de Herberay, Seigneur des Essarts, of a noble family of Picardy, who has already come under our notice as a translator from the Spanish[2]. The favour with which it was received encouraged Herberay to continue the work, and he produced in succession seven more books corresponding to books ii—iv, v, vii and ix of the Spanish *Amadis*[3]. The eighth book was published in 1548, and then the translator, being out of health, stayed his hand.

---

[1] It became the property of Baron Seillière and was sold at his sale (Seillière Cat. no. 23).

[2] See *ante*, pp. 50, 51. For Herberay see La Croix du Maine, and Du Verdier, and Niceron, XXXIX. He also translated Josephus's *Jewish War*, but the work was not published till after his death, in 1557.

[3] Books vi and viii of the Spanish *Amadis* were never translated into French.

After his death, which took place about the year 1552, the work was continued by others, till by 1574 the French version had reached fourteen books and the Spanish original with all its continuations was exhausted. But the appetite of the French public was not yet satisfied. Invention supplied the place of translation, or recourse was had to Italian originals. On rolled the interminable romance. By the year 1579 the tale of books had been increased to twenty-one. Then there was a long pause, till in 1615, the year, curiously enough, in which the second part of *Don Quixote* was published, the publication of three more books finally completed the vast work[1].

With these late books we have nothing to do. All that concerns us is the work of Herberay des Essarts. Judged as an original composition it is of great merit and thoroughly deserves the commendation of Estienne Pasquier, who says that the French tongue is not a little indebted to the translators of Francis I's reign, Dolet, Jean Martin and Le Maçon, but "above all to Nicolas de Herberay in the eight books of *Amadis de Gaule*, especially the eighth, a romance from which you can cull all the fair flowers of our French tongue[2]." The most striking characteristic of Des Essarts's style is the precision with which he chooses the right word, the word which expresses at once most forcibly and most simply the exact shade of meaning that he requires. And this virtue tends to another, namely enonomy of language. There is no waste of words because every word tells. It follows from this that it is a particularly clear style. It is also one of considerable variety, being equally successful in ordinary narrative, or in vigorous descriptions of murderous encounters, or in scenes of tender pathos. Finally it shews considerable proficiency in the art of constructing periods, and the rhythm, if seldom brilliant, is

[1] Book ix was translated by Gilles Boileau, and revised by Claude Colet, books x, xi, and xiii by Jacques Gohorry, xii by Guillaume Aubert, xiv by Antoine Tiron, who also wrote xv. Books xvi—xxi were translated by Gabriel Chappuys, probably from the Italian, and xxii—xxiv by an unknown writer, professedly from the Spanish. There is a duplicate translation of book xvi by Nicolas de Montreux.

[2] *Recherches*, VIII. 5.

always harmonious. Thus it is a style which is admirably
adapted to its purpose, that of carrying the reader through a
long narrative. It interests without exciting, and stimulates
without fatiguing. Here are two specimens, one a brilliant
description of the encounter between Amadis and King Abies
in which one almost seems to hear the clash of the strokes on
the combatants' harness, and the other an account of how
Oriana received the report of Amadis's death:

Or estoient ces deux Cheualiers si animez l'vn sur l'autre, tant pour
leur honneur, que pour la consequence, dont estoit leur combat, sans
interualle, ne reprendre leur alaine, frapoient & se chamailloient, de sorte
qu'à ouyr les coups, l'on eust iuge ce combat estre fait par plus de vingt
personnes ensemble, & bien monstroient le peu de bien qu'ilz se vouloient:
car à l'entour d'eux l'on voyoit la terre tainte de leur sang, les pieces de
leurs escutz, les lames de leur harnois espandues & semées, & leurs
heaumes si enfondrez, que pour estre leurs armes si endommagées, ilz ne
tiroient gueres de coups à faute, mais se saignoient trescruellement du
trenchant de leurs espées : ce neatmoins ilz auoient le courage si entier,
qu'ilz n'en sentoient rien. Et à ceste cause se maintenoit l'vn enuers
l'autre si brauement que l'on ne pouuoit cognoistre qui auoit le meilleur,
ou le pire[1].

Helas, mes amis, ne me destournez du chemin de la mort! si vous
desirez mon repos, & consentez que i'aille bien tost trouuer en l'autre
monde celuy qui n'eust sceu viure vn iour en cestuy cy sans moy.
Proferant ce mot elle se print tellement à renforcer son pleur, que
c'estoit grand' pitié de la voir, puis reprenant alaine, elle disoit : Ah, ah,
seul miroer de toute cheualerie! vostre mort est tant grieue & insuportable,
que non moy seule, mais le reste du monde y doit auoir regret, ayant
perdu ce qui plus l'honoroit en bonté, prudence, hardiesse, & toutes les
vertuz que tous les grands se peuuent desirer. Toutesfois, si en vous y a
encores quelque sentiment, ie suis seure, que vous n'auez regret à la vie
perdue, sinon pour l'amour de moy que vous voyez si affligée : car vous
auez tant laissé d'honneur en ce monde, & tant aquis de reputation en ce
peu de temps que vous y auez esté, que contant voz merites vous estes
mort vieil, mais bien estes demeuré immortel, & moy y seiournant apres
vous, ne sçaurois aquerir sinon bruit de malheureuse & ingrate[2].

As a translation the French *Amadis* is extremely unfaithful.
The Seigneur des Essarts was evidently not much of a Spanish
scholar ; whenever he comes to a passage of any difficulty he
makes no attempt to translate it, but substitutes for it some-

[1] Book I. c. 10.   [2] *ib.* c. 21.

thing of his own.   He is very fond too of introducing whole
passages, descriptions or flights of oratory, of which not a
trace is to be found in the original.   But his worst offence is
that he never misses an opportunity of giving rein to his
prurient imagination.   The Spanish *Amadis* cannot be called
a moral book, but it is reserved and decorous in tone, so that
the licentious passages introduced by the translator are a
thorough violation of its spirit.

It may be said that he has forestalled criticisms of this sort
by his statement that he had found part of an old Picard
manuscript, from which he believed the Spanish version to
have been taken, though it by no means followed the original.
But no one now believes in this Picard version.   The reference
to an old manuscript newly discovered in some out of the
way cabinet was a common fiction with compilers of romances,
which deceived nobody, and was probably meant to deceive
nobody[1].

But it was just this infidelity of the French *Amadis*, this
adaptation of its spirit to French soil, this clothing of the staid
Castilian romance with 'gay garments,' which made it so
popular in its new home.   " Never," says Pasquier, " was a book
received with such favour as this one for the space of twenty
years."   Its popularity brought other Spanish romances into
favour.   In 1546 a French translation appeared of *Palmerin
de Oliva*, first printed in Spain in 1511, the progenitor of
numerous descendants which in Spain at any rate almost
rivalled the *Amadises* in popularity.   The most famous of
these was *Palmerin of England*[2], which it may be recollected
was the only romance besides the original *Amadis* thought
worthy to escape the *auto-da-fé* of Don Quixote's library.   A
French translation by Jacques Vincent, secretary to the
Bishop of Le Puy, was printed in 1552–3 and in 1554
the same busy translator published a translation of *Flores
y Blancaflor*[3].   A few years previously, namely in 1550,

---

[1] Compare the elaborate introduction to the romance of *Perceforest* cited by
Scott in his *Essay on Romance* (*Misc. Prose Works,* vi.).

[2] *Palmerin de Inglaterra*, Toledo, 1548.

[3] This represents a poem of the 12th cent. which is also the origin of Boccaccio's
Filocolo.

another romance of the Palmerin series, *Primaleon of Greece* (son of Palmerin), had appeared in a French translation. The popularity of these Spanish romances led to the production of new ones of a similar character. The translator, as he professes to be, but doubtless really the author of *Gerard d'Euphrate*, published in 1549, says that he was encouraged to publish it by the success of *Amadis*. Though it is connected in subject-matter with the Charlemagne cycle, the hero being represented as a son of Doon of Mayence, the influence of Amadis is very apparent[1].

According to La Noue these romances had their greatest vogue during the reign of Henry II. " I believe that if any one at that time had tried to find fault with them he would have been spat at, seeing that so many persons found in them instruction and entertainment." To the Huguenot soldier their influence seemed as harmful to the young as that of Machiavelli to the old[2]. Their popularity continued with but little abatement under the remaining princes of the house of Valois, and Henry III is said to have placed a copy of *Amadis* in his library between the works of Aristotle and Plato. In the reign of Henry IV it was called the King's Bible[3]. But Estienne Pasquier, writing about the end of the reign, says that the memory of *Amadis* had almost perished. Its influence however remained. The heroic romances of the seventeenth century, the *Grand Cyrus* and *Clélie* of Mademoiselle de Scudéry and the *Cléopâtre* of La Calprenède, are its direct descendants ; even *La Princesse de Clèves*, the parent of the modern novel, breathes no small measure of its spirit.

---

[1] He professes to have translated it from a Walloon poem, but see Gaston Paris, *Hist. poétique de Charlemagne*, 325, n. 2. Gerard d'Euphrate is evidently a corruption of Gerard de Fratte.

[2] *Discours politiques et militaires* VI. (written during his imprisonment, 1580—1585).

[3] P. de l'Estoile, Journal, IX. 134.

BIBLIOGRAPHY.

EDITIONS.

Le premier livre d'Amadis de Gaule mis en françois par le Seigneur des Essars, Nicolas de Herberay, fo. Paris, Denys Janot, 1540. With woodcuts.

The other seven books translated by Des Essarts appeared in successive years, except that book viii. was not published till 1548. After Janot's death in 1545 his printing establishment was carried on first by his widow and then from 1547 by her second husband, Estienne Grouleau. This establishment made a *spécialité* of books with woodcuts, and according to A. F. Didot, *La gravure sur bois*, surpassed all the Paris printers of the time in this class of work.

A complete set of the original editions is very rare. The British Museum has only one of book iv. The passages given in my text are printed from an 8vo edition with woodcuts published at Paris in 1550 by Vincent Sertenas.

The best edition is that printed by Plantin for Jean Waesberghe, 12 vols., Antwerp, 1561 ; it contains books i—xii. There is no modern edition.

TO BE CONSULTED.

SIR WALTER SCOTT, *Miscellaneous Prose Works*, XVIII. 1—43, Edinburgh, 1835 (from the *Edinburgh Review* for Oct. 1803, a review of Southey's translation of *Amadis*) ; E. BARET, *De l'Amadis de Gaule*, 1853 ; 2nd ed. 1873 ; PASCUAL DE GAYANGOS, *Discurso preliminar* prefixed to *Libros de Caballerias* (*Bibliotheca de autores Españoles* XL.), Madrid, 1874 ; L. BRAUNFELS, *Amadis von Gallien*, Leipzig, 1876.

CHAPTER X

RABELAIS

1. *His life.*

THE early years of Rabelais's life are veiled in obscurity. To begin with we do not know in what year he was born. The traditional date of his birth is 1483, the year in which Louis XI died and Luther and Raphael were born. If this is correct, Rabelais must have been over forty when he left Fontenay-le-Comte and when Tiraqueau spoke of him as a man learned beyond his years[1]; he must have been forty-seven when he matriculated at Montpellier as a medical student; he must have been forty-nine when he began his literary career, and finally he must have been seventy when he died, although no contemporary speaks of him as an old man. On these grounds it seems reasonable to abandon the traditional date of his birth, which after all only depends on vague statements that he was seventy at the time of his death, and to adopt the view now generally prevalent that he was born about 1495.

There is practically no doubt about the place of his birth. According to his own statement, *Ego Franciscus Rabelæsus Chinonensis*, he was born at Chinon, a town of Touraine which lies wedged in between the river Vienne and the lofty castle-crowned rock[2]. We may therefore disregard an old local tradition that he was born at La Devinière, about three miles to the S.W. of Chinon, where his father is said to have had a

---

[1] *Vir supra aetatem...utriusque linguae omnifariaeque doctrinae peritissimus* (*De legibus connubialibus*, 2nd ed., 1524).

[2] Here our Henry II died, and here the Maid of Orleans had an interview with the Dauphin, the future Charles VII.

property[1]. Another tradition that his father, Thomas Rabelais, was an innkeeper doubtless arose from the fact that his house at Chinon, at the sign of the Lamprey, was afterwards turned into an inn, but this very circumstance, which is recorded in some Latin verses by De Thou[2], proves that this was not its original condition. According to Le Roy François had barely attained his tenth year when his father determined to make him a Franciscan[3], and there is fairly good evidence that he received his early education as a novice in the Franciscan convent of La Baumette near Angers[4]. The conspicuous part which the Cluniac abbey of Seuillé or Sully, close to La Devinière, plays in *Gargantua* as the abbey which brother John saved from destruction makes one inclined also to accept the tradition that Rabelais received some schooling here before going to La Baumette.

But it is not till the year 1519 that we meet with a piece of unimpeachable evidence for a fact in Rabelais's life. In a contract for a purchase of land made by the Franciscan convent of Fontenay-le-Comte in Poitou and dated April 5 of that year Rabelais appears as a signatory, and is qualified as *frere mineur*[5]. Some time, therefore, before this date he had definitely become a Franciscan friar. His residence at Fontenay-le-Comte is chiefly remarkable for the Greek studies which he carried on in conjunction with his brother monk Pierre Amy[6]. This involved them in an annoying persecution

---

[1] A.-F. le Double, *Rabelais anatomiste et physiologiste*, 1899, pp. 321, 322.

[2] *Mémoires*, Amsterdam, 1713, pp. 327, 328.

[3]   *Bis quintum attigerat vix annum Cordigerum esse*
        Vult pater arridens. Le Roy, *Rab. elogia.*

[4] Tradition in this case is supported by the evidence of one Bruneau, a lawyer of Angers, who died at an advanced age in 1626 (Rathery, p. 3). The tradition that among his schoolfellows were Guillaume and Jean du Bellay and Geoffroy d'Estissac is clearly wrong, for the Du Bellay brothers, certainly, and D'Estissac, probably, were never at La Baumette, which was a purely conventual school. The Du Bellays were at the University of Angers, but it is hardly likely that Rabelais can have made their acquaintance. (L. Séché in *Rev. de la Renaissance*, I. 236.)

[5] B. Fillon, *Poitou et Vendée*, p. 45.

[6] Rabelais calls him Amy (*Pant.* iii. 10), but he signed his own name Lamy Le Double, *op. cit.*, p. 27).

at the hands of their obscurantist brethren, but they were encouraged in their somewhat up-hill task by letters from the great Budé, with whom Amy began a correspondence, in which Rabelais also took part[1]. They had also a warm friend and sympathiser in André Tiraqueau, a distinguished jurist, who was lieutenant of the bailiwick of Fontenay. About the year 1524, and probably in that very year, Rabelais left the convent, having obtained permission from Clement VII to enter the neighbouring Benedictine monastery of Maillezais[2]. The bishop of Maillezais was his friend Geoffroy d'Estissac, who seems to have resided chiefly at his priory of Ligugé near Poitiers. A little room in the prior's *château* was set apart for Rabelais, and here he spent a considerable portion of his time garnering up in peace and quiet the stores of his encyclopædic learning[3]. Poitiers, which was only five miles from Ligugé, was something of a literary centre, and among his friends was Jean Bouchet, a relic of the *rhétoriqueur* school of poetry, who, as we have seen, had retired to Poitiers at the beginning of the reign of Francis I, where he continued to produce reams of jog-trot verse[4].

Between Rabelais's admission to the convent at Maillezais and his matriculation at the University of Montpellier in September 1530 there is a gap in the record. But it can be partially filled up by conjecture, which for some of the circumstances amounts almost to certainty. From the words of Rabelais's supplication to Paul III, *eoque per annos plures*

[1] The first letter is one from Amy to Budé, dated August 14, 1521; the last one is from Budé to Rabelais, dated Jan. 27 [prob. 1523].

[2] *Supplicatio pro apostasia* (Marty-Laveaux, III. 336 ff.). There is nothing to shew that Rabelais, like his friend Amy (*Pant.* iii. 10), left the convent in an irregular way (see Niceron, XXXII. 340). As for the date, Clement VII became Pope on Nov. 19, 1523, and it would have taken a little time for Rabelais to get an answer to his request. Moreover Tiraqueau, in the passage of the second edition of the *De leg. connub.* to which I have referred, and which was published in 1524, still speaks of Rabelais as *sodalis franciscanus*. On the other hand his departure from Fontenay can hardly have taken place later than 1524.

[3] See *Epistre à Bouchet* (Marty-Laveaux, III. 298 ff.) and Bouchet's answer (*ib.* 303 ff.).

[4] *Ante*, p. 53. See also A. Hamon (l'abbé), *Un grand rhétoriqueur Poitevin, Jean Bouchet*, 1902, and P. Laumonier in *Rev. de la Ren.*, IV. 65 ff., 1903.

mansit, we may infer that he remained for at least two or three years nominally an inmate of the abbey of Maillezais. Further, we know that he was admitted to the degree of Bachelor of Medicine at Montpellier two and a half months after his matriculation, and that as recently as 1526 that University had made a statute that only a course of study at the University of Paris should be recognised for their degrees in medicine[1]. The period of study required for the degree of Bachelor at Montpellier being twenty-four months of attendance at lectures[2], this leaves twenty-two months of lectures to account for at Paris. This implies that Rabelais must have been a medical student of the Paris University from July 1528 at the latest to September 1530, a view which is supported by the fact that his Second book, published at least as early as 1533, and probably towards the close of 1532, shews an intimate knowledge of Paris.

Supposing therefore that Rabelais left Maillezais early in 1527 the gap is now reduced to a year and a half. But his biographer Le Roy tells us that in his amusing and graphic description of Pantagruel's visits to various provincial Universities he is relating his own experience[3]. Now the way in which he refers to Bourges in several passages makes it highly probable that he knew the place, and if we combine with this the statement that Pantagruel "profited very much in the Faculty of the Laws," we may reasonably infer that Rabelais must have been at Bourges when Alciati was teaching there, that is to say after the beginning of 1528[4]. It also appears from the Second book that he was well acquainted with Orleans, and it is therefore probable that he was also a student of that University. But whether he went from Orleans to Bourges or, like Pantagruel, from Bourges to Orleans, it is impossible to say. Finally, coming more and more into the region of conjecture, it is not unlikely that he began his

---

[1] *Cartulaire de Montpellier,* I. xxii.

[2] *ib.* i. 351.

[3] *Gallicas omnes...academias sub Pantagruelis nomine peragravit.* See *Pant.* ii. cc. 5–7.

[4] Alciati in some Latin verses says that he left Bourges at the end of 1532 after being five 'summers' there. (Mazzuchelli, *I scrittori d' Italia.*)

student's career at Poitiers. This step may have been taken with the permission of the authorities at Maillezais, but by the time he began to study medicine at Paris he must have exchanged his Benedictine habit for that of a secular priest.

To leave inference for well-established facts, on September 17, 1530, Rabelais matriculated as a student of medicine in the University of Montpellier, and on December 1 of the same year was admitted to the degree of Bachelor of Medicine[1]. In accordance with the requirements of the University he gave a three months course of lectures on certain treatises of Hippocrates and Galen. A novel feature of the lectures, which attracted a large class, was the introduction of textual criticism, Rabelais having in his possession a Greek manuscript of Hippocrates[2]. Documentary evidence shews that he was still at Montpellier on October 23, 1531, but by Easter 1532, or soon after, he must have migrated to Lyons, for on June 3 we find him dedicating to his friend André Tiraqueau a volume of Latin letters of Manardus, a physician of Ferrara, which he had edited for Sebastian Gryphius[3]. The same publisher also employed him to edit the treatises of Hippocrates and Galen upon which he had lectured at Montpellier[4], and two Latin legal documents, a contract of sale, and a will, which Rabelais called 'relics of venerable antiquity,' but which turned out to be modern fabrications[5].

At the same time he found employment with Claude Nourry, a printer and publisher of popular vernacular literature, on a very different sort of work. It was for Nourry that he wrote, or rather revised, a burlesque romance of chivalry

---

[1] Marty-Laveaux, III. 308. Facsimiles in Dubouchet, pp. 28 and 38; by mistake Rabelais has written November for December.

[2] The library of University College, Sheffield, has a copy of Galen, *Opera omnia*, 5 vols., Venice, 1525, with Rabelais's autograph on the title-page of each volume.

[3] Marty-Laveaux, III. 309.

[4] *ib.* 319.

[5] *ib.* 320. Only two copies of this work are known, one in the *Bib. Nationale*, the other in the Christie library, Victoria University, Manchester (see Christie, *Selected Essays and Papers*, p. 60, n. 5).

entitled *Les grandes et inestimables Croniques du grant et
enorme geant Gargantua,* which had an immense success[1].
" More copies of it have been sold in two months than there
will be Bibles in nine years," says Rabelais in the prologue to
what was ostensibly a continuation, entitled *Les horribles et
espouentables faictz et prouesses du tresrenomme Pantagruel Roy
des Dipsodes, filz du grand geant Gargantua composez nouvellement par Maistre Alcofrybas Nasier*[2]. Rabelais finished writing
this new work in September 1532, apparently while he was on
a visit to Chinon[3]. It was published at Lyons by Claude
Nourry, probably before the end of the year. Its success was
even greater than that of its predecessor. The publishers
immediately set to work to pirate it; it was printed three
times at Paris and once at Poitiers in the following year
(1533)[4]. Then in the same year 1533 François Juste of Lyons,
who had succeeded to Nourry's business, brought out a slightly
revised but carelessly printed edition in a volume of that
peculiar shape—about 5 inches by 2¼—characteristic of his
press, which is known as the *format Jeanne d'Arc*[5]. It was
inevitable that so attractive a book should come under the
notice of the Sorbonne. In October it was put upon the
Index[6].

To return to the year 1532. In this same productive year
Rabelais also composed for Nourry an Almanac and a *Pantagrueline Prognostication* for the coming year, 1533. The
Almanac seems to have been the first of a series which he
wrote annually down to 1550[7]. Like the other almanacs of

---

[1] Brunot, *Recherches*, 2me partie, pp. 1—29 ; Marty-Laveaux, IV. 22—56.

[2] See Appendix C.

[3] *Icy je feray fin à ce premier livre...les registres de mon cerveau sont quelque
peu brouillez de ceste puree de Septembre* (*Pant.* ii. 34). Herr Birch-Hirschfeld was,
I believe, the first to call attention to this indication of the date (*op. cit.*, p. 224).
The prologue was written at Chinon (*mon pays de vache*), and probably after the
rest of the book. We also learn from the passage quoted above that it was written
two months after the publication of *Les grandes croniques*.

[4] Brunot, *Recherches*, pp. 50—64.

[5] See Appendix C.

[6] See a letter of Calvin, written in October 1533. *Se pro damnatis libris
habuisse obscoenos illos Pantagruelem...et ejus monetae* (Herminjard, III. 110).

[7] A fragment of the Almanac for 1541 is preserved in the *Bib. Nat.* It is

the day it not only gave the dominical letter and other information of this sort, but purported to be a prophecy, founded on astrological science, of the events of the year. But though Rabelais in his first Almanac calls himself Professor of Astrology, he protests against the folly of the so-called science, and disclaims all knowledge of the future. "These are secrets of the close counsel of the eternal King, who rules, according to his free will and good pleasure, everything that is and that is done[1]." All the fragments of his Almanacs that have come down to us are entirely serious in tone. The *Prognostication* on the other hand, which is a prophecy of much greater length than those contained in the Almanacs, is purely humorous: and is written in the exuberant style which characterises his great work[2]. Several editions of it were published in the author's lifetime, the date being altered to suit the year, till in 1542 Juste substituted *l'an perpetuel* for the date of the particular year.

On the 1st of November 1532 Rabelais had been appointed physician to the hospital of Pont du Rhône at Lyons at an annual stipend of forty *livres*[3], and on the last day of the same month we find him writing a remarkable Latin letter to Erasmus, in which he expresses to him in terms of the warmest devotion the debt which he owes to his writings. *Pater mi Humanissime* is the fitting salutation of the greatest voice of the French Renaissance to the great humanist to whom that Renaissance owed so much[4]. His duties at the hospital seem

---

reproduced by Marty-Laveaux, III. 261 ff. Copies of parts of the Almanacs for 1533 and 1535, and of the titles of those for 1546, 1548 and 1550, have also been preserved (*ib.* 253—271).

[1] Almanac for 1533 (*ib.* 256).

[2] Marty-Lavaux, *ib.* 229 ff. Several satirical *pronostications*, or skits on the astrological prophecies which found so much favour at this time, are printed in the *Anc. poés. franç.* See esp. the *Pronostication nouvelle* (XII. 144) and *Plenostication de Soncgereux* (*ib.* 168 ff.), between which latter and the *Prognostication* of Rabelais the editors notice many points of similarity.

[3] Marty-Laveaux says 1531, but the date of the first payment of his stipend is Feb. 15, 153⅔.

[4] *ib.* 322. M. Ziesing has shewn conclusively that this letter is addressed to Erasmus and not to Bernard Salignac (whoever he is). There are two copies of it at Zurich, one in the University Library, made 1750-60, and the other in the

to have sat on him somewhat lightly. At the beginning of
1534 he went to Rome in the suite of Jean du Bellay, who had
been sent on a mission to the Pope in the matter of Henry VIII's
divorce. The party reached Rome on the 2nd of February[1].
Having formed the intention of writing a description of the
eternal city, Rabelais at once proceeded with characteristic
energy to make himself acquainted with every nook and corner
of it. *Nulli notam magis domum esse suam quam Romam mihi
Romaeque viculos omnes puto.* But before he had begun to
write his book he learned that a similar work by an Italian,
named Marliani, entitled *Topographia Antiquae Romae,* was in
process of publication. He thereupon renounced his project
and contented himself with writing a preface, addressed to
Jean du Bellay, for an edition of Marliani's work, which was
published in September by Gryphius[2]. He must have got
back to Lyons, if he travelled with Du Bellay, as he probably
did, on April 14[3].

Never before had there seemed so fair a prospect of the
peaceful acceptance of religious reform. The evangelical
preachers had been drawing large congregations in the Louvre
itself. Their bitterest foe, Beda, the pillar of the Sorbonne,
had been put into prison. What wonder if Rabelais thought
it a favourable moment for introducing into a new edition of
Pantagruel, which he was revising for Juste's press, a little
extra mirth at the expense of the Sorbonne, in return for their
having had his book put upon the Index? He then set to
work upon a new volume, which was to take the place of the
Grandes Croniques, as a history of Gargantua. It was published by Juste in the *format Jeanne d'Arc,* but as the title-
page of the only known copy is missing we cannot be sure

town library among a collection of letters and documents, original and copies, of
the 16th and 17th centuries, made by J. H. Hottinger of Zurich (1620—1667).
M. Ziesing believes this latter copy to be the original, and this view is generally
accepted. The letter first appeared with the heading *Bernardo Salignaco* in
the *Clarorum virorum epistolae centum ineditae* (Amsterdam, 1702). See
Th. Ziesing, *Erasme ou Salignac,* 1887.

[1] P. Friedmann, *Anne Boleyn,* I. 276, 1884.
[2] Marty-Laveaux, III. 329 ff.
[3] *Letters and Papers of the reign of Henry VIII,* VII. 200.

either of the year of its publication or of its exact title. But it was probably published before the end of the year 1534 and under the same title as that of the edition of 1535, namely, *La vie inestimable du grand Gargantua, pere de Pantagruel*[1]. Soon, if not immediately, after its publication Rabelais again left Lyons, and by the middle of February 1535 he had been so long absent that applications began to be made for his post at the hospital. A meeting of the governors was held on February 23. Some were for proceeding to an election at once, others were for waiting till Easter to see if Rabelais returned or not. One elector had heard that he was at Grenoble, but no one knew for certain where he was. The meeting was adjourned to March 5, when Rabelais's post was filled up by the appointment of Pierre du Castel. We read in the minutes that it was the second occasion on which Rabelais had been absent without leave[2]. On this occasion it is not difficult to account for his absence. The affair of the Placards (October 18, 1534) had resulted in a vigorous persecution of the French Protestants. It was not till the edict of Coucy (July 16, 1535) that the king began to relent. Before that date the author of *Gargantua* may well have thought it desirable to have no address.

He was not long without employment. In July 1535 he again accompanied Jean du Bellay, lately made a Cardinal[3], to Rome, this time in the capacity of physician. On his way he stopped at Ferrara, where he must have met Clement Marot, who was now residing at the ducal court as secretary to the Duchess[4]. While at Rome he kept up a correspondence

[1] See Appendix C. The type is the same as that of the edition of 1535. The book was probably sent to press before the news of the affair of the Placards (Oct. 18, 1534) reached Lyons, for after that date Rabelais would hardly have ventured on its publication. If so, the printing would naturally have been finished before the end of the year. Possibly Rabelais dated Grandgousier's letter (c. xxix.) Sept. 20 because he happened to be writing it on that day. The edition of 1535, which bears the publisher's name, cannot have been published before July 16, the date of the edict of Coucy, for no attempt is made in it to tone down the Protestant passages.

[2] Marty-Laveaux, III. 326 ff.

[3] May 21, 1535.   [4] *Ante*, p. 67.

with his old friend, the Bishop of Maillezais, telling him the latest political news and local gossip, or giving him directions about various seeds and plants which he had sent him[1]. Nor did he neglect his own interests. Conscious of having committed great irregularities with regard to his Orders he took occasion of this visit to Rome to set himself right with the Church. Accordingly he addressed to the Holy Father a petition in which he stated his offences with great candour. He had, he says, abandoned the habit of his Order for that of a secular priest, had led a wandering life, had studied medicine and taken a medical degree, had lectured and practised, and had celebrated Mass and taken part in other services of the Church in an occasional and irregular way. For this he expressed extreme penitence and begged the Holy Father to give him absolution for the past, and to allow him to re-enter any Benedictine monastery that would receive him, and hold any benefice that might be conferred on him, and at the same time to continue the practice of medicine provided that he took no fees, and did not cauterise or use the knife[2]. The required permission was granted without much delay[3].

In March 1536 Cardinal du Bellay, having made a hurried flight from Rome to avoid assassination, returned to France, and doubtless Rabelais returned with him[4]. In March of the

---

[1] *Les Epistres de Maistre François Rabelais, escrites pendant son voyage d'Italie,* 1651. The brothers Scévole and Louis de Sainte-Marthe, the authors of *Gallia Christiana,* who edited these letters, make sixteen of them. But they really form only three dispatches, each dispatch being divided into several parts written on different occasions. The dates of the dispatches are December 30, [1535]; Jan. 28, 1536; Feb. 15, 1536. The editors wrongly assigned the first dispatch to 1536. These extant letters are evidently only a portion of the whole correspondence, as Rabelais refers to letters written by him on Oct. 18 and 22, 1535, and on Nov. 29, 1535. The authenticity of the letters has been recently examined by M. Jacques Boulenger (*Rev. des Études Rab.,* I. 97 ff.) and shewn to be beyond doubt.

[2] Marty-Laveaux, III. 336 ff. There is no date to the petition, but Rabelais in his first letter to the Bishop of Maillezais (Dec. 30, 1535) refers to it as having been sent.

[3] *ib.* 348 ff.

[4] Heulhard, p. 88. See also *Letters and Papers of the reign of Henry VIII,* X. 203. "The Bishop of Paris is come from Rome suddenly and secretly and glad that he might so escape. March 20, Paris." A letter from the Cardinal de Tournon to the Chancellor Du Bourg, dated from Lyons, August 10, in which he

following year we find him at Paris taking part in that dinner in honour of Dolet of which mention has been made in an earlier chapter[1]. It will be remembered that Dolet, in his account of it, describes Rabelais as "the glory of the healing art," and for the next two years he devoted himself almost entirely to medicine. Returning to Montpellier he took his degree of Licentiate in April or May of 1537, and that of Doctor on the following 22nd of May[2]. Having been appointed one of the four *professores ordinarii* of the Faculty of Medicine, he chose as the subject of his lectures for the winter term (October 18 to the eve of Palm Sunday) a book of the *Prognostics* of Hippocrates[3].

The next recorded fact about him is that on November 17, 1537, a gold crown was paid to the proctor on his behalf for an 'anatomy,' or demonstration on a human body in the medical theatre[4]. A similar demonstration which he gave at Lyons in the following year was commemorated by Dolet in a Latin poem[5]. It must be remembered that the dissection of the human body, though it had been practised in Italy for two centuries, was still a rare event in France. At Paris, in accordance with an immemorial custom, four bodies a year were allowed to be dissected. At Montpellier the statutes of 1340 provided for an 'anatomy' at least every two years[6], and the Faculty of Medicine were entitled to the body of one criminal a year[7]. But these rare dissections were performed in a perfunctory and ignorant manner, being left entirely to the barber-surgeon who acted as prosector to the professor.

refers to Rabelais as being in that town, is almost certainly to be assigned to 1536. (Desmarest and Rathery, I. 36.)

[1] *Ante*, p. 25.

[2] Marty-Laveaux, III. 372; Dubouchet, pp. 55—57, with facsimiles opp. pp. 53 and 64. Rabelais paid his fees for the licence on April 3.

[3] Dubouchet, pp. 69—72.

[4] *ib.* p. 73.

[5] *Cuiusdam epitaphium qui exemplo edito strangulatus publico postea Lugduni sectus est, Francisco Rabelæso, medico doctissimo, fabricam corporis interpretante.* *Doleti carmina*, Lyons, 1538, p. 164.

[6] *Cartulaire de Montpellier*, I. 344.

[7] *ib.* 680. This right is referred to by Guillaume Bouchet in his *Sérées*, ed. 'Roybet,' III. 59.

The professor himself seldom, if ever, handled the knife ; and
he was generally less competent to do so than even the barber-
surgeon. Vesalius, who attended Sylvius's lectures at Paris
between 1533 and 1536, and for part of this time acted
as prosector to Jean Günther of Andernach, records the
difficulties which surrounded a student of human anatomy in
this early dawn of the science. He says that he never saw a
knife in Günther's hands except at meals[1]. Sylvius, it is true,
made certain discoveries which he could only have arrived at
by practical work[2], but Vesalius speaks of the unsatisfactory
nature of the dissecting work at his demonstrations, the
anatomical preparations being confined to the bones of dogs[3].
Vesalius himself used to prowl round the gibbet at Montfaucon
and fight with the dogs for the arm or leg of a criminal[4].
There is no reason for supposing that Rabelais's knowledge
of anatomy was superior to that of Günther or Sylvius, and
doubtless his regard for his Orders went so far as to prevent
him from actually using the knife himself at his demonstrations,
but the fact of his lecturing on the human body at all stamps
him as one of the most advanced men of science of his time[5].

Rabelais left Montpellier in 1538, probably soon after
Easter, when his course of lectures was finished. About this
time he was appointed by his friend Cardinal du Bellay to a
canonry in his recently secularised Benedictine abbey of Saint-
Maur des Fossés, near Paris, " a paradise of salubrity, amenity,
serenity, convenience, delights, and all honest pleasures of
agriculture and country life[6]." Close by was the magnificent
château which Philibert de l'Orme was building for the
Cardinal. But the new canon was "tortured by a con-

---

[1] Quoted by M. Roth, *Andreas Vesalius*, Berlin, 1892, p. 67.

[2] I owe this information to Professor Macalister.

[3] See the preface to the *De humani corporis fabrica*, 1543, 3, r°, and comp.
Noel du Fail, *Contes d'Eutrapel*, ed. C. Hippeau, II. 15, where there is an
interesting account of Sylvius's lectures.

[4] Vesalius, *Opera* (Leyden, 1725), II. 680.

[5] It is noteworthy that Gargantua in his famous letter to Pantagruel is made to
say, "*Par frequentes anatomies acquiers toy parfaicte congnoissance de l'autre monde,
qui est l'homme.*"

[6] Letter to the Cardinal de Châtillon prefixed to Book IV.

scientious scruple" (*angitur scrupulo conscientiae*). The late Pope, Clement VII, had, as we have seen, given him leave to enter a Benedictine monastery, and if he had been already admitted to Saint-Maur at the date of the papal Bull which authorised its secularisation (June 13, 1533), he would have become a Canon with the rest of the monks. But he had not been admitted and its position was therefore irregular. Accordingly he addressed a petition to Paul III begging that this might be set right[1].

In July 1540 we find him at Turin in the service of Guillaume du Bellay, now governor of Piedmont[2]. Here he employed part of his time in writing a Latin account of his patron's military exploits[3]. He doubtless accompanied his patron on a temporary visit to France, which extended from November 1541 to May 1542[4], for in the first half of 1542 he was at Lyons seeing through the press a new edition of *Gargantua* and *Pantagruel*. It was a work which required considerable care and discretion. Since the treaty of Nice (June 1538), Francis had been resolute in his purpose of extirpating heresy from his kingdom. Rabelais therefore, who, as he frankly tells us, was a martyr *jusques au feu exclusivement*, went carefully through his two books expurgating all dangerous words and phrases, and especially all references to the Sorbonne. Judge then of his disgust when almost immediately after the publication of Juste's revised edition there appeared another from the press of his friend Dolet, which, while it purported to be revised and largely augmented by the author, was in fact a mere reproduction of the old text. He was naturally furious, and taking advantage of a re-issue of Juste's edition by his successor in business, Pierre de Tours, he wrote a notice from the printer to the reader, in which not only Dolet's special

---

[1] Marty-Laveaux, III. 369. We have not the Pope's reply, but it was doubtless favourable.

[2] There are extant three letters from G. Pellicier, then ambassador at Venice, to Rabelais, the earliest dated July 23, 1540, and the latest May (Heulhard, p. 143) 20, 1541, all of which were evidently addressed to Turin (*ib*. 382—386).

[3] Du Verdier, III. 51, says that a French translation of this work by Claude Massuau was published in 1542. The original does not exist.

[4] Heulhard, p. 153.

offence against himself, but his whole character as a scholar and a printer, were dealt with in lively and expressive language[1].

On January 10, 1543, Rabelais stood by the death-bed of his friend and patron, Guillaume du Bellay. He died at Saint-Symphorien near Lyons[2]. During this and the two following years the Third book of *Pantagruel* was written, and by the autumn of 1545 it was nearly ready for publication[3]. The times were more dangerous than ever. Dolet was lying in the *Conciergerie* awaiting his sentence of death; Marot had died in exile a year previously; and in the spring the terrible massacre of the Vaudois had taken place. A man had been burnt at Chinon, Rabelais's birthplace, and at the beginning of the year a secretary of the Cardinal du Bellay had been burnt at Paris. If the Cardinal could not protect his secretary, how was he to protect his physician? Pondering these things Rabelais armed himself with a privilege for ten years from the King, in which it was duly set out that our beloved and trusty Master François Rabelais having written "two volumes of the heroic deeds and sayings of Pantagruel, no less useful than delectable," had, owing to the perversion of the text in various places by the printers, abstained from publishing the continuation of the same; but that "being daily importuned by the learned and studious men of our kingdom" to publish the said continuation, he has now petitioned us to grant him a privilege[4]. Was there ever such delightful humour in an official document? The advantage of it was that it enabled Rabelais to lay the blame of any heretical passages in his earlier books on the wicked printers. The new volume appeared in 1546, printed and published by Chrestien Wechel, with the author's name for the first time on the title-page[5]. But in spite of his precautions Rabelais, either shortly before or shortly after its publication, judged it prudent to make a

[1] See Appendix C.

[2] *Pant.* iii. 21; iv. 27.

[3] The 21st chapter could not have been written till after Du Bellay's death, and probably the book was not begun till then or even later.

[4] Dated Sept. 19, 1545; Marty-Laveaux, III. 387 ff.

[5] See Appendix C.

hasty flight. The place of his refuge was Metz, where he was appointed physician to the town at an annual stipend of 120 *livres*. He held the post from Easter 1546 to Midsummer 1547[1]. By July 10, 1547, he had apparently returned to Paris, for a passage in the *Sciomachie* seems to point to his presence at the celebrated duel between Jarnac and Chataigneraie[2]. The great work still progressed. In 1548 a fragment of a new book, consisting of a prologue and eleven chapters, was published at Lyons, without the printer's name[3]. In June of that year Rabelais was again at Rome with Cardinal du Bellay[4]. Once more it was a good time to be absent from France. In December of the previous year the *Chambre ardente*, the newly instituted Criminal Court of the Paris Parliament for the trial of heresy, had begun its sessions, and they had not been barren[5].

---

[1] An extract from the town accounts runs as follows :—1547, *payé à Mr. Rabellet p. ses gages d'un an c'est à savoir à la saint Remy* 60 *livres, à Pasques darien passé* 60 *livres comme plus con lui ont donné p. le quart d'an de saint Jean* 30 *livres* (Marty-Laveaux, IV. 401, from Paul Ferry, *Observations séculaires*). There are extant two letters which relate to this incident. One is from Rabelais to Jean du Bellay (Marty-Laveaux, III. 390), dated Feb. 6, in which, writing from Metz, he speaks of himself as being in great pecuniary distress. The year is not given, but the expressions used in the letter shew that it was written in 1546, and not in 1547, as by that time he had got a good appointment and had received half-a-year's stipend. Rabelais therefore must have fled from Paris not later than January, 1546. The other letter is from Sturm to Jean du Bellay, and is dated March 28, again without giving the year, which no doubt is 1546. It contains the following passage : *Tempora etiam Rabelaesum eiecerunt e Gallia φεῦ τῶν χρόνων. Nondum ad nos venit. Metis consistit ut audio, inde enim nos salutavit. (Latinae et gallicae clarorum virorum epistolae ad Joannem Cardinalem Bellaium. Bib. Nat., anc. fonds lat. 8584.)* See for the whole incident Ch. Abel, *Rabelais, médecin stipendié de la cité de Metz* (Metz, 1870). He assigns Rabelais's letter to 1547, and thinks it possible that he came to Metz and was appointed physician in 1545. Both of these views seem to me untenable. Nor can I agree with M. Heulhard, who interprets the passage from the accounts as meaning that Rabelais held his post from Easter 1547 to Easter 1548 (*op. cit.* p. 233).

[2] See Moland's edition of Rabelais, p. xxxiii.

[3] See Appendix C. This fragment comprises cc. 1, 5—12, 16—24, and half of 25 of the complete edition, but some additions to these chapters were made afterwards. It was probably begun at Metz on June 9, the day on which Pantagruel put to sea. Chapters 5 and 18 seem to have been written just before the sixth session of the Council of Trent, which opened on July 29, 1546.

[4] Heulhard, p. 262.

[5] Weiss, *La Chambre ardente*, pp. 418—422.

In March 1549 Rabelais sent a series of letters to the
Cardinal of Guise giving an account of the festivities held by
the Cardinal du Bellay in the Piazza di SS. Apostoli, where his
palace was situated, to celebrate the birth of a son to Henry II.
They were published by Gryphius in the same year under the
title of *La Sciomachie et festins faits a Rome*[1]. It was probably
by Du Bellay's advice that Rabelais addressed himself to the
Cardinal of Guise or, to call him by the title by which he is
best known and which he assumed on his uncle's death in the
following year, the Cardinal of Lorraine. For not only was
he all-powerful under the new King, but he was a discerning
patron of men of letters. The prudent Rabelais also acquired
at this time another protector in the Cardinal Odet de Châtillon,
the nephew of Guise's rival, the Constable of Montmorency,
and like Guise a good friend to literature and learning. His
old patron, Jean du Bellay, was now out of favour, so that he
had need of new protectors, especially at this time, when he
was the object of a virulent personal attack from a monk of
Fontevrault named Gabriel de Puits-Herbault. In a Latin
dialogue entitled *Theotimus* he had introduced a passage repre-
senting Rabelais as a glutton, a drunkard, and a dangerous
heretic[2].

Rabelais probably returned to France with Du Bellay,
arriving in July 1550. In the previous January he was
appointed by his patron to the cure of Meudon in the diocese
of Paris, and probably at the same time to that of Saint-
Cristophe du Jambet in the diocese of Le Mans, of which
Du Bellay was also at this time bishop. He must have dis-
charged the duties of this latter parish through a *vicaire*[3], for
he resided at Meudon, and a century later Antoine le Roy
found there traditions, possibly legendary, of the diligent care
with which he tended his flock. The Fourth book was now

[1] Marty-Laveaux, III. 391 ff.

[2] *Putherbei, Turonici, professione Fontebaldei Theotimus, sive de tollendis et
expurgandis malis libris, iis praecipue quos vix incolumi fide ac pietate plerique
legere queant*, 1549, pp. 180—183.

[3] See H. Chardon, *Rabelais, Curé de Saint-Cristophe du Jambet*, Le Mans,
1879.

approaching completion[1]. Rabelais had as usual taken every precaution. Already in August 1550 he had obtained a fresh privilege, in which the wickedness of the printers in corrupting his text was insisted on even more strongly than in the former one. A new prologue was substituted for the one prefixed to the eleven chapters published in 1548, and a letter to the Cardinal de Châtillon was written by way of preface, in which Rabelais protested most stoutly that there was no heresy in his book. The printing was finished on January 28, 1552. In spite of the author's precautions, immediately the book appeared, it was pounced upon and censured by the Faculty of Theology, and the Paris Parliament prohibited its sale for a fortnight pending the King's pleasure (March 1, 155½)[2]. In a second and revised edition the epithets *grand, victorieux et triomphant* were introduced in the prologue before the King's name in honour of his conquest of the three bishoprics[3]. But this flattery did not avail to remove the interdict on the book ; the revised edition appeared without mention of publisher or place of publication, as did an edition of the four books which appeared in 1553[4]. Just before the printing of the Fourth book was finished, on January 9, 1552, Rabelais had resigned both his livings[5]. The reason for this step is impossible to divine. It may have been due to pressure from without, or have been in some way or other connected with the publication of the fourth book. This is the last specific act of Rabelais's life that is known to us, but we hear of him again in November 1552, when Denys Lambin, the well-known scholar, writing from Lyons to a friend at Paris on the third of that month, says that he has heard a rumour that Rabelais has been thrown into prison. A few days later he writes to Henri Estienne

---

[1] Chap. 32 must have been written at any rate after the appearance of Puits-Herbault's book in 1549, and perhaps after the publication of Calvin's *De Scandalis* in 1550 ; chap. 48 after Feb. 8, 1550, the date of the election of Julius III.

[2] Marty-Laveaux, III. 420.

[3] Henry entered Toul on April 13, and Metz on April 18. The revised edition appeared in 1552 with *reueu et corrigé pour la seconde edition* on the title-page. There is a copy in the British Museum (Grenville library).

[4] See Appendix C.

[5] Marty-Laveaux, III. 418 f., and see Chardon, *op. cit.*

that he believes the rumour to be a mere fable, and on
December 5 he tells the same correspondent that he has heard
nothing on the subject of Rabelais[1]. According to an old
tradition his death took place in the year 1553[2]; we know at
any rate for certain that he died before May 1, 1554, for an
epigram by Jacques Tahureau on *Rabelais trespassé* must have
been written before that date[3]. Colletet says that he died
at Paris in the *Rue des Jardins*, and that he was buried in the
cemetery of Saint-Paul.

Such, shorn of all legend, is the life of Rabelais. One
feature of it especially worthy of attention is the high esteem
in which he was held by his contemporaries. His relations to
Guillaume and Jean du Bellay and Geoffroy d'Estissac are
those of a trusted friend rather than of a dependent. His
correspondence with Guillaume Pellicier is on a footing of
perfect equality. With another bishop and ambassador,
Georges d'Armagnac, he also entertained friendly relations.
All these were men in high place and station, the patrons and
princes of Humanism. By those who were more of his own
rank he was regarded with a like respect and affection.
Among his most intimate friends were the distinguished
jurists, André Tiraqueau and Jean de Boyssonne. Marot,
Salmon Macrin, Voulté and Sussanneau addressed French
or Latin verses to him, testifying their friendship and admiration. To these contemporaries he was known as one of the
most eminent physicians of the day, as a man of great and
varied learning, as a warm friend, a delightful companion, a

[1] These references to Rabelais have been recently discovered by M. Henri
Potez in a Latin MS. of the *Bib. Nat.* (*Rev. des Études Rab.*, I. 57, 1903).

[2] The oldest reference to this is in the *Trésor chronologique*, 1647, of the Père
de Saint-Romuald, who was born in 1585. Guy Patin, writing in 1660, gives the
same date (*Lettres*, III. 223). The additional statement that he died on the 9th of
April appears for the first time in a note in the margin of the 1710 edition of
Les lettres de Rabelais escrites pendant son voyage d'Italie (Rathery, I. 64 n.).
In the original edition of this work, published in 1651, the editors, though they
mention the statement of the Père de Saint-Romuald, say that the date of Rabelais's
death is uncertain.

[3] This indication of date has been recently printed by M. Abel Lefranc in the
Rev. des Études Rab., I. 59 ff. May 1, 1554, is the date of the dedicatory letter
prefixed to Tahureau's poems published at Poitiers in that year.

bon vivant and a wit. They also knew him as the author of
a popular and amusing book. That it was the greatest book
that had yet been written in France had naturally not occurred
to them.

2. *His Book.*

We have seen that in 1532 Rabelais revised for a Lyons
publisher, adding some characteristic touches of his own, a
burlesque romance of chivalry which embodied the popular
traditions relating to a beneficent giant named Gargantua[1].
It was apparently while he was engaged upon this work that
it occurred to him to use it as a starting point for an original
work dealing with the history of Pantagruel the son of
Gargantua. This, as we have seen, appeared probably before
the end of the year 1532. Encouraged by its success Rabelais
determined to write a new and worthier account of Gargantua,
yet without altogether rejecting the materials of the popular
story. The description of Gargantua's clothes, the marvellous
mare which he rode, the story of his carrying off the bells of
Notre Dame at Paris—all have their origin in *Les grandes
chroniques.*

The new *Gargantua* opens with an account of the hero's
birth and childhood, and the first thirteen chapters—with the
exception of the inimitable *Les propos des bienyvres*, commonly
known as *Les propos des buveurs*, and the amusing chapter on
Gargantua's hobby-horses—are of no great interest except to

---

[1] There was until recent years considerable discussion as to whether Gargantua
was invented by Rabelais or whether he already existed in popular tradition.
But the mention of him by Claude Bourdigné in the *ballade* prefixed to the
Legende Pierre Faifeu, which he finished writing on March 31, 1531 (prob. 1532),
and which was printed in 1532, conclusively proves his prior existence. Equally
conclusive are Sebillot's investigations of the traditional lore on the subject in the
various districts of France. Stories relating to Gargantua are most plentiful in
Brittany, which agrees with the fact that he is connected in *Les grandes chroniques*
with the Arthurian cycle (see P. Sebillot, *Gargantua dans les traditions populaires,*
1883).

a thorough-going Pantagruelist, but they serve to show the extraordinary verve and overflowing vitality of the writer. It is with the account of Gargantua's education that the real interest begins. This occupies the next eleven chapters (xiv–xxiv), and includes the famous episode of the carrying off of the bells of *Notre Dame*, and the speech of Maître Janotus de Bragmardo, who is sent by the University of Paris to demand their restitution. This part is at once a good-humoured but thoroughly effective satire on the old learning and an exposition of Rabelais's own views on education.

The next and longest section of the book (cc. xxv–li) is occupied by the account of the war between Grandgousier and his neighbour Picrochole. Some of the chapters are models of narrative style (cc. xxv and xxvi) and even of historical narrative (cc xlvii and xlviii), while Grandgousier's letter (c. xxix) and the speech of his envoy Gallet to Picrochole (c. xxx), though perhaps more open to criticism, are noble specimens of eloquence. The account of the war is mainly a satire on schemes of universal conquest, but it also contains some of Rabelais's most effective attacks on monasticism and pilgrimages, and generally on the principle of substituting religious observances for work and the duties of a citizen. We are here also introduced to the celebrated Friar Jean des Entommeures, whose presence on the scene is always the signal for exuberant gaiety. Then there is an exceedingly comic episode in the account of how Gargantua ate six pilgrims in his salad (c. xxxviii). Finally, after ridiculing the monastic system, Rabelais gives us his own idea of a collegiate society in the form of the famous abbey of Thelema.

It is almost universally agreed that the first book of *Pantagruel* was written before *Gargantua*. Rathery alone among Rabelais's commentators has maintained that there was an earlier version of *Gargantua* other than *Les grandes chroniques*, which was written before *Pantagruel*. The arguments in favour of the accepted view are briefly as follows. Firstly, in the prologue to *Pantagruel* Rabelais refers to *Les grandes chroniques* and not to *La vie tres-horrifique du geant*

Gargantua as having preceded it ; secondly, in the last chapter of *Pantagruel* he distinctly calls it *ce premier livre* ; thirdly, several topics, such as the infancy and education of the hero, which are briefly touched on in *Pantagruel*, are developed at length in *Gargantua* ; fourthly, characters such as Friar John, Ponocrates and other attendants of Gargantua who figure in the third and fourth books do not appear at all in the first book of *Pantagruel*, for the good reason that they have not yet been called into existence. A less definite though hardly less convincing argument for the priority of *Pantagruel* is its inferiority. *Gargantua* is perhaps on the whole the finest of all the books. If it is less philosophical than the later books, it has greater freshness, more action, more genuine fun, less display of learning. *Pantagruel*, on the other hand, bears evident marks not only of haste, but of a hand not yet warmed to its work. Some of the best episodes are not original, several of the chapters are decidedly dull, and though it has the distinction of introducing Panurge to us, much that relates to that worthy forms the coarsest and most repulsive part of the whole work.

The book opens, like Gargantua, with an account of the hero's birth and childhood (cc. i–iv). Then follows his encounter with the Limousin student, one of whose speeches is identical with a passage in Tory's *Champ fleury*[1]. The next chapter contains the well-known burlesque catalogue of the library of Saint-Victor. Then comes the admirable letter of Gargantua, which contains the germ of that contrast between the old and the new methods of education which is worked out at much greater length in *Gargantua*. In chapter ix we are introduced to Panurge : chapters x–xiii, which relate how Pantagruel gave judgment in a law-suit between two great lords, are a somewhat ponderous, though occasionally amusing, satire on the legal procedure of the day. After this Panurge becomes for a time the most prominent figure in the story. His acts and deeds, including his discomfiture of the Englishman Thaumaste in a disputation carried on by signs, occupy the next nine chapters (xiv–xxii). Then follows the account

---

[1] *Ante*, p. 33.

of the war against the Dipsodes, for the most part written in
the giant-story vein (cc. xxiii–xxxi), the best chapter of the
section, which relates Epistemon's experiences in the other
world (c. xxx), being directly inspired by Lucian. Two
chapters follow of somewhat commonplace foolery, one of
which is a developement, with the help of another reminiscence
of Lucian, of an episode in *Les grandes chroniques*, and then
with an address to the reader the book ends.

Between the publication of *Gargantua* and that of the
Third book, which continues the story of Pantagruel, nearly
twelve years elapsed, and probably there was a considerable
interval between their composition. At any rate the Third
book shews a marked difference in character. There is less
action and more argument, less practical suggestion and more
philosophy. The whole tone is consequently more serious,
and if it is not on that account less provocative of laughter,
it is no longer the laughter of broad farce, but of genuine
humour. To Rabelais as to all other men of genius "years
had brought the philosophic mind." In conformity with this
more serious spirit the framework of a giant-story with
which Rabelais had set out is now definitely abandoned.
Pantagruel henceforth appears no longer as a giant, but as an
ordinary mortal, raised above his fellows only by his superior
wisdom and virtue.

After an exceedingly witty discussion between Pantagruel
and Panurge as to the advantage of being in debt, which gives
occasion to one of Rabelais's most brilliant lyrical outbursts,
we are introduced to what now becomes the central theme of
the work, the question of Panurge's marriage. Panurge has
no particular lady in his eye, but he is matrimonially inclined.
But first he would like to be assured that his marriage will
be successful, and particularly as regards three points : first,
whether his wife will be faithful ; secondly, whether she will
beat him ; and thirdly, whether she will rob him. He accordingly resorts to various methods of ascertaining the future,
sortes Virgilianae, dreams, a Sibyl and a mute. In each case
he receives an answer which to everyone but himself appears
perfectly unambiguous on every point. His wife will be un-

faithful, she will beat him, and she will rob him. Panurge, however, invariably interprets the answers in a contrary sense. Next he consults an old dying poet named Raminagrobis (said to stand for Cretin), who gives him a completely ambiguous answer, and then an astrologer, Herr Trippa (Cornelius Agrippa), who assures him that his wife will be unfaithful. Still Panurge is not satisfied. Accordingly a theologian, a doctor, a lawyer and a philosopher are invited to dinner, and the question is propounded to them in turn. The theologian's advice is excellent and practical, the physician's wholly irrelevant, and the philosopher's absolutely colourless. The lawyer, Judge Bridoye, or Bridlegoose, did not appear, being engaged in defending before a superior court a judgment which he had recently delivered. The company accordingly adjourn to hear him. His case was a very simple one. His sight not being so good as it was, he could no longer distinguish clearly the pips of the dice which it was his habit to consult before giving judgment.

After this delightful interlude, which occupies five chapters, Panurge continues his quest and consults Triboulet, the famous court fool. His answer being interpreted in different senses by himself and Pantagruel, they determine to consult the oracle of the Bottle. The book concludes with the famous description, extending to four chapters, of the virtues of the herb Pantagruelion.

The Fourth book is occupied with the voyage to the Divine Bottle. The first notable incident is that of Panurge and the sheep, one of the most humorous stories in the whole of Rabelais, the idea of which is borrowed from Merlin Coccaye. The voyagers visit in turn the islands of Medamothi (Nowhere), Ennasin, where the noseless ones dwell, Cheli, the land of lip-service and false compliment, the island of the Chiquanous or Catchpoles, the islands of Tohu and Bohu (Waste and Void), where in the account of the death of the giant Bringuenarilles we have another hit at schemes of universal conquest. Then follows the well-known description of the storm, remarkable for the wonderful gusto of the language rather than for the accuracy of its observation; then

the visit to the island of the Macreons or Long-lived, in the
account of which Rabelais introduces the story of the death
of Pan, taken from Plutarch's treatise on Oracles.   Next the
voyagers come to the island of Tapinois, where, under the
figure of Quaresmeprenant, the practice of fasting is attacked.
The *Isle Farouche*, inhabited by the Andouilles (Chitterlings),
which they next visit, and where they have to fight against
the inhabitants, represents the land of the opponents of fasting,
either Switzerland or some other Protestant country.   The
island of Ruach (the Hebrew word for wind) is their next
halting-place, and this is followed by another satire on the
two opposing religious parties, the account of the Papefigues
and Papimanes (cc. xlv–liv).   The last part of the book is
somewhat inferior to the rest.   It comprises the account of
the frozen winds, borrowed from Antiphanes, and the ingenious
but somewhat laboured panegyric on Messer Gaster, the
source of all inventions, concluding with five chapters of little
interest, which, like the last chapters of the second book, gives
one the idea that they were written merely to make the book
of the required length.

We now come to the Fifth book, and to the vexed question
as to whether it is by Rabelais or not.   The facts of its publication are as follows.   In the year 1562, nine years after
Rabelais's death, there appeared without name of publisher or
printer or place of publication a thin octavo volume of thirty-
two leaves entitled *L'isle Sonnante par Francois Rabelais.*   It
consisted of sixteen chapters, being the first fifteen chapters of
the fifth book as it is now generally printed and a chapter
entitled *L'isle des Apedeftes*[1].

In 1564 appeared the complete Fifth book with the title of
Cinquiesme et dernier livre.   It contained forty-seven chapters,
that on the Apedefts being omitted.   On the last page is a
quatrain beginning *Rabelais est il mort, Voicy encour un livre,*
and signed *Nature quite,* which is said to be an anagram of
Jean Turquet[2].   There is no publisher's name and no place of

---

[1] See Appendix C.

[2] See Appendix C.   The well-known Turquet de Mayenne, physician to
James I and Charles I, was the son of a Jean Turquet of Lyons, who in 1570

publication, but the type is identical with that used for a
re-impression which appeared in the following year with the
name of Jean Martin of Lyons. In another edition by the
same publisher, of 1567, the chapter on the Apedefts is inserted
as the seventh chapter. Besides the printed editions of the
fifth book there is a manuscript of it in the *Bibliothèque
Nationale*. It omits the chapter on the Apedefts and also
chapters xxiii and xxiv (the account of the game of chess),
but has after what is now chapter xxxii an entirely new chapter
entitled *Comme furent les dames lanternes servies à souper*, and
a different and much longer ending for the last chapter[1]. The
prologue is represented by a short fragment, less than a third
of the length of the one in the printed text, and ending
abruptly after the word *entre* and before the words *cette aage
courante l'an mil cinq cens cinquante* of the prologue as
printed.

The circumstances of the publication of the Fifth book were
therefore peculiar and calculated to arouse suspicion. The
only express statements on the subject by persons who were
alive at the time of the publication are the two following.
The bibliographer Antoine du Verdier, who was born in 1544,
says in his *Prosopographie* (1604) that the *Isle Sonnante* was
the work of (*faicte par*) a student of Valence. Louis Guyon,
a physician of great learning, who died in 1630 at an advanced
age, is equally explicit. In the thirtieth chapter of his *Diverses
Leçons*, published in the same year as the *Prosopographie*, after
speaking of Rabelais's religious opinions, he says: "As for
the last book that is put with his works, entitled *L'isle
Sonnante*, which seems openly to blame and ridicule the
functionaries of the Catholic Church, I protest that he did

married the daughter of Antoine le Maçon, the translator of the *Decameron*.
There was also a Louis Turquet, who translated *El Menosprecio de la Corte, Le
grand Olympe* (1583), and the *De vanitate* of Cornelius Agrippa.

[1] *MS. français* 2156, *Cinquiesme livre de Pantagruel, fragment de prologue*,
126 leaves, v°. of last leaf blank, written in the same hand throughout, which is
certainly not Rabelais's. The numbering is peculiar. After c. 12 the numbering
is by a different hand. After c. 14 it runs as follows: 38-15 (= xv of Marty-
Laveaux's edition), 39-16 (= xvi), 50, 51, 52, 53 (= xvii-xx), 4 chapters not
numbered (= xxi, xxii, xxv, xxvi), 58 (= xxvii); the rest are not numbered.

not write it, for it was written (*se fit*) a long time after his
death. I was at Paris when it was written, and I know well
who the author was. He was not a physician." It will be
noticed that both these writers speak of the *Isle Sonnante*,
the title under which the first instalment of the book appeared,
though Guyon apparently uses the term as signifying the
whole book.

It is said that neither of their testimonies is worthy of
credence, Du Verdier's because in his account of Guillaume
des Autels in his *Bibliothèque*[1] he says that when he was a
scholar at Valence he wrote an imitation of Rabelais, but does
not mention the *Isle Sonnante*; Guyon's because it forms part
of a defence of medical men against the charge of impiety.
But there is little force in either of these objections. The
statements at least prove that two contemporaries, one of
whom was a professed bibliographer, did not accept Rabelais's
authorship. On the other hand the Fifth book has generally
been accepted as Rabelais's genuine work from the time of its
appearance till within the last half century. As early as 1584
we find Étienne Tabourot, who was born in 1549, quoting in his
Bigarrures a passage from chapter xii as by Rabelais[2]. Again,
Vauquelin de la Fresnaye, who was born in 1536, in a passage
written about the same time as Tabourot's refers to Rabelais
as the creator of Grippeminaud[3].

Coming to the next century we find the physician Guy
Patin, who was a great admirer of Rabelais and had a portrait
of him in his dining-room, unhesitatingly accepting the Fifth
book as by him[4]. On the other hand Colletet, a contemporary
of Patin, in his life of Rabelais only speaks of four books.
Clearly the external evidence is not conclusive either for or
against the authenticity. We must therefore have recourse to
the internal evidence. First of all we find passages in the

---

[1] IV. 64.

[2] See Marty-Laveaux, IV. 324.

[3] *Œuvres*, ed. Travers, p. 251. In the *Contes d'Eutrapel* of Noel de Fail,
published in 1585 but probably written some years before, there are two references
to Frère Fredon (ed. Hippeau, I. 129, II. 4) and the phrase *Passons outre* occurs
(I. 138).

[4] *Lettres*, 3 vols. 1846, II. 451.

book which must in all probability have been written after Rabelais's death. The reference in chapter xviii to Julius Caesar Scaliger's *Exercitationes contra Cardanum* must be later than 1557, when that work was published, and the tedious repetition of the words *Or ça* in chapters xii and xiii looks very much as if it were borrowed from the twenty-first story of Des Periers's *Joyeux devis*, which did not appear till 1558[1]. Secondly there are passages, even whole chapters, which are repetitions from the earlier books. The strongest instance is the prologue, in the latter part of which occur several passages which are repeated almost verbatim from the prologue to the third book. But also the greater part of chapter ix (*L'isle des Ferrements*) is borrowed from the earlier books. In chapter xvii we have another shipwreck, which is possibly a first sketch of the famous shipwreck in the fourth book. Other suspicious circumstances are that the manuscript, the partial edition of 1562 and the complete edition of 1564, each give a different version of the opening of the first chapter, and that in chapter xvi there is no account of how Panurge was nearly killed to correspond to the heading of the chapter. But one need not continue this line of argument. All critics are at any rate agreed that the Fifth book is not as it left Rabelais's hands ; indeed, anyone acquainted with the methods of sixteeeth century editors would expect to find not only passages interpolated but possibly whole chapters.

But can we go further than this and say definitely, as some critics do, that Rabelais did not write the Fifth book[2]? Here the manuscript comes in to help us. Though it is evidently the work of an unlearned and unintelligent scribe, there can be no doubt that in some places it alone gives, at any rate approximately, the true reading. I will mention some of the most striking instances. In chapter xx the reading of the manuscript is *fontaine de jovence*, of the printed text *fontaine*

---

[1] The monosyllabic answers of the Frère Fredon in c. xxvii may be taken from the 38th story of the *Joyeux devis*, but the idea occurs in the *Dialogue de Messieurs de Mallepaye et de Baillevent*, published in an edition of Villon's poems in 1532.

[2] *Die...Fortsetzung des Romans hat er nicht geschrieben*, Birch-Hirschfeld, *op. cit.* p. 257.

de jeunesse, the right reading being of course *fontaine de Jouvence.* Again, in chapter xxxix the manuscript has *echo, les meurs et les esprits,* which the editor has corrected to *echo, paroles, meurs* ; but if we turn to Pliny, *n. h.* 35. 10. 98, we see that it ought to run *ethe* ($\dot{\eta}\theta\eta$), *les meurs et les esprits.* Another comparison with Pliny (*n. h.* 34. 8. 55) shows that the reading of the manuscript in chapter xlii, in a passage referring to the canon of Polycletus, *par l'aide de l'art* (artis opere), is absolutely right, while the editor by reading *apprendre de l'art* has made nonsense of it. So in the same chapter the printed text has *Pompeie Pauline,* while the manuscript has *Lullie Pauline,* which is right with the exception of a single letter, the true reading being *Lollie Pauline,* as we see by reference not only to Pliny but to the *Hypnerotomachia Polyphili,* which is evidently the immediate source of the passage. In chapter xxix the printed text has *Henry Clerberg,* while the manuscript has *Hans Clebeir,* the true reading being *Hans Cleberg* (i.e. Kleberg), the name of a German merchant who lived at Lyons. In chapter xxxiii the printed text has *les orangiers de Suraine,* where the true reading *San Remo* is revealed by *San Rame* of the manuscript. Finally it may be noticed that in a few places a blank is left in the manuscript, evidently because the scribe failed to decipher the words, and that in the printed text either no attempt is made to supply the blank or a pure conjecture is adopted. An instance occurs at the close of chapter viii, where the manuscript has *un païsant en* followed by a blank.

We learn then from these and other variations between the manuscript and the printed text that in certain parts of the Fifth book the manuscript is a copy of an original draft written by someone who was not the editor of the printed text; further, that this unknown writer was a man of considerable classical learning decidedly greater than that of the editor ; and lastly, that he was acquainted with the *Hypnerotomachia Polyphili.*

This last fact carries us a stage further. The work of Francesco Colonna was certainly known to Rabelais, for he mentions it in the ninth chapter of *Gargantua* and in the

Briefve declaration appended to the fourth book. Moreover, as Mr W. F. Smith has pointed out, some of the details in the description of the abbey of Thelema seem like reminiscences of the same work[1]. Now, as he and others have shewn, not only is the whole of chapters xxiii and xxiv (the games of chess) taken from the *Hypnerotomachia*, but long passages in chapters xxxvi–xliii come from the same source[2].

On the combined evidence then of the manuscript, of Rabelais's acquaintance with Colonna's book, and of the thought and language, I should regard from chapter xxxii to the end as the genuine work of Rabelais, intended by him to form the conclusion of his book. With regard to the evidence from thought and language I am well aware how illusory this is, and that what may appear to one man as bearing the infallible stamp of authenticity may be as unhesitatingly rejected by another as on the face of it spurious. I may add that in the delicate operation of testing the style I have used as criteria Rabelais's practice with regard to syntax and to the order of his words, and especially his unfailing ear for a harmonious cadence. On similar evidence I would assign to him chapters xxiii and xxiv, which contain the account of the game of chess.

With regard to the rest of the book it is far more difficult to form a judgment. There are a considerable number of passages, varying in length from nearly a whole chapter to only a few lines, which one may with little hesitation regard as Rabelais's work. Some of these may be fragmentary notes, which Rabelais had intended to work up into a complete narrative ; others may be first drafts which he had deliberately discarded in favour of improved versions which appeared in the earlier books. In this latter category I would include nearly the whole of chapter xi, the close of chapter xiii, and possibly part of chapter xv. At the very beginning of the episode of the *chats fourrez* (chapter xi) the manuscript has,

[1] *Modern Quarterly*, April 1899, 238 ff. Compare *Gargantua*, c. 55 with *Hypnerotomachia*, f[1] r° and g[2] v°.

[2] W. F. Smith, *loc. cit.* and H. K. Söltoft-Jensen in *Rev. d'hist. litt.* III. 608 ff. The latter considers this as strong evidence against the authenticity of this part, but I do not think that anyone well acquainted with Rabelais's methods would agree with him.

in place of a reference to the island of Cassade, the words *avoit battu le Chiquanous passant procuration*, which looks as if this part was originally meant to follow after chapter xvi of the Fourth book. It may well have been inspired by the *Chambre Ardente*, which had begun its work in December 1547, shortly before the publication of the Fourth book in its original form. In the same way I should regard the fourth chapter, most of which seems to me genuine, as matter which Rabelais had not cared to use, while the seventeenth is possibly a first draft of the storm. Of the other chapters the seventh (the apologue of the charger and the ass), the twenty-fifth (island of Odes) and possibly the twenty-second seem to me to be Rabelais's work with some additions[1]. How much of the rest is unfinished or rejected work and how much is positively spurious is very difficult to determine. One thing at any rate is clear. We must not assert in a sweeping and dogmatic way that the whole Fifth book is or is not by Rabelais. Each chapter must be tested separately. That Rabelais's manuscript was more or less tampered with must be evident to everyone, especially to those who are acquainted with the unscrupulous ways of sixteenth century editors and publishers. We know that in 1548 a Parisian bookseller published an unauthorised edition of Noel du Fail's *Propos rustiques* with a considerable amount of interpolated matter[2], and that large additions equally spurious were made to the tales of Bonaventure des Periers. Finally we know that in 1549 an impudent attempt was made to palm off as a fifth book by Rabelais a patchwork made out of two old and well-known works[3].

---

[1] In c. xxv the MS. reading *les voyagiers* souvent es *habitans du païs demandoient* is clearly right, that of the printed text being nonsense.

[2] See A. de la Borderie's edition, pp. vi, vii.

[3] See H. Stein, *Un Rabelais apocryphe de* 1549, 1901; A. Tilley, *A spurious book of Pantagruel, Modern Language Quarterly* IV. 91, 1901; H. Schneegans, *Der Münchener "Rabelais" aus dem Jahre* 1549, *Zeitschr. franz. Spr.* XXIV. 262, 1902; and especially A. Lefranc, *Un prétendu vᵉ livre de Rabelais, Rev. des Études Rab.* I. 29 ff., 122 ff., 1903, where it is conclusively shewn that the greater part is a mere reproduction of certain chapters of the French translation of Brant's *Ship of Fools*, while the rest is taken from a work entitled *Les Reynars traversant les voyes perilleuses des folles fiances du monde*, which appeared under the name of Brant but was really written by Rabelais's friend, Jean Bouchet.

The problem too is complicated by the appearance in 1538 of a work entitled *Le voyage et navigation que fist Panurge disciple de Pantagruel,* and generally known as *Le disciple de Pantagruel*[1], which is certainly not by Rabelais, but which has a chapter on the *Andouilles,* and one describing the arrival of the voyagers in the country of the Lanterns followed by a banquet given by the Queen of the Lanterns. It was reprinted at Rouen in 1545 under the title of *La navigation du compagnon à la bouteille*[2].

There has been a tendency in recent years to represent Rabelais as a grave person who, under colour of a buffoonery wholly alien to his character, was solely concerned with the teaching of profound philosophic truths. This is perhaps the natural result of a reaction against the old view that Rabelais was a mere buffoon, but it goes too far in the other direction. Rabelais's laughter is as much a part of him as his philosophy:

> *Mieulx est de ris que de larmes escrire,*
> *Pource que rire est le propre de l'homme.*

As in the case of Molière, his main purpose was none the less serious because he loved laughter.

It is perhaps therefore well to insist at the outset on the comic side of his book. There is much in it that is neither witty nor humorous, but simply ludicrous. The account of how Gargantua ate the six pilgrims in his salad, the description of his perplexity as to whether he should laugh for joy at the birth of his son or weep for sorrow at the death of his wife, the derivation of La Beauce from *je trouve beau ce,* the whole scene between Panurge and the sheep-merchant, the sayings and doings of brother Jean des Entommeures—all these proceed from sheer gaiety of heart and exuberant spirits. For in all these episodes the fun lies less in the conception than in the execution, in the natural bubbling over of irrepressible merriment.

---

[1] Reprinted in 1875 with a notice by P. Lacroix.

[2] See Brunet, *Recherches* pp. 113–116; and for the various titles under which it was frequently reprinted, Arnstädt, p. 69; Schneegans, pp. 272–278.

But Rabelais's fun has some defects. It is occasionally
tedious, as in the account of the disputation by signs, and it is
too often not only coarse but indecent. It may be said in his
defence that he is never immoral or licentious, that indecency
was habitual to his age, and that in a book which was ostensibly
written for the amusement of a large public it was almost
de rigueur. All this is perfectly true, but it does not altogether
clear Rabelais. One expects a man of his intellectual stature
to be in advance of his age, whereas in this respect he is, as
a matter of fact, behind it. The fault may be trifling, but
the misfortune is infinite, for the result is that no writer of
anything like his importance is so little read. By a large
and growing class of readers, that of women, he is not read
at all.

The real excuse for him lies in his monastic education, and
the absence from his life of all female influence[1]. Though
the presence of virtuous women is a prominent feature of the
Abbey of Thelema, it is remarkable how insignificant a part
woman plays in the rest of his work. "When I say woman
I speak of a sex so frail, so variable, so changeable, so inconstant and imperfect that Nature appears to me (speaking
of her with all respect and reverence) to have strayed far from
the good sense by which she had created and formed all
things when she framed woman[2]." "Little I care for her or
for any other woman," he says, in relating the death of
Gargamelle, the wife of Grandgousier[3].

This contempt for women was, like the obscenity, a relic
of the mediæval literary tradition which hung about Rabelais[4].
To the same cause may be ascribed the cruelty which disfigures some of the incidents of his narrative; such as the
drowning of the sheep-merchant and the shepherds, an
unnecessary conclusion to the story which Rabelais did not
find in Folengo; the relation of how Panurge whipped the

---

[1] It may be noted here that he had a son, named Théodule, who was born at
Lyons and died when two years old. Nothing is known of its mother.
[2] iii. 32.   [3] i. 37.
[4] M. Faguet truly says, *D'humeur Rabelais est moyen âge, et d'esprit il est
Renaissance.*

pages without mercy to help them on their way; the cruel treatment of the Chiquanous.

Rabelais's learning is as exuberant as his gaiety. It is poured forth in season and out of season, and with such perfect simplicity that it can hardly be called pedantry. It is, like his mirth, the overflow of a full reservoir. For none of his contemporaries applied himself with greater avidity than Rabelais to the fountains of literature which the revival of learning had set running. He was, as a contemporary calls him, a veritable *heluo librorum*. And he read the ancients for their subject-matter rather than for their form. The influence indeed exercised by Greek as well as by Latin models on his style is manifest, but of Greek restraint or Latin elaboration there is no trace. Neither does it appear from his book that he fully appreciated the beauty of the ancient masterpieces. He calls Homer the 'paragon of all philologers[1]' and though he speaks of Plato's *beaux dialogues* he mentions them in the same breath with Pausanias and Athenæus[2]. But on the whole it is the learning of the ancients rather than their literary art which attracts him. Historians and scientific writers, Herodotus, Livy, Suetonius, Aristotle, Hippocrates, Galen, are frequently quoted. Works of a miscellaneous or encyclopædic character such as those of the elder Pliny, Aulus Gellius, Athenæus, Julius Pollux, and Ælian, are frequently laid under contribution. There are two ancient writers however, to whom he was especially indebted, Plutarch and Lucian. From Plutarch be borrowed the account of the island of the Macræons, the story of the death of Pan, and the advice given to King Picrochole by his counsellors. But his greatest debt is to Lucian. The whole idea of Pantagruel's voyage, and especially that of the island of Ruach, come from his *True history*; the account of Epistemon's experiences in the other world from his *Nekyomanteia*; the idea of prayers ascending to Jupiter through a trap-door from his *Icaromenippus*; the

---

[1] i. Prol.

[2] ii. 8 (Gargantua's letter). Elsewhere (iv. 37) he speaks of the 'divine Plato.' His copy of Plato, the *editio princeps* of the complete Greek text, Aldus 1513, is in existence (see A. Lefranc in *Bull. du Bib.* 1901, pp. 105 ff. and 169 ff.).

story of the countryman and his axe from his *Timon*. Rabelais was also well acquainted with works of miscellaneous
learning by Renaissance scholars, such as the *Antiquarum
lectionum libri xvi* of Cælius Rhodiginus (Lodovico Ricchieri
of Rovigo), a protégé of Francis I, who died in 1525, and the
De dictis factisque memorabilibus of Battista Fregoso, some-
time Doge of Genoa, who was living at Lyons in 1509. He
also makes use of the *Apophthegmata* of Erasmus and the *De
vanitate scientiarum* of Cornelius Agrippa.

But his reading was by no means confined to books
written in a learned tongue. He was familiar with the
literature of his own country. He quotes Coquillart and
Marot, he often refers to *Pathelin*, he evidently appreciated
Villon, while to one of Raulin's sermons he owes the story of
Panurge and the church-bells. His knowledge of the contemporary literature of Italy was considerable. Colonna, as
we have seen, furnishes the chess-tournament and many other
passages, Aretino the story of the camp of Stockholm, Berni
the discussion between Pantagruel and Panurge as to the
advantage of being in debt; Ariosto, Machiavelli, Castiglione,
all contribute their quota to the great hodge-podge[1].

But the contemporary Italian writer to whom he owes
most is Girolamo Folengo, otherwise called Merlin Coccaye,
who, like Rabelais, was once a monk, and whose principal
work, like Rabelais's, though to a far greater extent, is a
burlesque of the favourite romances of chivalry[2]. There are
three explicit references to him in *Pantagruel*. In the library
of St Victor figures *Merlinus Coccaius de patria diabolorum*,
and his book is mentioned in another place under the same
title, while in the list of Pantagruel's ancestors we have
Fracassus, *duquel a escript Merlin Coccaie*[3]. As has been
already mentioned both the episode of Panurge and the

---

[1] See P. Toldo, *L' arte italiana nell' opera di F. Rabelais* in *Archiv neuer. Spr.*
c. 103 ff., 1898.

[2] There are good accounts of Folengo and his work in J. A. Symonds, *Renaissance in Italy*, v. 334–354, and G. Saintsbury, *The Earlier Renaissance*, pp. 64 ff.
He was born *circ.* 1490, fled from his convent in 1515, and published his book in
1519. His name in religion was Théophile.

[3] II. ii; III. ii; II. i.

sheep-merchant and the famous description of the storm are borrowed from his work. The following passage will serve to shew how Rabelais developed the ideas which he borrowed:

Fraudifer ergo loquit pastorem Cingar ad unum,
Vis compagne mihi castronem vendere grassum?
Sum contentus ego, vendam, pegorarius inquit,
Da mihi quinque tronos si vis, aut quattuor ad plus,
Absque sothiezza mercati Cingar eidem
Sborsavit numos tolto castrone dolosos,
Sub terra quoniam falsos impresserat illos,
Hic Mercadantes optant rei cernere finem,
Expectat Baldus fraudem, ridetque Lonardus,
Nam bene squadrabat quod erat malus ille ghisellus.
Cingar per binas castronem brancat orrechias,
Quod butat in medio cernentibus æquora cunctis.
Illico (nam mos est ovium seguitare priorem)
Omnis grex sequitur, præcepsque nodare caminat
Postque caporalem certatim mandra ruinat,
Immo gaudenti cantabant carmine be be.
Non fuit una quidem quæ non scampasset in undas.
Totum lanigeris impletur piscibus Æquor[1].

Thus Rabelais with his many-sided learning was the true child of an age in which men were contented with nothing less than the whole of knowledge for their domain. But it is especially characteristic of him that he was deeply imbued with the scientific spirit, that to the knowledge which comes from books he added the knowledge which comes from personal observation. We have seen how celebrated he was as a physician, and how his knowledge of anatomy was derived not merely from books but from the study of the human body[2]. But he was also an ardent botanist, he had a considerable knowledge of architecture and he appears to have been something of a mechanician[3].

Rabelais was an observer of human nature rather in the

[1] *Macaronea* xi (*Opus Merlini Cocaii poetae Mantuani Macaronicorum*, Amsterdam 1692). There is a modern edition of his works in 3 vols., Mantua, 1883–89.

[2] *Ante*, p. 176.

[3] If we may believe Le Roy's statement that he was the author of some of the mechanical contrivances which he describes in the *Sciomachie*.

large than in the little, a student of man in general rather
than of individual men. As might be expected therefore
his book is no great store-house of characters, and these
are for the most part types rather than distinct individuals.
Of all of them except Panurge and Friar Jean des Entommeures it may be said that they are embodiments of an
idea rather than living creations. Thus Pantagruel is the
embodiment of Rabelais's idea of a good and enlightened
monarch. He is wise, learned and intelligent, a model of
good breeding and urbanity, patient and good-natured even
to a fault. *C'estoit le meilleur petit et grand bon homet, que
oncques ceigneït espee. Toutes choses prenoit en bonne partie,
tout acte interpretoit à bien. Jamais ne se tourmentoit, jamais
ne se scandalisoit*[1].

Panurge is a more genuine creation of flesh and blood
and Rabelais's conception of him is more definite and distinct.
He was about thirty-five years of age, of middle height with
a slightly aquiline nose shaped like the handle of a razor;
he had sixty-three methods of finding money when he was in
need, of which the most honourable and the most common
was by way of secret larceny; he was an evil-doer, a sharper,
a drinker, a roysterer, a libertine, if ever there was one in
Paris: for the rest the best fellow in the world[2].

It is probable that the idea of this unlovely character was
suggested to Rabelais by that of Cingar in the *Macaronea*:

> *Perfectus ladro, promptus mala guida viarum.*

Cingar has all Panurge's dexterity and readiness of resource;
he has the same complete indifference to moral considerations:
like him he is cruel, unscrupulous, and cowardly: like him he
has one redeeming quality, fidelity to his master.

Another literary character who belongs to the same family
is the celebrated Til Ulespiegle, whose adventures had, as we
have seen, appeared in a French translation just before the
publication of *Pantagruel*. He, like Panurge, is most fertile in
resource, and like him is malicious, vindictive and cruel. The

---

[1] III. ii.

[2] II. xvi. The words, *Au demourant le meilleur filz du monde*, are borrowed
from Marot's *Epistre pour avoir été desrobé*.

Repues franches or apocryphal anecdotes about François Villon were probably also in Rabelais's mind. But personal intercourse with the needy students who frequented Paris and the other French Universities no doubt helped to give definiteness to his conception. For it is one of the features which distinguish Panurge from his literary compeers that he is a scholar. Like Postel, like Amyot, he had acquired his learning in the face of poverty and hardships, and it is the thought of the hard, loveless life that he had experienced which makes us to some extent forgive him the cruelty and vindictiveness which are the most unpleasant features in his character.

The other great character in Rabelais is Friar Jean des Entommeures. He is far less complex than Panurge. He is the type of a man of action, practical, energetic and fearless, wholly devoid of intellectual interests, and of all men least fitted to lead the sleepy inactive life of a monk. "Young, gallant, frisk, lusty, nimble, bold, adventurous, resolute, tall, lean, wide-mouthed, long-nosed, a rare mumbler of matins, a rare unbridler of masses and scourer of vigils ; in a word, a very monk, if ever there was one, since the monking world monked a monkery. For the rest a clerk to the teeth in matter of breviary[1]."

It is well said by M. Faguet that these three characters, Pantagruel, Panurge, and Brother John, represent in a measure three sides of Rabelais's own character[2]. Pantagruel is the grave, wise, and learned physician whose portrait hangs in a room of the *Faculté de Médecine* at Montpellier ; Brother John is the unfrocked monk, the vigorous, adventure-seeking man of action ; Panurge is the needy student who loves a bottle of wine and a broad jest. But of these three, though it is Panurge who is most often made the mouthpiece of Rabelais's

---

[1] *Jeune, gallant, frisque, de hayt, bien à dextre, hardy, adventureux, deliberé : hault, maigre, bien fendu de gueule, bien advantagé en nez, beau despescheur d'heures, beau desbrideur de messes, beau descroteur de vigiles: pour tout dire sommairement, vray moyne si oncques en feust depuis que le monde moynant moyna de moynerie. Au reste, clerc jusques es dents en matiere de breviaire.* I. xxvii. *Entommeures* is formed from *entommer*, another form of *entamer*. Mr W. F. Smith well renders by Friar John of the Trencherites.

[2] *Seizième siècle*, p. 95.

own reminiscences, it is Panurge, it need hardly be said, who resembles him least.

Of the less important characters there is not much to be said. Grandgousier and Gargantua represent Pantagruel in less advanced states of intellectual development. Grandgousier has little or no learning, Gargantua has some learning, but he is not, like Pantagruel, a philosopher. Both like him are thoroughly kind-hearted and virtuous, and govern their kingdom with model wisdom and justice. Pantagruel's followers have little individuality, except perhaps Epistemon, whose constant appeals to classical authority in moments of difficulty give a certain consistency to his character. But of the minor characters the two who stand out most distinctly are Judge Bridoye or Bridlegoose, who decided his cases by the help of dice[1], and the good bishop Homenaz, who believed so firmly in the virtue of the Decretals[2]. They are creations of true humour, for true humour sympathises while it ridicules.

To the great majority of Rabelais's contemporaries his book seemed no doubt, as it did to Montaigne, one *simplement plaisant*, to be classed with the *Decameron*, or the *Basia* of Johannes Secundus. Yet in the prologue to *Gargantua* he had warned his readers to look beneath the surface. Just as Socrates behind his ugly face, ridiculous bearing, and rustic apparel concealed a more than human understanding, marvellous virtue, invincible courage, "so the matters treated on here are not such buffoonery as the title shewed forth....You must interpret in a higher sense what perhaps you thought was spoken of only in gaiety of heart....Did you ever see a dog with a marrow-bone?...With what diligence he sucks it.... What induces him to do this?...Nothing more than a little marrow....In imitation of this dog it becomes you to be wise, to smell, feel and value these goodly books of high import (*de haute gresse*)...for you will find another taste, and a more abstruse learning, which will reveal to you very high sacraments and dread mysteries, as much in that which concerns our religion as also the public polity and domestic economy."

But before, using Rabelais's metaphor, we proceed to

---

[1] III. xxxix—xliii.   [2] IV. xlix—liv.

' suck the substantial marrow ' of his book, it is important to
bear in mind two things: first, that he was twenty years
writing it, and that it is inevitable that his opinions on many
subjects must have undergone considerable modification during
this long period ; secondly, that he writes as a satirist and a
poet, not as a practical reformer or a professed philosopher.
His constructive reforms are professedly Utopian in character,
counsels of perfection to which the human race may one day
attain, but not to be rashly taken in hand by an imperfect
age.   So, too, we must not expect from him, any more than
from Shakespeare or Montaigne, a complete or consistent
system of philosophy. His deepest thoughts often find expression in an emotional outburst, which is none the less
lyrical because it is expressed in prose.

    With this proviso then let us first consider his teaching in
matters connected with 'the public polity.'   As regards the
form of government he seems to have been in favour of
monarchy, but he held most distinctly that monarchs, like
other members of the body politic, have duties to perform, the
neglect of which ought in extreme cases to be punished with
deposition.   Picrochole and Anarche, the two bad rulers of
his book, end their days, one as a day-labourer, the other
as a hawker of green sauce[1].   " It is the greatest folly," says
Rabelais, " to suppose that there are stars for Kings, Popes,
and great Lords, any more than for the poor and afflicted[2]."
He is especially severe on wars undertaken solely for the
sake of conquest.   In the days of Charles V and Francis I he
dared to say boldly that " the time had gone by for conquering
kingdoms to the loss of our nearest Christian brother: this
imitation of the Alexanders, Hannibals, and Cæsars of old is
contrary to the profession of the Gospel."   The whole of
chapter xxxiii of *Gargantua* is an exquisite satire on the
schemes of universal conquest.   He holds that a conquered
country should receive lenient treatment, and refers to the
advice of Machiavelli that it should be ruined, as Capua and
Carthage were by the Romans, as " the erroneous opinion of
certain tyrannical minds[3]."

[1] I. xlvi.   [2] *Prognostication*, c. v.   [3] III. i ; see *Principe*, c. vi.

A good deal of Rabelais's satire is directed against the administration of justice as it was carried on in his days. Without taking into account the episode of the *Chats fourrés* in the Fifth book, there are plenty of passages to shew that his views on the subject were as bold as they were enlightened. The delightful account of Judge Bridoye is a satire at once on the inordinate length of law-suits, and on the obscurity of the law. "Thirdly," says the good old judge, "I consider, *comme vous autres Messieurs*, that Time ripeneth all things; by Time all things become evident; Time is the Father of Truth. Therefore it is that, *comme vous autres Messieurs*, I adjourn, defer, and delay the judgment, that the suit being well ventilated, sifted and threshed out, may, by process of Time, come to its maturity, and that the hazard of the dice ensuing thereupon may be more lightly borne by the condemned parties[1]." The chief cause of the law's obscurity in Rabelais's eyes is the ignorance of the *Glossators* or the mediæval commentators on the Pandects. In his attacks on them he shews himself a thorough-going follower of Alciati, whose lectures, as we have seen, he had probably attended at Bourges. In the account of how Pantagruel decided a law-suit between M. Baisecul and M. de Humevesne he speaks of "the foolish opinions of Accursius, Baldus, Bartolus...and those other old mastiffs, who never understood the least law of the Pandects, and were nothing but great tithe-calves, ignorant of all that is necessary for the understanding of the laws. For they had no knowledge of either Greek or Latin, but only of Gothic and Barbarian[2]." The speeches of the two suitors and the judgment which Pantagruel delivers are in their utter unintelligibility satires on the legal jargon of the day.

His views with regard to monks and friars need not detain us. His voice, though one of the loudest, is only one in the general chorus of disapproval, and his experience of the monastic life was derived from a convent of that order which, at any rate in France, bore the worst reputation, namely the Franciscans. But it may be pointed out that his chief objection

[1] III. xl.   [2] II. x.

to the monks and friars was their idleness. This view is ex-
pounded in chapter xl of *Gargantua.* "A monk (I mean one
of those idle monks) doth not labour like the peasant ; doth
not guard the country like the soldier ; doth not heal the sick
like the physician ; nor preach to and instruct the world like
the good evangelical doctor and the pedagogue ; he doth not
import goods and things necessary for the commonwealth like
the merchant. That is the reason why by all men they are
hooted at and abhorred." " True," said Grandgousier, " but
they pray to God for us." "Nothing less," answered Gargantua.
"True it is that they disturb the whole neighbourhood with
the jangling of their bells. They mumble a great store of
legends and psalms in no ways understood by them. They
count a number of paternosters, interlarded with long Ave
Marias, without thinking of or understanding them. And
that I call a mockery of God and not prayer."

And he has the same objection to pilgrimages, that they
take men away from their work. " Go your ways, poor men,"
says Grandgousier to the pilgrims, " go your ways in the name
of God the Creator, and may He be your perpetual guide.
And henceforth do not lend yourselves to these idle and un-
profitable journeys. Maintain your families, labour every one
of you in his vocation, instruct your children, and live as the
good apostle St Paul directeth you[1]."

The famous abbey of Thelema is based entirely on the
negation of the monastic system. Because all abbeys were
strongly walled, it is to be built without walls; because all
monasteries were regulated by fixed hours, there is to be no
clock ; because men were not admitted to convents of women,
men and women are to live in common ; because monks and
nuns, after their year of probation, had to remain monks and
nuns all their lives, the brothers and sisters of Thelema are to
be at liberty to depart when they please ; because members of
the religious orders took a threefold view of chastity, poverty
and obedience, at Thelema everyone may marry, everyone
may be rich, everyone may live as he pleases.

How strongly Rabelais objected to idleness, how thoroughly

[1] I. xlv.

he grasped the idea that from the point of view of society idleness is the greatest sin, may be seen from the picture of an ideal education which he gives in *Gargantua*[1], and which supplements the admirable summary of the aims and aspirations of Humanism which is contained in Gargantua's letter to Pantagruel. This is how Gargantua spent his day. He got up at four and repeated his lessons of the preceding day while he was being dressed; then he had a book read to him, accompanied no doubt by explanations, for three hours. This was followed by some form of moderate exercise, such as tennis. Then came dinner, probably at nine. During the meal a book was read, and there was learned conversation. The hour of digestion was devoted to gentle instruction in the mathematical sciences, such as the solution of arithmetical problems with the help of dice and cards, the drawing of geometrical figures, a lesson in astronomy, and vocal and instrumental music[2]. Then came hard study again for three hours, consisting partly of repetition of the morning lesson, partly of a continuation of the book lectured on in the morning, partly of a writing lesson. This was followed by exercise on horse-back and various military manœuvres. Then the pupil and tutor, after changing their dress, walked home through the meadows, botanising on the way. It was now time for supper, the principal meal of the day. Probably this was at five o'clock. Like dinner, it was accompanied by reading and improving conversation. The evening was spent in music, or games of cards or dice, varied by visits to learned men or travellers. Then came a lesson in practical astronomy, and finally the pupil gave a brief account to his tutor of all he had read, seen, learnt, and done during the day, which ended, as it had begun, with prayer and thanksgiving.

We are not told what books were read at the long morning and afternoon lectures, but we may safely infer from Gargantua's letter, and from Rabelais's own enthusiasm for the new studies, that they were principally Greek and Latin

---

[1] I. cc. xxiii, xxiv.

[2] Arithmetic, geometry, astronomy and music together formed the *quadrivium* of mediæval education.

authors, with the addition probably of Hebrew and history. On wet days, instead of out-door exercise, there was carpentering, painting, sculpture, and visits either to various workshops in the town or to the fencing-rooms, where they shewed themselves masters of every form of the art. Once a month there was a whole holiday, which was spent in an excursion into the country, to Chantilly or Saint-Cloud. But even on these days, though there were no books or lectures, instruction was not forgotten. For they recited passages from Virgil's *Georgics* or Hesiod, or they composed Latin epigrams and then translated them into French *ballades* or *rondeaux*.

According to our ideas this never-ceasing round of instruction seems grotesque enough. A modern boy who was made to break off in the middle of his games in order to collect the passages of ancient writers which bore on the subject would, if he were not disgusted with learning altogether, develope into a monstrous prig. But the enthusiasm for learning in Rabelais's scheme of education is not priggish, because in that age it was perfectly natural. Moreover, it must be borne in mind that the scheme, like that of the abbey of Thelema, is an ideal one, and that it pre-supposes a pupil endowed with a physical and intellectual capacity more than human ; in short, a giant like Pantagruel.

Further, it should be noticed that in many respects it is little more than a general outline, with little attempt to go into detail either as regards method or subjects, and with no attempt to discriminate between the various stages of intellectual developement. Perhaps the most remarkable and original feature of the whole scheme is the prominence that is given to physical exercise. Never in France has the training of the body played so important a part in an educational system. The next most remarkable feature, one which in Rabelais's day was hardly less original, is the care that is taken to develope the faculty of observation. Morning and evening the pupil has to note the face of the sky and the position of the stars : at dinner everything on the table is made a subject for instruction : in the afternoon there is a practical lesson in botany, or if the day is wet there is a visit to the druggist and the apothecary to see how they adulterate their goods, or visits to the work-shops of every kind of trade, workers in metal, jewellers, clock-makers, printers, dyers, etc.   Thirdly, we should notice the part played by repetition.   Three times a day the pupil repeats by heart some passage from the book that has been read to him.   Then twice a day he goes over with his tutor the work of the previous morning or afternoon.   Thus the memory and the intelligence are exercised with equal care.

The whole scheme is so remarkable for its good sense, for its entire freedom from those fads to which educationalists of all ages have been prone, that one is apt to overlook its originality, and to forget sufficiently to admire the man who, fighting in the forefront of those who were storming the citadels of knowledge, was cool-headed enough to remember that the business of education is not so much to fill a man with learning as to train both his mind and his body.   In short, Rabelais's views on education are essentially characteristic of his genius, of a genius which was none the less bold, none the less original, because it was always controlled by the dictates of moderation and common sense.

It has been often said, and with considerable confidence, that Rabelais was not at heart a Christian.   But those who speak so confidently with regard to Rabelais's, or indeed any man's, religious views should ponder the following words of M. Gebhart: "The lowest depths of a conscience are often hidden from the bearer of it, but they are impenetrable to the eyes of others.   Even in the case of members of a religious sect there is no rigorous proof of their sincerity, apart from martyrdom.   The same question applied to Erasmus, to Leo X, to Montaigne, to a hundred others will only lead to an uncertain answer[1]."   "The wise man," says Lord Beaconsfield, "never tells his religion," and Rabelais was essentially a wise, that is a prudent, man.

But we may say with confidence that he had a profound belief in the power and wisdom of God.   "Believe in this year that there will be no other governor of the universe but

[1] *Rabelais*, p. 100.

God the Creator," he says in the *Prognostication*[1], and in
another place he speaks of the "unique and supreme affection
which man owes to God[2]." He believes too in the efficacy of
prayer. "All true Christians," says Gargantua, "of all conditions, in all places and at all times pray to God, and the
Spirit prays and intercedes for them, and God is gracious to
them[3]." And again, "I have hope in God that He will hear
our prayers, seeing the firm faith in which we make them;
and that He will accomplish our wishes, provided they
be moderate[4]." So too with regard to immortality. He
represents the old poet Raminagrobis declaring, as he lay on
his death-bed with "a joyous open countenance and bright
look," that he was already contemplating and tasting the
"happiness and felicity which the good God has prepared for
His faithful and elect in the other life, which is eternal[5]."

But we may go further than this. His actual language in
many places, especially when he is speaking by the mouth of
Pantagruel, would warrant us in supposing that he accepted
the broad features of Christianity, above all the divinity of
Christ. Nor is there anywhere any satire, open or covert, of
the principal doctrines of the Roman Catholic Church, of the
worship of the Virgin Mary and the Saints, of Purgatory or
Confession or the Mass. But it is said that this is a mere
outward conformity, dictated by the prudence of a man
who wished to secure immunity for his book, and had no
desire "to be burnt like a red herring." It may be so, but
the matter requires a closer examination.

We have seen that the great majority of the French
humanists looked at first with favour on the new doctrines
preached by Lefèvre d'Étaples and his friends, and would
gladly have welcomed a reform of the Church within and by
the Church. Rabelais indeed went further than most of
them. In Calvin's words he welcomed the preaching of
the Gospel (*gustavit Evangelium*)[6], and his book *Gargantua,*

[1] c. i, and comp. c. viii.   [2] *Pant.* III. xxxv.
[3] I. xl.   [4] Prologue to book IV.   [5] III. xxi.
[6] *Alii ut Rabelaysus gustato Evangelio eadem caecitate sunt percussi* (*De
scandalis,* 1550, *Opera* VIII).

which he finished writing, as we saw, almost certainly in the
autumn of 1534, has a decided Protestant tinge. The reference
to the need of divine grace and the Protestant use of the
phrase "Christ our Redeemer" without the definite article
in Grandgousier's letter, the inscription over the door of
the abbey of Thelema, and some phrases in the Enigma,
all bear out this assertion. But between the publication of
this book and that of the Third book nearly twelve years
elapsed, and Rabelais's religious opinions underwent considerable change. First came the affair of the Placards, and
the consequent breach between the thorough-going and the
moderate Reformers, between those who would reform the
Church at all costs and those who would reform it only from
within. Then came the publication of Calvin's *Institution*,
which must have convinced Rabelais of the profound diver-
gence of their views. For while Calvin went even beyond St
Augustine in his belief in the innate corruption of man,
Rabelais, like the other leaders of the Renaissance, had a firm
conviction in his virtue and dignity. It is true that Grandgousier in his letter to Gargantua is made to say that man's
free-will and understanding cannot fail to be evil if they are
not continually guided by the divine grace, but Rabelais's
inmost belief is better represented by the *Fay ce que vouldras*
which was the only regulation of the abbey of Thelema, and
by the explanation that "men who are free, well-bred, well-
educated, conversant with honest company, have by nature
an instinct and spur which always impels them to virtuous
actions and draws them away from vice; and this they call
honour." It is easy to press too far this foretaste of the *honnête
homme* theory of the seventeenth century, for after all Rabelais
only describes honour as furnishing an impulse towards virtue,
but it indicates a highly aristocratic theory of human nature
which is considerably at variance with the teaching of
Christianity. Whether it is more at variance with it than the
equally exclusive theory of Calvin is another question[1].

Another important point in which Rabelais differed pro-

---

[1] See Calvin, *Inst. Chrét.* ii. 1. 8; iii. 6. 3 (text of 1560). The contrast
between the two views is well brought out by M. Brunetière.

foundly from Calvin was the question of religious tolerance. In the abbey of Thelema there was complete liberty of conscience ; there was not even a chapel for common worship; in religion as in other matters each member of the community might act according to his pleasure and free-will. Rabelais, like the other humanists, had welcomed Protestantism as a vindication of the right of free inquiry, and nothing can have helped to repel him more than the rigid discipline alike in thought and action which Calvin demanded. In fact, the chief defect in Rabelais's theory of life, as in that of the whole Renaissance, is that in its devotion to intellectual progress it overlooks the importance of moral discipline. It forgets that it is by self-restraint and self-discipline that the characters of strong men are built up. Pantagruel has every virtue but that of sternness. He is too lenient to Panurge.

But while the increasing influence of Calvin definitely alienated Rabelais from Protestantism, he did not become a more submissive son of the Catholic Church. In the Third book, with the exception of the excellent advice which the theologian gives to Panurge on the subject of his marriage, and the scathing denunciation of monks by the dying Rami-nagrobis, there is little about religion. Then followed his hasty flight, his exile at Metz, and his third journey to Rome. When he returned to France in 1550 with his Fourth book nearly finished, there had been five years of savage persecution. It is not surprising if his satire on the Church acquired a sharper sting. In the Fourth book we have the onslaught on Lent (*Quaresmeprenant*) and fasting (which was at that time regarded as one of the surest tests of orthodoxy) and the account of the island of the *Papimanes* with its biting satire on the more extravagant pretensions of the Papacy. It is true that in this latter episode Rabelais hardly goes beyond what might be considered permissible in a loyal supporter of the Gallican Church and an opponent of the temporal power; but when he asserts, as he does in his letter to the Cardinal de Châtillon, that there is not a word of heresy in his book, he protests too much.

The real truth of the matter would seem to be that

Rabelais during the last fifteen or sixteen years of his life, disgusted on the one hand by the corrupt condition of the Catholic Church, and yet even more opposed to the dogmas of Calvinism, steered mainly by his own compass. But if he subjected the doctrine of the Catholic Church to a somewhat large interpretation, the more one reads in his book the more one is impressed by the essentially Christian note of many of its passages. It is to irreverence, not to scepticism, that we should ascribe those sallies which point to a contrary conclusion. For he was by temperament a jester, but no sceptic[1]. He held certain religious beliefs with a deep-seated conviction, and if with regard to others his creed was less clearly defined, this does not justify us in asserting that he was a disloyal servant of the Church which he professed to serve and the rites of which he for a time actually administered.

It is in Panurge's quest that some of Rabelais's commentators have professed to find the key to his philosophy. But it is doubtful whether the allegory rests on any such systematic plan as this implies. At any rate we may be sure that like all great allegories it has more than one interpretation. Primarily it is no more than a satire on those who are perpetually asking advice without taking it unless it coincides with their own wishes. But it may also have a deeper meaning and be directed against those who cry out for a new revelation, who are not satisfied unless they have convincing proofs as to the final destiny of man. The only two sound pieces of advice that are given to Panurge come from Pantagruel and the theologian. Pantagruel's opinion is that in marriage "everyone ought to be arbiter of his own thoughts and take counsel of himself." The theologian tells Panurge that, if God pleases, his wife will be faithful to him, and on his expressing dissatisfaction with this conditional form of statement, he adds that if Panurge chooses for his wife the daughter of virtuous parents who has been brought up in the fear of God, and if he himself sets her an example of a chaste and virtuous life, invoking continually the grace of God,

---

[1] "For the man doth fear God, howsoever it seems not in him by some large jests he will make," *Much Ado About Nothing.*

she will not be unfaithful. But this is not at all what Panurge
wants. He wants to be assured of the future without any
reference to his own actions. He declines to accept the view
that man is the maker of his own destiny. He must have a
fresh revelation, he must consult the oracle of the Divine Bottle.

The only answer vouchsafed to Panurge by the Bottle is
the single word 'Drink.' But when Panurge in obedience to
this command has drunk a flagon of Falernian wine, the
priestess says: " Here we maintain that not laughter but
drinking is the special property of man; I do not say
drinking simply and absolutely, for so also drink the beasts:
I say drinking good and fresh wine. Note, my friends, that
by wine man becomes divine...for it has power to fill the soul
with all truth, all knowledge and philosophy[1]." Finally when
the friends take leave of her she says, "When you come to
your world, bear witness that under the earth are great
treasures and wonderful things. Your philosophers who
complain that all things have been described by the ancients,
and that nothing new has been left them to invent, are very
clearly in the wrong. All that the earth has produced for you
is not comparable to that which is still concealed in it[2]."

The message then is one of hope based on a profound
belief in the progress of knowledge and discovery. Whether
this be Rabelais's message or that of some great unknown
philosopher, it is exactly in accordance with the whole spirit
of Rabelais's book, with his belief in the goodness of God and
in the future of the human race. *Bon espoir y git au fond.*

But the priestess Bacbuc has another lesson to teach.
"We place," she says, "supreme good, not in taking and
receiving, but in imparting and giving, and we count ourselves
happy, not if we take and receive much from others as perhaps
the sects of your world decree, but if we are always imparting
and giving much to others[3]." This again is in accord with
Rabelais's whole teaching, especially as expressed in the
celebrated discussion between Pantagruel and Panurge as to
the advantage of debts, where Rabelais after satirising spend-
thrifts in the person of Panurge, suddenly passes to his side

[1] v. xlvi.					[2] *ib.* xlviii.					[3] *ib.*

and breaks forth into a magnificent pæan in praise of human fellowship, painting an ideal world, in which all are debtors and all are lenders, in which there are no law-suits, no wars, no quarrels, but Charity alone reigns, rules, and triumphs[1].

This social element in Rabelais's theory of life distinguishes it from the somewhat exaggerated individualism of Renaissance thought in general. It is, he holds, by helping our fellow men that we can best work out our individual salvation. It is only by a life of active beneficence that we can attain to that excellent state of mind to which he has given the name of Pantagruelism, and which he defines as "a certain gaiety of spirit built up of disregard of things fortuitous[2]," and of which Pantagruel, the wise beneficent ruler, who is always ready to help his fellow-creatures, is the living embodiment.

Such is some of the marrow that may be extracted from Rabelais's book, if we but read it with that attention which he invites us to bestow on it. But most readers must feel as they read that it has many mysteries still unrevealed to them, mysteries which they cannot penetrate, because they cannot plumb the depths of Rabelais's mind.

It is a less difficult task to speak of Rabelais's style, to consider the qualities in virtue of which his countrymen have assigned to him the first place among the French prose writers of his century and a foremost one among those of every age. The conditions under which he wrote were anything but favourable. Ever since the beginning of the fifteenth century the French had been struggling with the problem of how to develope out of the simple picturesque prose of the middle ages a style suited to the expression of complex ideas or deep emotions. In order to effect this they had rightly gone to Latin literature for their models, but as yet their efforts had been only moderately successful. Their prose in its endeavour to become more like Latin had almost ceased to be French. Another difficulty arose from the loss of the case inflexions, which necessitated new methods of structure for the sentences. Thus vocabulary and syntax alike had fallen

---

[1] III. iv and see the whole of chapters iii and iv.
[2] IV. prologue.

into disorder. Nor was Rabelais the man to reduce them to order. His genius was too luxuriant and unmethodical. He loves variety and inconsistency, he uses archaisms and Latinisms just as it suits him, and triumphs in the very disorder which to weaker men is a stumbling-block. His power of building up a long and complicated sentence without the sacrifice of clearness is marvellous, and it is but rarely that he is betrayed like the rest of his contemporaries into the abuse of the parenthesis and the ellipse. He has also the merit of being able to write in a great variety of styles, from the simplest narrative to the noblest harmony of concerted eloquence. His account of the war between Grandgousier and Picrochole has the straightforward brevity of Thucydides[1]. Here is a specimen :

L'aduis feut trouué bon. Adoncques produict toute son armee en plain camp, mettant les subsides du cousté de la montee. Le moyne print auecques luy six enseignes de gens de pied, & deux cens hommes d'armes, & en grande diligence trauersa les marays, & gaingna au dessus le puy iusques au grand chemin de Loudun. Ce pendent l'assault continuoit, les gens de Picrochole ne sçauoient si le meilleur estoit sortir hors & les recepuoir, ou bien guarder la ville sans bouger. Mais furieusement sortit auecques quelque bande d'hommes d'armes de sa maison : & là feut receu & festoyé à grandz coups de canon qui gresloient deuers les coustaux, dont les Gargantuistes se retirerent au val, pour mieulx donner lieu à l'artillerye. Ceulx de la ville defendoient le mieulx que pouoient, mais les traictz passoient oultre par dessus sans nul ferir. Aulcuns de la bande sauluez de l'artillerie donnerent fierement sus nos gens, mais peu profiterent, car tous feurent repceuz entre les ordres, & là ruez par terre. Ce que voyans se vouloient retirer, mais ce pendent le moyne auoit occupé le passaige. Parquoy se mirent en fuyte sans ordre ny maintien. Aulcuns vouloient leur donner la chasse, mais le moyne les retint, craignant que suyuant les fuyans perdissent leurs rancz, & que sus ce poinct ceulx de la ville chargeassent sus eulx. Puis attendant quelque espace, & nul ne comparant à l'encontre, enuoya le duc Phrontiste pour admonnester Gargantua à ce qu'il auanceast pour gaigner le cousteau à la gauche, pour empescher la retraicte de Picrochole par celle porte.

Ce que feist Gargantua en toute diligence, & y enuoya quatre legions de la compaignie de Sebaste, mais si tost ne peurent gaigner le hault, qu'ilz ne rencontrassent en barbe Picrochole & ceulx qui auecques luy s'estoient espars[2].

---

[1] See especially I. xxv, xxvi, xlvii and xlviii.   [2] I. xlviii.

It is impossible to wish for anything clearer or more concise
in the way of a military narrative than this.

In contrast with this let us take as a specimen of lofty
eloquence the following passage from the speech by Ulrich
Gallet, Grandgousier's ambassador to Picrochole:

> Quelle furie doncques te esmeut maintenant, toute alliance brisee,
> toute amitié conculquee, tout droict trespassé, enuahir hostilement ses
> terres, sans en rien auoir esté par luy ny les siens endommaigé, irrité, ny
> prouocqué? Ou est foy? Ou est loy? Ou est raison? Ou est humanité?
> Ou est craincte de dieu? Cuyde tu ces oultraiges estre recellés es esperitz
> eternelz, & au Dieu souuerain, qui est iuste retributeur de nos entre-
> prinses? Si le cuyde, tu te trompe, car toutes choses viendront à son
> iugement. Sont ce fatales destinees, ou influences des astres qui voulent
> mettre fin à tes ayzes & repous? Ainsi ont toutes choses leur fin
> & periode. Et quand elles sont venues à leur poinct suppellatif, elles
> sont en bas ruinees, car elles ne peuuent long temps en tel estat demourer.
> C'est la fin de ceulx qui leurs fortunes & prosperitez ne peuuent par
> raison & temperance moderer[1].

Here it will be noticed that both vocabulary and construction are somewhat Latinised. This tendency is more
marked in other parts of the same harangue, and in the later
books wherever Rabelais aspires to a tone of grave eloquence
it is carried to an exaggerated pitch. This is how Pantagruel
writes to his father Gargantua:

> Pere tresdebonnaire, comme à tous accidens en ceste vie transitoire
> non doubtez ne soubsonnez, nos sens & facultez animales patissent plus
> enormes & impotentes perturbations (voyre iusques à en estre souuent
> l'ame desemparee du corps, quoy que telles subites nouuelles feussent à
> contentement & soubhayt) que si eussent au parauant esté propensez
> & preueuz: ainsi me a grandement esmeu & perturbé l'inopinee venue de
> vostre escuyer Malicorne. Car ie n'esperoys aulcun veoir de vos dome-
> sticques, ne de vous nouuelles ouyr auant la fin de cestuy nostre voyage.
> Et facilement acquiesçoys en la doulce recordation de vostre auguste
> maiesté, escripte, voyre certes insculpee & engrauee on posterieur
> ventricule de mon cerueau: souuent au vif me la representant en sa
> propre & naïfue figure[2].

This is hardly more like French than the utterances of the
Limousin student.

---

[1] I. xxxi. For another example in the same style comp. Grandgousier's letter
(I. xxix).
[2] IV. iv.

On the other hand when Rabelais, without thought of Latin models, trusts to his natural vein of eloquence he can produce such perfect writing as the following:

Tel disoit estre Socrates: par ce que le voyans au dehors & l'estimans par l'exteriore apparence, n'en eussiez donné vn coupeau d'oignon: tant laid il estoit de corps & ridicule en son maintien, le nez pointu, le reguard d'vn taureau, le visaige d'vn fol: simple en meurs, rustiq en vestimens, pauure de fortune, infortuné en femmes, inepte à tous offices de la republique, tousiours riant, tousiours beuuant d'autant à vn chascun, tousiours se guabelant, tousiours dissimulant son diuin sçauoir. Mais ouurans ceste boyte: eussiez au dedans trouué vne celeste & impreciable drogue, entendement plus que humain, vertus merueilleuse, couraige inuincible, sobresse non pareille, contentement certain, asseurance parfaicte, deprisement incroyable de tout ce pourquoy les humains tant veiglent, courent, trauaillent, nauigent & bataillent[1].

The Third and Fourth books are distinguished from the earlier ones by the frequent introduction of short stories. It may be remembered that just before the publication of the Third book, Le Maçon's translation of the *Decameron* had given additional impetus, at any rate among the court circle, to the popularity of the short story, and in this, as in so many other respects, Rabelais shews his readiness to fall in with the literary fashions of the day. It must be confessed that he is not altogether a master in this art: his short stories, which unlike those of his contemporaries, Des Periers and Margaret of Navarre, are all drawn from literary sources, are told as a rule with almost too great brevity and without much humour. He has given us however one masterpiece in this line, the story of how Seigny Joan, a celebrated Paris fool of the middle ages, decided a dispute between a porter and a roast-meat seller[2].

But Rabelais as a rule requires a larger canvas for the display of his story-telling art. The story of the little devil of Papefiguière, which La Fontaine has versified in one of his *Contes*, is excellent[3]. But the most characteristic of all is

---

[1] *Gargantua*, prologue.

[2] III. xxxvii. For the origin of the story see P. Toldo in *Rev. des Études Rab.* I. 13 and E. Langlois, *ib.* 222 ff.

[3] IV. xlv—xlvii.

that of the countryman and his axe which occupies the
greater part of the prologue to the Fourth book.   Here
Rabelais gives full play to his humour, and tells his story with
a verve and exuberance of spirits, and a dazzling *bravoure* of
style which even he has never surpassed.   This is the opening
of it :

De son temps estoit vn paouure homme villageois natif de Grauot
nommé Couillatris, abateur & fendeur de boys, & en cestuy bas estat
guaingnant cahin caha sa paouure vie.   Aduint qu'il perdit sa coingnee.
Qui feut bien fasché & marry ce fut il.   Car de sa coingnee dependoit
son bien & sa vie : par sa coingnee viuoit en honneur & reputation entre
tous riches buscheteurs : sans coingnee mouroit de faim.   La mort six
iours apres le rencontrant sans coingnee, auecques son dail l'eust fausché
& cerclé de ce monde.   En cestuy estrif commença crier, prier, implorer,
inuocquer Iuppiter par oraisons moult disertes (comme vous sçauez que
Necessité feut inuentrice d'Eloquence) leuant la face vers les cieulx, les
genoilz en terre, la teste nue, les bras haulx en l'air, les doigts des mains
esquarquillez, disant à chascun refrain de ses suffrages à haulte voix
infatiguablament.   Ma coingnee, Iuppiter, ma coingnee, ma coingnee.
Rien plus, ô Iuppiter, que ma coingnee, ou deniers pour en achapter vne
autre.   Helas, ma paouure coingnee[1].

M. Stapfer in his book on Rabelais well says that there
are two classes of great writers, those who use style solely to
express their thoughts, and those who use style for its own
sake, and that Rabelais certainly belongs to the second class,
that of the artists.   Of no writer may it more truly be said
that the style is the man; like the man, it is exuberant,
boisterous, joyous, full of energy and movement, a style in
which art and nature are so happily intermingled, that it is
impossible to say whether the most daring flights are the
result of elaborate science, or the outburst of a sudden inspiration.   Some of the best examples of these flights will be
found in the account of the plant Pantagruelion (III. li), and in
Panurge's panegyric of debtors (III. iii and iv).   The following
is from the latter :

Au contraire representez vous vn monde autre, on quel vn chascun
preste, vn chascun doibue, tous soient debteurs, tous soient presteurs.

---

[1] It is difficult to suppose that the story of the Charger and the Ass in book v.
(chap. vii.) is not by the same hand.

O quelle harmonie sera parmy les reguliers mouuemens des Cieulz. Il
m'est aduis que ie l'entends aussi bien que feit oncques Platon. Quelle
sympathie entre les elemens. O comment Nature se y delectera en ses
œuures & productions. Ceres chargée de bleds : Bacchus de vins : Flora
de fleurs : Pomona de fruictz : Iuno en son aër serain seraine, salubre,
plaisante. Ie me pers en ceste contemplation. Entre les humains Paix,
Amour, Dilection, Fidelité, repous, banquetz, festins, ioye, liesse, or,
argent, menue monnoie, chaisnes, bagues, marchandises, troteront de
main en main. Nul proces, nulle guerre, nul debat : nul n'y serà vsurier,
nul leschart, nul chichart, nul refusant. Vray Dieu, ne sera ce l'aage
d'or, le regne de Saturne? L'idée des regions Olympicques : es quelles
toutes autres vertus cessent : Charité seule regne, regente, domine,
triumphe. Tous seront bons, tous seront beaulx, tous seront iustes[1].

It is noteworthy that, while Rabelais's verse is in the
highest degree prosaic, his prose in these dithyrambic outbursts has the imaginative sweep, the emotional vibration, the
concerted music of lyrical poetry. It is not the prose of one
whose habitual instrument is verse and who tries to force from
prose the same effects that he is accustomed to produce in
verse, but it is the prose of one who in that medium finds the
most natural expression for his poetic feeling[2].

One of the most striking features of Rabelais's prose is his
prodigious vocabulary. It is drawn from all sources. Local
words and expressions are used in abundance, and as if the
French language were not rich enough to supply his needs, he
borrows freely from Latin and Greek, coining with careless
prodigality hundreds of words, of which some have taken their
place among the permanent possessions of the language, while
the greater part scarcely survived their birth. The long lists
of verbs, substantives or adjectives strung together without
any connecting particle in which he so much delights, testify
to his superlative enjoyment in the manipulation of words.
And he loves words not merely for their philological interest
but for their sound, and for their sound not only by themselves
but in combination. He has an unfailing ear for the harmony
of prose. For the sake of a harmonious cadence he will often
sacrifice the logical structure of a sentence. This passion for

[1] III. iv.
[2] See an admirable essay by Hazlitt (the first of *The Plain Speaker*) on *The prose style of poets*.

harmony grew upon him. In his later books, especially in
the Fourth, it is always harmony and not clearness of expression which determines the order of the words. Hence an
exaggerated use of inversion and other archaic forms of
syntax which were being fast abandoned by other writers[1].

Rabelais is one of those few chosen writers who represent
their whole age. He represents not only the French Renaissance but the whole Renaissance, in its earlier, fresher and
healthier manifestations, in its devotion to classical learning,
in its many-sided curiosity, in its belief in the high destinies
of the human race. He belongs also to that even smaller
band who unite creative power of the highest order to
deep philosophic insight. He is—to keep to modern writers—
with Dante, Shakespeare, Cervantes, and Goethe. Of these
he is most equally matched with Cervantes, and a comparison
between the two great prose representatives of the creative
genius, both of whose works had for their starting point the
popular romances of chivalry, would be interesting. But it is
with Goethe that he has the closest spiritual affinity. His
interest and belief in science, his gospel of work for the benefit
of mankind, his unshaken optimism, his doctrine of serenity
as the goal of individual developement, all these he shares
with the great German writer who dominates the nineteenth
century. If his mirth often shew traces of the mediæval
atmosphere by which he was so long stifled, in his thought
he is surprisingly modern.

BIBLIOGRAPHY.

EDITIONS.

For the original and other important editions of *Gargantua* and
Pantagruel see Appendix C.

The principal later editions are the following:—5 vols. Amsterdam,
1711, with notes by J. le Duchat and Bernard de la Monnoye ; 3 vols. *ib.*
1741, with notes by Le Duchat and Pierre Motteux ; *Variorum edition,*

---

[1] See E. Huguet, *Syntaxe de Rabelais*, p. 422 ff. for an excellent account of
Rabelais's method of constructing his sentence and for the general features of his
style.

ed. Esmangart and Eloi Johanneau, 9 vols. 1823-26; ed. Burgaud Des Marets and E. J. Rathery, 2 vols. 1857-58; 2nd ed. 1870 (perhaps the most serviceable edition, with good notes at the bottom of the page, but the spelling of the text is arbitrary); ed. A. Montaiglon and L. Lacour, 3 vols. 1868-72 (the Fifth book is printed from the MS. text); ed. P. Jannet, 6 vols. 1867-68; 2nd ed. 7 vols. 1873-74 (a convenient little edition); ed. Ch. Marty-Laveaux, 6 vols. 1868-1903 (the best text; vol. IV. contains the notes, the scope of which is intentionally limited, V. and VI. the life, a full and excellent glossary, and a bibliography). The best edition in one volume is that of L. Moland, 1881.

See for the early editions J. C. Brunet, *Recherches bibliographiques et critiques sur les éditions originales de Rabelais*, 1852.

PANTAGRUELINE PROGNOSTICATION...*pour lan* 1533 [Lyons, 1532] (in six chapters); *pour lan* 1535, Lyons, Juste, 1534 (in ten chapters); *pour lan perpetuel*, Juste, 1542 (in ten chapters).

Of Rabelais's series of ALMANACS only fragments of those for the years 1533, 1535 and 1541 with titles of three others have been preserved. —See Marty-Laveaux, III. 255—271.

LA SCIOMACHIE *et festins faits à Rome au Palais de mon seigneur reuerendissime Cardinal du Bellay, pour l'heureuse naissance de mon seigneur d'Orleans*, Lyons, 1549.

LES EPISTRES *de Maistre François Rabelais, docteur en medecine escrites pendant son voyage d'Italie...avec des observations historiques et l'abregé de la vie de l'autheur*, 1651 (ed. by Scévole and Louis de Sainte-Marthe); reprinted with some additional notes, Brussels, 1710.

Printed by Jannet in *Œuvres de Rabelais*, VI. and by Marty-Laveaux, III. 340 ff. from a 17th century MS. in the *Bib. Nat.* entitled *Trois lettres de M. François Rabelais, transcriptes sur les originaux, escrites de Rome*, 1536.

There is another MS. of the 2nd letter formerly in the possession of M. Benjamin Fillon and now in the Morrison collection, London. M. Boulenger believes this to be a 16th century copy of the original letter and shews that it is the source of the text printed by the brothers Sainte-Marthe. (See A. Lefranc and J. Boulenger in *Rev. des Études Rab.* I. 93 ff. with a facsimile.)

TRANSLATIONS.

The first book [and the second book] *of the Works of Mr Francis Rabelais, Doctor in Physic: containing five books of the lives, heroic deeds and sayings of Gargantua and his son Pantagruel...Translated into English*, by S.T.U.C. [Sir Thomas Urquhart], 2 parts, 1653; *The Works of F. Rabelais, M.D....Done out of French by Sir Tho. Urchard, Kt and others*, 3 vols. 1694, 1693 (the third book is by Urquhart and was edited by Pierre Motteux in 1693; in the following year he reprinted the original edition of the first two books and added a translation of the fourth and fifth books by himself); *The whole works of F. Rabelais, M.D.*, 2 vols. 1708.

This celebrated translation has been several times reprinted in recent years, notably in the series of Tudor Translations with an introduction by Charles Whibley, 3 vols. 1900.

Rabelais, the five books and minor writings together with letters and documents illustrating his life. A new translation with notes by W. F. Smith, 2 vols. 1893.

Notes and translation are alike excellent: see I. pp. xiv—xix for an account of the preceding work and its translators.

Mention should also be made of the German translation by Gottlob Regis, 2 parts, Leipsic, 1832–41, which is furnished with numerous notes and a good bibliography. For the free rendering of *Gargantua* by Johann Fischart, published in 1575, see Arnstädt, *F. Rabelais und sein Traité d'Éducation*, c. iv.

LIFE.

Nearly all the original documents relating to Rabelais's life are printed in vol. III. of Marty-Laveaux's edition. In the seventeenth century Antoine le Roy, a devoted admirer, who retired to Meudon during the Fronde, wrote a long rigmarole account of him in Latin entitled *Rabelæsina elogia*. It remains in manuscript (*Bib. Nat.* MSS. *latins* 8704), but a portion of it was published as a preface to his *Floretum Philosophicum* (1649) under the title of *Illustre Meudonium sub clarissimo Francisco Rabelæso*. Unfortunately neither this, nor the longer work from which it was extracted contains many facts. The same must be said for Colletet's life, printed by G. Brunet (Philomneste junior), Geneva, 1867.

The first really critical life was that by Rathery, prefixed to his and Des Marets's edition. This has formed the basis of subsequent accounts, of which the best are those of L. Moland at the head of his edition, P. Stapfer, *Rabelais, sa personne, son génie, son œuvre*, pp. 1–88 (1889), A. Birch-Hatzfeld, *Geschichte des französischen Litteratur*, pp. 212–252, and Ch. Marty-Laveaux (vol. v. of his edition). Special mention should also be made of the life by Niceron (*Memoires*, XXXII. 337 ff.), in which for the first time the serious side of Rabelais's character was insisted on, and the traditional stories of his buffoonery were rejected. The life in Chaufepié's Dictionary is based mainly on Niceron.

Several obscure points in his life have been elucidated by A. Heulhard, *Rabelais, ses voyages en Italie, son exil à Metz*, 1891.

TO BE CONSULTED.

E. Gebhart, *Rabelais, la renaissance et la réforme*, 1877, re-published with alterations in 1897 as a volume of the *Classiques populaires*

(much of it excellent, especially the chapter on Rabelais's religion);
J. Fleury, *Rabelais et ses œuvres*, 2 vols. 1877 (a popular but com-
prehensive and useful summary); W. Besant, *Rabelais*, 1879 (Foreign
Classics for English Readers); G. Martinozzi, *Il Pantagruele di
Francesco Rabelais*, Citta di Castello, 1885; P. Stapfer, *Rabelais, sa
personne, son génie, son œuvre*, 1889 (distinguished by good sense and
appreciation of Rabelais's humour); R. Millet, *Rabelais*, 1892 (*Les grands
écrivains français*). The books of Delécluze, Meyrargues, and E. de Noel
are of little or no value. E. Faguet's essay in his *Seizième siècle*, in spite
of his position that Rabelais's character is a very simple one and some
other rather astonishing propositions, is well worth reading, and
C. Whibley's introduction to Urquhart's translation (see above) is sensible
and sympathetic. See also F. Brunetière in *Rev. des deux mondes* for
Aug. 1, 1900. H. Schneegans in his *Geschichte der grotesken Satire*,
Strasburg, 1894, deals with the character of Rabelais's humour in a somewhat heavy and pedantic fashion.

The following works relate to special points :—T. Ziesing, *Erasme ou
Salignac*, 1887; Ch. Abel, *R. Médecin stipendié de la cité de Metz*,
Metz, 1870; R. Gordon, *F. Rabelais à la faculté de Médecine de Montpellier*, Montpellier, 1876; A. Dubouchet, *Rabelais à Montpellier*, 1530-38,
ib. 1887 (adds little or nothing of importance to Gordon); A. F. Le Double,
Rabelais anatomiste et physiologiste, 1899; F. A. Arnstädt, *F. Rabelais
und sein Traité d'Éducation*, Leipsic, 1872; G. Compayré, *Hist. critique
des doctrines de l'Éducation en France*, 2 vols. 1879 (I. 55-82); A. Coutaud,
La pédagogie de Rabelais, 1899; H. Ligier, *La politique de Rabelais*, 1880
(sensible but slight); Ch. Lenormant, *Rabelais et l'architecture de la
Renaissance*, 1840; E. Cartier, *La numismatique de Rabelais* in *Revue de
Numismatique*, XII. 336-349, 1847; Th. Baudement, *Les Rabelais de
Huet*, 1867 (an account of Huet's manuscript notes in the margins of two
of his copies of Rabelais); G. d'Albenas, *Les portraits de Rabelais*,
Montpellier, 1880.

The *Rev. des Études Rab.* I. 188 ff. gives a list of German commentaries
on Rabelais which have appeared since about 1870.

In 1886 a society was formed on the initiation of F. Audiger under
the title of *Société des Amis et Admirateurs de Rabelais* with its head-
quarters at Tours. Its publications consist of two pamphlets by Audiger
and six notices of its annual congress from 1886 to 1892. After the latter
year it was dissolved (see *Rev. des Études Rab.* I. 79 ff.).

In 1903 the *Société des Études Rabelaisiennes* was founded at Paris
with M. Abel Lefranc for president, and the first number of its review,
Revue des Études Rabelaisiennes, which is published quarterly, appeared
in July of that year. The Society contemplates among other lesser
undertakings an edition of Rabelais's complete works worthy of the
great nation of which he is so illustrious an ornament.

CHAPTER XI

CALVIN

IF Rabelais is unquestionably the first writer of French prose during the reign of Francis I, Calvin is as unquestionably the second. He is not like Rabelais a great artist; but inferior though he is in the highest qualities of style, in imagination and harmony and colour, he is superior in the more homely, but more essential qualities of clearness and precision; and it was he and not Rabelais who determined the future of French prose and prepared the way for Pascal, and Bossuet, and Voltaire. Before Rabelais and Calvin French prose had been mainly narrative and descriptive. Alain Chartier had taught it eloquence; Jean Le Maire had given it strength and dignity, but no one had yet taught it to reason. Comines is not a master of any style, but as a narrator he writes tolerably well; when he tries to reason, he stutters, and stumbles. Then came Rabelais with *Pantagruel* and *Gargantua* and for the first time revealed to his countrymen the capabilities of the instrument on which he played. Still his triumphs are greatest in the domain of narrative and description; when he leaves the world of fact for that of ideas, he writes as an imaginative philosopher rather than as an analytical reasoner. Moreover when Calvin translated the *Institution* into French, Rabelais had not yet written his Third or his Fourth book, the part of his work in which he is most concerned with abstract questions.

Jean Calvin was born on July 10, 1509, at Noyon in Picardy. It is noteworthy that the majority of those who played leading parts in the early developement of French Protestantism came from Picardy or the neighbouring province of Artois ; Lefèvre d'Etaples and his friends Gerard Roussel, Michel d'Arande, and François Vatable, who started the movement at Meaux, Calvin's cousin and fellow-townsman Pierre Olivetan, the translator of the Protestant Bible, and Jean Crespin, the author of the Protestant Martyrology. Calvin's real name was Cauvin, but having Latinised it after the fashion of the day into Calvinus he adopted Calvin as the French form. His father, Gerard Cauvin, was a lawyer who held several posts connected with the Chapter at Noyon, and who was thus enabled to make a comfortable provision for each of his three sons[1]. Jean, who was the second, received as his portion before he was twelve years old the chaplaincy of one of the Cathedral chapels. At the age of fourteen he was sent to Paris where he attended the Latin classes of Maturin Cordier, the educational reformer, at the College of La Marche[2]. When he was sufficiently advanced to begin the academic course in arts, he joined the College of Montaigu, which with Noel Beda for its Principal was, as we have seen, a stronghold of the obscurantist party in the University[3].

In 1527 he was presented by the Chapter of Noyon to a living, but early in the following year, when he had completed his course in arts, his father, who had begun to have sundry differences with the Chapter, came to the conclusion that the Law offered a more promising career than the Church. Calvin was accordingly sent to Orleans to study law, and took his degree of Licentiate in that University. But either before or after this event he migrated to Bourges, attracted by the fame of Alciati's lectures[4]. Here also he studied Greek under Melchior Wolmar, who had already taught him at

---

[1] There was a fourth who died in childhood.

[2] *Ante*, p. 17.

[3] The usual course in arts was three years and a half; he therefore probably joined the College of Montaigu after Easter in 1524.

[4] In a document of Feb. 14, 153½, he is described as a Licentiate. The regular course for the Licence being two years, he may have taken his degree at the beginning of 1530. Alciati began to lecture at Bourges in 1528, and was appointed Professor in 1529 (*ante*, p. 22).

Orleans[1]. On the death of his father in May 1531 he gave up all thoughts of a legal career, and having determined to devote himself to humanistic studies returned to Paris where he attended the lectures of Pierre Danès, the royal professor of Greek. The firstfruits of his studies was a commentary on Seneca's *De clementia*, which he published in April 1532 at his own expense[2]. Soon after its publication he returned to Orleans, remaining there till after June 1533.

He was now a Protestant, his conversion which had begun in 1528 having been completed in 1532[3], and before long his new opinions were the occasion of a public scandal. On November 1, 1533, the usual Latin oration was delivered by the Rector of the Paris University, Nicolas Cop. To the indignation of his audience it contained a passage expressing open approval of the doctrine of justification by faith. It soon became known that Calvin, who was Cop's friend, had written his speech for him. He was in Paris at the time and had to seek safety in flight. The winter was spent at Angoulême, where he lived in the house of a young canon, Louis du Tillet, under the name of Charles d'Espeville[4]. In the spring he paid a visit to the aged Lefèvre d'Etaples at Nerac. We next find him at Poitiers[5], and then at his native Noyon, where after resigning his benefices on May 4, 1534 he was imprisoned from May 26 to June 3 for exciting a tumult in a church. The preface to his next work, the *Psychopannychia*, is dated from Orleans, 1534, and he was probably residing in that town when the affair of the Placards took place (October 18, 1534). The persecution which ensued made flight from France imperative. He accordingly made for Basle by way of Metz and Strasburg. It was in Basle on August 23, 1535, that he put the last touch to the *Christianae Religionis Institutio*. It was published in the following year. In that year, after a short visit for the purpose of regulating

---

[1] See the letter to Wolmar prefixed to the Commentary on the Second Epistle to the Corinthians (*Opera*, XII. 364).

[2] The preface is dated from Paris, April 4, 1532.

[3] See Doumergue, I. 337—352.

[4] Herminjard, *Corr. des réformateurs*, III. 156.   [5] *ib.* 201 n.

his affairs, he left his native country for ever and went to
Geneva with the intention of stopping there for a night on
his way to Strasburg. But Guillaume Farel, by whose efforts
the establishment of the reformed religion had, after a sharp
struggle with the Catholic party, been recently proclaimed at
Geneva, constrained him to remain.

The great work which Calvin carried on at Geneva lies
outside the scope of these pages. It is only with his work
as a writer of French prose that we are now concerned.
His masterpiece, the *Institution Chrestienne*, was published
in its French form in the year (1541) in which he made
his triumphal re-entry into Geneva (September 13) and
took up the reins of government never again to lay them
down till his death. This first version of the French translation of the *Institution* was made by Calvin himself from
the second Latin edition of 1539, a greatly enlarged form
of the original edition of 1536, the original six chapters
being increased to seventeen and the matter being more
than trebled. In the eighth and final Latin recension
of 1559 there were again very considerable alterations and
additions, making the work five times as long as it was
in its original form, and for the first time the division
into four books and eighty chapters was adopted. In the
following year 1560 a corresponding French version, the
seventh, was produced[1]. Calvin began the work himself,
dictating it to a secretary, but after making practically a
fresh translation for the first seven chapters he seems to
have contented himself with patching up the old translation,
and to have left to Nicolas Colladon the work of revising
the proofs[2]. It follows that from a literary point of view

---

[1] Table of principal editions :

Latin.			*French.*		
I. 1st. Basle .	.	1536			
II. 2nd. Strasburg .		1539	1st. [Geneva] .	.	1541
3rd. ,,	.	1543	2nd. Geneva	.	1545
III. 8th. Geneva	.	1559	7th. ,,	.	1560

In the Latin edition of 1543 the number of chapters was increased to twenty-one.

[2] See *Opera*, I. xli. The editors of this edition consider that, with the possible

the *Institution Chrestienne* of 1560 is a careless piece of work from which, except in the preface and the first seven chapters, it is impossible to get a true idea of Calvin's style.

As Nisard says in his history of French literature, Calvin's *Institution* is the first French book written on a regular plan. The four books into which it is divided in its final shape correspond to the four divisions of the Athanasian creed. The subject of the first book is God as Creator and Sovereign Ruler of the world, or God the Father; of the second God as Redeemer, or God the Son; of the third the means of Grace, or God the Holy Ghost; and of the fourth the Church. The execution of this plan is on the whole worthy of its conception. Sometimes indeed the argument is obscured by a too luxuriant overgrowth of learning and illustration, and sometimes it is abandoned for the sake of polemical digressions. But every paragraph testifies to the lucid and logical mind of the writer. If the defects of his religious system are due to that exaggerated regard for logic which is so marked a characteristic of the French nation, the same logic carries him triumphantly through the task of making that system intelligible to others.

Another feature of his style is its austere simplicity, its entire freedom not only from rhetoric but from all literary ornament. Though it is by no means what is called a personal style, it gives one the feeling of being face to face with the writer. Nor does this austerity prevent it from rising at times under the impulse of strong feeling to flights of real eloquence. Take for instance the close of the sixth chapter of the third book, which with the four following ones formed the conclusion of the original French edition:

Mais pource que cependant que nous conversons en ceste prison terrienne, nul de nous n'est si fort et bien disposé, qu'il se haste en ceste course d'une telle agilité qu'il doit: et mesme la pluspart est tant foible et debile qu'elle vacile et cloche, tellement qu'elle ne se peut beaucoup

exception of the first seven chapters, the French *Institution* of 1560 is not Calvin's work at all (III. xxv–xxvii). But the real facts of the case have been pointed out by M. Lanson in the *Rev. historique* LIV. (1894) 60 ff.; he pleads for a reprint of the 1541 edition, of which there are very few copies in existence.

avancer: allons un chacun selon son petit pouvoir, et ne laissons point de poursuivre le chemin qu'avons commencé. Nul ne cheminera si povrement, qu'il ne s'avance chacun jour quelque peu pour gagner pays. Ne cessons donc point de tendre là, que nous profitions assiduellement en la voye du Seigneur: et ne perdons point courage pourtant, si nous ne profitons qu'un petit. Car combien que la chose ne responde point à nostre souhait, si n'est-ce pas tout perdu, quand le jourdhuy surmonte celuy d'hier. Seulement regardons d'une pure et droite simplicité nostre but, et nous efforçons de parvenir à nostre fin: ne nous trompans point d'une vaine flaterie, et ne pardonnans à noz vices: mais nous efforçans sans cesse, de faire que nous devenions de jour en jour meilleurs que nous ne sommes, jusques à ce que nous soyons parvenus à la souveraine bonté: laquelle nous avons à chercher et suyvre tout le temps de nostre vie pour l'apprehender, lors qu'estans despouillez de l'infirmité de nostre chair, nous serons faits participans pleinement d'icelle: assavoir quand Dieu nous recevra à sa compagnie[1].

There are many eloquent passages in the fifth chapter of the first book (= c. I, 12—19, with large additions, of the 1541 edition), which treats of the power of God as revealed in the creation and government of the world, and the prefatory letter to Francis I is justly celebrated for its manly and simple eloquence. Here are the opening sentences:

Au commencement que je m'appliquay à escrire ce present livre, je ne pensoye rien moins, o tres noble Roy, que d'escrire choses qui fussent presentees à ta Majesté: seulement mon propos estoit d'enseigner quelques rudimens, par lesquels ceux qui seroyent touchez d'aucune bonne affection de Dieu, fussent instruits à la vraye pieté. Et principalement vouloye par ce mien labeur servir à noz François: desquels j'en voyoye plusieurs avoir faim et soif de Jesus Christ, et bien peu qui en eussent receu droite cognoissance. Laquelle mienne deliberation on pourra facilement appercevoir du livre, entant que je l'ay accommodé à la plus simple forme d'enseigner qu'il m'a esté possible. Mais voyant que la fureur d'aucuns iniques s'estoit tant eslevee en ton royaume qu'elle n'avoit laissé lieu aucun à toute saine doctrine, il m'a semblé estre expedient de faire servir ce present livre, tant d'instruction à ceux que premierement j'avoye deliberé d'enseigner, qu'aussi de confession de foy envers toy: dont tu cognois quelle est la doctrine contre laquelle d'une telle rage furieusement sont enflambez ceux qui par feu et par glaive troublent aujourd'huy ton royaume. Car je n'auray nulle honte de confesser que j'ai icy compris quasi une somme de ceste mesme doctrine laquelle ils estiment devoir estre punie par prison, bannissement, proscription et feu: et

---

[1] Text of 1560, but altered hardly at all from that of 1541.

laquelle ils crient devoir estre dechassee hors de terre et de mer. Bien
say-je de quels horribles rapports ils ont remply tes oreilles et ton cœur,
pour te rendre nostre cause fort odieuse: mais tu as à reputer selon ta
clemence et mansuetude, qu'il ne resteroit innocence aucune n'en dits
n'en faits, s'il suffisoit d'accuser[1].

It will be noticed that this passage is full of Latinisms,
not in the vocabulary, but in the structure of the sentences
and the order of the words. Some of these features indeed,
the inversions and the omissions of the article and the pro-
noun, were common to every writer of Calvin's day, being
part of the inheritance of mediæval French from Latin, but
the form of the sentences is due to Calvin's close study of
Latin. He writes, as has been said, like a man who, on
theological subjects at any rate, habitually thought in Latin.
But from both forms of Latin influence he gradually shook
himself free. Even. in the earlier period, when he is not
translating from the Latin but is writing original French, as
for instance in the remarkable letter written to the Duchess
of Ferrara in 1541, and in the two letters, known as the *Traité
des superstitions*, written in 1540 and published in 1543, the
Latin features in his style are much less noticeable. In his
latest work, such as the *Confession de foy* of 1563, there is
hardly a trace of them. But Calvin's debt to Latin is a great
one. From no other language could he have learnt so well
the secret of clause-architecture which was so essential to his
work of exposition. While the older writers had gone to
Latin models for eloquence and dignity, Calvin had learnt
from them terseness, lucidity and precision. His peculiar
relation to Latin is well put by Petit de Julleville and Rébelliau. "His method of construction in French is an admirable adaptation of the Latin method: his French is not a
natural product, it is not a developement and a new phase of
mediæval French; it is taken directly from the fountain-head
of classical Latin. But with an art, which is all the more
sure because it is instinctive, he does not Latinise beyond the
intelligence of educated Frenchmen; if his language is not
altogether natural, it is perfectly simple. The result is that,

---

[1] Text of 1541, practically unaltered in 1560.

while Latinising much more than Ronsard ever did, he is never like Ronsard, pedantic; and his style, which is to some extent artificial, or at any rate quite different from the spoken tongue, never seems affected, and in fact is not[1]."

The *Institution* is not only an expository treatise, it is also a polemic; it is not only an exposition of the Christian religion according to Calvin, it is an attack on the Church of Rome. Indulgences, purgatory, monastic vows, and especially the mass, are all condemned with that violence of language which characterises most of the controversial writing of the period. But if the tone to which Calvin too often condescends strikes a note of discord in a grave work like the *Institution*, it must be confessed that in the various pamphlets which were called forth by the numerous controversies in which he was engaged the vigour of his onslaught gives force and point to his style. When he is attacking individuals like a *certain cordelier suppost de la secte des Libertins* or a *certain belistre nomme Anthoine Cathelan*, he is perhaps too furious to be really effective. But when he is fighting against principles rather than individuals, when he has not the sense of personal injury to excite his anger, his controversial style is excellent. The popular *Traité des reliques* is somewhat heavy in its irony, but the three pieces which deal with the so-called Nicodemites, those reformers who bowed their knee to Baal, are masterpieces of vigorous and searching polemic. I will quote a passage from the *Excuse aux Nicodemites*, which is admirably written and which represents Calvin's nearest approach to playfulness:

Il y a puis apres une seconde secte. Ce sont les prothonotaires delicatz, qui sont bien contens d'avoir l'Evangile, et d'en deviser ioyeuse-ment et par esbat avec les Dames, moyennant que cela ne les empesche point de vivre à leur plaisir. Ie mettray en un mesme ranc les mignons de court, et les Dames qui n'ont iamais apprins que d'estre mignardées, et pourtant ne savent que c'est d'oyir qu'on parle un peu rudement à leur bonne grace. Ie ne m'esbahy pas si tous ceux là font une bende contre moy; et comme s'ilz avoient serment ensemble, condamnent tous d'une

---

[1] Petit de Julleville, III. 347. All classical Latin prose, with the exception of Petronius and perhaps Cicero's *Letters*, is in the same way "to some extent artificial, or at any rate different from the spoken tongue."

bouche ma trop grande austerité. Et de faict, ie m'y suis bien attendu devant le coup. Et maintenant il m'est avis que les oy: Qu'on ne nous parle plus de Calvin: c'est un homme trop inhumain. Comment? si nous le voulions croire non seulement il nous feroit belistres mais il nous merroit[1] incontinent au feu. Y a-il propos de nous presser en telle sorte? S'il veut que chacun le ressemble, et s'il est marry de nous voir plus à notre aise qu'il n'est, que nous en chaut-il? nous sommes bien icy: qu'il se tiene là où il est, et qu'il laisse chacun en repos. La conclusion est que ie ne say que c'est du monde. Quand ilz ont bien compté pour se flatter l'un l'autre, il leur semble qu'ilz se sont bien vengé de moi. Voire: mais que feront-ilz à Dieu, auquel ie les renvoye, et lequel les adiourne au son de la trompette? Un prothonotaire se pourra bien moquer du crucifix, aux despens duquel il meine ioyeuse vie, en banquetz, en ieux, en danses et en toute braveté. Car ce n'est qu'un marmoset. Mais Dieu ne se laisse pas moquer en cette façon[2].

The same subject is handled in one of the four sermons published in 1552, but here again the tone is one of anger rather than of irony. I must however quote a passage which, whatever may be thought of its taste, is certainly most vigorous and effective, and is a good instance of the homely but racy expressions which form the only garnish to Calvin's otherwise dry and unpicturesque writing:

Il ne me chault des mocqueurs qui disent que nous en parlons bien à notre aise: car ce n'est point à moy qu'ils s'attachent, d'autant qu'il n'y a rien yci de mon creu, comme on le voit. Autant en di-ie de tous ces philosophes, qui en prononcent leur sentence sans sçavoir comment; car, puisqu'ils ne veulent escouter Dieu, lequel parle à eulx pour les enseigner, ie les adjourne devant son siege iudicial, là où ils orront sa sentence, contre laquelle il ne sera plus question de replicquer. Puisqu'ils ne daignent maintenant l'ouïr comme maistre, ils le sentiront alors iuge en despit de leurs dents....

Les beaux tiltres ne feront yci rien pour exempter personne, sinon que messieurs les abbez, prieurs, doyens et archediacres seront contraincts de mener la danse en la condamnation que Dieu fera. Si messieurs les courtisans ont accoustumé de contenter les hommes par leur eau beniste, qu'ils n'attentent pas de faire le semblable à Dieu. Que tous gaudisseurs se deportent de donner leurs coups de bec, et iecter leurs brocards accoustumez, s'ils ne veulent sentir la main forte de celuy à la parolle duquel ils debvoyent trembler[3].

[1] meneroit, 1566.   [2] Opera, VI. 598-9.
[3] ib. VIII. 390-1; Œuvres françoises, p. 229.

Finally I will add a passage in a very different style, which describes in modest and simple language how he was constrained by Farel to abide at Geneva:

Pource que pour aller à Strasbourg, où ie vouloye lors me retirer, le plus droit chemin estoit fermé par les guerres, i'avoye deliberé de passer par yci legerement, sans arrester plus d'une nuit en la ville. Or un peu au paravant la Papauté en avoit este chassee par le moyen de ce bon personnage que i'ay nommé[1], et de maistre Pierre Viret : mais les choses n'estoyent point encore dressees en leur forme, et y avoit des divisions et factions mauvaises dangereuses entre ceux de la ville. Adoncques un personnage, lequel maintenant s'est vilenement revolté et retourné vers les Papistes, me descouvrit et feit cognoistre aux autres. Sur cela Farel (comme il brusloit d'un merveilleux zele d'avancer l'Eavangile) feit incontinent tous ses efforts pour me retenir. Et apres avoir entendu que i'avoye quelques estudes particulieres auxquelles ie me vouloye reserver libre, quand il veit qu'il ne gaignoit rien par prieres, il veint iusqu'à une imprecation, qu'il pleust à Dieu de maudire mon repos et la tranquillité d'estudes que ie cherchoye, si en une si grande necessité ie me retiroye et refusoye de donner secours et aide. Lequel mot m'espovanta et esbransla tellement, que ie me desistay du voyage que i'avoye entreprins : en sorte toutesfois que sentant ma honte et ma timidite, ie ne voulus point m'obliger à exercer quelque certaine charge[2].

The defects of Calvin's style are what we should naturally expect in a writer who took no pains except to be clear and convincing. It is sometimes long-winded and it is often rough, shewing that he had neither the leisure nor the desire to put an artistic finish on his work. Besides this it is wanting in colour and harmony; it is the style of a man devoid of imagination. As was the man, so is his style.

Calvin's Commentaries on the Epistle to Titus are dedicated to "two eminent servants of Christ, Guillaume Farel and Pierre Viret." In noble and touching words he compares his relation to these two with that of Titus, the head of the Church of Crete, to St Paul. For it was Farel and Viret who, with the help of Antoine Froment, had founded the reformed church at Geneva, but who on the arrival of Calvin

[1] Guillaume Farel.
[2] *Opera*, XXXI. 26 (Preface to the *Commentary on the Psalms*).

persuaded him to stay there, and left it to him to complete
their work.   They themselves were shortly afterwards called
to other spheres of activity, Farel to Neuchatel, Viret to
Lausanne.

Farel[1] was the senior by twenty-two years.   A native of
Gap in Dauphiné, and a student and professor of the Paris
University, he was one of the earliest men in France to
embrace the new religion, and he had been working in its
service for already ten years, when in the year 1531 he encountered Viret, then a young man of twenty, living in his
native town of Orbe in the canton of Vaud, and made a
convert of him.   Farel was chiefly celebrated for his eloquence,
but unfortunately no record of his sermons, which he always
delivered extempore, has been preserved.   Some of his shorter
writings however, such as the *Forme d'oraison* and the *A tous
cœurs affamés*[2], enable us to some extent to judge of his powers.
The latter especially is full of eloquent passages remarkable
for their well-balanced and rhythmical periods ; a few lines
deserve quotation as a specimen :

> Reduisez en memoire tout ce que Iesus a faict & dit, tous ses tormens
> & angoisses, & icy vous iettez à terre & criez de tout ce qui est en vous,
> iettez tout vostre cueur en Dieu, tout sens, puissance, vertu, & entende-
> ment, de tresardente affection criez sans cesse : Ha! Seigneur Dieu &
> Pere, la grande multitude de nos pechez, de nous, & de nos peres, te
> pressera elle tant, que tu n'ayes pitié de nous, & que tu uses de telle
> rigueur sur nous, que nous soyons delaissez comme poures brebis esgarées
> & sans pasteur : & Seigneur, o Seigneur, ayes souuenance de la mort &
> passion de ton trescher filz, qui estant esgal a toy, d'une mesme puis-
> sance, authorité, essence, & diuinité, pour nostre salut a pris nostre
> chair, & esté faict vray homme, comme il estoit vray Dieu, prenant ce
> qu'il n'estoit point, & ne laissant point ce qu'il estoit eternellement.

But except under the influence of strong emotion Farel is
not a good writer.   *C'était une flamme, rien de plus.*

Pierre Viret[3] had a far greater natural aptitude for

---

[1] b. 1489—d. 1565.

[2] Both written and published in 1545, and reprinted in the volume containing
Du vray usage.

[3] b. 1511—d. 1571.

literature. If Calvin was the theologian of the reformed religion, and Farel the orator, Viret was the pamphleteer[1]. An easy and rapid writer he produced during the course of some twenty years (1544–1564) a large number of volumes, some of which had considerable popularity. His style, if it lacks the incision and nervous force of Calvin, has all his clearness and much of his skill in managing his periods. But, like most rapid writers, Viret is careless and slovenly, diffuse, and given to repetition. Born of the people—his father was a cloth-worker—and writing for the people, he adopts a popular tone, and makes a liberal use of colloquial words and phrases. At the same time he shows himself to be well furnished with learning, adorning, not to say over-loading, his treatises with quotations from a wide range of ancient literature. His writings may be divided into two classes, expository and polemical. The chief work of the expository class is the *Instruction Chrestienne*, a bulky work in two volumes composed of various earlier treatises with little or no attempt at unity. Calvin's *Institution* is more for instruction than for pleasure, but Calvin watered down to the comprehension of the multitude by a writer of greatly inferior powers is beyond the range of literature. Viret is rather more readable in his polemical or satirical works, of which the best is *Le monde à l'empire et le monde demoniacle*, composed of ten dialogues; but even this need not detain us. The dialogue form which Viret adopted for all his works, with the view of making them more popular, does not seem very effective when the speakers are little better than dummies. But it was certainly popular in Viret's day, and in the second half of the sixteenth century was used alike by Protestant controversialists, by the pamphleteers of the wars of religion, by Henri Estienne, and by Agrippa d'Aubigné.

---

[1] Lenient calls him the *commis-voyageur* of the Reformed Church.

BIBLIOGRAPHY.

I. CALVIN.

Editions.

JEAN CALVIN. *Opera quae supersunt omnia,* ed. G. Baum, E. Cunitz,
E. Reuss, 59 vols. (*Corpus Reformatorum* XXIX—LXXXVII), Brunswick,
1863—1900 (I—IV comprise the various recensions of the *Institutio,* V—
IX the minor treatises, X—XX the correspondence, XXI the three recensions of Beza's life of Calvin, XXII—LVIII the Commentaries and
Sermons, LIX the indexes and bibliography). *Recueil des opuscules c'est à
dire petits traictez de M. Jean Calvin,* ed. Beza, Geneva, 1566. *Œuvres
françaises,* ed. P. Lacroix, 1842 (a selection, including the spurious translation of the *Psychopannychia*). *Lettres françaises,* ed. J. Bonnet, 2 vols.
1854. *Institution de la religion chrétienne, revue et corrigée sur l'édition
française de* 1560 *par* F. Baumgartner, Geneva, 1888. The following are
his principal French writings :

1537. *Instruction et confession de Foy. Op.* XXII. An unique copy
discovered in 1877 by H. Bordier and published as *Le Cathéchisme
français,* Geneva, 1878 ; the editors of the *Corpus* think that the *Confession*
is by Farel and only the *Instruction* by Calvin.

1541. *Institution de la religion Chrestienne.* First French edition[1].

1541. *Petit traicté de la saincte cène. Op.* V. *Œuvres franç.* 181 ff.

1543. *Traicté des reliques. Op.* VI. *Œuvres franç.* Reprinted
(from 1599 edition), Geneva, 1863.

1543. *Traité des superstitions. Op.* VI. First published in this year
under the title of *Petit traicté monstrant que c'est que doit faire un homme
fidèle cognoissant la vérité de l'Evangile, quand il est entre les papistes,
avec une Epistre du mesme argument* (the letter, written after the *traicté,*
is dated Sept. 12, 1540). Reprinted in 1551 with another treatise, written
in 1544, on the same subject, entitled *Excuse de Iehan Calvin à messieurs
les Nicodemites, sur la complaincte qu'ilz font de sa trop grand' rigueur.
Op.* VI.

1544. *Brieve instruction...contre les erreurs...des anabaptistes. Op.* VII.

1545. *Contre la secte...des Libertins qui se nomment Spirituels.
Op.* VII.

1547. Reprint of the preceding with *Une epistre de la mesme manière
contre un certain Cordelier. Op.* VII. *Œuvres franç.* 293 ff.

1549. *Advertissement contre l'Astrologie. Op.* VII. *Œuvres franç.*
107 ff.

---

[1] See notes to the text of 1560, *Op.* III. IV.

1552. *Quatre Sermons avec exposition du Pseaume* 87. *Op.* VIII. *Œuvres franç.* 211 ff.

1554. *Declaration pour maintenir la vraye foy...de la Trinité...contre les erreurs detestables de Michel Servet.* *Op.* VIII.

1556. *Réformation pour imposer silence à un certain belistre nommé Antoine Cathelan.* *Op.* IX. *Œuvres franç.* 313 ff. Assigned to this year by Colladon in his life, but no copy of an edition of this date is known to exist.

1562. *Response à un certain Hollandois.* *Op.* IX.

1564. *Confession de foy au nom des églises réformées de France.* *Op.* IX. *Œuvres franç.* 330 ff.

Besides these treatises there are over two thousand *Sermons*, of which the most celebrated are those on Job (*Op.* XXXIII—XXXV); *Commentaries* on nearly every book of the Bible, the prefaces to some of which, especially that to the Commentary on the Psalms (1558, *Op.* XXXI), are of great merit ; and the voluminous correspondence (*Op.* X—XX).

See A. Erichson, *Bibliographia Calviniana*, Berlin, 1900 (reprinted with additions from vol. LIX of the *Opera*). It gives only short titles of most of the treatises.

An English translation of the *Institution* by Thomas Norton was published in 1561.

LIFE.

The basis of all the modern lives is that of Beza of which there are three recensions :—(1) *Discours contenant en bref l'histoire de la vie et mort de maistre Jean Calvin*, Geneva, 1564 (also prefixed to the *Commentaries on Joshua* ; this life in its original form was written in the year of Calvin's death and is of a highly panegyrical character) ; (2) *L'histoire de la vie et mort de feu maistre Jean Calvin, ib.* 1565 (also prefixed to a new edition of the *Commentaries on Joshua*; this recension of the life was revised and enlarged by Nicolas Colladon, and is the most important of the three for Calvin's private life) ; ed. A. Franklin, Paris, 1864 ; (3) *Vita Calvini*, Lausanne, 1575 (further revised and turned into Latin by Beza).

One of the best modern accounts of Calvin's life is that by H. Bordier in the 2nd edition of *La France Protestante* 1881, though for his early life it must be supplemented by A. Lefranc, *La jeunesse de Calvin* 1888, the same writer's article in *La grande encyclopédie* 1889, and E. Doumergue, *Jean Calvin. Les hommes et les choses de son temps*, Lausanne, I. 1899.

There are also good accounts by Ch. Dardier in Lichtenberger's *Encyclopédie des sciences religieuses* 1877, and by R. C. Stähelin in the 3rd ed. of Herzog's *Realencyclopädie für prot. Theologie und Kirche*, Leipsic, 1897. F. W. Kampschulte, a Roman Catholic professor at Bonn, published at Leipsic in 1869 (2nd ed. 1899) the first volume of his *Johann Calvin seine Kirche und sein Staat in Genf* which goes down to the year 1546, but owing to his early death it was never completed; it is excellent as far as it goes.

TO BE CONSULTED.

A. Sayous, *Études littéraires sur les écrivains français de la réformation*, 2 vols. 1841; 2nd ed. 1854, I. 67—180; II. 349—386. E. Renan, *Études d'histoire religieuse* 1862 (a review of Bonnet's *Lettres françaises*). E. Faguet, *Seizième siècle* 1894, and Petit de Julleville and A. Rébelliau in Petit de Julleville III. 319—345, 1897. F. Brunetière, *L'œuvre littéraire de Calvin* in *Rev. des deux mondes* for Oct. 15, 1900.

2. FAREL AND VIRET.

Editions.

GUILLAUME FAREL. *Summaire et briefve declaration* 1534 (only 3 copies known); ed. T. G. Baum, Geneva, 1867; the original edition printed in 1524–1525 has completely disappeared. *Epistre envoyee au duc de Lorraine* 1543 (Brit. Mus.). *Le glaive de la parole veritable*, *ib.* 1550 (a copy in the public library of Geneva). *Du vray usage de la croix*, 1560 (copies at Geneva and in the Bodleian); reprinted with other treatises by Farel, Geneva, 1865.

As mentioned above the Confession to the *Instruction et Confession de Foy* (Calvini *Op.* XXII.) is believed by the editors of the *Corpus Reformatorum* to be by Farel. In recent years an addition has been made to his writings by the discovery and publication of a MS. containing an account of the famous *Dispute de Rive* of 1535 and entitled *Le recueil et conclusion* &c., which is assigned to him on apparently good grounds (*Mém. et doc. de la Société d'hist. et d'arch. de Genève*, 2me série, II. 201—240).

PIERRE VIRET. *Disputations chrestiennes* (in 3 parts), Geneva, 1544. *Metamorphose chrestienne faite par dialogues*, Geneva, 1552. *Le monde à l'empire et le monde demoniacle fait par dialogues, revu et augmenté*, *ib.* Jacques Bres, 1561 (10 dialogues), also *ib.* Berthet, 1561; this work in its original form was part of the *Dialogues du desordre qui est a present au monde*, 2 vols. *ib.* 1545. *Instruction chrestienne*, 2 vols. *ib.* 1564.

TO BE CONSULTED.

La France Protestante, 2nd ed. VI. (Farel), 1st. ed. IX. (Viret); A. Sayous, *op. cit.* I. 1—65 (Farel), 181—241 (Viret); C. Lenient, *La Satire en France* I. 194—203, 1877 (Viret). For Swiss writers generally see J. Senebier, *Histoire littéraire de Genève*, Geneva, 3 vols. 1786; V. Rossel, *Hist. litt. de la Suisse Romande*, 2 vols. Geneva, 1889 (somewhat superficial and inaccurate); P. Godet, *Hist. litt. de la Suisse française*, 1890, pp. 33—112 (a good sketch).

CHAPTER XII

MEMOIRS AND CHRONICLES

DURING the reign of Francis I the humanistic impulse, though it led, as we have seen, to the translation of several Greek and Roman historians, had but little effect on the production of national history. Throughout the reign the two popular histories of France were the translation, with additions, by Pierre Desrey of Gaguin's *Compendium*, and the longer work of Nicolas Gilles. Both alike were based on the great collection of chronicles, known as the *Grandes chroniques*, formed at St Denis, and they reproduced the mediæval character of these chronicles[1]. But in the third year of the reign there appeared a Latin history of France which was modelled on the pattern of the classical historians, especially of Livy. It was the work of an Italian, Paolo Emilio, of Verona, who had come to France on the invitation of Louis XII. At first in four books only, it had reached ten, bringing it down to the year 1488, at the author's death in 1529[2]. It was continued down to the death of Francis I by the French scholar and jurist Arnoul Le Ferron[3], and in 1556 was introduced to a wider circle of readers in a French translation by Jean Regnart[4]. It was only in form that the work of Paolo Emilio with its imaginary speeches and colourless classical style differed from those of Gaguin and

---

[1] The oldest known edition, the second, of Gaguin's *Compendium super Francorum gestis* is of 1497, but it appeared originally in 1495 and the translation in 1514; the latter was also often published under the titles of *Miroir historial de France* and *La mer des croniques et miroir historial*. Gilles' work appeared in 1492, but the oldest known edition is of 1525.

[2] *De rebus gestis Francorum libri* IV. [1517]; *libri* X. 1539.

[3] For Le Ferron (1515—1563) see Christie, *E. Dolet*, pp. 123 ff.

[4] Originally of five books only; the most complete edition, which includes Le Ferron's continuation, is of 1581.

Gilles. Its material was derived from the same sources, and was handled with equal lack of criticism. Of a similar humanistic type, but written in French, was Dolet's *Les gestes de Francoys de Valois, Roy de France* (1540), a paraphrase of a Latin poem on the wars of Francis I which he had published in the previous year[1].

Meanwhile the distinguished soldier and statesman Guillaume du Bellay had written a Latin history of the reign in eight books or, as he called them, *Ogdoades*, based on his own intimate knowledge, and at the request of the King had translated them into French. But at his death in 1543 only a small portion of the work could be found. His brother Martin therefore determined to supply its place by writing a history, or, as he modestly entitled it, memoirs, of the reign on his own account, incorporating the existing fragment of the *Ogdoades*. His work, however, was not published till after his death, in the year 1569, the editor being René du Bellay, Baron de la Lande, the son-in-law of Guillaume and the heir of Martin. Books i–iv and ix and x are the work of Martin, while books v–viii, being a portion only of a single *Ogdoade*, the fifth, are by Guillaume[2]. Martin's memoirs are not ill-written, but they are commonplace in style as well as thought. Guillaume's are evidently the work of a man of a higher order of intelligence, but they are stiff and long-winded. Moreover both alike lack the personal element which makes for literature. On the other hand the memoirs of Robert de la Marck, Seigneur de Fleuranges, *le Jeune Adventureux* of Francis I's boyhood[3], are true memoirs, making no pretence to be history, but written with considerable liveliness, and containing some interesting gossip. They served to beguile the writer's imprisonment in the *château* of L'Écluse. Like the Du Bellay memoirs, they were not published in the reign of Francis I, in fact not till the eighteenth century[4].

---

[1] See Christie, *op. cit.* pp. 365—369.

[2] The Latin text of the first book of the first *Ogdoade* is preserved in the *Bib. nationale*. See B. Hauréau, *La première ogdoade de Guillaume du Bellay*.

[3] b. 1492 or 3—d. 1536.

[4] First printed by the Abbé Lambert in 1753 in vol. VII. of his edition of the Du Bellay memoirs.

From the point of view of literature the most interesting
quasi-historical work written in France during this period is
the life of Bayard by the anonymous secretary who calls
himself *Le Loyal Serviteur*[1]. The interest inherent in the
character, sublime in its simplicity, of its hero is heightened by
the charm of a lively narrative and the *naïve* admiration of
the writer. Moreover there is no better document on the
spirit of chivalry. The wide distinction between rich and
poor, or rather between gentleman and 'villain,' the dis-
proportionate value which is set on a knight's life compared
with that of an ordinary foot-soldier, the deviations from the
Christian code which the code of honour permitted to a hero
sans reproche, are all extremely instructive. Many of the
events are admirably described, such as Bayard's combat
with Don Alonso (c. 21), his attempt to capture Pope Julius II
(c. 43), his illness at Brescia (c. 51), and his death (c. 64).
On the whole however the general character of the book and
the style of writing is more akin to the spirit of mediæval
literature, to that of Froissart for instance, than to that of
the Renaissance. A life of Bayard was also written by
Symphorien Champier, but it need not detain us; still less
need a life of La Trimouille (who was killed at the battle of
Pavia a year after Bayard) by Rabelais's friend, Jean Bouchet.

Two journals kept by citizens of Paris during the reign of
Francis I have come down to us, and were published in the
middle of the last century. But of these one, entitled by its
editor *Journal d'un bourgeois de Paris*[2], is devoid of all literary
merit, while the other, *Cronique du roi François I*[3], if written
in a somewhat more lively style and with more eye for
interesting details, still lacks the personal note which is the
salt of literature. To find this in the chroniclers of this
period we must go to Geneva, where the stirring events which
preceded the establishment of Calvinism produced numerous

[1] *Histoire de Bayart par Le Loyal Serviteur*, ed. J. Roman. M. Roman on the
evidence of an entry in the catalogue of the *Bib. Mazarine* thinks that the oldest
known edition of 1527 was preceded by one printed in 1524, the year of Bayard's
death, in which the name of the writer appeared on the title-page as Jacques de
Mailles.

[2] Ed. L. Lalanne, 1854.   [3] Ed. G. Guiffrey, 1860.

memoirs and journals. Many of these have no literary value; but three writers stand out among the rest, all of whom have a full share of that lively spirit which characterised the gay and pleasure-loving city of Geneva before it passed under the austere rule of Calvin. These are Jeanne de Jussie, Antoine Froment and François Bonivard.

Jeanne de Jussie was a nun of St Claire, who became abbess of the community after its removal to Annecy and died at an advanced age towards the close of the sixteenth century. Her account of the religious troubles at Geneva was published after her death under the title of *Le levain du Calvinisme, ou Commencement de l'Hérésie de Genève*[1]. Though not completed till 1547 the greater part of it, so minute and graphic are the details, must have been written as a journal day by day. In addition to its interest as giving the Roman Catholic point of view of the religious revolution at Geneva it has real literary merit. Jeanne de Jussie is by no means a correct or practised writer, but she atones for her deficiencies in grammar and style, which are not after all very great, by the actuality of her narrative. Simply by force of that power of close observation which women as a rule possess in a greater degree than men, and of the lively directness with which she reports the results of her observation, she has produced a narrative which always charms by its *naïveté* and often impresses by its dramatic force. She lets her characters, the Abbess and her nuns on the one hand, the Syndics and their officers on the other, speak, as in a drama, for themselves, while the part of the chorus is represented by the animated and racy language of her indignant comments. She is at her best in the account of the entry of the Lutherans into the convent and the examination of the Abbess and her nuns. Here is the portrait of Marie Dentiere, the first wife of Antoine Froment:

En celle compagnie estoit vne Moine Abbesse fausse, riche, et langue diabolique, ayant mary et enfans, nommee Marie d'Entiere, de Picardie, qui se mesloit de prescher, et de peruertir les gens de deuotion. Elle se va mettre entre les Sœurs pour trouuer Sœur Collette Mesuere, et

[1] Chambéry, 1611; *Le levain du calvinisme* is the editor's title for it.

demandoit à l'vne, puis à l'autre, estes vous sœur Collette, ma fille, nous voulons vous parler: et la premiere à qui elle s'adressa c'estoit elle mesme: mais elle la repoussa du costé disant, ie ne suis pas celle que tu cherches, va la chercher autre part: et de chacune auoit quelque reproche disant, vat'en Moine reniee, et langue enuenimee. Mais pour l'enuie qu'elle auoit d'en peruertir aucune, ne faisoit conte des reproches, et disoit, hé pauures creatures! si vous sçauiez qu'il fait bon estre aupres d'vn ioly mary, et comment Dieu l'a aggreable; l'ay long temps esté en ces tenebres et hypocrisie ou vous estes, mais le seul Dieu m'a faict cognoistre l'abusion de ma chetiue vie, et suis paruenüe à la vraye lumiere de verité. Considerant que ie viuois en regret: car en ces religions n'y a que cagoterie, corruption mentelle, et oysiueté, et pour ce sans differer ie prins du thresor de l'Abbaye iusques à cinq cens ducats, et me suis retiree de ce malheur, et graces au seul Dieu, i'ay desia cinq beaux enfans, et vis salutairement.

It is interesting to compare this account of the nuns by one of their own body with that of a writer of the opposite party :

Dauantage les Sindicques et plusieurs du Conseil voyans l'obstination de ces Dames de Sᵗᵉ Clayre, et affin qu'elles n'eussent excuse d'ignorance, ou occasion de se plaindre de Geneue, les ont bien voullu encore derechef admonester et prier de voulloir viure selon l'Euangile, de laysser leurs superstitions, leurs ceremonies papalles accoustumees, et d'assister à la predication comme les aultres : et ce faysant, la Seigneurie s'offroit à les tracter en maniere qu'elles eussent heu occasion de se contenter. Mais toutes, d'ung commun accort, furent de cette resolution de s'en aller et d'absenter la ville, excepte une, qui descouurit, ce que dict Clement Marot, le pot aux roses, laquelle d'empuys apres fust mariee à ung Prebstre de Sᵗ Gerves, Messire Thomas Genotz, laquelle a vescu fort honnestement en mariage, durant sa vie ; et luy furent baillés mille flourins de mariaige, du bien du Convent de Sᵗᵉ Clare.

The above passage is from Antoine Froment's *Les Actes et Gestes merveilleux de la cite de Geneve*[1], an account of events from 1532 to 1536 which he wrote about the year 1550, but which were not printed till three hundred years later. Froment had helped to establish the reformed religion at Geneva, but he gave a great deal of trouble to his co-reformers by his conceit, want of judgment, and disorderly habits. In 1549 he was at Bonivard's request appointed to assist him in

---

[1] Ed. G. Revilliod, 1854. Froment (b. *circ.* 1509—d. 1581) was, like Farel, a native of Dauphiné.

the work of preparing the *Chroniques de Genève* for the press, and this put it into his head to write a continuation on his own account. His narrative, as we might expect from a man of his character, is anything but a grave historical work; it is neither philosophical, nor impartial, nor accurate. The style, too, is far from correct, and in a long sentence becomes hopelessly involved. But it has life and movement; and with its dramatic touches and free use of colloquialisms and *patois* it is well suited to story-telling. The account of the conversion of a *bourgeoise* named Claudine Levet (c. iii) opens exactly in the manner of a *conte*. The next chapter, which contains a report *in extenso* of a sermon preached by Froment in the *place du Molard*, the principal public square of Geneva, is interesting as a specimen of the more popular pulpit oratory of the reformers. Throughout the work Froment himself plays a prominent part. Whether as a preacher, or as narrowly escaping a ducking in the Rhone, he figures joyously on his own canvas. Egotism however is the breath of autobiography, and it is the personal element in Froment's narrative which gives it its chief interest. But we must pass on to a greater man.

François Bonivard is probably known by name to a greater number of English people than any other writer except Calvin who has been mentioned in this history. And he is not only known by name but in connexion with a historical fact, his imprisonment in the castle of Chillon. 'The prisoner of Chillon' however was a very different sort of person to the melancholy captive portrayed in Byron's poem. His six years' imprisonment was merely an episode in a long and active life, an episode which, judging by the way in which he himself mentions it, does not seem to have made much impression upon him[1]. Born in 1493 at Seyssel in Savoy of a noble and ancient family he succeeded at the age of seventeen to the rich and independent priory of St Victor, which his uncle had vacated in his favour. His position

---

[1] *Chroniques des Ligues de Stump*, addition by Bonivard, cited by Chaponnière in *Mem. et Doc. de la Soc. d'Hist. et Arch. de Genève* iv. 267–8; *Chroniques de Genève* ii. 407 (quoted *post*, p. 248).

brought him into collision with the Duke of Savoy, whose claim to seignorial rights he refused to recognise, and whose displeasure he further incurred by actively assisting the city of Geneva in its just resistance to his pretentions. In 1519 he was arrested and confined in the castle of Grolée for two years, and deprived of his priory, which he never afterwards regained. On his release he espoused more warmly than ever the cause of the burghers of Geneva, with the result that when the duke caught him again he shut him up in the castle of Chillon. Here he remained for six years from 1530 to 1536 till on the capture of the castle by the army of Berne, which had made common cause with Geneva, he was set at liberty. He returned to Geneva to find the religious revolution accomplished, and he became a protestant like his neighbours. This step put the recovery of his lost revenues out of the question, but the republic out of gratitude for his services made him a member of the Council of Two Hundred, and assigned him a house and an annual pension of 200 crowns, which was afterwards increased to 400, his debts to the amount of 800 crowns being paid in addition. In spite of his avowed preference for living under a republic he could not have felt quite at ease at Geneva. He cared for liberty less as a lofty political abstraction than as a personal possession, and of this latter sort of liberty there was very little in the good city of Geneva. It must have been intolerable to the *ci-devant* prior of St Victor, who had ruled absolutely over a considerable domain, that he could not play at backgammon with a brother man-of-letters for five sous without being summoned before the Consistory[1]. He had probably not brought more than a moderate amount of theological fervour into his change of religion, and austerity was distasteful to him. He was virtuous, but he did not think virtue incompatible with cakes and ale.

However, he managed to keep on good terms with the Consistory, and on the whole they treated him with considerable indulgence from their point of view. In 1542 he was charged with the task of writing a history of Geneva, a work

---

[1] See *ante*, p. 72.

to which he brought great zeal and industry and which occupied him actively from 1546 to 1551. But owing to the request of the Consistory that some passages should be omitted and that the style generally should be made less familiar, a delay took place in the printing, and, so far as is known, the work remained unprinted till the last century[1].

On the whole the *Chroniques de Genève* partakes more of the nature of a Chronicle than of a history. There is little sense of proportion, things important and unimportant being related in equal detail. But the narrative is interesting and intelligent, and bears some traces of a true historical spirit. There is plenty of citation, and some criticism of authorities ; and occasionally there is a good review of the political situation, or a business-like summary of antecedent events. In the two latter of the four books which deal with the period within Bonivard's memory (1514–1532) events are related at greater length.

With the exception of some youthful and very poor verses and a translation of Postel's *De magistratibus Atheniensium* the *Chroniques* was apparently Bonivard's first literary work. But after its completion his pen was seldom idle. His next work, which was entitled *Advis et devis de l'ancienne et nouvelle police de Genève*, was completed in 1556[2]. It was a defence of Calvin's government against the party of the *libertins*. It contains a good many stories to the discredit of Calvin's opponents, which lose none of their flavour in the telling. *Amartigenée* (ἁμαρτιγένεια), a rambling philosophical treatise on the origin of sin, was presented by him in 1562 to his fourth wife three weeks after their marriage. It was followed up by a philological treatise, equally rambling, called *Advis et devis des lengues*, the philology of which is naturally absurd, but which shows a good deal of learning and contains some good stories. Between these two grave treatises was written *Advis et devis de la source de l'idolatrie*

---

[1] An edition was published in 1831, but it does not give a complete text and has been superseded by the excellent one of Chaponnière and Revilliod.

[2] It was presented to the Consistory in that year (Senebier, *Cat. Raisonné*, p. 380).

et tyrannie papale, which is anything but grave, and which should rather have been entitled Scandal about the Popes, for it consists of short biographies, after the manner of Tallemant des Réaux, of the eleven popes from Alexander VI to Pius IV who had worn the tiara in Bonivard's lifetime. Many of the stories are no doubt apocryphal, but they are all *ben trovato*. Then after pelting the popes he showed his impartiality by throwing stones into the Protestants' garden, and in a short treatise entitled *Advis et devis des difformes reformateurz* he pointed out that a good many persons had embraced the reformed religion from purely interested motives, giving as instances various champions of reform, notably the Landgrave Philip of Hesse and Henry VIII of England, whose morals had stood greatly in need of reformation. Anticipating by an ingenious use of Boccaccio's story of the Marquise de Montferrat and the King of France (1. 5) Voltaire's comparison between religions and sauces, he declares that whatever our religion may be we still remain children of Adam.

On the whole we get the most favourable idea of Bonivard's style from the *Chroniques*. It is evidently more carefully written than any of the *Advis et devis*; the style is more equal, and, as may be seen from a comparison of the passage on monarchy, aristocracy, and democracy[1] with the corresponding passage in the *Advis et devis de noblesse*[2], it is less familiar. Considering that Bonivard's works were written in the home of Calvin some years after the publication of the *Institution Chrestienne*, it is perhaps singular that they should show little or no trace of Calvin's influence. Bonivard's style is in fact a complete contrast to Calvin's; the merits and defects of the two writers are exactly opposite, and what is lacking in the one is the distinction of the other. Bonivard is often neither clear nor logical, and he is an easy prey to the common pitfalls of sixteenth century writers, the overloading and obscuring of the main thought with parenthetical matter, and the piling up of clauses without any central architectural idea to govern them. On the other hand he has the qualities

[1] 1. 50—52.　　[2] pp. 287—289.

which Calvin lacked, colour and imagination: he is fond of quaint expressive phrases such as *les choses etaient en tel grabuge,* and *ceux qui ne danceoient selon la note que le dict peuple sonnoit, estoient en danger de recevoir de la pantoufle*; he sometimes strikes a really poetic note, as in *ne restoit que Dieu qui faisoit le guet pour Geneve tandis quelle dormoit.* His picturesque touches often remind one of La Fontaine, and make one feel how thoroughly La Fontaine would have appreciated him if he had known him. Like La Fontaine he uses *patois* and old-world expressions which, to borrow a French metaphor, *sentent le terroir,* a habit which makes his style look more mediæval than it really is. For though it is far less modern than Calvin's, it is scholarly and correct, and in ordinary narrative well constructed. As Littré has pointed out, it is akin to Rabelais's in syntax. I will quote as a specimen the passage in the *Chroniques* in which Bonivard relates his capture and imprisonment:

Mais quant nous fusmes pres Saincte Catherine sus le Iurat, voicy le capitaine du chastel de Chyllon, nomme Messire Anthoine de Beaufort, seigneur de Bierez, avec ung bailly de Thonon nomme Rosey, qui estoient embusches au boys auec douze ou quinze compaignons, qui sortent de lembusche sur moy. Ie cheuaulchoie lors une mulle de mon guide ung puissant cortaut; ie luy dis: "Picque, picque!" & picquay pour me sauluer, & mis la main a lespee. Mon guide, au lieu de picquer auant, tourne son cheual & me saulte sus, & auec ung coustel quil avoit tout prest me couppa la caincture de mon espee. Et sur ce ces honnestes gens arriverent sur moy & me feirent prisonnier de la part de Monseigneur. Et quelque saufconduict que leur monstrisse (*sic*), me menerent lie & guerrote a Chillon, ou ie demeuray non plus longuement de six ans, iusque Dieu, par les mains de Mess. de Berne accompaignez de plusieurs de Genesve, me deliura des mains de ces honnestes gentz, comme verrez quant parlerons de la prise du pays de Sauoye. Et voyla ma seconde passion[1].

There is a touch of Rabelais in this account of the death of Leo X: *Or ce poltron de pape se revoltant contre les Francoiz par ces menees leur fit perdre Milan, de quoy il fut si esioui que riant, beuvant et bancquettant il mourut de joye soubdainement,* and in this: *A un basteleur est bien seant tourner les yeux ça et*

---

[1] II. 407.

la, bien dancer, sauter, gambader, bien iouer de souplesse[1]. In fact there are not a few reminiscences of Rabelais in his writings; Rabelais's book was evidently well known to him and is several times referred to; another contemporary whom he often quotes is Marot. But his most frequent references are to ancient literature, in which he had evidently read widely, historians, philosophers, poets, fathers. He also knew German and Italian and Spanish, though, judging from his quotations in these languages, with no great accuracy. He had a fine collection of books, which he bequeathed to the public library at Geneva: it included the *editiones principes* of Apuleius and Ammianus Marcellinus[2]. He has been called the Montaigne of Geneva: I should be rather tempted to compare him with Rabelais, for he belongs both as a man and as a writer to the same generous race.

BIBLIOGRAPHY.

EDITIONS.

ROBERT III DE LA MARCK, SEIGNEUR DE FLEURANGES. *Mémoires*, ed. Petitot, 1re série, XVI; ed. Michaud and Poujoulat, V.

Histoire composee par le loyal serviteur des faiz gestes triomphes et prouesses du bon chevalier sans paour et sans reprouche le gentil seigneur de Bayart, Paris, 1527; ed. J. Roman for the *Soc. de l'Hist. de France*, 1878.

JEANNE DE JUSSIE. *Le Levain du Calvinisme ou Commencement de l'Hérésie de Genève*, Chambéry, 1611; ed. G. Revilliod, Geneva, 1853; ed. Ad.-C. Grivel, *ib.* 1865.

ANTOINE FROMENT. *Les Actes et Gestes merveilleux de la cite de Geneve*, ed. G. Revilliod, Geneva, 1854.

FRANÇOIS BONIVARD. *Histoire veritable...de quatre Jacobins de Berne heretiques et sorciers*, [Geneva], 1549; reprinted, *ib.* 1867 (a translation of part of Stumpf's *Chroniques des Ligues*). *Chroniques de Genève*, ed. J. J. Chaponnière and G. Revilliod, 2 vols. *ib.* 1865. *Advis et Devis de la source de lidolatrie et tyrannie papale, suivis des difformes Reformateurz de ladvis et devis de menconge et des faulx miracles du temps present*, ed. J. J. Chaponnière and G. Revilliod, *ib.* 1856. *Advis et*

---

[1] *Advis et devis des lengues*, p. 60.

[2] As Gaullieur has shewn, he was not the founder of the library, as he is often said to be (*Histoire et description de la libraire publique de Genève*, Neuchâtel, 1850).

Devis des Lengues suivis de Lamartigenee, ed. G. Revilliod, *ib.* 1865.
*Advis et Devis de l'ancienne et nouvelle police de Genève suivis de l'advis
et devis de noblesse, ib.* 1865. (In 1549 permission was granted to
Bonivard to print the *Advis et devis de la noblesse*; and Senebier says
that he had seen a copy of an edition of 1549; as the existing MS.
mentions the accession of Charles IX, Dec. 5, 1560, we must suppose
that Bonivard made later additions to it.)

To be consulted.

A. Rilliet, *Notice sur Jeanne de Jussie,* Geneva, 1866; E. and E. Haag,
La France Protestante (2nd ed.), vol. VI. (Froment); Senebier, *Histoire
littéraire de Genève,* I. 131—139, 1790; J. J. Chaponnière, notice prefixed
to *Chroniques de Genève*; E. Littré, *Littérature et histoire,* pp. 286—301,
1875; A. Sayous, *Les écrivains français de la réformation,* I. 359—367
(2nd ed.), 1881.

CHAPTER XIII

RETROSPECT

THE period of production covered by the preceding chapters extends roughly from 1525 to 1550. It is true that several of the works mentioned had not been published by the latter date, but they had nearly all been written, and had for the most part been circulated in manuscript. We have seen that it was about the year 1525 that the popularity of the old school of poetry began to decline in favour of the new. In the year 1529 Humanism may be said to have definitely triumphed; it was the year of the publication of Budé's *Commentarii linguae graecae* and of the establishment of the royal professorships. In 1532 the seal was set on Marot's growing popularity by the publication of a collected edition of his poems, and almost certainly before the end of the same year appeared the first instalment of Rabelais's great work. In 1540 was published the first book of Herberay des Essarts's translation of *Amadis*, and in the following year the French version of the *Institution*. The remaining years of the reign of Francis I, with their policy of severe repression of heresy, were hardly favourable to the production of literature. On July 1, 1542, the Parliament of Paris issued a long edict concerning the supervision of the press, and in 1544 the Sorbonne published its first *index expurgatorius*, which included Lefèvre's translation of the New Testament, Marot's Psalms, and above all *Gargantua* and *Pantagruel*.

In 1545 however the author of *Pantagruel* managed to

obtain from the King, whose conscience was perhaps beginning to trouble him for the massacre of the Vaudois, a fresh privilege. Armed with this he published in 1546 a third book with his name for the first time boldly set out on the title-page. But when it appeared, or at any rate soon afterwards, Rabelais was no longer on French soil. In the same year Margaret of Navarre put into execution the project which she had conceived about five years earlier of forming a collection of tales on the model of the *Decameron*; and, though the result was not published till twelve years later, her stories were doubtless circulated at this time.

Thus by the close of the reign of Francis I, not only had French literature been enriched by several masterpieces, but its whole character had been changed. The lumbering verse of the *grands rhétoriqueurs* had been replaced by verse which, if not of the highest quality, was at any rate natural, graceful, and harmonious; their stilted prose gave way to a prose style which not only exhibited these qualities, but in the hands of Rabelais attained a brilliance and variety, and in those of Calvin a precision and lucidity hitherto unknown in French literature. This change was due primarily to the Renaissance spirit, to that quickening of the interest in human life which revealed itself on the one hand in the spirit of free inquiry, and on the other in individualism. For the root of the difference between what passed for literature at the beginning of the reign of Francis I and the literature which flourished at its close lay in the fact that, while the former was in the main a mere putting together of words in obedience to mechanical rules, the latter was a direct representation of life shaped according to the temperament and the artistic conception of the individual writer.

As has been pointed out in the previous chapters, the new writers owed something to foreign models, chiefly to Latin and Italian ones. We have seen that Margaret of Navarre borrowed the plan of her *Heptameron* from Boccaccio, that Marot's Eclogues and Epistles were modelled on Virgil and Horace, that Des Periers was indebted to Lucian for the form of his *Cymbalum Mundi*, and that Rabelais owed to the same writer the framework of his later books. Lastly, the syntax and the clause architecture of both Rabelais and Calvin are the result of a close familiarity with Latin models. But the debt, at any rate on the part of these five principal writers of the period, is almost entirely one of form; the spirit of their work is thoroughly French. It is this strong national flavour in the literature which, as we shall see, distinguishes the reign of Francis I from that of his successors.

Of the individual writers Rabelais stands head and shoulders above the rest; he is the only one who takes rank with the great creators of the world, who gives us noble thoughts in a noble form. The second place, especially in a history of literature, undoubtedly belongs to Marot. His is the success which comes from knowing one's own powers; though his poetry is not of the highest kind, of its kind it could hardly be better. Common sense, great literary tact, and an intuitive knowledge of the genius both of his nation and its language, enabled him to clear French poetry from the mists which for half a century had surrounded it, and to restore the literary taste of his countrymen to a healthy condition.

Margaret of Navarre had a less direct influence than Marot on the developement of the literature, but her chief work, the *Heptameron*, is distinguished by almost the same qualities as his poetry, *viz.* common sense, lucidity and literary tact. Thus, like his poetry, it illustrates the most distinctive qualities of the national genius. Nor must it be forgotten that, if her verse is often dull and tiresome, it shows here and there distinct traces of the loftier sentiment and the more elaborate harmony which it was the work of the Pleiad to introduce into French poetry.

Charles Nodier, in his enthusiasm for a writer whom he claimed not altogether without reason to have discovered, declared in confident tones that next to Rabelais the greatest literary representative of the reign of Francis I was Bonaventure des Periers. Des Periers has certainly left three or four poems which for true lyric power are superior to anything of Marot's; his tales, judged purely as tales, and putting style

out of the question, are far superior to Margaret's, while the
Cymbalum Mundi, with all its crudeness of thought and
roughness of execution, is perhaps, next to *Pantagruel*, the
most original production of the reign.   But in spite of his
greater originality, he is not, whatever he might have become
had not his life been cut prematurely short, so important a
figure in French literature as either Marot or Margaret.

Calvin stands altogether apart : he was a theological reformer first, and a man of letters afterwards.   The merits of
his style, its differences from that of Rabelais, and its influence
on the French prose of the future have been sufficiently
discussed, nor is it necessary to recapitulate here what has
been said about Rabelais as a prose writer.   Next to these
in merit as prose writers come Margaret of Navarre and
Herberay des Essarts, who resemble each other in this, that
they both nearly always write well, and not, like so many
writers of the sixteenth century, sometimes well and sometimes very ill.   Margaret is the more equal writer of the
two : she is always clear, graceful, dignified, and harmonious.
Her defect is that she has only one note ; she wants force
and passion and picturesqueness.   Des Essarts, though less
uniformly meritorious and though a little deficient in dignity,
is on the whole more interesting, because he has more variety.
Both have the somewhat rare merit of combining distinction
with simplicity.   You could no more parody them than you
could parody Caesar.

The lesser prose writers of the reign have neither the
distinction nor the equality in execution which mark these
two.   Bonivard, though the most unequal, has the most
character ; Viret, though without character, has much of
Calvin's gift for clear and logical utterance, while Le Maçon
has some of the lively and natural charm of his original.
Des Periers, as we have seen, is admirable in mimicking the
speech of common people or in telling a droll story, but he
cannot construct a period or write with dignity.   His translation of Plato's *Lysis* is vulgar and slangy.   Dolet's translations
of Plato are better, but all his prose lacks distinction and even
character.   However his *Gestes de Françoys de Valois* shows

that he had a fairly good style for narrative purposes; it is simple and on the whole clear.

The second place among the poets of the reign belongs to Saint-Gelais. He is not a poet to arouse enthusiasm, or even to excite sympathies, but he has one saving quality which has often stood French poets in good stead, and which coupled with a fair amount of sensibility has in many cases been productive of better poetry than a deeper vein of inspiration. With far less capacity for emotion than either Margaret or Des Periers, his *esprit* saves him from writing commonplace doggerel like Margaret, or trivial nothings like Des Periers. Moreover, apart from his claim as the probable introducer of the sonnet, he distinctly added a new string to the French lyre. The kind of poetry in which he excelled, a compound of half sentiment and half art, may not be the highest kind, but it is one which since his day has often flourished in France.

It will be noticed that of one important kind of literature, the drama, nothing has been said beyond a bare mention of the dramatic productions of Margaret of Navarre. The reason is that it was still of a purely mediæval type; it is not till the year 1552, the year which saw the production of Jodelle's *Cléopatre* and *Eugène*, that the Renaissance drama can be said to begin.

APPENDIX A.

1. LADOLESCENCE CLEMENTINE. Autrement, Les Oeuures de Clement Marot de Cahors en Quercy, Valet de Chambre du Roy, composees en leage de son Adolescence. Auec la Complaincte sur le Trespas de feu Messire Florimond Robertet. Et plusieurs autres Oeuures faictes par ledict Marot depuis leage de sa dicte Adolescēce. Le tout reueu, corrige, & mis en bon ordre. On les vend a Paris, deuant Lesglise Saincte Geneuiefue des Ardens. Rue Neufue nostre Dame. A Lenseigne du Faulcheur. Auec Priuilege pour Trois Ans.

On the *recto* of the last leaf: Ce present Liure fut acheue dimprimer le Lundy .xij. iour Daoust . Lan . M.D.XXXII. pour Pierre Roffet, dict le Faulcheur. Par Maistre Geofroy Tory, Imprimeur du Roy.

8vo. Collation: A—O⁸P⁴; 4 ll. not numbered (last blank)+115 ll. numbered + 1 l. not numbered.

British Museum; *Bib. Nat.*

Le Petit, p. 27; Picot, I. no. 596.

In some of the later editions Marot's preface is dated August 12, 1530, but 1530 is certainly a misprint for 1532. The edition of 1532 is therefore the first authorised edition of Marot's collected works. In the library of Fernando Colombo, the son of Columbus, there was a copy of a work entitled *Les Opuscules et petitz Traictez de Clement Marot*, which must have been published between the autumn of 1530 and the spring of 1535, and which may have been one of the unauthorised editions of Marot's early works of which he complains in the preface to the *Adolescence*. (See Harrisse, *Excerpta Colombiniana*, pp. 131—133.)

Three new editions were printed by G. Tory in the course of 1532 and 1533, containing *Autres œuvres faictes en sa dicte maladie* (see Bernard, *G. Tory*, pp. 182–3). A copy of the 2nd edition (November 13, 1532) which was in the *Bib. Mazarine* has disappeared.

2. LA SUITE de l'adolescence Clementine dont le contenu s'ensuyt, Les Elegies de L'autheur, Les Epistres differentes, Les Chantz diuers, Le Cymetiere, Et le Menu.

On les věd a Paris en la rue neufue nostre Dame, deuant L'esglise Saincte Geneuiefue des Ardens, a l'enseigne du Faulcheur. Auec priuilege pour trois ans.

8vo. Collation: A⁴ a—h⁸ of 4 ll. numbered (one blank) + 125 pp. numbered + 3 pp. not numbered. The privilege is granted to the widow of Roffet who died in the early months of 1533.

Bib. Nat.

Le Petit, p. 31.

This edition must be earlier than either of the 1534 editions, of which there are copies in the Rothschild library (Picot, I. nos. 598 and 601), for it contains less matter; but from the fact that Juste's edition of Feb. 23, 153¾ does not contain the *Suite* I infer that this edition was published only a little before it, too late for Juste to avail himself of it.

Juste, Boullé, and other Lyons publishers, brought out several pirated editions both of the *Adolescence* and the *Suite* from 1533 to 1535. A formal protest against them appears on the title-pages of the editions of the widow Roffet and of Bonnemere, published at Paris in 1536.

3. LES Oeuures de CLEMENT MAROT DE CAHORS, Valet de chambre du Roy. Augmentées de deux Liures d'Epigrammes : Et d'ung grand nombre d'aultres Oeuures par cy deuant non imprimées. Le tout songneusement par luy mesmes reueu, & mieulx ordonné.

A Lyon : au Logis de Monsieur Dolet. MDXXXVIII. Auec priuilege pour dix ans.

8vo. Gothic letter. Collation : a—k⁸ l¹⁰ ; 90 ll. numbered in Roman numerals, (*Adolescence*) : a—m⁸ ; 96 ll. similarly numbered, (*Suite*) : A—B⁸ C¹⁰ ; 26 ll., (translation of the first book of Ovid's *Metamorphoses*) : Aa—Da⁸ ; 32 ll., (Epigrams).

Bib. Nat.

Le Petit, p. 33.

There is an almost identical edition printed with the same type, with Gryphius's name as printer (see Picot, I. no. 605). Guiffrey's explanation is that Marot, having agreed with Gryphius that he should publish an enlarged and revised edition of his works, withdrew the edition from him after its publication and gave it to his friend Dolet, who had recently obtained a *bel et ample priuilege* dated March 6, 153⅞ (Guiffrey, II. 7; Christie, *E. Dolet*, p. 375 n. 1).

4. LES OEVVRES DE CLEMENT MAROT, DE CAHORS, VALLET DE CHAMBRE DU ROY. Plus amples, & en meilleur ordre que parauant.

A Lyon, a l'enseigne du Rocher, 1544.

8vo. Collation: 1st part, a—z⁸, A—H⁸; 479 pp. numbered + 17 pp. not numbered (table); 2nd part (translations), aa—qq⁸ rr⁴; 264 pp. numbered.

Printed by Antoine Constantin whose mark is on the title-page.

British Museum; *Bib. Nat.* (with date of 1545).

Le Petit, p. 35; Picot, I. no. 609.

This was the last edition published in Marot's lifetime. The poems are arranged in a new order which has been retained in all subsequent editions.

APPENDIX B.

THE AUTHORSHIP OF THE JOYEUX DEVIS.

Des Periers's authorship of the *Joyeux devis* has been questioned by no less an authority than Gaston Paris[1]. A careful examination of the evidence thus becomes necessary.

External evidence.

Estienne Tabourot says in his *Bigarrures* (1572) that the author was Jacques Peletier; La Croix du Maine says in his *Bibliothèque Française* (1584) that, though some of the tales were perhaps by Des Periers, the principal authors were Peletier and Nicholas Denisot. On the other hand Estienne Pasquier writes to Tabourot that he is mistaken. "Peletier," he says, "was one of my greatest friends, and being very jealous of his reputation would certainly have told me had he been the author. They were written by Des Periers[2]."

Of these witnesses Pasquier is the most deserving of credit, for when the *Joyeux devis* were published he was a man of twenty-nine, living at Paris in the midst of literary society, while Tabourot and La Croix du Maine were only children. The fact that La Croix was a native of Maine carries little or no weight, for, so far as we know, Peletier never returned to his native province after 1546.

Internal evidence.

We may leave Denisot out of account, for, so far as we can judge from his poetry, the prologue and the best stories of the *Joyeux devis* are far beyond his capacity.

It is rightly pointed out that the scene of eight of the stories is laid in Peletier's native province of Maine, and of eight more either

---

[1] *Journal des Savants*, 1895.
[2] *Lettres*, VIII. 12.

in Poitou or in Poitiers itself, where he lived for two or three years, and that Des Periers, so far as we know, had no connexion with either of these provinces. Against this it may be said that we are specially warned in the prologue not to suppose that the stories necessarily happened in the places assigned to them. The names of the places may well have been added or changed at the time of publication.

Certain events are mentioned which took place after Des Periers's death, namely, the deaths of René du Bellay (1546) in xxvii, of Jacques Colin (1547) in xlvii, and of Pierre Lizet (1554) in xvii. Here again these may be additions on the part of the editor. In the same way may be explained a reference at the end to the Third Book of *Pantagruel* (c. xxviii.), which was published in 1546.· In fact the words, *Pantagruel le dit bien*, read very like an addition, for the remark is so obvious that there is no reason to suppose that it is borrowed from Rabelais, especially as it is expressed in different language.

But a passage at the beginning of the prologue enables us to fix the date when the writer of the tales collected them for publication. *Je vous gardoys ces joyeux propos à quand la paix seroit faicte...mais quand j'ay veu qu'il s'en falloit le manche et qu'on ne sçauoit par où le prendre, j'ay mieux aymé m'avancer.* This must surely refer to the Treaty of Nice (June 18, 1538) by which, in default of a peace, a truce of ten years was agreed to between Francis I and Charles V. Now this date suits Des Periers perfectly well, but not Peletier, who at this time was only twenty-one.

An examination of the style leads to the conclusion that the stories in the original edition, with the exception of the last (xc)[1], are practically all by the same hand. Some of course are of no great merit, but there are very few which do not show the same lively treatment. In fact the only one which I should be disposed to question on the score of style is xxxviii, the scene of which is laid in Maine. More particular points of style are a fondness for parenthetical explanations, a peculiar way of ending the story with some little remark to the reader, and a frequent use of such forms as *caillettois, regnardois, vieillois, villenois, jurois, beguois, pageois,* which may be paralleled by Rabelais's *pensarois* (language of the thoughts) and *bibarois.*

---

[1] Note the long moralising introduction, and the inartistic handling of the story, which is another version of *nouv.* xxxvi. of the *Heptameron.* In the edition without date published by Galiot du Pré it is placed at the head of the *Additions* or spurious stories.

The evidence then practically disproves alike the assertion of Tabourot that Peletier was the author of the *Joyeux devis*, and that of La Croix du Maine that the principal authors were Peletier and Denisot. On the other hand there is no valid reason for doubting Pasquier's express statement, coinciding as it does with that of the title-page of the volume, that Des Periers was the author. The mention of certain events which happened after his death, and the introduction of one or more spurious stories, are only in accordance with the usual licence which sixteenth-century editors allowed themselves.

Charles Nodier in the article on Des Periers referred to above (p. 114) attributed to him a collection of miscellaneous essays, entitled, *Discours non plus mélancoliques que divers* (Poitiers, 1556). There is not a shadow of evidence for this attribution. According to Du Verdier the essays are the joint work of Peletier and Élie Vinet (a well-known professor of the College of Guyenne at Bordeaux), and M. Chenevière (*Des Periers*, pp. 211 ff.) has shewn conclusively that he is right.

APPENDIX C.

BIBLIOGRAPHICAL DESCRIPTION OF THE ORIGINAL AND
OTHER IMPORTANT EDITIONS OF GARGANTUA AND
PANTAGRUEL, AND OF LES GRANDES CRONIQUES.

1. LES GRANDES CRONIQUES. Les grandes et inestimables
Cronicq̃s : du grant et enorme geant Gargantua : Contenant sa
genealogie, La grandeur et force de son corps. Aussi les merueilleux faictz darmes quil fist pour le Roy Artus, cõme verrez cy
apres. Imprime nouvellement. 1532. (At the end) a Lyon.
Small 4to. Gothic letter. Collation: A⁴—D⁴ of 16 ll. not
numbered.
Bib. Nat. (the only known copy); it has a leaf missing, viz. A³ ;
bound up in the same volume with *Pantagrueline Prognostication pour
lan* 1533. Printed by Claude Nourry.
For a reproduction of the title-page see Le Petit, p. 37; Marty-
Laveaux, IV. 23.
The *Bib. Nat.* has a copy of another edition printed at Lyons,
but undated, and the Royal Library at Dresden has a copy of
an edition also printed by Nourry, and the date of 1533.

2. PANTAGRUEL. Les horribles et espouẽtables faictz et
prouesses du tresrenõme Pantagruel Roy des Dipsodes, filz du
grand geãt Gargantua, Cõposez nouuellement par maistre Alco-
frybae (*sic*) Nasier. On les vend a Lyon en la maison de Claude
Nourry, dict le Prince pres nostre dame de Confort.
Probably printed at the end of 1532.
Small 4to. Gothic letter. Collation : A⁴—Q⁴ of 64 ll. not num-
bered.
Bib. Nat.
Le Petit, p. 40.

3. PANTAGRUEL. JESUS MARIA. LES HORRIBLES ET ESPOU-
uentables faictz et prouesses du tresrenõme Pantagruel, Roy des

Dipsodes, Filz du grāt geant Gargantua, Cōpose nouuellement par maistre Alcofrybas Nasier. Augmente et Corrige fraichement par maistre Jehan Lunel, docteur en theologie. MDXXXIII. On les vend a Lyon en la maison de Francoys Juste. Demourant deuant nostre Dame de Confort.

8vo. Gothic letter. Collation: A⁸—L⁸; 1 l. not numbered+86 ll. numbered irregularly 2 to 95 + 1 l. not numbered.

Royal Library, Dresden. Bound up in the same volume and printed with the same type as the 1533 edition of *Les grandes croniques* (see *ante*, no. 1), and a *Prognostication*, of which the first and last leaves are missing, but which must be for the year 1533, for it has only six chapters.

A facsimile of this edition of *Pantagruel* has recently been published by L. Dorez and P.-P. Plan.

It is in 24 chapters, of which three are numbered ix, while there is no x. The text differs from that of no. 2 in several unimportant particulars, but sufficient to shew that it is a new and revised edition. It is very carelessly printed. For the differences see Regis, II. 1289—1316.

4. PANTAGRUEL. ΑΓΑΘΗ ΤΥΧΗ. LES HORRIBLES FAICTZ et prouesses espouëtables de PANTAGRUEL roy des Dipsodes, composes par M. ALCOFRIBAS abstracteur de quinte essence. MDXXXIIII. Monogram of Fr. Juste on the title-page.

16mo. Gothic letter. Collation: A⁸—L⁸ M⁴; 88 ll. numbered + 4 ll. not numbered, of which the last is blank.

A copy of this very rare edition was sold at the Sunderland sale (*Bib. Sund.* no. 10470, bound up with no. 6) to the late M. Morgand of Paris, who kindly shewed it to me with nos. 10472—10479 from the same sale and five or six other interesting editions. It has since been re-sold, but I do not know the name of the present possessor.

See Le Petit, p. 43, for a reproduction of the title-page of M. Morgand's copy.

This edition is in 29 chapters, c. x of the earlier editions being divided into three chapters, and cc. xiii, xiv, and xv into two each. There are also considerable additions and alterations in the text.

5. GARGANTUA. [Title-page missing in the only known copy.]
8vo. 14 × 6 cm. Gothic letter. Collation: A⁸—M⁸ N⁴; 100 ll. not numbered. [1534.]

Bib. Nat. The only known copy, of which the first and eighth leaves are missing.

This edition is printed with the same type and the same capitals as no. 6, but the impression is much fresher. It is therefore certainly prior in date.

6. GARGANTUA. ΑΓΑΘΗ ΤΥΧΗ. LA VIE INESTIMABLE DU GRAND Gargantua, pere de Pantagruel, iadis cõposée par L'abstracteur de quĩte essẽce. Liure plein de pantagruelisme. MDXXXV.
On les vend a Lyon chès Frãcoys Juste devãt nostre Dame de Confort.
8vo. 13 cm. Gothic letter. Collation: A⁸—M⁸ N⁶; 102 ll. not numbered. Title printed in red and black.
Bib. Nat. See *Bib. Sund.* no. 10470.
Le Petit, p. 45.
Compared with no. 5 this edition shews several changes, all unimportant, but evidently made by Rabelais's own directions. As no attempt is made to tone down the strong Protestant flavour of certain passages, we may infer that it was not published until after the Edict of Coucy (July 16, 1535) had stayed the prosecutions for heresy resulting from the affair of the Placards. It is very incorrectly printed. Doubtless Rabelais did not revise the proofs himself; in July he left France for Rome, and earlier in the year he was apparently in hiding.

In 1537, after Rabelais's return from Rome, Juste published a new edition, but with only a few unimportant changes from the text of 1535.

7. PANTAGRUEL and GARGANTUA. Pantagruel, Roy des Dipsodes, restitue a son naturel, auec les faictz et prouesses espouentables: cõposes par feu M. Alcofribas abstracteur de quinte essence. MDXLII.
On les vend a Lyon chez Françoys Juste deuãt nr̃e Dame de Cõfort.
16mo. 11 cm. Collation: A⁸—S⁸ T⁴; 145 numbered ll. + 3 ll. not numbered, of which the last is blank.
This part contains the *Prognostication pour l'an perpetuel.*
La vie treshorrificque du grand Gargantua, pere de Pantagruel, iadis cõposée par M. Alcofribas abstracteur de quinte essence. Liure plein de Pantagruelisme. MDXLII.
On les vend &c.
16mo. 11 cm. Collation: A⁸—T⁸ U⁴; 155 ll. numbered + 1 leaf blank.
Brit. Mus. *Bib. Nat.* Bound up in the same volume is *Le disciple de Pantagruel.*

This edition of Gargantua and Pantagruel was re-issued in the same year by Pierre de Tours, with a fresh title-page—Grandes Annales Tresueritables des Gestes merueilleux du Grãd Gargantua &c. 1542. A Lyon par Pierre de Tours—and with 3 ll. of an *imprimeur au lecteur* containing the attack on Dolet.

Bodleian Library. There was a similar copy in the Sunderland Library (*Bib. Sund.* no. 10472), but with the date of 1543 on the new title-page.

It is evident that P. de Tours acquired Juste's business.

8. THIRD BOOK. Tiers liure des FAICTZ ET DICTZ Heroïques du noble Pantagruel : cõposez par M. Franç. Rabelais, docteur en Medicine, & Calloïer des Isles Hieres. A Paris, par Chrestien Wechel. MDXLVI. Auec privilege du Roy, pour six ans.

8vo. 16 cm. Collation : a⁴ A⁸—Y⁸ Z⁴ ; 8 pp. not numbered + 355 pp. numbered + 5 pp. not numbered.

Bib. Nat. (Bishop Huet's copy) ; the last leaf is missing.

In forty-six chapters ; the last chapter is numbered 47, but there is no 27.

Le Petit, p. 47 ; Picot, II. no. 1511.

9. FOURTH BOOK. Le Quart Liure des faicts & dictz Heroiques du noble Pantagruel. Composé par M. François Rabelais, Docteur en Medicine, & Calloier des Isles Hieres. A Lyon, Lan mil cinq cens quarante & huict.

16mo. Collation : A⁸—F⁸ ; 48 ll. not numbered, with woodcuts ; badly printed.

Bib. Nat. The only other known copies are in the Rothschild collection (Picot, II. no. 1513) and the Royal Library at Dresden.

First edition of the Fourth Book, in eleven chapters ; printed by P. de Tours.

10. THIRD BOOK. Le Tiers Liure des Faicts et Dicts Heroïques du bon Pantagruel : Composé par M. Fran. Rabelais, docteur en Medicine. Reueu, & corrigé par l'Autheur, sus la censure antique. ...A Paris, De l'imprimerie de Michel Fezandat, au mont S. Hilaire, a l'hostel d'Albret. 1552. Auec privilege du Roy.

8vo. 16·5 cm. Collation : A⁸—V⁸ Y⁴ ; 11 ll. not numbered + 159 ll. numbered 2 to 48, 50—57, 57—89, 100—170 + 4 ll. not numbered.

Bib. Nat.

Picot, II. no. 1514.

In fifty-two chapters, cc. 26, 33, 36, 40, 45 and 49 of the edition of 1546 being severally divided into two. With considerable additions, especially in cc. 10, 15, and 25.

In an edition of the four books published in 1556, without place of publication, this book has forty-eight chapters, which presupposes an edition, now lost, intermediate between that of 1546 and that of 1552. (See Brunet, *Recherches*, p. 97.)

11. FOURTH BOOK. LE QUART LIVRE DES FAICTS et dicts Heroiques du bon Pantagruel. Composé par M. François Rabelais, docteur en Medecine. A Paris, de l'imprimerie de Michel Fezandat 1552. Auec privilege du Roy.

8vo. Collation: A⁸—Y⁸ Z¹; 20 ll. not numbered + 143 ll. numbered 2 to 144 + 14 ll. not numbered (for *table* and *briefve declaration d'aulcunes dictions plus obscures*).

Brit. Mus.; *Bib. Nat.* (wants the *briefve declaration*, as do other examples, *e.g.* that in the collection of the late Baron de Ruble).

Le Petit, p. 50; Picot, II. no. 1514.

In sixty-seven chapters with a new prologue.

12. FOURTH BOOK. Same title with the addition of *Reueu et corrigé pour la seconde edition*, 1552. No place of publication.

16mo. Collation: a⁸—z⁸, A⁸—D⁸; 24 ll. not numbered + 375 pp. numbered + 9 pp. not numbered.

Brit. Mus.

The prologue contains the words, *grand victorieux et triumphant*. Printed with different type to no. 13, probably by Fezandat.

13. THE FOUR BOOKS. Les Oeuvres de M. François Rabelais, Docteur en Medicine, contenans la vie, faicts, & dicts Heroiques de Gargantua & de son filz Panurge: Auec la Prognostication Pantagrueline. MDLIII.

16mo. Collation: a⁸—z⁸, A⁸—Z⁸, AA⁸—NN⁸ O⁵; 933 pp. numbered (two pp. are numbered 191 and two 255, but there is no 192) + 21 pp. not numbered.

Brit. Mus. Bound in two volumes, with the monograms of Louis XIII and Anne of Austria. Bought at the Destailleur sale in 1891. Former owners were M. Chedeau of Saumur and M. Joseph Renard of Lyons (see *Cat. Renard*, no. 449).

Reproduces for books I and II the 1542 edition of F. Juste, for book III Wechel's edition of 1546 in 46 chapters. The title of book IV has *reueu et corrigé pour la seconde edition*. Not printed by Fezandat, or the 1552 edition of book III would have been followed.

Another copy was sold at the sale of M. de Ruble's library (*Cat. Ruble*, no. 437).

14. FIFTH BOOK. L'ISLE SONNANTE PAR M. FRANÇOYS RABELAYS qui n'a point encore este imprimee ne mise en lumiere: en laquelle est continuee la nauigation faicte par Pantagruel, Panurge et autres officiers. Imprime nouuellement. MDLXII.
Small 4to. Collation: A⁴—H⁴; 32 ll.
Bib. Sund. no. 10478. Bought by Morgand for £26. I do not know who is the present possessor.
In sixteen chapters, the last being entitled *L'Isle des Apedeftes*; a MS. note at the beginning of this copy says that this chap. is a satire on the *Chambre des Comptes*.

15. FIFTH BOOK. LE CINQUIESME ET DERNIER LIVRE DES FAICTS ET DICTS Heroïques du bon Pantagruel, composé par M. François Rabelais, Docteur en Medecine. Auquel est contenu la visitation de l'Oracle de la Diue Bacbuc, & le mot de la Bouteille: pour lequel auoir, est entrepris tout ce long voyage. Nouuellement mis en lumiere. MDLXIIII.
16mo. 11 cm. Collation: A⁸—M⁸ N⁶; 97 ll. numbered 1 to 16 and 33 to 113 + 5 ll. (for *table*) not numbered.
Bib. Nat.
Le Petit, p. 53.
In forty-seven chapters, that on the Apedefts being omitted.

16. THE FIVE BOOKS. LES OEUURES de M. François Rabelais, docteur en medecine, côtenans cinq livres de la vie, faicts et dits Heroïques de Gargantua et de son fils Pantagruel: Avec l'oracle de la Diue Bacbuc et le mot de la Bouteille. Plus la Prognostication Pantagrueline. A Lyon. MDLXV.
8vo. Collation: a⁸—z⁸, A⁸—C⁸ D⁶; 418 pp. numbered + 10 pp. not numbered (books I and II, Prognostication, and table): aa⁸—zz⁸, AA⁸—LL⁸; 533 pp. numbered + 11 pp. not numbered (books III and IV and table): A⁸—N⁸; 97 ll. numbered + 7 ll. not numbered (book v, Epistre du Limosin, La cresme philosophalle, and table).
Bodleian Library.
There is a separate title-page to book v, which is a repetition of that of no. 15 with the addition of "appelle vulgairement l'Isle Sonnante." The bottle is figured on the verso of p. 92. This part also contains *Epistre du Limosin* and *La cresme philosophale*.

APPENDIX D.

ON THE BEGINNING OF THE YEAR IN FRANCE BETWEEN 1515 AND 1565.

On the 1st of January 1565, the practice of beginning the year on the 1st of January came into legal force in France. This was in accordance with an edict of Charles IX issued in January 1563 (clause 39) and registered by the Parliament of Paris on December 22, 1564.

Prior to this, at any rate since the fourteenth century, the legal year had begun on Easter-eve. But soon after 1500 the new method began to be adopted in France by publishers and others for private documents. Thus we find the publisher, Jean Petit, in the *Opus quadragesimale* of Olivier Maillard, the printing of which was finished on February 1, $150\frac{6}{7}$, using both methods, the old in the imprint, and the new in his preface. So the printer Josse Bade (Jodocus Badius) dates the *Apologia* of Noel Beda, published on February 15, $15\frac{19}{20}$, *secundum Parrhisiorum supputationem* MDXIX.

Again, to take another class of instances, Louise of Savoy uses the new method in her Journal, and says in one place *l'an* 1519 *et selon la coutume de France* 1518 *le* 31 *de Mars*, Easter-day in 1519 being on April 24. So Fleuranges, who wrote his memoirs in 1525, speaks of the 1st of January 1515 as *le jour de l'an*.

It follows from this that between 1515 and 1565, while the privileges of books, being public documents, are dated according to the old method, the date of publication follows sometimes the old and sometimes the new, the new method however becoming more and more common.

But the practice being thus uncertain, a difficulty in determining the date is liable to arise in the case of any book published between the 1st of January and Easter. Sometimes it can be determined by internal evidence, sometimes by the date of the privilege or the preface, sometimes by a knowledge of the practice, supposing it to be constant, of the particular publisher or printer. In any case there is a problem to be solved.

PART II

1550–1580

THE PLEIAD

CHAPTER XIV

VALOIS AND MEDICI

WE have seen that during the reign of Francis I there was a large influx of Italian artists and men of letters into France. The greater number were Florentine refugees; the Arno flowed into the Seine. At the court of Henry II and Catharine de' Medici this foreign influence made itself sensibly felt, and the Renaissance began to wear an Italian aspect. Unfortunately the Italy which thus took France captive was a decadent Italy, decadent alike in politics and morals, in art and literature. Rosso and Primaticcio, to whom Francis I entrusted the decoration of his new palace at Fontainebleau, were with all their learning and invention mannerists and eclectics. They largely influenced various departments of art, and their influence reached even literature. It is to them that we may trace the love of mythological ornament which is so marked a characteristic of the poetry of the Pleiad, and which retained its hold on French poetry throughout the classical period. Italian literature was on the whole less worthily represented at the French court than art. It is true that among the recipients of the royal favour were Matteo Bandello and Luigi Alamanni, both of whom have an assured place on the roll of Italian literature: but the great majority of the hungry aspirants for place and profit who found their way across the Alps were third-rate Petrarchists like Gabriele Simeoni or Giulio Camillo, whose very names have fallen into oblivion.

But there was a good side to this Italian influence. Italian literature of the first half of the sixteenth century is

marked by a strong sense of style. There are few long
poems in which the style is sustained at so high a level as in
the *Orlando Furioso*; there is hardly another in which it is
sustained with so little apparent effort. Even in the colder
and more artificial productions of the age, such as the poems
of Bembo and the other Petrarchists, it is inspiration rather
than style that is lacking. Now style was the very quality in
which French poetry was deficient. Marot has charm and
grace in abundance, but he lacks distinction, which is but
another name for style. Contact therefore with writers who
paid an almost excessive devotion to style was no bad thing
for French poetry.

Already in the reign of Francis I at least one poet, Mellin
de Saint-Gelais, had, as we have seen, come under the spell
of Italian models. He had spent some years in Italy and was
on terms of familiarity with several of the Italian poetasters
who frequented the French court. But he only partially
learnt his lesson; it was reserved for his rivals and successors,
the poets of the Pleiad, thoroughly to complete the work of
introducing style into French poetry. And they were all the
more fitted to appreciate its value because their first lessons
had been learnt from greater masters than the Italians, from
Homer and Pindar and Sophocles. The older French
humanists, and Rabelais among them, had drunk greedily of
classical literature, and especially Greek literature, as the
fountain-head of all knowledge. They had cared little for its
beauty. When Rabelais calls Plato divine, he is probably
thinking less of his language than of his philosophy. But
Ronsard and his fellows worshipped the Greek writers for
their style.

This change in the spirit in which the classics were
studied was accompanied by a greater diffusion of classical
knowledge. Latin, and to some extent Greek, began to be
recognised as a necessary part of the education, not only of
an ecclesiastic, but of an ordinary French gentleman who
was destined for a civil career. The well-known passage, in
which the future magistrate and diplomatist, Henri de Mesmes,
describes his life at college, may be taken as no unusual

picture of education among this class at the close of the reign of Francis I. In the year 1542, he tells us, when he was in his eleventh year, he was sent with his younger brother to the College of Burgundy under the charge of a private tutor. When he left, a year and a half later, he sent in two thousand Greek verses, and many Latin ones, and recited in public some Greek and Latin declamations and the whole of Homer[1]. In his fourteenth year he was sent to the University of Toulouse, where he spent three years chiefly in the study of law. "We were up at four; and, having said our prayers, went at five to lecture, our huge books under our arms, our writing-cases and candlesticks in our hands. We heard various lectures up to ten o'clock without a break. Then, after half an hour spent in hastily correcting our notes of the lectures, we dined. After dinner we read for amusement Sophocles or Aristophanes or Euripides, sometimes Demosthenes, Cicero, Virgil, or Horace. At one to lecture again; at five back to our lodgings, to go over our notes and look up the passages referred to in the lectures. This took till past six; then we had supper, and read Greek or Latin[2]."

In the same year (1545), in which Henri de Mesmes joined the University of Toulouse, the cause of education was greatly strengthened at the Paris University by the appointment of a remarkable man to the headship of the College of Presles. Pierre Ramus, the descendant of a noble Flemish family named De la Ramée, but the son of a day labourer, had obtained his education at the College of Navarre by acting as servant to a wealthy fellow student[3]. In 1536 at the age of twenty-one, when he was a candidate for the master's degree, he had electrified the University by supporting, unshaken by the attacks of his opponents, the paradoxical thesis that everything written by Aristotle was false, and in 1543 he had followed this up with a detailed and severe criticism of

---

[1] *Récitay Homère par cœur d'un bout à l'autre.* I cannot believe this statement.

[2] E. Fremy, *Mémoires inédits de H. de Mesmes* (1898), 136 ff. The passage is quoted by Rollin in his *Traité des Études*, II. c. 2.

[3] For Ramus (1515—1572) see C. Waddington, *Ramus*, 1855; John Owen, *The Skeptics of the French Renaissance*, 1893, pp. 491 ff.

the Aristotelian logic (*Aristotelicae animadversiones*). The
partisans of Aristotle were up in arms; Ramus's book was
sentenced to be burnt, and he himself was forbidden to lecture
on philosophy. This was the man who in spite of the attacks
of his opponents succeeded in raising the College of Presles
from one of the most obscure to one of the most popular
colleges in the University. Thanks to the good offices of
his old fellow-student, the Cardinal of Lorraine, Henry II
restored to him full liberty of writing and lecturing, and in
1551 appointed him to the new royal professorship of
eloquence and philosophy, which was created expressly for
him[1]. Two thousand persons came to hear his inaugural
address. His lectures became the most famous in Paris,
surpassing even those of Turnèbe in reputation, who, as
Brantôme quaintly puts it, had not *telle piaffe de parler en
seigneur, comme Ramus.*

In a preface written in the last year of his life Ramus
speaks of the reform of dialectic as the achievement by
which he wished especially to be remembered. But nearly
every department of study in the University profited by
his reforms, which consisted chiefly in the substitution of
humanistic methods of teaching for the old scholastic ones.
He encouraged the study of Greek and improved that of
Latin; but what concerns us more especially is that he took
a warm interest in his own language, writing a French
grammar, remarkable for its bold innovations in method,
and entitled *Gramerȩ* in accordance with the new system
of orthography which he proposed[2], and publishing his
Dialectique[3], the first philosophical work written in French.

We have seen that in his struggle with his opponents
Ramus found a supporter in Henry II. The new king had,
as Tavannes puts it, *plus de vertu corporelle que de spirituelle,*
and his chief interests lay in hunting and jousting and tennis,

---

[1] Pasquier, *Recherches de la France*, IX. 18.

[2] See F. Brunot in Petit de Julleville, III. 741 ff. The first edition (1562) is
very rare. Brunot gives a facsimile of two of its pages, *ib.* 773.

[3] Paris, Wechel, 1555. M. Brunot does not seem to know of this edition,
which is mentioned by Waddington as being in Victor Cousin's library.

in all of which he was extremely proficient. But he also loved
ceremony and display, and at the instigation of those about
him, especially of the Cardinal of Lorraine, gave ready
encouragement to learning and literature. The tutors for
his sons were chosen from the first scholars in the kingdom,
Danès for the Dauphin, Amyot for the future Charles IX and
Henry III. His elderly and all-powerful mistress, Diane de
Poitiers, loved books chiefly for the sake of their binding, and
was a distinguished connoisseur in every branch of art. The
vast sums which she extracted from her royal lover were
spent in building a sumptuous palace at Anet, the work of
Philibert de l'Orme, and in filling it with works of art of every
kind. The Constable of Montmorency, who was second only
to Diane in the King's affections, and her equal in greed,
had for all his rough and brutal manners a keen eye for
artistic merit. He recognised the genius of Palissy and
Bullant when they were comparatively obscure. His magnificent *châteaux* at Écouen and Chantilly, and his four *hôtels* at
Paris were store-houses of art. Though no scholar, he was
fond of history and military commentaries, and he had a fine
library which was especially rich in manuscripts[1].

Catharine de' Medici competed with Diane for architects,
and rivalled her in the richness of her bindings. She was also
an energetic collector of books and manuscripts. Her library
at her death numbered about 4,500 volumes, of which nearly
two-thirds were manuscripts. These included 800 Greek and
Latin manuscripts from the library of her cousin Piero
Strozzi, which she had annexed on his death at the siege
of Thionville[2]. As might be expected from her love of
building, architecture was well represented in her collection,
which included Fra Giocondo's edition of Vitruvius, and the
works of Serlio, Alberti, and Philibert de l'Orme. There were
over 500 works of a historical character, the majority being
French chronicles, and there was a considerable amount of

---

[1] See F. de Lasteyrie in the *Gazette des Beaux Arts*, XIX. 305 ff. and XX. 97 ff.
(1879).
[2] Brantôme, I. 434. Catharine promised to pay Strozzi's heirs for the library,
but never did so.

French poetry and drama, the latter consisting almost entirely of mediæval plays. There were also numerous romances of chivalry and novels, including five copies of Boccaccio in French. Finally one is not surprised to find a choice collection of works on astrology[1].

Of the other French princesses the King's sister, Margaret, Duchesse de Berry, was a woman of real learning and an enlightened patroness of letters[2]. The attainments of the Dauphin's wife, Mary Stuart, are well known, but they were equalled by those of her sisters-in-law, the princesses Elizabeth and Margaret, and Diane, the daughter of Henry II and Diane de Poitiers. Apart from the royal family the chief patrons of literature were the Cardinal of Lorraine and the Cardinal of Châtillon, to the one or the other of whom a large proportion of the books published during the reign of Henry II were dedicated.

Under the genial influence of all this illustrious patronage the artistic spirit of the Renaissance bore manifold fruit. Jean Bullant, Pierre Lescot and Philibert de l'Orme in architecture, Jean Goujon and Germain Pilon in sculpture, François Clouet and Corneille de Lyon in portrait-painting, were all at the height of their powers during the reign of Henry II. The minor arts were illustrated with equal distinction. Engraving on copper was represented by Jean Duvet and Estienne Delaulne, enamelling by the Penicauds, Pierre Reymond and Léonard Limosin, the potter's art by Palissy and the *faïence* of Saint-Porchaire[3]. The jewellery and the furniture of the period shew the same careful workmanship and refined taste. Indeed, in all these various forms of artistic production we find more or less the same characteristics, elegance, refinement, reverence for detail, and a general feeling for style. On the other hand, there is a certain lack of originality and creative energy. There are of course exceptions, but it is noticeable that these are chiefly to

[1] See Le Roux de Lincy, *Notice sur la bibliothèque de C. de Médicis*, 1859. The library is now incorporated in the *Bib. Nat.*

[2] See R. Peyre, *Une princesse de la Renaissance*, 1902.

[3] Formerly known as Henri Deux ware.

be found in the minor arts, notably in the work of Palissy
and Duvet.

It was much the same with literature. In the days when
copyrights could be infringed with impunity, and the publication of a popular work was the signal for a succession of
pirated editions, an author counted less on the sale of his
book than on the munificence of some royal or noble patron.
Literature was therefore hardly less dependent than art on
the patronage of the great. But it suffered more from the
dependence. The panegyrics and official poems which the
author laid at the feet of an actual or possible patron, if not
the most likely channels of inspiration, might, and sometimes
did, contain passages of excellent workmanship. A more
fruitful source of inferior work was the constant demand in
connexion with court performances for eclogues and masquerades and similar productions, or the orders for poems from
royal patrons who had their own ideas of literary art. "If
I had composed," says Ronsard, "the greater part of these
elegies to please myself, and not by express order of Kings
and Princes, I should have aimed at brevity; but I had to
satisfy the wishes of those who have power over me[1]." A
court, however cultivated, is no better judge of literature
than an ignorant public, or any other body the judgments of
which are influenced mainly by the fashion of the moment.
If then the poetry of the Pleiad, by which French literature is
chiefly represented during the reign of Henry II, is with all
its merits somewhat deficient in the two highest qualities of
poetry, creative energy and seriousness of purpose, this is in
some measure due to its dependence on a frivolous and
pleasure-loving court, in which national ideals had been
corrupted by contact with a decadent Italy.

The fatal accident in the lists of the Tournelles by which
Henry II lost his life proved also the death-blow to that
prosperity and plenty which France had enjoyed since the
beginning of the century. The lavish expenditure of Francis I
and his son, swelled by the immense sums which the latter
had distributed amongst his favourites, was now beginning to

[1] *Œuvres*, VI. 210.

tell its tale in the shape of an impoverished exchequer.
Forced economy and increased taxation added to the unpopu-
larity of the Guises, and the malcontents, fanning the sparks
of the religious controversy, rose in open rebellion.   The con-
spiracy of Amboise in 1560 and a constant succession of
local tumults between the Catholics and the Protestants fore-
shadowed the civil war which broke out in February 1562.
At first this religious warfare took the form of a series of short
wars separated by longer intervals of peace, and it was not
till after the massacre of St Bartholomew, when the intervals
of peace became shorter, that the unhappy condition of the
country began visibly to affect the production of literature
and art.

That strange unhappy being, Charles IX, had a real taste
for poetry, and his relations with Ronsard are the one bright
spot in his life.   He even interchanged verses with the 'prince
of poets':

> Tous deux egalement nous portons des couronnes;
> Mais, roy, je la reçus; poète, tu la donnes[1].

He not only consented to be 'protector' of the Academy of
poetry and music founded by Jean-Antoine de Baïf, but he
joined the institution as a 'listener' (*auditeur*) or uninitiated
member.   Similar favour was shewn to the Academy by
Henry III, who had the reputation of being a good speaker
and a good judge of literature.   His favourite poet was
Desportes, and his chief literary advisers were the two
Florentines, Jacopo Corbinelli and Baccio Delbene, but, if we
may believe D'Aubigné, he grew tired of the graceful nothings
of the later Pleiad school, and preferred to them the more
serious and more imaginative poetry which came from the
court of Navarre.   "I like," he said, "a wine with body; if
you only want something to pour down your throat, you had
better drink water[2]."

But as the reign of Henry III grew older neither kings nor
academies could avail to support literature.   It had to stand

---

[1] Unfortunately the piece which contains these lines is said to have been
touched up by other than the royal hands.

[2] D'Aubigné, *Œuvres* (ed. Réaume and Caussade), I. 459.

by itself or not at all. The long continued civil wars were the
death blow of that cultivated worship of form and beauty which
had flourished under the patronage of the house of Valois.
The great artistic movement, which had borne such various
and exquisite fruit, rapidly declined from want of nourish-
ment. Jean Goujon had already died in exile¹. François
Clouet died in the year of the massacre. The building of the
Louvre and the Tuileries came to a standstill, and by 1578 the
three great architects of the French Renaissance, Bullant,
Lescot and De l'Orme, were all dead. No one was left but
Palissy and Pilon and that shadowy figure, Jean Cousin.
Poetry fared little better that art. Ronsard retired from the
court in 1574: though he lived for another eleven years, he
had practically done his work. His successor Desportes
carried on the traditions of the Pleiad, but on less imaginative
lines. With him begins the return to an era of prose².

¹ He died at Bologna between 1564 and 1568.

⁸ Two recent publications of great importance for the subject of Italian
influence on the French Renaissance are E. Picot, *Influence des Italiens à la cour
de France*, 1903 (reprinted from the *Bull. italien*) and L. Dimier, *French painting
in the sixteenth century*, 1904.

CHAPTER XV

SCHOLARS AND ANTIQUARIES

1. *Amyot.*

ONE of the last official acts of Francis I was to appoint Jacques Amyot to the abbey of Bellozane, vacant by the death on March 16, 1547, of François Vatable, one of the royal professors of Hebrew. On the same day as Vatable there died another royal professor, Jacques Toussain, one of the professors of Greek, and his post was filled by Adrien Tournebus[1], known better as Turnebus, or as Turnèbe. The difference between the two men is typical of the change which was taking place in the whole character of French Humanism. Toussain, like all the humanists of the reign of Francis I, like Budé and Rabelais and Sylvius, was a man of great erudition ; he was, as his friends called him, a living library, ranging over the whole field of the ancient world. But with the growth of knowledge came the necessity for the division of labour. The humanists of the next generation, of the period from the accession of Henry II to the massacre of St Bartholomew, were what we should call specialists, men who devoted themselves to some one department of ancient learning.

In two of these departments France now took a decided lead, *viz.* in jurisprudence and the editing of classical texts. Cujas, Hotman, Baudouin, and Doneau ; Turnèbe, Lambin, Dorat, and Henri Estienne ; these were the great doctors of French jurisprudence and French scholarship during this

---

[1] His name was Latinised into Turnebus and then Gallicised back into Turnèbe.

golden age. Of these, Cujas and Turnèbe rank the highest,
the former as the founder of the historical school of jurisprudence, the latter as the first critical editor of classical
texts. To both alike the professors of several German
universities were wont to pay the same tribute of admiration,
that of raising their caps whenever they mentioned their
names in their lectures[1]. Turnèbe's editions of Aeschylus and
Sophocles are still regarded with respect by scholars, and his
Adversaria, or collections of notes, may still be searched with
profit[2]. Of his colleague, Denys Lambin, Munro says in his
edition of Lucretius that "his knowledge of Cicero and the
older Latin writers, as well as the Augustan poets, has never
been surpassed and rarely equalled." Dorat will come before
us in the next chapter in connexion with the Pleiad, while
Henri Estienne demands a more extended notice in this. He
alone of these four great scholars belongs to literature by
virtue of his own writings as well as by the stimulus that he
gave to others. But first we must return to Amyot, who, if
his inferior as a scholar, holds a higher place in the history of
French literature.

Jacques Amyot[3], the man who made Plutarch a Frenchman, was born at Melun on the Seine in 1513[4]. At fifteen he
was sent by his father, a small tradesman, to the University
of Paris, where he attended the Greek lectures of Jean
Bonchamp (Evagrius) at the College of Lemoine. Two years
later he took advantage of the appointment of the new royal
professors to sit at the feet of Danès and Toussain. It was a
hard struggle to support life, and when after taking his
master's degree he migrated to Bourges to study law, he was
glad to accept the post of tutor to the nephews of Jacques
Colin, who was now abbot of St Ambroise of Bourges (1535).

[1] Pasquier, *Recherches*, IX. c. 18.
[2] For Turnèbe see Montaigne, *Essais*, I. c. 24, *le plus grand homme (de lettres) qui fust il y a mille ans*; Legay, *A. Tournebus, Lecteur Royal*, Caen, 1877 ; L. Clément, *De A. Turnebi praefationibus et poematis*, 1899.
[3] b. 1513—d. 1593.
[4] A full account of the authorities for Amyot's life will be found in Blignières, pp. 400 ff. The most important are the abbé Lebeuf in *Mémoires sur l'histoire civile et ecclésiastique d'Auxerre* (2 vols. 1743), I. 618 ff., and Bayle.

Soon afterwards he was appointed by Margaret of Navarre to a professorship at the University. His first publication, the printing of which was finished on February 15, 1547, was a translation of the *Story of Aethiopia* by Heliodorus, that well-known Greek novel of the close of the fourth century, which relates the loves and adventures of Theagenes and Chariclea. It was as a reward partly for this translation, and partly for that of some of Plutarch's *Lives*, still in manuscript, that Amyot received from Francis I the abbey of Bellozane.

He spent the next four years in Italy, working in the libraries of St Mark and the Vatican. In the former he rediscovered five books of Diodorus, of which all trace had for many years been lost, and in the latter he found a manuscript of Heliodorus with a better text than that which he had used for his translation. Before his return to France Odet de Selve and the Cardinal de Tournon sent him to the Council of Trent with a letter from the king of France, which after some discussion he was permitted to read to the assembled prelates. The modest part which he played on this occasion, and of which he himself has given an amusing account, has been transformed by the historian De Thou into that of a bold champion of Gallican liberties[1]. In 1554 he was appointed tutor to the future Charles IX and Henry III[2], and in the same year he published a translation of the books of Diodorus (xi–xv) which he had rediscovered at Venice, and two others (xvi, xvii). But he still worked steadily at the *Lives* of his favourite Plutarch, and the complete translation appeared in 1559, about six months before the death of Henry II, to whom it was dedicated. A translation of Longus's novel, *Daphnis and Chloe*, which Amyot had made many years before, was published in the same year. Almost the first act of Charles IX as king was to appoint his tutor to the office of the highest dignity in the kingdom, that of grand almoner (1560)[3], and

---

[1] VIII. vii ; Blignières, pp. 77 ff.

[2] Charles was four, and Henry three.

[3] Charles IX ascended the throne on December 5, and Amyot was appointed on the following day. The grand almoner ranked immediately after the princes of the blood.

ten years later he made him bishop of Auxerre. Encouraged by the favour with which the *Lives* were received[1] Amyot went on to translate the rest of Plutarch, and not long before he was made a bishop he sent to the press the *Œuvres morales et meslées*. They appeared in 1572.

Contrary to what might have been expected from a man who was so passionately devoted to learning and letters, and in an age in which episcopal duties were so lightly brushed aside, Amyot made an excellent bishop, devoting himself to the administration of his diocese and to theological studies. For nearly twenty years he led an ideal life of peaceful and contented activity, and then the storm of anarchy broke over him (1588). For the remaining five years of his life he had to endure the 'slings and arrows of outrageous fortune,' calumny, sedition, the pillage of his property, even attempts on his person. He died in February 1593, five months before the abjuration of Henry IV made possible the return of order to the kingdom.

When Joubert says that 'in France Amyot's translation of Plutarch has become an original work,' he is speaking the literal truth. Without this complete transformation it would never have obtained its remarkable influence. For it is no exaggeration to say that, excepting Luther's Bible and our own Authorised Version, no translation has ever had so great an influence. Two hundred and fifty years later it was still a living force[2].

But it concerns us rather to note its influence on the literature of the sixteenth century. "Above all things," says Montaigne in a well-known passage, "I am grateful to Amyot for having had the wit to select so worthy and so suitable a book to present to his country. We ignorant folk had been lost had this book not lifted us out of the mire ; thanks to it we now dare speak and write, and ladies give lessons out of it to schoolmasters ; 'tis our breviary[3]." And besides

---

[1] A second and revised edition appeared in 1565 and a third in 1567, both printed by Vascosan.

[2] For the influence of Plutarch in France see O. Gréard, *De la morale de Plutarque,* 2nd ed. 1874, pp. 328 ff.   [3] *Essais,* ii. 4.

popularising the knowledge of the ancient world, it had the effect of setting before a wide circle of readers the example of noble and well-ordered lives. Those *âmes frappées à la médaille antique*, who rose superior to the "school of treason, inhumanity, and brigandage" in which they were brought up, were nourished on Amyot's Plutarch. The influence of the moralist was even greater than that of the biographer. In this capacity Plutarch appealed strongly to a nation like the French with its inborn, if undeveloped, capacity for the study of man on his moral side. The seed fell indeed on congenial soil, but one has only to compare the literature of the last twenty years of the sixteenth century with that of the previous eighty, to realise the bias that was given to it by Amyot's Plutarch.

Plutarch is also an admirable *conteur*, and with all his seriousness of purpose can appreciate in a kindly way the ridiculous side of things. Under this aspect too he found a sympathetic audience in France. His charming essay on Marriage had attained great popularity in its French dress[1], and possibly gave the impulse which, helped by Amyot's translation, determined the form not only of Montaigne's *Essays*, but of the writings of men like Noel du Fail, Guillaume Bouchet, and Beroalde de Verville, who, though generally spoken of as *conteurs*, are in reality more or less essayists.

But what is the secret of Amyot's success, and how did he come to perform that rare feat of re-creating a translation as an original work? Montaigne tells us that one day at Rome when he was dining with the French ambassador in company with Marc-Antoine Muret and other scholars, they began to criticise Amyot's scholarship and pointed out two instances in which he had gone astray[2]. Similar criticisms have been made at other times, especially by a learned academician of the seventeenth century, Bachet de Meziriac. Such criticisms are quite beside the mark when we are judging of Amyot's work as a literary performance, but it may be well to point out here that, after allowing for some cases in which Amyot

---

[1] A new translation by Grévin appeared in 1558.
[2] *Journal de Montaigne*, 1774, II. 152.

adopted a different reading from that which is now generally accepted, and for a few palpable mistakes, his translation is accepted by those best qualified to judge as that of a competent scholar[1]. The one important particular in which he differs from his original is the redundancy of his language. The following passage, in which I have italicised all his additions, will enable us to judge of this. It is the well-known account of the death of Mark Antony, whose life was one of the last which Plutarch wrote, and one of the last which Amyot translated :

Quand il sceut qu'elle vivoit encore, il commanda de grande affection à ses gens qu'ilz y portassent son corps, et fut ainsi porté entre les bras de ses serviteurs jusques à l'entree : toutefois Cleopatra ne voulut pas ouvrir les portes, mais elle se vint mettre à des fenestres *haultes*, et devalla en bas quelques chaisnes et cordes, dedans lesquelles on empacqueta Antonius, et elle avec deux de ses femmes seulement qu'elle avoit souffert entrer avec elle dedans ces sepultures, le tira amont. Ceulx qui furent presens à ce spectacle, disent qu'il ne fut onques chose si piteuse à voir : car on tiroit ce *pauvre homme* tout souillé de sang tirant aux traicts de la mort, et qui tendoit les deux mains à Cleopatra, et se soublevoit *le mieulx qu'il pouvoit.* C'estoit une chose *bien* malaisée *que de le monter, mesmement* à des femmes, toutefois Cleopatra en grande peine *s'efforceant de toute sa puissance*, la teste courbee contre bas[2] sans jamais lascher les cordes, *feit tant à la fin qu'elle* le monta *et tira à soy*, à l'aide de ceulx d'abas qui luy donnoient courage, et tiroyent autant de peine *à la voir ainsi travailler*, comme elle mesme. Apres qu'elle l'eust en ceste sorte tiré amont, et couché *dessus au lict*, elle *desrompit et* deschira adonc les habillemens sur luy, batant sa poictrine, et s'esgrattignant *le visage et* l'estomac : puis luy essuya le sang qui luy avoit souillé la face, en l'appellant son seigneur, son mary et son Empereur, oubliant presque sa misere *et sa calamité* propre, pour la compassion de celle ou elle le veoit. Antonius luy feit cesser sa lamentation, et demanda a boire du vin, fust ou pource qu'il eust soif, ou pource qu'il esperast par ce moyen plus tost mourir. Apres qu'il eust beu, il *l'admonesta* et luy conseilla qu'elle meist peine à sauver sa vie, si elle le pouvoit faire sans honte *ne deshonneur*, et qu'elle se fiast principalement en Proculeius plus qu'à nul autre de ceulx qui avoyent credit autour de Cesar : et quant à luy qu'elle ne le lamentast point pour la *miserable* mutation de la fortune sur la fin de ses jours, ains

[1] George Long, an English translator of Plutarch, says of Amyot, "It is surprising to find how correct this old French translation is."

[2] The Greek, κατατεινομένη τῷ προσώπῳ, really means 'straining the muscles of her face.'

qu'elle l'estimast *plus tost bien* heureux pour les *triumphes et* honneurs qu'il avoit receuz *par le passé* : veu qu'il avoit esté *en sa vie* le plus glorieux, *le plus triumphant* et le plus puissant homme de la terre, et que lors il avoit esté vaincu, non laschement, *mais vaillamment,* luy qui estoit Romain par un autre Romain aussi. (c. lxxvii.)

The additions denoted by the italicised words are dictated, it will be noticed, by two considerations : first, a desire to heighten the pathos or the picturesqueness of the situation ; secondly, by a natural tendency to redundancy of language characteristic of the sixteenth century no less in France than in England. This redundancy also shews itself in Amyot's habit of using many more words than Plutarch to express the same idea. In one case a single Greek word is rendered by *et tiroyent autant de peine à la voir ainsi travailler, comme elle mesme.* But it must not be forgotten that by this means Amyot succeeds in a remarkable way in bringing out the whole meaning of the original. Compare him with a rival translator of Plutarch, Estienne de la Boétie, and you see that, if he is less concise, he gives the meaning better[1]. From an artistic point of view there can be little doubt that Amyot was right. It must be remembered that he was dealing with an author whose style, if unaffected, is singularly wanting in distinction. It lacks relief and precision, colour and harmony ; moreover, his Greek virtue of terseness is not always accompanied by the other Greek virtue of lucidity[2]. Had Amyot been as terse as Plutarch, his work would have seemed unfamiliar to his countrymen. It was by resolutely writing like a Frenchman of his own day, with a rich fulness of expression and an eye for picturesque effect, that he was enabled to give to his translation the air of an original work. This illusion is further helped by his constant care to make himself intelligible to the ordinary reader. Just as Plutarch gives the Greek meaning of a Roman technical term, Amyot gives the French one, and by a happy anachronism translates

---

[1] La Boétie translated the *Precepts of Marriage* about fifteen years before Amyot.

[2] Amyot in his preface to the *Lives* speaks of Plutarch's style as *plus aiguë, plus docte et pressée, que claire, polie ou aisée.*

names of ancient usages into their nearest modern equivalents. For he was no antiquary seeking to reconstruct the past, but an artist who cared for the permanent features of human interest, and who endeavoured to give to Frenchmen of the sixteenth century the same pleasure which Plutarch gave to Greeks of the first and second.

It has been objected that Amyot in thus interpreting Plutarch's work has misinterpreted Plutarch himself, imparting to him too large a share of his own *bonhomie*[1]. But as a matter of fact *bonhomie* was by no means foreign to Plutarch's character. Beneath his fussiness and his pedantry he was at bottom a genial kind-hearted man. It is his interest in the minor traits of character which atones for his deficiency in the power of drawing a finished portrait, and which gives the charm to his work.

If Amyot's other translations are of considerably less importance, yet through them two of the chief representatives of Greek romance, the *Story of Æthiopia* and *Daphnis and Chloe*, exercised a decided influence on French literature. That of the *Story of Æthiopia* was more immediate, for the romantic adventures of Theagenes and Chariclea appealed at once to readers fresh from *Amadis of Gaul*. In the next century they furnished Alexandre Hardy with the plot of an interminable drama, they influenced the pastoral romance of D'Urfé and the heroic romances of Gomberville and La Calprenède and Mlle de Scudéry, and they were the favourite reading of Racine when he was a boy at Port-Royal and suggested to him a tragedy which he afterwards abandoned[2].

The popularity of *Daphnis and Chloe*, with its pagan instead of Christian inspiration, was of a slower growth. It was the Regent Orleans who brought it into favour more than a hundred and fifty years after its first publication by having an illustrated edition printed at his own expense. Throughout the eighteenth century it kept its vogue, and, though in 1813 Paul-Louis Courier brought out a skilful

[1] See Sainte-Beuve, *op. cit.* pp. 467 ff.
[2] See life by Louis Racine in *Œuvres*, ed. P. Mesnard, I. 212 and 220.

revision of it, which reflected more faithfully the tone of the original, Amyot's version still holds the field[1].

If in *Daphnis and Chloe* Amyot mastered the art of a simple narrative style, he had a far harder task in dealing with the more complicated structure of Plutarch. But like a true artist he was always learning. It is by comparing his translations of the earlier *Lives* with those of the later ones, Numa, for instance, and Lycurgus and Themistocles with Cicero and Demosthenes and Antonius, that we can judge of his progress during the dozen years or more of his work on the *Lives*. It is especially visible in his management of his periods. In the earlier *Lives* they are weak and involved in construction; in the later ones they are built up with a firm and easy hand into a structure of graceful strength and perfect balance. Just as that other *bonhomme* La Fontaine was France's greatest artist in verse, Amyot comes very near to being her greatest artist in prose. *Je donne avec raison, ce me semble, la palme à Jacques Amiot sur tous noz escrivains François; non seulement pour la naïfveté et pureté du langage, en quoy il surpasse tous autres*[2]. This is the verdict of the writer of genius who was Amyot's contemporary, and in a measure his disciple. But even in the middle of the next century, when the literature of the sixteenth century had gone wholly out of fashion, and an age of imagination had been succeeded by an age of reason, we find one of the high-priests of reason, the grammarian Vaugelas, appreciating Amyot's prose in almost the same terms as Montaigne. *Quelle obligation ne lui a point notre langue, n'y ayant jamais eu personne qui en ait mieux su le génie et le caractère que lui, ni qui ait usé des mots, ni de phrases si naturellement françoises*[3]. Nor even in the age of Louis XIV was Amyot forgotten. 'Amyot is read,' says La Bruyère[4].

---

[1] In 1810 Courier had published an edition of Amyot's work with his own translation of the new fragment which he had discovered at Florence, but only sixty copies were printed.

[2] Montaigne, *Essais*, II. iv.

[3] Preface to the *Remarques* (1647). It is true that he also says that they had struck out half his words and phrases.

[4] *Des ouvrages de l'esprit.*

Amyot's fame as a translator is so great that critics have
decided somewhat hastily that he was incapable of good work
without the support of a model. Sainte-Beuve, for instance,
sweepingly condemns all his original writing. But this is
unjust. Amyot's prefaces to the *Lives* and the *Moral Works*
are no doubt somewhat long-winded, but there is firmness and
dignity in the style, and good sense, if no great originality, in
the thought[1]. It is however the treatise entitled *Projet de
l'éloquence royale*, composed for Henry III and first printed in
1805, which most deserves our attention. From this we may
learn what importance Amyot attached to the more delicate
refinements of style. No clause, he says, should exceed the
length of four Alexandrine lines[2]; not only the words themselves should be chosen for their harmonious sound, but they
should be arranged in a harmonious order[3]. And the style
of the treatise corresponds to its precepts ; it is a model of
well-ordered grace and harmony. We learn from it, better
perhaps than from any of his other work, how true an artist
Amyot was.

The only other translators of classical literature during
this period who demand a passing notice are Pierre Saliat, the
secretary of Odet de Châtillon, whose translation of Herodotus
appeared in 1556[4], and more particularly Louis or Loys Le
Roy, the translator of Demosthenes, Plato, and Aristotle.
Born at Coutances in 1510 of parents as poor and humble as
those of Amyot, he came to Paris about 1530, a year or two
later than Amyot, and attended the lectures of the new royal
professors. In 1535 he went to Toulouse to study law,
supporting himself meanwhile by acting as secretary to Jean
de Pins, the Bishop of Rieux[5]. He returned to Paris in 1540
in time to follow Budé's body to the grave, and he wrote his life
in excellent Latin. Then he obtained a small place at court,
travelled in Germany, Italy and England, and, after devoting
nearly twenty years to the work of translating Greek prose

[1] Blignières's judgement is far more favourable (pp. 268 ff.).
[2] *Projet*, p. 43.   [3] *ib.* pp. 44 and 46.
[4] Ed. E. Talbot, 1865.
[5] See *ante*, p. 23.

authors, succeeded Lambin in 1572 as royal professor of
Greek. In 1577 he ended a life of honourable poverty and
untiring industry[1]. His translations consist of the *Olynthiacs
and Philippics* of Demosthenes (1551–1575), Plato's *Timæus*
(1551), *Phædo* (1553), *Symposium* (1559) and *Republic* (1600),
Aristotle's *Politics* (1568) and some treatises of Isocrates and
Xenophon[2]. Le Roy was not a great artist like Amyot[3], but
he was a competent translator, who understood his author's
meaning, if he could not always express it in graceful French.
But his style sometimes strikes a higher note, notably in the
praise of Love at the close of the first book of his commentary
on the *Symposium*. M. Becker cites from it a passage of
considerable beauty, which shews evident traces of the study
of Rabelais[4].

Another service performed by Le Roy for his native
language was the delivery of lectures on a learned subject,
namely Demosthenes, in the vernacular, following in this the
examples of Ramus, and of Forcadel the mathematician. In
his preliminary lecture (1576), after paying due tribute to the
ancient languages, he makes an eloquent attack on those
scholars who entirely neglected their native language and all
modern topics[5]. But we must pass on to one who was a
greater scholar than either Amyot or Le Roy, and whose
services to his native language were second only to Amyot's.

2. *Henri Estienne.*

Henri Estienne[6] was the knight-errant of scholarship.
He was ever in the thick of the fray, ransacking the libraries

---

[1] See a sonnet on his death by Antoine de Cotel (*Les poètes franç.* v. 72).

[2] See Becker, *Loys Le Roy*, pp. 386 ff.

[3] Becker prints parallel translations by Le Roy and Amyot of a passage
from Plutarch's *Moralia*, Le Roy's being a little earlier in point of date (*ib.*
pp. 120 ff.).

[4] *ib.* pp. 150, 151.

[5] *ib.* 173 ff.; F. Brunot in Petit de Julleville, III. 649 ff.

[6] b. 1531—d. 1598. Many scattered biographical details will be found in the
garrulous and egotistical prefaces to his editions and other books, and 27 letters

of Europe for manuscripts, editing and printing classical texts, attacking with impetuous pen the vices of his age, or defending the language which he loved, if possible, better than Greek. He was the eldest son of Robert Estienne, and there seems no reason to doubt the statement of his uncle Charles, agreeing as it does with his own, that he was born in 1531[1]. In the preface to his edition of Aulus Gellius (1585) he gives an interesting account of his father's household, in which, owing to the various nationalities of those who were employed on the work of the press, Latin was used as a common language even by the maid-servants. He thus picked up Latin colloquially as a child, but by his own request he began to learn Greek first as a serious study. At twelve he became by special favour the private pupil of Pierre Danès, and two years later he began to attend the lectures of Toussain. In the spring of 1547, when he was barely sixteen, he went to Italy, where he spent three years in collating manuscripts and in intercourse with learned men[2]. In 1550 he visited England, and then Flanders, where he learnt Spanish. In the following year he went to Geneva to join his father, who had settled in that city in the preceding November. In 1552 and 1555 he again went to Italy, gleaning new manuscripts even in that closely reaped field. The chief result from the point of view of French literature was an *editio princeps* of the so-called "Anacreon," which, as we shall see in the next chapter, had a considerable influence upon the poets of the Pleiad. His father dying in 1559, he became under his will owner of his famous press, subject however to a condition which had the effect of keeping it at Geneva, under the stern supervision of the Geneva Council.

Henri would gladly have returned to France and Paris, for staunch Protestant though he was, the Geneva atmosphere

written by him to John Crato of Crafftheim between 1570 and 1584 have been printed (ed. F. Passow, 1830). The older secondary authorities are Janssen van Almeloveen, *De Vitis Stephanorum*, Amsterdam, 1683, and Maittaire, *Stephanorum Historia*, London, 1709.

[1] This date is adopted by L. Clément, *Henri Estienne et son œuvre française*, p. 468; the date of 1528 suggested by Renouard is purely arbitrary.

[2] For his travels from 1547 to 1556 see Clément, *op. cit.* pp. 463 ff.

was as little congenial to him as it was to Bonivard or Marot. The first trouble arose in connexion with his first work written in the vernacular, the *Apologie pour Hérodote*. It was ready for the press towards the close of 1566, but he was ordered by the Council to make certain alterations before publication[1]. In the following April he published, without any authorisation, an *Avertissement* or defence of his book, which was more ingenious than ingenuous, followed by a summary of the chapters and an index, the latter containing matter which aggravated the offence[2]. The author was imprisoned for some days, and then after a severe admonition released.

The full title of the work is *L'introduction au traité de la conformité des merveilles anciennes avec les modernes, ou Traité preparatif à l'apologie pour Hérodote*. It was characteristic of its author that he should have written a preparatory treatise which filled nearly six hundred pages, and that the main work for which this was meant to be an introduction should never have been written. The title gives no clue to its actual contents, though it represents pretty accurately the purpose with which Henri Estienne began to write it. Already in a Latin preface to a revised edition of Valla's Latin translation of Herodotus which he had published earlier in the year he had defended the credibility of the Father of history, and the new treatise was more or less an expansion of this preface. His object, he says, is to shew that in his own and in the preceding century men did things which for wickedness and folly were even more incredible than the stories related by Herodotus. His book thus becomes an attack on the vices of his age, Herodotus being practically left out of account. But the design is carried out without any attempt at method or logical construction. The sermons of the popular fifteenth-century preachers, Maillard, Menot, and the Italian Bareletta, are the

[1] Some copies had already been sent to Lyons, and some of these had already been sold. . Two copies only of this uncancelled edition are known to exist; one belongs to the Comte Roger du Nord, and the other formed part of the library of the late Baron Alphonse de Ruble (*Cat. Ruble*, no. 528).

[2] The only known copy is that sold at the Turner sale in 1888 (no. 1096). Turner had 50 copies printed from it (London, 1860).

chief sources for the earlier chapters. But other sources are soon added without any pretence at testing their authority. Before long it becomes clear to the reader that the author's indignation at the vices of his age is, like that of many another satirist, considerably mitigated by his relish for scandalous stories, and in the fifteenth chapter he begins to give full rein to the story-telling spirit, which from this point becomes the chief business of the book. His stories are drawn from various sources, from Boccaccio, Poggio, the *Heptameron*, Bandello; from Erasmus and Pontanus and Battista Fregoso; from Froissart and Comines. Some are probably founded on a manuscript collection of *fableaux* which he had in his possession, while a considerable number are based either on oral tradition or on recent anecdotes. As a story-teller Henri Estienne has no claim to rank with the masters of the art, with Boccaccio and Antoine de la Sale and Bonaventure des Periers. He is a lively and to some extent graphic narrator, but he is too rapid a writer for artistic composition. The pregnant brevity of the *Joyeux Devis* and the long-drawn sweetness of the *Heptameron* are alike wanting to him.

The nineteenth chapter of the first part ends with the words, *Mais c'est assez parlé des meschancetez des hommes laiz: il faut venir à celles de ceux qui se font appeler gens d'église*, which shews that the author's intention would have been correctly expressed if he had entitled his work 'A satire on human society and particularly on the Roman Catholic Church.' The second part is no more effective as an attack than the first. Three years after the Council of Trent had concluded its sittings, even though the Counter-reformation had not begun to make its effects felt in France, it was a little late in the day to trot out time-worn stories of the ignorance and immorality of the clergy. On other grounds, too, the book is ineffective; its satire lacks precision and concentration, while its extreme desultoriness makes continuous reading of it impossible. But those who dip into it will find much to amuse and interest them; they will learn not a little about the manners and fashions of the age; they will hear about those highly entertaining persons, the popular preachers of the close of the fifteenth century; finally, amongst many stories which have been told better elsewhere they will meet with several new ones told with considerable spirit and in excellent French[1].

In 1572 Henri Estienne published the work on which his fame as a scholar mainly rests, the *Thesaurus Graecae Linguae*. From the point of view of financial success it was damned by being in five volumes, but it was the greatest attainment that Greek scholarship had yet achieved in Europe. Alas! it appeared in the very year in which that scholarship received its death-blow in France. The outbreak of the religious wars in 1562 had already made France an undesirable place of residence for peaceful scholars, but the massacre of St Bartholomew was fatal alike to philosophy, to scholarship, and to jurisprudence. Ramus perished in the massacre, Lambin died of fright, Hotman, Doneau, and Joseph Scaliger, the rising hope of French scholarship, fled to Geneva, the two former never to return. Baudouin died in the following year; Turnèbe had been dead for some years. When Scaliger returned in 1574, there was no one left of the great scholars and jurists who had made France illustrious except Cujas and Dorat. It is significant of the utter decay which now fell upon Greek scholarship in France that Scaliger could say of Pierre Pithou, perhaps the ablest scholar left in France after his own final departure to Leyden in 1593, that "he was nothing of a Greek scholar[2]."

But to return to Henri Estienne. The other works besides the *Apologie* which he wrote in French were all concerned with the French language. The first of these, *Traité de la conformité du langage françois avec le Grec*, had already appeared in 1565[3], dedicated to Henri de Mesmes. In this the author maintains the superiority of French to all languages except Greek, which he regards as the ideal language. Especially he asserts the superiority of French over Latin for the purpose of translating Greek. The cause

---

[1] There is a good appreciation of the book in Lenient, *La Satire en France au XVIᵉ siècle*, new ed. 1877, I. 100 ff.

[2] *P. Pithou nec Franciscus n'entendoient guères au Grec. Scaligerana altera*, p. 188.

[3] The first edition has no date; it was reprinted in 1569.

of French as against Latin, of the vernacular against the learned language, thus found in him a vigorous champion. But it was as much against Italian as against Latin that he was fighting. In the preface, which is the most interesting part of the book, he attacks the *françois italianizé et espagnolizé* of the Court and it is against Italian that the other two treatises are directed.

We have seen how Italian artists and men of letters had been welcomed by Francis I and freely admitted to a share of the good things of his kingdom, and how the marriage of his son with Catharine de' Medici had given a fresh impulse to the movement. After her assumption of the regency on the accession of Charles IX, it was to her Italian advisers and her Machiavellian policy that the miserable condition of the country was freely ascribed ; and it was remembered that at the fateful conference on the eve of St Bartholomew the only persons present besides the members of the royal family and Tavannes were those Italians. Henry III on his return from Poland to France had amused himself for two months in Italy, and was a warm advocate of Italian fashions.

This Italian influence had invaded even the language, and it was this latter invasion which Henri Estienne set himself to stem in his *Deux dialogues du nouveau langage françois italianizé* published in 1578. The work is chiefly interesting to the philologist, but the student of manners and fashions will find some entertainment, especially in a longish passage which is devoted to dress[1]. There is also some scattered criticism on the poetry of the Pleiad, of which Henri Estienne was a friendly but far from enthusiastic admirer[2]. But on the whole the most noteworthy passage, because it deals with a subject of permanent human interest, is the advice how to act in order to appear grander and more important than you really are, a subject which forms the chief theme of D'Aubigné's satire *Les aventures du baron de Feneste*[3].

---

[1] Ed. Lizeux, I. 174—238.

[2] The Lyons library has a volume of J. du Bellay's poetry which is covered with manuscript notes by H. Estienne. See Clément, *op. cit.* pp. 142—182.

[3] Ed. Lizeux, II. 201—211.

The publication of the *Dialogues* brought Henri Estienne into a fresh dispute with the Geneva Council, and to avoid their censure he went to France and resided at the French Court from the autumn of 1578 to that of 1579. It was at the instigation of Henry III that he wrote and saw through the press in three months his *Projet du livre intitulé De la pré-cellence du language François*, 1579. Again a mere preface fills a volume of three hundred pages, and again the work which the preface announces was never written. The superiority of the French language is shewn by comparing it with Italian, at that time generally considered to be the first of modern languages. One does not look for fair treat-ment of Italian in so pronounced an adversary, and the best part of the book is that which deals with the positive merits, especially the richness, of the French language[1]. Treating as it does almost exclusively of linguistic matters, the work can hardly be said to be of general interest; but there is some interest in the account of French words and terms derived from hunting, falconry and tennis, and in the collection of French proverbs[2]. Henry III having expressed doubts as to the genuineness of some of them, the author published in 1594 *Les Premices ou le I livre des Proverbes epigrammatizez*[3].

The last twenty years of Henri Estienne's life were years of increasing trouble. From 1580 he became more and more of a wanderer. The large sums which he had spent, first on his *Thesaurus* and then on the *Plato* which he issued from his press in 1578, had almost ruined him, and his long journeys were undertaken partly in the hope of procuring patrons and purchasers. In 1597 he left Geneva for the last time. After visiting Montpellier, where his son-in-law Casaubon was now professor, he started for Paris, but was seized with sudden illness at Lyons and died there at the end of January 1598.

Henri Estienne's chief merit as a writer is his style. His treatises on the French language are too technical, his *Apologie pour Hérodote* too desultory, to take high rank as

---

[1] Ed. Huguet, pp. 116—253.

[2] *ib.* pp. 116—150; 201—252.

[3] Very rare and never reprinted; there is a copy in the Arsenal library at Paris.

literary works, but his style, though lacking the artistic feeling and the careful workmanship of the great masters, raises him far above the level of the ordinary writer of his age. For it has the saving quality of individuality ; it is the natural mirror of a strong personality. Perhaps the most remarkable feature of it is the vocabulary. We can see from the *Dialogues* and the *Précellence* that Henri Estienne had a real genius for words. He knew little about their derivation and anatomical structure, for philology was still an unborn science, but he had an extraordinary knowledge, partly acquired by much reading, but in a large measure intuitive, of their precise signification. It is said by competent scholars that his knowledge of Greek, especially as shown in the *Thesaurus*, was of the same character. And to this knowledge of words he united a lively and vigorous fancy. Hence a style which is easy, picturesque, forcible and, on the whole, clear. Perhaps the single epithet that would describe it best is 'racy.' So rapid a writer is naturally not free from the common faults of his age, such as the abuse of parenthesis, and the undue weighting of a clause to the destruction of its balance. But the conversational tone which he generally adopts saves him to a great extent from the interminable sentences which are the besetting sin of sixteenth century prose. Finally it should be noted that his syntax, unlike Amyot's earlier work, shews few traces of archaisms, such as the omission of the article and inversion. This is to be accounted for mainly by the fact that he did not begin to write in French till 1565, nearly twenty years later than Amyot, but also to some extent by his connexion with Geneva. For though, owing to some similarity in temperament between the two men, his style may remind one at times of Rabelais, he belongs by association to the school of Calvin. He thus unites to the sensuous picturesqueness of the older school something of the logical precision of the new. The following passage from the *Apologie pour Hérodote* is an average specimen of his style :

Je di donc premièrement que si nous voulons parler de la qualité des viandes avant que de la quantité (c'est à dire de la friandise avant de la

gourmandise), il ne nous faut que considérer ce qu'on appelle vin théologal, et ce qu'on appelle pain de chapitre. Car quand il est question
d'exprimer en un mot un vin bon par excellence, et fust-ce pour la bouche
d'un roy, il faut venir au vin théologal. Pareillement s'il est question de
parler d'un pain ayant toutes les qualités d'un bon et bien friand pain
(voire tel que celuy de la ville Eresus, pour lequel Mercure prenoit bien
la peine de descendre du ciel, et en venir faire provision pour les dieux,
si nous croyons au poëte Archestrate), ne faut-il pas venir au pain de
chapitre? Je di, au vray pain de chapitre, dont celuy que vendent à Paris
les boulengers a retenu le nom, mais non la bonté, sinon qu'en partie. Or
est-ce là bon commancement: car la feste ne peut estre mauvaise où il y
a bon pain et bon vin. Quant à la pitance, en premier lieu il est certain
que ce qu'on dit *Traité en commissaire, de chair et de poisson*, mériteroit
bien mieux d'estre dict *traité à l'ecclésiastique.* Car pour qui achète-on
quelquesfois les gros brochets six escus, sinon pour la bouche de nostre
mère saincte église? Qui pensons-nous qui a premièrement faict courir
les chassemarées, sinon nostre mère saincte église? Mais je confesse
bien qu'ils ne mangent pas chair et poisson l'un parmi l'autre (comme
aussi les médecins ne leur conseillent pas de ce faire). Ains attendent
volontiers qu'ils soyent si saouls de chair qu'ils commencent à crever:
comme les Flamens, quand ils veulent faire leur grand gaudeamus, font
conscience de taster du vin qu'ils ne soyent yvres de bière[1].

To some extent this gift of style was hereditary.   In
the answer which his father, Robert Estienne, sent to the
Sorbonne from Geneva, and which he published first in Latin
and afterwards in French (1552), he shews a considerable
faculty for clear and forcible statement with some skill in the
management of the period[2].

[1] Ed. Ristelhuber, II. 33—35.
[2] The preface to *Les Censures des Théologiens de Paris* in printed in A. A.
Renouard's *Annales de l'Imprimerie des Estienne*, 2nd ed. 1843, pp. 545 ff.

3. *Pasquier*[1].

Thirteen years before Henri Estienne began to champion his native tongue and to maintain its superiority to Latin, another writer who had had a classical training had expressed similar views in a letter addressed to Turnèbe. "What? Shall we bear the name of Frenchmen, that is to say of free men, and yet bow our minds to the yoke of a foreign language? Have we not expressions as suitable as Latin ones, are we not as well equipped for eloquence as this ancient Latin[2]?" The author of this letter, which was written in 1552, was Estienne Pasquier, a young man of twenty-three, who not long before (November 1549) had made his *début* at the Paris bar. He had studied under the greatest jurists, under Hotman and Baudouin at Paris, under Cujas at Toulouse, and under Alciati at Pavia. Before long he began gradually to make his way in his profession, but his progress was interrupted by a long illness, and it was not till 1564 that his defence of the University of Paris against the Jesuits raised him at a bound to the front rank. He had already begun to make a name in literature, having published in 1554 a volume in prose, with a few poems interspersed, on the fashionable subject of love, entitled *Le Monophile*, and having added to the second edition which appeared in the following year a small collection of poems[3]. In 1560 he published the first book of the work by which he is best known, *Les Recherches de la France*, together with the *Pourparler du Prince*[4]. A second book was added in 1565[5]. In 1585 he was raised to the magistracy as advocate-general in the Chambre des Comptes,

---

[1] b. 1529—d. 1615.   [2] Pasquier, *Les Lettres*, 1586, fo. 3 v°.

[3] *Recueil de rimes et proses. La Jeunesse d'Estienne Pasquier et sa suite*, 1610, contains besides poems and *Le Monophile* two short prose pieces, *Colloques d'amour* and *Lettres amoureuses*, which first appeared in 1567.

[4] In 1564 he published anonymously another volume on the same subject as *Le Monophile*, but of a more joyous character. It was reprinted by Techener in 1833 in a collection entitled *Joyeusetez, facéties et folâtres imaginations*. See Pasquier's letters, II. 5.

[5] Books i. and ii. were republished in 1569 and again in 1581.

and in the year 1588 he was one of the deputies for the Third
Estate at the Estates of Blois. True to his loyalist principles
he remained at Tours during the occupation of Paris by the
League, and it was not till the entry of Henry IV into Paris
in 1594 that he returned to the capital and resumed his official
position. He retired in 1604, and died in 1615 at the age of
eighty-five. His enforced leisure at Tours had been chiefly
employed in literary pursuits, and in 1596 he republished his
Recherches with four additional books. A seventh book was
added in an edition of 1611, the last published in his life-time,
and finally in 1621, after his death, the number of books was
increased to ten[1]. The last book however, which treats chiefly
of Fredegonde and Brunehaut, properly belongs to the fifth
book, and is printed as such in the edition of 1665.

At the opening of his seventh book Pasquier briefly and
correctly describes the subject-matter of the first six books as
particularités concernant nos anciens Gaulois et Français (i),
les polices tant séculières (ii) *qu'ecclésiastiques* (iii) *de notre
France, quelques anciennetés qui regardent l'État en son général*
(iv), *une mélange d'exemples signalés qui peuvent servir d'édi-
fication au lecteur* (v, vi). The remaining books deal respectively with French poetry (vii), the French language (viii),
and the French Universities, especially that of Paris (ix).
Ranke speaks of Pasquier as an important and trustworthy
authority on those subjects on which from his position he was
competent to speak, namely the Parliament and University of
Paris, and the relations of the Church to the Crown[2]. But
from the point of view of literary history the most interesting
and instructive part of his work is the seventh book, especially
that part of it from the sixth chapter onwards in which he
gives an account of the Pleiad school and which has often
been cited in these pages. If his appreciation of the school,
of which he was proud to be a member, and especially of its
leader, Ronsard, is more enthusiastic than critical[3], and if,

---

[1] There is another edition in ten books of 1633.

[2] *Zur Kritik neuerer Geschichtschreiber* (2nd ed. 1874), pp. 142–3.

[3] Both here and in one of his letters (xviii. 14), he speaks of the *Amours de
Marie* and *Amours d'Hélène* as only inferior to the *Amours de Cassandre*.

like Henri Estienne, he boldly compares the poetry of his countrymen with that of modern Italy and ancient Rome, no one will think the worse of him for his patriotism. For it is just this patriotism which is one of the most admirable features of his character, and which lies at the bottom of all his antiquarian researches[1].

The first five chapters of this book, in which he treats of mediæval French poetry, though naturally superficial, shew that at any rate he took an interest in the earlier literature of his country. In the eighth book, which deals mainly with questions of language and the explanation of current phrases and proverbs, he gives an analysis of the farce of *Pathelin* and devotes a short chapter to Villon.

Pasquier's other important work besides the *Recherches* is his collection of Letters. Like the letters of his models, the younger Pliny, Symmachus, and Sidonius Apollinaris, in ancient times, and Poliziano, Erasmus, and Budé in modern, they are addressed to posterity, or at any rate to the contemporary public, rather than to his nominal correspondents. Pasquier, however, agreed with Erasmus that letters which are destined for publication, should be really sent to their nominal address. One important innovation he made. Hitherto the humanists with a view to displaying their scholarship had written their letters in Latin or even in Greek; Pasquier for the first time used his native language, sensibly remarking that Cicero and Pliny had done the same. He published the first ten books of his letters in 1586[2]; the remaining twelve did not appear till after his death in the complete edition of André Duchesne (1619).

Many of the letters are detailed narratives of public events, and as such rank among our more important sources for the history of the period. Thus book iv deals with the years 1557–1564, and book v with the years 1567–1570, while a large proportion of letters in books xi—xvii are concerned with the struggle between the Crown and the League from

[1] The whole of book vii, with the exception of c. 2 and the three concluding chapters, is given in Feugère's selection.

[2] Re-published 1597, 1598, and 1607.

1587 to 1592. To a true patriot like Pasquier the civil wars
were hateful, and he rightly regarded a religious war as the
worst form which a civil war could take (x. 6). Questions of
literature and language form the subject of several letters.
He gives an account of the first book of Monluc's *Commentaires* (xviii. 2), he advises La Croix du Maine on the subject
of his proposed *Bibliothèque* or bibliographical dictionary (ix.
7), and Jean de Serres on that of his proposed history (xv. 18
and 19); he writes to Tabourot saying he had read *Les Bigarrures* with pleasure (viii. 14), and he thanks his publisher for
sending him an anonymous treatise on eloquence, of which
the author was Du Vair (xv. 10). Nothing can be more
sensible than his letter (ii. 12) on the true standard of purity
in language, and on the extent to which foreign words and
provincialisms may be imported. Like Henri Estienne, he
objects to the effeminate Italianised pronunciation of the
Court and declares that neither there nor in the Law-courts is
the true standard to be found. There is a long letter to
Ramus on the vexed subject of orthography, in which he
points out that one great difficulty in the way of phonetic
spelling is that each reformer, Meigret, Peletier, Baïf, and
Ramus himself, proposes a different system, because each pro-
nounces according to the standard of his own province (iii. 4)[1].

Among the more interesting letters on miscellaneous
subjects are one to his son Theodore on joining the bar, in
which he points out the path which an honourable advocate
should trace (ix. 6), and one on the prevalent fashion of
duelling, in which he takes a similar view to that of Montaigne.
*Je souhaiterois que la noblesse de France ne trompetast point
tant le point d'honneur sur lequel elle fonde toutes ses actions, ou
qu'elle y apportast moins d'hypocrisie a le soustenir.* And he
points out that the practice of having seconds who fight without any cause of quarrel is as much a sign of cowardice on
the part of the principal as it is of folly on that of the second

---

[1] *Combien que decochiez toutes vos fleches a un mesme blanc, toutesfois nul de
vous ny a sceu atteindre, ayant chacun son orthographe particuliere, au lieu de celle
qui est commune à la France...Qui me fait dire que pensants y apporter quelque
ordre, vous y apporterez le desordre.*

(x. 4). There is a charming letter written about 1612 to his old friend Achille de Harlay, the former First President of the Parliament of Paris, in which he describes his life as an octogenarian, confined more or less to his room, but having by his side his books, his pen, his thoughts, and a good fire (xxii. 9). He had already given a similar account of his retirement to his friend Antoine Loisel, *cet autre lui-même*, as he calls him, who had written a book entitled *Pasquier, ou dialogue des avocats du Parlement de Paris* (xix. 8 and 9). Among his other intimate friends, most of whom appear among his correspondents, were Pierre Pithou, Guy du Faur de Pibrac, Scévole de Sainte-Marthe, and a considerably younger man, Louis Servin, advocate-general of the Paris Parliament. From the more intimate letters we can form a good idea of Pasquier's character. We see his honesty, his patriotism, his manly common-sense, and on the other hand we can detect a dash of egotism and vanity, with a touch of that *naïve* self-satisfaction which the consciousness of a well-spent life sometimes gives.

Perhaps the best-known and the most interesting of all his letters is the one in which he describes the death of Montaigne, though not as an eye-witness, and passes criticism on the famous *Essays* (xviii. 1). For his remarks serve to some extent as a measure of his own critical powers. "I love," he says, "I respect and honour his memory as much as any man; and as for his *Essays*, which I call masterpieces, there is no book which I have so greatly cherished. I always find something in it to please me. 'Tis a French Seneca." Earlier in the letter he describes how he met Montaigne at Blois in 1588, and how he pointed out to him the Gasconisms in his book, and how he was much surprised to find that Montaigne did not correct them in his next edition. And then entirely missing the whole point of the book he objects that a large proportion of it is an account of Montaigne's habits and character. The letter is all the more interesting because up to a certain point there is a considerable similarity between the two men. They both had the same classical and legal training; they both belonged to that middle party in

the state which was so intensely conservative in its attachment
to the throne and the Gallican Church, and yet partly by
reason of that very conservatism proved itself to be the true
liberal party by its willingness to grant liberty of worship to
the Protestants; both were men of active and inquiring minds,
both cared for the manner as well as for the matter of their
discourses, both were remarkable for their shrewd and robust
common sense.   Yet they are separated by all the immeasur-
able distance between genius and ability.

It is hardly necessary to add that in the matter of style
Pasquier is a long way inferior to Montaigne.   Yet his style
has considerable merits; it is easy and clear, and, though in
some of the letters it becomes a trifle stilted, while in others
there is a somewhat forced attempt at playfulness, it is on the
whole unaffected.   Moreover it is redeemed from monotony
by picturesque and happy expressions which, as Sainte-Beuve
says, would honour Montaigne, and which testify to the
poetical side of Pasquier's nature better than his actual
poetry[1].   The syntax of his earlier letters is that of the older
school, and the sentences are somewhat long and cumbrous.
As time goes on he gradually drops many of his archaisms,
and his sentences become shorter and more manageable.
But in its general character his style changed singularly little
throughout the sixty years of his literary life.

In the first book of his *Recherches* Pasquier threw considerable doubt on the current view that the Franks were
descendants of the Trojans.   Twenty years later his contemporary Claude Fauchet[2], first president of the *Cour des mon-
naies*, bringing to bear upon the question more systematic
researches and a more matured mind, pointed out in the first
part of his *Recueil des antiquitez Gauloises et Françaises*, published in 1579, that the Trojan origin of the Franks had
absolutely no evidence to support it and that in reality they

---

[1] *Il est moins vif et moins court-vêtu que Montaigne....Son style est de robe
longue, même dans ses Lettres où il ne vise point à être pompeux ; mais, à tout
moment, il rachète ces défauts réels, ces longueurs de phrase, par des expressions
heureuses qui honoreraient Montaigne. Causeries*, iii. 257.

[2] b. 1530—d. 1601.

were a German tribe closely connected if not identical with the Sicambri, which is not very far from the truth[1]. For the rest of his life he continued his researches in the early history of his country. The last instalment of his work, which was published in 1602, the year after his death, brought it down to the close of the Carolingian dynasty and the election of Hugh Capet. Fauchet's book, lacking as it does the qualities of style or literary charm, does not come within the scope of this history, but we have only to read a few chapters of it to realise that we are in the presence of a really critical mind, of a writer who is able to distinguish between good and bad evidence, and who has an unfailing instinct for the most trustworthy authorities.

A work of Fauchet's which more nearly concerns us is his *Recueil de l'origine de la langue et poesie françoise*, which he published in 1581, and which though of no great extent is a notable contribution to the subject. In the first book he discusses the origin of the French language and shews himself so far superior to the general philological standard of his age that he recognises its Latin origin, though he still believes in the mixture of a Gallic element[2]. The second and longer book is the more important, for here he gives a summary account with numerous extracts from their writings of a hundred and twenty-seven French poets who lived before the year 1300, a task which implies a very considerable study of manuscripts.

[1] Book i. c. 1. Hotman's *Francogallia*, in which the German origin of the Franks is stated in a masterly fashion, was published in 1573, but it does not appear that Fauchet was acquainted with it.
[2] It may be noted that he cites the Strasburg Oaths.

BIBLIOGRAPHY.

EDITIONS.

JACQUES AMYOT, *L'Histoire Æthiopique*, 1547; with notes by P.-L. Courier, 4 vols. Didot, 1822–25. *Les amours pastorales de Daphnis et Chloé*, 1559; numerous modern editions. *Les Vies des Hommes Illustres*, 1559; 2 vols. 1565–72; 6 vols. 1567 (a beautiful edition in 8vo.). *Les Œuvres morales et meslées*, 1572; 7 vols. 1574 (uniform with the 3rd ed. of the *Vies*). *Projet de l'Éloquence Royale composé pour Henri III, Roi de France*, Versailles, 1805.

HENRI ESTIENNE, *Traité de la conformité du langage françois avec le grec* [Geneva, 1565]; ed. L. Feugère, 1853. *L'introduction au traité de la conformité des merveilles anciennes avec les modernes, ou Traité preparatif à l'Apologie pour Hérodote*, 1566; ed. Le Duchat, 3 vols. The Hague, 1735; ed. P. Ristelhuber, 2 vols. 1879. *Deux dialogues du nouveau langage françois italianizé* [Geneva, 1578]; reprinted by Liseux, 2 vols. 1883; ed. P. Ristelhuber, 2 vols. 1885. *Projet du livre intitulé De la précellence du langage françois*, 1579; ed. L. Feugère, 1850; ed. E. Huguet, 1896. There is an English translation of the *Apologie* by R. C. entitled *A world of wonders*, 1607.

ESTIENNE PASQUIER, *Les Recherches de la France* (book i), 1560; in ten books, 1621. *Les Lettres* (ten books), 1586; in twenty-two books, edited by André Duchesne, 3 vols. 1619. *Œuvres*, 2 vols. Amsterdam, 1723 (incorrectly printed and incomplete, omitting the *Ordonnances d'amour*, the *Exhortation aux Princes*, 1561, which will be found in the *Mémoires de Condé*, II. 613 ff., the *Congratulation au roi sur sa victoire*, 1588, and the *Catéchisme des Jésuites*, 1602). *Œuvres choisies*, ed. L. Feugère, 2 vols. 1849.

CLAUDE FAUCHET, *Recueil de l'origine de la langue et poesie jrançoise ryme et romans. Plus les noms et sommaire des œuvres de cxxvii poetes François vivans avant l'an MCCC*, 1581. *Recueil des antiquitez Gauloises et Françoises*, 1579 (books i, ii); *Les antiquitez Gauloises et Françoises augmentées de trois livres*, 1599 (books i–v). *Œuvres*, 1610.

TO BE CONSULTED.

A. de Blignières, *Essai sur Amyot et les Traducteurs français du xvie siècle*, 1851. (The author of this excellent book died two months after its publication in his twenty-seventh year.) C.-A. Sainte-Beuve, *Causeries du Lundi*, IV. 450 ff. A.-H. Becker, *Loys Le Roy*, 1896. A.-A. Renouard, *Annales de l'Imprimerie des Estienne*, 2nd ed. 1843. *Nouv. Biogr. Gén.*

1856 (by A.-F. Didot, a long and important article). L. Feugère, *Essai sur la vie et les ouvrages de Henri Estienne*, 1853; republished in a somewhat abridged form in *Caractères et portraits littéraires*, 2 vols. 1849; new ed. 2 vols. 1875. Mark Pattison, *Essays*, I. 67 ff., 1889. L. Clément, *Henri Estienne et son œuvre française*, 1899 (deals very thoroughly with his services to the French language).

A. Loisel, *Pasquier ou Dialogue des Advocats du Parlement de Paris*, 1652; ed. Dupin aîné in Loisel's *Opuscules*, 1844. L. Feugère, *Étude sur la vie et les ouvrages d'Estienne Pasquier*, prefixed to the *Œuvres choisies* (see above). Ch. Giraud, *Notice sur E. Pasquier*, prefixed to Pasquier's *Interpretation des Institutes de Justinien*, 1847. C.-A. Sainte-Beuve, *Causeries du Lundi*, III. 249 ff., 1851. T. Froment, *Essai sur l'histoire de l'éloquence judiciaire en France avant le dix-septième siècle*, pp. 79—147, 1874. E. de Brémond d'Ars, *Un Gaulois à l'école de Rome* in the *Rev. des deux mondes* for May 1, 1888.

Niceron, *Mémoires*, XXV. (Fauchet). J. Simonnet, *Le Président Fauchet, sa vie et ses ouvrages* in *Rev. hist. de droit français et étranger*, IX. 425—470, 1863.

A very full bibliography of Pasquier will be found in L. Feugère, *Caractères et portraits* (see above), 1849, I. ccvii ff.

CHAPTER XVI

RONSARD AND DU BELLAY

1. *The beginnings of the Pleiad.*

WE have seen that Thomas Sibilet published in the year 1548 an *Art poétique* which based its precepts mainly on the practice of Marot and his followers. Within a year of its publication there appeared a treatise which poured contempt on the whole Marotic school, and which invited aspirants to Parnassus to look elsewhere for their models. The author of this manifesto of revolution was Joachim du Bellay, but it expressed more or less the common ideas of a group of young University students, whose acknowledged leader was Pierre de Ronsard.

The chief poet of the French Renaissance, the 'Prince of Poets,' as his contemporaries acclaimed him, was born on September 11, 1524, at his father's manor-house of La Possonnière near the village of Couture in the Vendômois. His father, Loys Roussart, was a *chevalier* of the order of St Michael and *maître d'hôtel* to the royal princes[1]. At the age of nine

---

[1] A life of Ronsard by his friend Claude Binet was published in 1586; it is printed, with some omissions, by Becq de Fouquières in his *Poésies choisies de Ronsard*. See also Du Perron's *Oraison funèbre* (*Œuvres*, ed. Blanchemain, VIII. 181 ff.) and Ronsard's *Élégie à Remy Belleau*, addressed originally to Pierre Paschal (*ib.* IV. 296 ff.), in which he gives an account of his early life. In this poem he says:

> L'an que le roy François fut pris devant Pavie,
> Le jour d'un samedi, Dieu me presta la vie,
> L'onzieme de Septembre...

Now the battle of Pavia was fought on February 24, 152⅘. Was Ronsard reckoning according to the old or the new method of beginning the year? Both Binet and Pasquier (*Recherches*, VII. x) say he was born in 1524, but Bertaut in his poem *Sur le trespas de M. de Ronsard* (*Œuvres*, ed. Chenevière, p. 123) gives the

the future poet was sent to the College of Navarre, but he only remained there for six months. On August 4, 1536, being then nearly twelve, he was appointed page, first to the Dauphin, and then after that prince's sudden death six days later to his younger brother Charles, Duke of Orleans. In April 1537 he sailed for Scotland with James V and his bride Madeleine of France, who died within fifty days of her arrival and six months of her marriage. He remained at the Scottish court for two years, and after spending six months in England returned to France in October 1539. In May 1540 he was attached to the mission of Lazare de Baïf, the French representative at the meeting of the German Protestant Princes at Hagenau[1]. On his return to France (August 1540) he frequented the Court, where he was remarked for his fine physique and his skill in athletic exercises. But a serious illness, which left deafness behind it, compelled him to give up all idea of a career in arms or diplomacy. He accordingly took orders, receiving the tonsure at Le Mans on March 6, $154\frac{2}{3}$[2]. At the same time he determined to devote himself to literature, and after the death of his father in June 1544 began to share the Greek lessons of Lazare de Baïf's young son Jean-Antoine, whose tutor was the distinguished Greek scholar Jean Dorat.

Dorat[3] is known as a scholar for his excellent work on

date as seven months after the battle, or 1525. But as Ronsard also says in the same elegy that at the end of May 1540 he was barely sixteen, the evidence is conclusive in favour of the earlier year. In neither year was the 11th of September on a Saturday. (See P. Laumonier, *La jeunesse de Pierre de Ronsart*, *Rev. de la Ren.* I. 97—99. He points out that he signed himself *Ronsart*.)

[1] For L. de Baïf see *ante*, p. 20. Like Ronsard's, his home was in the valley of the Loir. The Protestant meeting had originally been fixed to take place at Speier.

[2] See L'abbé Froger, *Ronsard ecclésiastique*, p. 7, n. 1.

[3] b. 1501 or 2 (at Limoges)—d. 1588 ; appointed a royal professor of Greek in 1560. There is some discrepancy in the statements as to his family name, but the facts appear to be that his father's name was Dorat, that he Latinised his name into Auratus, and that he was called by his contemporaries variously Dorat and Daurat. Disnemandy (= Disne-matin) seems to have been a surname borne by his branch of the family. (See Marty-Laveaux, pp. vi, vii of his edition of Dorat's works in *La Pléiade française*; La Croix du Maine, I. 444 n.; Goujet, XIII. 287 ; and for Dorat generally P. Robiquet, *De J. Aurati vita*, 1887 ; M. Pattison, *Essays*, I. 206, 210.)

the text of Æschylus, but he only concerns us as a teacher of
genius who inspired his pupils with an enthusiasm for classical
literature, especially for Greek poetry. He had been tutor
in several noble families and to some of the royal princes
before becoming tutor to Jean-Antoine de Baïf. Soon after
Ronsard became his pupil he was appointed Principal of the
College of Coqueret at Paris, which opened out to him a
wider field for his powers of teaching. Ronsard and Baïf
joined the college, and spent at least five years there[1], and
it was there that Ronsard formed his great project for the
reform of French poetry. It was probably in July 1547
that he obtained a new and important recruit in Joachim
du Bellay, whom he met accidentally in an inn between
Poitiers and Paris[2]. An interchange of literary ideas took
place with the result that Du Bellay joined the College of
Coqueret.

Joachim du Bellay was somewhat older than Ronsard,
having been born in 1522[3] at his father's *château* of Turmelières,
near the hamlet of Liré in Anjou. His father was first
cousin to Guillaume and Jean du Bellay. Both his parents
dying when he was a boy he was left to the guardianship of
his elder brother, who paid little attention to his education[4].
He had originally intended to follow the profession of arms,
but the death of Guillaume du Bellay (January 1543), on
whom he had counted for advancement, turned his thoughts
to a civil career[5]. Accordingly he joined the University of

---

[1] In the original version of the *Élégie à Belleau* Ronsard says *cinq ans*, but he
afterwards altered this to *sept ans*.

[2] M. Séché reasonably suggests that Du Bellay was on his way home from
Poitiers after the end of term (*Rev. de la Ren.* I. 83). Binet places the meeting
in 1549, but this is clearly too late.

[3] In the Latin epitaph written by his intimate friend Pierre de Paschal it is
stated that he was thirty-seven at the time of his death, Jan. 1, 1560. (Marty-
Laveaux, *La langue de la Pléiade*, II. 383.) With this De Thou (XXVI. xxvi)
agrees. On the other hand Sainte-Marthe states that he was thirty-five at his
death, and Du Bellay says himself that he thought he was a little younger than
Ronsard (*Regrets*, sonnet 26). M. Chamard, p. 19, n. 1, gives some additional
evidence for the earlier date, which makes it practically certain. M. Séché however still holds to the traditional date of 1524 (*Rev. de la Ren.* I. 73–4).

[4] His brother died in 1552.

[5] Du Bellay gives some account of his early life in a Latin poem addressed to

Poitiers as a law-student, and it was apparently just after the completion of his studies that the eventful meeting with Ronsard took place. He had already received an impulse towards literature from Jacques Peletier, who, meeting him in 1546, had urged him to write odes and sonnets[1].

The appearance of Sibilet's treatise was the signal for more active measures on the part of the reformers. They were annoyed alike by the moderation of its tone, by its whole-hearted admiration for Marot and his followers, and by the fact that it anticipated some of their favourite ideas[2]. Accordingly in March 1549 Du Bellay put forth a manifesto of a very different character, under the title of *La Deffence et Illustration de la langue Françoyse*[3].

The twofold title of Du Bellay's treatise corresponds to the two books into which it is divided[4]. The first book is a defence of the French language; the second shews how lustre may be conferred on it. The French language, says Du Bellay, is potentially as good as Greek or Latin for literary purposes, but it wants cultivating. Much good work has already been done by the translation of Greek and Latin, Italian and Spanish authors, but something more than translation is needed. Take the example of the Romans. They did not confine themselves to the translation of Greek masterpieces; they produced masterpieces of their own by imitating the

his friend Jean Morel (printed by Becq de Fouquières in *Œuvres choisies*, pp. xxi ff.). There is a good deal of personal matter in his various prefaces. M. Chamard, p. 24, is right in putting his severe illness at a later period of his life.

[1] Preface to the 2nd ed. of *Olive*. Peletier may have come to Poitiers after the death of the Bishop of Le Mans, René du Bellay, with whom he had been living as secretary.

[2] The view, which is undoubtedly correct, that the *Deffence* was suggested by Sibilet's treatise was first put forward by M. Roy in the *Rev. d'hist. litt.* II. (1895) 237, and IV. (1897) 420. It is developed by M. Chamard, pp. 90 ff.

[3] Par I.D.B.A. 1549. The privilege is dated March 20, 154$\frac{8}{9}$, the dedicatory letter February 15, 1549, that is, undoubtedly, 154$\frac{8}{9}$. See Chamard, pp. 96 ff.

[4] Du Bellay mentions Aristotle, Horace and Vida (II. ix), but it does not appear that he was acquainted with Aristotle's *Poetics*. A French edition of Vida's Latin poetry was published at Lyons in 1548; his *De arte poetica* first appeared in 1527. Du Bellay is also indebted to Quintilian and Cicero, especially to the former.

Greeks. In the same way Frenchmen must imitate the Greeks and Romans, but they must do this not in Greek or Latin, but in French. Having thus sufficiently proved (so he says) his general proposition that it is only by imitation of the Greeks and Romans that the French language can acquire the excellence and lustre of her more famous sisters, Du Bellay in his second book goes more into detail. He begins by giving his opinion of "our French poets." The whole of French poetry before the sixteenth century is dismissed as not worth reading, with the solitary exception of the *Roman de la Rose*, which may be read as a venerable specimen of the older language. He has a good word for Jean le Maire, and then he comes to the moderns, the present representatives of the poetic art. Not that he has any intention of criticising them himself, but he will just mention some rather severe judgements which he has heard passed on three or four of the best. One, they say, lacks the first elements of good writing, namely learning; moreover his fame would have been greater if his book had been shorter[1]. That for Marot. Another, besides the poverty of his rhyme, is so devoid of charm and poetical ornament, that he deserves to be called a philosopher rather than a poet. That for Héroet. A third—and here he is undoubtedly aiming at Saint-Gelais—sustains his reputation by never publishing anything, while a fourth, Maurice Scève, in his desire to avoid what is common, has reached an obscurity such as even the most learned cannot enlighten[2].

After this oblique criticism of his elders, in which he gives an indication of his talent for pointed satire, he insists that a natural gift for poetry is not sufficient. Without study

---

[1] *Et auroit augmenté sa gloire de la moitié, si de la moitié il eust diminué son Liure.*

[2] I. c. ii. There can be no doubt that Du Bellay is here aiming at individuals, nor, I think, that the third poet criticised is Saint-Gelais. It may be said that Saint-Gelais had published a volume of poems in 1547, but, as we have seen, it was quickly withdrawn from circulation so that Du Bellay, who was at Poitiers at the time, may never have seen it or even heard of it. A strong argument for this view is that Marot, Saint-Gelais, Héroet and Scève are with Salel the very poets whom Sibilet singles out as the best models for the beginner.

or hard work you cannot produce an immortal poem. He then goes on to recommend in the best known and most important chapter of the book the kinds of poetry which should be cultivated. "Leave," he cries, "to the Floral games of Toulouse and the *Puy* of Rouen[1] all the old forms of French poetry; the *rondeaux, ballades, virelais, chants royaux, chansons* and other rubbish (*épiceries*) which corrupt the taste of our language and only serve to shew our ignorance." Write epigrams like Martial, tender elegies like Ovid, Tibullus and Propertius, odes, hitherto unknown to French poetry, epistles and satires like Horace, sonnets like Petrarch, eclogues like Theocritus, Virgil, and Sannazaro, tragedies and comedies instead of moralities and farces[2].

In the next chapter he urges his countrymen to write a 'long poem,' like Homer and Virgil and Ariosto. In the sixth he states his views with regard to the enrichment of the French vocabulary for the purposes of poetry, an important subject to which I shall recur later, while the four succeeding chapters deal with various questions of versification. Finally, after inveighing against the petty rhymesters of the Marotic school, he concludes in a noble and eloquent chapter by extolling France as superior to all other modern countries, and by once more exhorting her learned men not to neglect their own language.

There is little argument in Du Bellay's treatise and there is less novelty than he seems to imagine. He might have found in Marot alone epigrams in the manner of Martial, elegies, eclogues, and even sonnets. But the importance of the treatise lies in its general tone rather than in its actual precepts. Marot and his followers had adopted the principles of the Renaissance in a conservative and somewhat half-hearted spirit. Du Bellay breaks absolutely—too absolutely—with mediæval tradition and proclaims without any reservation that the only good models are those of Greece and Rome and the country which had first been quickened by the Renaissance spirit—Italy. He recognises that the greatest poetry deals with lofty and serious themes in heightened and

[1] See *ante*, p. 69.		[2] II. c. iv.

imaginative language, and he urges his countrymen to write poetry of this stamp in place of the light and trivial pieces to which they were accustomed.

The lofty tone of the manifesto is set off by considerable merits of style. If Du Bellay occasionally lays himself open to attack by using Greek and Latin words where a good French one would have served as well, or by an abuse of Latin constructions, these are small blemishes on the general excellence of the writing, which is clear, forcible and eloquent.

Du Bellay did not confine himself to precept. Almost if not quite simultaneously with the *Deffence* he published a thin volume·entitled *Olive*[1], which contained fifty sonnets and thirteen odes, and in the month of November another little volume entitled *Recueil de Poësie*[2]. In the same year another member of the Brigade, Pontus de Tyard, published a volume of sonnets entitled *Erreurs amoureuses*. Then Ronsard, who up till now had published nothing but three single poems[3], was spurred on by the publication of Du Bellay's odes to give to the world his own experiments in that species of poetry, of which he considered himself to be the inventor. Accordingly at the beginning of 1550 there appeared a volume entitled *Les quatre premiers Livres des Odes de Pierre de Ronsard. Ensemble son Bocage*[4].

It must have been about this time that the *Pléiade*, or constellation of seven poets, was constituted in imitation of the Alexandrian Pleiad of the third century B.C. It was composed of Ronsard, Du Bellay, Baïf, Dorat, Pontus de Tyard, and two men whose names have not yet been mentioned,

---

[1] There is a tradition that Olive is the anagram of the family name, Viole, of Du Bellay's poetical mistress, but M. Séché suggests that the name really refers to the branch of olive which Margaret, sister of Henry II, had for her arms (*Rev. de la Ren.* I. 239—241).

[2] The privilege for the *Deffence* included the *Olive*. The privilege for the *Recueil* is dated Nov. 5, 1549, and the dedicatory epistle Oct. 24, 1549.

[3] *Epithalame d'Antoine de Bourbon et de Jeanne de Navarre* (II. 241), *Avant-entrée du Roy tres-chrestien* (VI. 297), and *Hymne de France* (V. 283). There is a unique copy of the *Epithalame* in the British Museum. An ode of Ronsard's had also appeared in Peletier's *Œuvres poétiques*.

[4] The privilege is dated Jan. 10, 15$\frac{4}{9}$. The *Ode de la Paix* which stands at the head of the volume was published separately soon afterwards.

Estienne Jodelle and Remy Belleau. The last to be admitted was Belleau[1]. The old name however of the Brigade was still retained for the larger band of those who followed Ronsard's lead[2].

It was not to be supposed that these revolutionary spirits would be allowed to overthrow the existing powers without a struggle. Early in 1550 the *Deffence* was attacked in a pamphlet with the pedantic title of *Le Quintil Horatian*, or the Quintilius of Horace[3]. The authorship was ascribed to Charles Fontaine, one of Marot's disciples, and it was only after the lapse of three centuries that M. de Nolhac discovered in 1883 a letter of Fontaine's in which he absolutely denies it, and says that the real author was Barthélemy Aneau, Principal of the Trinity College at Lyons[4]. Du Bellay's treatise must have touched Aneau sharply. He had been an intimate friend of Marot, and had achieved a considerable reputation not only as the guiding spirit of his college since its foundation, but as a writer of Greek, Latin and French verse, and as a translator of various Latin works. From the height of his superior knowledge it was not difficult for him to make points against his younger antagonist and to note sundry mistakes and inconsistencies in his treatise. But he

[1]   ...Belleau, qui vins en la brigade
             Des bons, pour accomplir la septiesme Pléiade.
                              (Ronsard, *Œuvres*, VI. 202.)

[2] Neither Pontus de Tyard nor Jodelle nor Belleau is mentioned in the *Voyage d'Hercueil* (Arcueil), which was written in the summer of 1549 (*ib.* VI. 358 ff.). On the other hand Du Bellay's remark in the preface to the second edition of his *Olive* (1550)—*encore moins à ce qu'ils disent, que j'ay reservé la lecture de mes escripts à une affectée demi-douzaine des plus renommez poëtes de nostre langue*—seems to imply the existence of the *Pléiade* at this date. M. Chamard, p. 49, n. 1, thinks that the later term superseded the earlier one, and that consequently the mention of the term *Brigade* as in use in 1552 (Ronsard, *Œuvres*, VI. 382 ; VII. 111) shews that the name *Pléiade* was not yet in existence.

[3] See Horace, *Ars Poetica*, 438.

[4] The earliest known edition of *Le Quintil Horatian* is of 1555, but it must have appeared between the publication of Ronsard's odes and that of the second edition of *Olive* (September 1550). Fontaine's letter (see P. Nolhac, *Lettres de J. du Bellay*, 1883, p. 71) is dated April 8, without mention of the year, which must be 1550. The *Quintil Horatian* therefore appeared in February or March (H. Chamard in *Rev. d'hist. litt.* V. (1878) 54 ff.).

dwells too much on unimportant details to be effective, and
his whole answer smacks of the angry schoolmaster[1].

Of superior merit were the answers of Sibilet and
Guillaume des Autels. Sibilet's was contained in a preface
to his translation of the *Iphigenia* of Euripides, published in
November 1549[2], in which he defended the practice of
translation, hinted broadly at Du Bellay's own lack of
originality and renewed his praises of Marot[3]. A more
complete and direct answer was made by Guillaume des
Autels in his *Replique aux furieuses defenses de Louis Meigret*,
a contribution to the great spelling controversy which appeared
in August 1550. Like Sibilet, only with greater plainness
of speech, he points out that there is little or no difference
between the practices of the new school who imitate a whole
sonnet of Ariosto and Petrarch or an ode of Horace, and
that of regular translators, unless it is that the theory of
imitation enables you to leave out what you cannot translate.
But the chief merit of his remarks lies in their fairness and
catholicity. He can admire odes and sonnets without pouring
contempt on the older forms of French poetry, and his high
opinion of Ronsard does not prevent him from recognising
the inimitable grace and natural charm of Marot[4].

Du Bellay replied to his critics in a haughty and well-
written preface which he prefixed to a second edition of his
Olive, now increased from fifty sonnets to a hundred and
fifteen[5]. He defends himself, not very satisfactorily, against
the charge of plagiarism, referring to Virgil, Ovid and Horace,
whom he had not copied, and to Petrarch, whom he copied
only a little, but making no mention of Ariosto and many

---

[1] He translated the third book of Ovid's *Metamorphoses*, the *Emblems* of
Alciat and More's *Utopia*. He was murdered in 1561 by the Lyons populace on
the suspicion that he was a Protestant. There is a just appreciation of his pamphlet by J. E. Spingarn in his *History of literary criticism in the Renaissance*,
p. 182.

[2] *L'Iphigene d'Euripide tourne de Grec en François par l'auteur de l'Art
poetique*, Paris, 1549.

[3] See Chamard, p. 146.

[4] See Chamard, pp. 147 ff.

[5] The privilege is dated Oct. 3, 1550.

other Italian poets from whom he had borrowed freely[1]. Finally he closes the controversy with the remark that "if any one wants to revive the farce of Marot and Sagon he is at liberty to do so, only he must find some one else to play the fool with him."

The indebtedness of Du Bellay to Italian models is an important fact in the history of the Pleiad, for it is typical of the whole school. In spite of their enthusiasm for Greek and Latin poetry, and the insight which they had gained from the study of classical masterpieces into the value of form and style, Ronsard and his friends, as recent research has made more and more evident, chose as their immediate models the Italians rather than the ancients. It is therefore highly probable that they were to some extent influenced in their ideas by the Italian poet, Luigi Alamanni, who in the early days of the Pleiad was still living and in high favour at the French court.

Less than three years before the appearance of the *Deffence* he had published at Paris his didactic poem *La Coltivazione*, and Du Bellay refers to it in his treatise as an example of the use of blank verse[2]. But it is his earlier volumes, the *Opere Toscane*[3], which are likely to have exercised an influence on the poets of the Pleiad. They comprise elegies, eclogues, satires, sonnets, *selve* (or occasional poems, the title of which is borrowed from the *Silvae* of Statius), a translation of the *Antigone*, and hymns imitated from Pindar's odes. It will be seen that these contents closely correspond with the kinds of poetry which Du Bellay urges his countrymen to

---

[1] Eighteen sonnets are inspired by Ariosto (Chamard, p. 176; Vianey in *Rev. d'hist. litt.* VIII. 153). M. Vianey further points out that the *Olive* contains imitations of no less than thirty poets whose works appeared in a collection entitled *Rime diverse di molti excellenti autori*, of which the first part appeared in 1545, printed in Venice by Giolito of Ferrara (a copy in the Brit. Mus.), the second in 1547, and the third in 1550. The editor was Luigi Domenichi, a friend of Aretino and an active translator and compiler. Other volumes, with various editors, making in all nine, were published down to 1560.

[2] *Comme le Seigneur Loys Aleman, en sa non moins docte, que plaisante Agriculture.* II. c. vii.

[3] 2 vols. Lyons, 1532, 1533

cultivate, and we may further note that Ronsard called some of his poems *Bocage* in evident imitation of the term *selve*, and that his Pindaric odes closely resemble Alamanni's hymns. Moreover Alamanni, though deficient in originality, was an ardent classicist with a strong sense of form and style, and therefore just the sort of poet to serve as a model in these matters to the eager young humanists who sat at the feet of Dorat[1].

In the year 1551 no addition seems to have been made to the published work of the new school. But the following year saw the publication of Ronsard's and Baïf's *Amours*, and of Du Bellay's translation of the fourth book of the *Æneid*; it also saw the memorable performance of the first Renaissance comedy, Jodelle's *Eugène*, and probably also that of the first Renaissance tragedy, Jodelle's *Cléopatre*[2].

2. *Ronsard.*

Thus the new school was now fairly launched, but it still had to encounter considerable opposition. The brunt of the battle fell upon Ronsard. Soon after the publication of his *Odes* Mellin de Saint-Gelais, the chief living representative of the Marotic school, had openly ridiculed them in the King's presence. But the princess Margaret, who, as we have seen, was celebrated for her learning and patronage of men of letters, had come to the rescue and the elder poet had been for the time discomfited[3]. In December 1552 we find Michel de l'Hospital, then Chancellor to the princess for her Duchy of Berry, advising Ronsard through their common

[1] For Alamanni (b. 1495—d. 1566) see F. Flamini, *Studi di storia letteraria*, pp. 268—285; H. Hauvette, *Luigi Alamanni, sa vie et son œuvre*, 1903, and esp. pp. 443—460 for his influence on the Pleiad. P. Laumonier in a review of the latter work (*Rev. de la Ren.* IV. 258 ff.) thinks that M. Hauvette has exaggerated this influence.

[2] The appearance of all the early productions of the Pleiad school from 1549 to 1553 is related by Ronsard in a poem addressed to Bastier de la Peruse (*Œuvres*, VI. 43).

[3] Ronsard refers to this in some stanzas which originally formed part of the second ode of book v. (published with the *Amours* in 1552) but which were omitted in the second edition (see *Œuvres*, VIII. 136-7).

friend Jean Morel to propitiate Saint-Gelais and Lancelot de Carle, the Bishop of Riez, by inserting in his next publication some lines addressed to them, and at the same time to conciliate the public by abstaining from new and unusual forms of verse[1]. Accordingly, a reconciliation between Ronsard and Saint-Gelais having meanwhile taken place, Ronsard inserted in the second edition of his *Amours*, published in May 1553, an ode addressed to him, while he prefixed to the volume a sonnet of Saint-Gelais's addressed to himself.

Carle also was by way of being a poet. He had written blazons and sacred poetry, and had begun a translation of the *Odyssey*, but his biographer Colletet expresses surprise 'that so great a prelate should have wished to pass for so little a poet.' He was however of considerable importance in the literary world, and the warm support which before long he gave to the new school must have been of considerable value[2].

In the year 1553 Ronsard began to solicit patronage in a systematic fashion[3]. He dedicated to the Cardinal of Lorraine the fine *harangue* of the Duke of Guise to his troops at Metz[4], and made favour with Catharine de' Medici and Odet de Châtillon. The first book of *Hymnes*, which appeared in 1555, contains a large amount of skilfully distributed panegyric. Besides the *Hymne de Henri II* there are four hymns dedicated to the Cardinal de Châtillon, and one apiece to the Cardinal of Lorraine, Lancelot de Carle, and Saint-Gelais. One great personage alone, the most important of all, Diane de Poitiers, turned a deaf ear to his offers of homage[5].

---

[1] See P. de Nolhac in *Rev. d'hist. litt.* VI. (1899) 351 ff.

[2] Carle died in 1568, '*assez âgé*.' He was a native of Bordeaux and brother-in-law to Estienne de la Boétie. See P. Tamizey de Larroque, *Vies des poètes bordelais et périgourdins par E. Colletet*, 1873, pp. 1–50.

[3] Ronsard's friend Pasquier remonstrated with him for his indiscriminate touting: '*Je souhaiterois que ne fissiez si bon marche de vostre plume a hault-louer quelques-uns que nous scavons notoirement n'en estre dignes.*' Pasquier, *Lettres*, I. 8 (written in 1555). It was the common practice of the poets of the Pleiad.   [4] *Œuvres*, VI. 28.

[5] *ib.* V. 330; I. 425. It is said that Diane bore a grudge against all poets

Thus gradually Ronsard succeeded in winning the ear of that public to which alone he appealed, the aristocracy of culture and learning. But he achieved this partly by descending somewhat from his lofty classical platform. He no longer wrote Pindaric odes, but gems like *Mignonne, allons voir si la rose*[1], and in his new volume of *Amours*—the *Amours de Marie*—published in 1555 he relieved the monotony of the sonnets by songs and other pieces. At the same time he lowered his style to a more natural tone. Defending himself where no defence was needed he said that a simpler style was better suited to love-poems[2]. Finally the publication of the second book of *Hymnes* in 1556 definitely established his reputation.

The year 1560 marks the close of the first period of Ronsard's poetical career. In that year his position as the 'prince of poets' is marked by the publication of a collected edition of his poems in four volumes. For the next fourteen years he is the poet-laureate of his country, the official poet of the Court, and even in some measure of the nation. He became a great favourite with Charles IX, who conferred on him the revenues of the Abbey of Bellozane, vacant by the resignation of Amyot. He already held sundry livings, canonries, and archdeaconries, and the post of royal almoner with an annual stipend of 1200 francs; and a few years later

on account of Voulté's insulting lines on her written in the previous reign, when she was the rival of Madame d'Etampes (*Vulteii Hendecasyllaborum lib. IV* (1538), 16 v° and 48 r°. It is more probable that she did not care to spend her money on poets.

[1] First published in the 1553 edition of the *Amours*.

[2] See the introductory *Élégie à son livre* :

    Or si quelqu'un après me vient blasmer de quoi
    Je ne suis plus si grave en mes vers etc. (I. 146).

and the first sonnet (*ib.* 147). This volume seems to have been inspired by two Maries, a *petite pucelle angevine*, and a lady whom he calls Sinope (Sonnets xxxviii. ff.) :

    D'une belle Marie en une autre Marie,
    Belleau, je suis tombé (I. 408).

But in Ronsard's imagination the two are often fused into one, as in the last line of the *Élégie à Marie, Que je vous ay six ans plus que mon cœur aimée* (I. 231).

he acquired by cession or exchange the priories of Saint-Cosme near Tours and Croix-Val in the Vendômois.

It is a question whether he ever took priest's orders, but the weight of the evidence is decidedly against it[1]. However, in view of the irregularities of his life, this was made one of the grounds of accusation against him in a violent attack which certain Protestant poets, especially Antoine de la Roche-Chandieu, a minister of Geneva, Jacques Grévin and Florent Chrestien, directed against him in 1563. Up to this time, though as a fervent royalist he was strongly opposed to Protestantism, he had recognised the fact that the Church greatly needed reform, and that the prevailing religious discontent was largely due to the scandalous neglect of their dioceses by the bishops. Thus in the *Élégie à Guillaume des Autels*, published in 1560, he has the following lines:

> Mais que diroit sainct Paul, s'il revenoit icy,
> De nos jeunes prelats, qui n'ont point de soucy
> De leur pauvre troupeau, dont ils prennent la laine,
> Et quelquesfois le cuir; qui tous vivent sans peine,
> Sans prescher, sans prier, sans bon exemple d'eux,
> Parfumez, decoupez, courtisans, amoureux,
> Veneurs et fauconniers, et avec la paillarde
> Perdent les biens de Dieu dont ils n'ont que la garde[2]?

But after the outbreak of the religious war his tone becomes less moderate, especially in the second *Discours des misères de ce temps*, written in December 1562, in which he throws the whole blame of the rupture on the Protestants. Then when they attacked him in their turn with personalities which had just enough truth in them to give them an additional sting, he loses all sense of moderation. His long *Remonstrance au peuple de France*, written in 1563, is almost an incentive to civil war, and concludes with a prayer for Condé's death[3].

---

[1] Froger, *op. cit.*; P. Bonnefon in *Rev. d'hist. litt.* II. 244 ff.; P. Laumonier in *Annales fléchoises* for Feb. 1904.

[2] *Œuvres*, VII. 42. The words *Sur le tumulte d'Amboise* were added to the title of this poem in 1562; M. Laumonier thinks that it was written before the Tumult. (*Rev. universitaire*, Feb. 15, 1903.)

[3] *ib.* 54 ff. See, for the whole question, P. Perdrizet, *Ronsard et La Réforme*, 1901.

In 1564 he published a new volume consisting largely of
elegies, and in 1567 a new collected edition of his poetry in
six volumes. Already at the outset of his poetical career he
had determined to write an epic, and had settled on the
Franciade as its title. In a versified epistle to the Cardinal
of Lorraine written about 1554 he promised him that, if only
he would procure him an abbey or some other source of
a modest revenue, a *Franciade* should be forthcoming which
should rival the *Iliad*, and which should contain life-like
portraits not only of the Cardinal's ancestors but of the
Cardinal himself. But it would take, he said, ten years of
hard work[1]. Ronsard was hardly as good as his word; he
received abbeys in abundance, but by the year 1572 he had
only written four books of his epic. The printing of these
was finished on the 13th of September, twenty days after the
massacre of St Bartholomew. It was an inauspicious moment
for the appearance of an epic poem, and Ronsard never continued it.

Early in the year 1574, being a martyr to gout, he retired
from Court, and soon afterwards lost his friend and patron
Charles IX (May 30). It was at this time that he wrote
the *Sonnets pour Hélène*[2] in honour of one of Catharine de'
Medici's waiting-women, Hélène de Surgères. During the
remainder of his life he lived chiefly in the country, either
at his priory of Saint-Cosme or at his abbey of Croix-Val,
hunting in the forest of Gastine or working in his garden.
When he visited Paris he generally stayed either with Baïf or
with his friend Jean Galland, Principal of the College of
Boncourt. Though not so great a favourite with Henry III
as he had been with Charles IX, his reputation had nothing
diminished. He was still the 'prince of poets.' In 1583
Mary Stuart sent him a magnificent sideboard with the

---

[1] *Epistre à Charles, Cardinal de Lorraine* (*Œuvres*, VI. 276 ff.).

[2]   Je chantois ces sonnets, amoureux d'une Helene,
          En ce funeste mois que mon prince mourut.
                              I. 366.

They were first published in the collected edition of 1578: Hélène was
apparently not beautiful (*Perroniana* s.v. *Gournay*).

inscription "To Ronsard, the Apollo of the Muses' fountain." He wrote little during this period, but he spent much time in revising his poems for a new edition, which appeared in a magnificent folio volume in January 1584. He died on December 27, 1585, at his priory of Saint-Cosme, having given to his art forty years of unstinted devotion.

In judging of Ronsard's poetry it will be most convenient to begin with his failures, and in the first place with the Pindaric Odes and the *Franciade*. In the preface to his volume of Odes he claims to have introduced to France both the name and the thing. But the name occurs in a poem of Jean le Maire published in 1511, and the second claim can only be conceded by using the term in a somewhat limited sense, namely that of a noble and elevated lyrical poem capable of being to music. In his earliest Odes, written in 1547, as in those of his friend Peletier published in the same year, the second qualification was wanting. But the Pindaric Odes, at any rate, were a novelty; they were modelled on Pindar, probably with the assistance of Alamanni's Hymns[1]. They are fifteen in number, the masterpiece in the judgment of Ronsard's contemporaries being the one addressed to Michel de l'Hospital. It is at any rate the longest, containing over 800 lines, but like the rest it shows a complete misconception as well of the structure as of the spirit of Pindar's immortal Odes[2].

The *Franciade* is an equal failure, especially in the more epic parts, such as the vision of the Kings of France. Ronsard's genius was, in fact, unsuited to an epic poem. Though he had studied Homer carefully he had not imbibed his spirit[3]; though he had seen many men and cities his

[1] See J. Vianey in *Rev. d'hist. litt.* VIII. (1901) 154, and P. Laumonier in *Rev. de la Ren.* IV. 258 ff.

[2] Until Pindar's metres were elucidated by Boeckh his Odes were printed as they appeared in the MSS, in lines of about equal length. Hence Ronsard uses a uniform line of eight syllables.

[3] For Ronsard's debt to Homer see E. Gandar, *Ronsard considéré comme imitateur d'Homère et de Pindare*, Metz, 1854. T. de Banville says quite truly, ' *Il écrira une Iliade impossible...mais il donnera une saveur homérique à ses élégies et surtout à ses sonnets.* ' (*Petit traité de poésie française*, p. 282.)

imagination was not sufficiently moved by the clash of active life to write a national epic. Moreover he handicapped himself first by too close an imitation of Virgil (whom rather than Homer he chose as his model), forgetting that the weakest part of the *Æneid* is where Virgil imitates Homer, and secondly by his use of the decasyllabic metre instead of the more stately Alexandrine. But though the poem is an utter failure judged as a whole, it contains some beautiful episodes, especially the meeting between Francus and Hyante in the fourth book.

The poems of Ronsard which perhaps won the greatest applause from his contemporaries were his Hymns. They were modelled on the Homeric hymns and those of Callimachus and Marullus, but they also contain imitations of Theocritus, Apollonius Rhodius, and Valerius Flaccus. They differ considerably from one another in subject, character, and treatment. The majority are written in Alexandrines, but some are in lyric measures ; some are didactic, some narrative, some, to use M. Faguet's term, symbolic ; some are purely classical in spirit, others are quite modern, while in several there is a strange mixture of pagan and Christian sentiment. It is the classical hymns, those, for instance, of Pollux and Castor[1], and of Calaïs and Zethes[2], which are the greatest failures. There is too much description and too little movement for epic narrative ; the poems are too diffuse and too loosely knit. Those of a more modern character are far better suited to Ronsard's genius. The best perhaps are the *Hymne de l'éternité*[3], which is a good example of his admirable handling of the Alexandrine, and the *Prière à la Fortune*[4], written in decasyllables and apparently the earliest in point of date. The *Hymne des Estoiles*[5] is a lyrical treatment of a subject, the influence of the stars, which he had already treated in a didactic form in *Des Astres*[6]. The Hymns to the Seasons, which his contemporaries admired most of all[7], are more

[1] *Œuvres*, v. 42 ff.   [2] *ib.* 19 ff.
[3] *ib.* 13 ff. ; imitated from Marullus.   [4] *ib.* 289 ff. Written in 1553 or 1554.
[5] *ib.* 148 ff. ; imitated from Marullus.   [6] *ib.* 276 ff.
[7] Du Perron, *Oraison funèbre* (VIII. 192) ; Pasquier, *Recherches*, VII. c. 6.

remarkable for ingenuity than for real poetic merit. Finally, mention must be made of the *Hymne de la Mort* (which Chastelard recited on his way to the scaffold), partly because it contains some fine passages, and partly because, in spite of its free use of pagan mythology, it is thoroughly Christian in tone, and is therefore difficult to reconcile with the view that Ronsard was at heart a pagan. The Epicureanism and the fear of death which are associated with the Renaissance are here resolutely set aside as unworthy of a Christian :

> Ne nous faisons donc pas de Circé les pourceaux,
> De peur que les plaisirs et les delices faux
> Ne nous gardent de voir d'Ithaque la fumée,
> Du ciel, nostre demeure à l'âme accoustumée,
> Où tous nous faut aller, non chargez du fardeau
> D'orgueil, qui nous feroit perir nostre bateau
> Ains que venir au port, mais chargez d'esperance,
> Pauvreté, nudité, tourment, et patience,
> Comme estans vrais enfans et disciples de Christ,
> Qui vivant nous bailla ce chemin par escrit,
> Et marqua de son sang ceste voye tres-sainte,
> Mourant tout le premier pour nous oster la crainte[1].

And the concluding lines are admirable alike in sentiment, in language, and in versification :

> Je te salue, heureuse et profitable Mort,
> Des extremes douleurs medecin et confort!
> Quand mon heure viendra, Déesse, je te prie
> Ne me laisse long temps languir en maladie,
> Tourmenté dans un lict; mais puis qu'il faut mourir,
> Donne-moy que soudain je te puisse encourir,
> Ou pour l'honneur de Dieu, ou pour servir mon Prince,
> Navré, poitrine ouverte, au bord de ma province[2]!

A good deal of Ronsard's time during the middle portion of his career was taken up with writing Masquerades and Challenges (*Cartels*), and other official pieces, those of a more miscellaneous character being grouped together in the edition of 1584 under the title of *Bocage Royal*[3]. In this class

---

[1] *Œuvres*, V. 243.   [2] *ib.* 248.

[3] The *Mascarades*, which include the *Cartels*, will be found in vol. IV., the *Bocage Royal* in III.

however we come upon a well-told narrative poem, entitled *Discours de l'équité des vieux gaulois*[1], and a poem addressed to Catharine de' Medici in 1560 or 1561, which contains some interesting autobiographical matter, a touching reference to Du Bellay's death, and some beautiful lines on Marguerite, Duchess of Savoy :

> Fleur et perle de prix, Marguerite parfaite,
> Après que la bonté de nature t'eut faite,
> Assemblant pour t'orner une confection
> De ce qui est plus rare en la perfection,
> Elle en rompit le moule, à fin que, sans pareille,
> Tu fusses icy-bas du monde la merveille[2].

Among the official or court poetry may be classed the Eclogues, six in number, in some of which the princes and princesses, in others Ronsard and his friends, play a part under the thinnest of-disguises.   Thus in the first, which is immensely long—for, as Ronsard says with reference to his elegies, *il a fallu satisfaire au desir de ceux qui avoient puissance sur moy, lesquels ne trouvent jamais rien de bon, ny de bien fait s'il n'est de large estendue*—the characters are the Dukes of Alençon and Anjou (the future Henry III), the King of Navarre, the Duke of Guise, and Marguerite de Valois[3].   In the third Eclogue written for the marriage of the Duke of Lorraine with the daughter of Henry II, the speakers are Du Bellay (Bellot), De l'Hospital (Michau) and Ronsard himself (Perrot)[4].   On the whole these Eclogues, if superior in style to Marot's, are more artificial, while even the style is somewhat monotonous in its unvarying sweetness.   But they contain passages of great beauty, especially the fifth, which is modelled on the singing-match of Virgil's third eclogue.   Here is a specimen :

> Un pescheur est assis au bord du gobelet,
> Qui courbé fait semblant de jeter un filet
> En la mer, pour pescher, et de toute sa force,
> Et de mains et de nerfs et de veines, s'efforce
> De le tirer de l'eau. Ses muscles, grands et gros,
> S'enflent depuis son chef jusqu'au bas de son dos ;

---

[1] *Œuvres*, III. 293 ff.   [2] *ib.* 369 ff.
[3] IV. 5 ff.   [4] *ib.* 54.

> Tout le front lui degoutte, et bien qu'il soit vieil homme,
> Le labeur toutefois ses membres ne consomme.
> Son reth est dessous l'eau, et diriez, à le voir,
> Qu'en tirant il ahanne et ne le peut ravoir.
> Ma levre au gobelet n'a touché pour y boire :
> Tu l'auras toutefois si tu as la victoire[1].

The *Discours*, in which Ronsard aspires to be the poet not merely of the court but of the nation, belong to a class of poetry which has always found more favour with French than with English readers, for it is a product of the reason rather than of the imagination. The opening lines of the *Institution pour l'adolescence de Charles IX* are found in nearly all selections from Ronsard:

> Sire, ce n'est pas tout que d'estre Roy de France,
> Il faut que la vertu honore vostre enfance;
> Car un roy sans vertu porte le sceptre en vain,
> Et luy sert d'un fardeau qui luy charge la main[2].

But the best of the *Discours* is the *Remonstrance au peuple de France*[3]. It is excellent in rhythm and movement, and successfully avoids the jerkiness, due to the want of connexion between the separate rhetorical flights, which is the chief fault of the others. The following passage is a favourable specimen of Ronsard's satirical powers:

> Il ne faut pas avoir beaucoup d'experience
> Pour estre exactement docte en vostre science;
> Les barbiers, les maçons en un jour y sont clercs,
> Tant vos mysteres saincts son cachez et couvers.
> Il faut tant seulement avecques hardiesse
> Detester le Papat, parler contre la messe,
> Estre sobre en propos, barbe longue, et le front
> De rides labouré, l'œil farouche et profond,
> Les cheveux mal peignez, le sourcy qui s'avale,
> Le maintien refrongné, le visage tout pasle,
> Se monstrer rarement, composer maint escrit,
> Parler de l'Eternel, du Seigneur et de Christ,
> Avoir d'un grand manteau les espaules couvertes,
> Bref, estre bon brigand et ne jurer que: Certes[4].

---

[1] *Œuvres*, IV. 94.   [2] VII. 33.
[3] *ib.* 54 ff.   [4] *ib.* 60.

But as a rule Ronsard is happy neither in irony nor in invective. He is heavy-handed and often vulgar. His rhetoric is better when it is untouched by satire. As M. Faguet points out, in these poems Ronsard is really original. "He has created a species of poetry, and one which is entirely in accordance with the character of the French, who are born orators, and who love more than any other people the *discours en vers*[1]."

To pass from the *Discours* to the *Amours de Cassandre*[2] is to go from France to Italy, from original work to imitation. Apart from the decided superiority in language and rhythm there is nothing to distinguish this volume from the other *Amours* or series of love-sonnets in imitation of Petrarch and the Italian Petrarchists which were produced at this time with such wearisome reiteration. They have nearly all the same three faults, coldness, insincerity, monotony. It has been said that the coldness is due to the fact that they are for the most part addressed to ideal mistresses[3]. But an imaginary passion, if it is also imaginative, can and does produce passionate poetry. Rather the coldness is to be ascribed to the same cause as the insincerity, to the fact that Ronsard and his fellows modelled themselves on a poet with whose feelings as a lover they had no sympathy. Ordinary sensual men, they used the language of spiritual love; lovers of a day, they imitated a man who loved for eternity[4]. The monotony of their poems is equally easy of explanation.

---

[1] E. Faguet, *Seizième siècle*, p. 254. See also F. Brunetière in *Rev. des deux mondes* for May 15, 1900. There is a good appreciation of Ronsard's satirical powers in Chalandon, pp. 145 ff.

[2] The first book of the *Amours*. It has been recently shewn that the name of Ronsard's mistress was Cassandre Salviati, afterwards Mme de Pré, a direct ancestress of Alfred de Musset. See P. Laumonier, *Rev. de la Ren.* III. (1902) 73 ff. and A. Longnon in *Rev. des quest. hist.* (1902) 224 ff.; also A. d'Aubigné, *Œuvres*, I. 457.

[3] The poetical mistress was generally some real person, often above the poet in social status, to whom he paid imaginary court.

[4] In several places Ronsard expresses his real feelings:

> Sotte est la jeunesse
> Qui n'est point éveillée et qui n'aime en cent lieux
>
> *Œuvres*, I. 158 (to Marie);

Their theme was one which only intensity of passion can save from being monotonous. When passion is absent and the poet has nothing but his poetic machinery to fall back on, then the allegory, the mythological learning, the antithesis, the points and the puns of the Petrarchian system become wearisome indeed[1].

In spite of these serious drawbacks to the *Amours de Cassandre* as a whole, a few of the individual sonnets are exquisite. It is noteworthy that one of the best is an almost literal translation of Bembo and that the translator has improved upon his original:

> Comme un chevreuil, quand le printemps détruit
> Du froid hyver la poignante gelée,
> Pour mieux brouter la fueille emmiellée,
> Hors de son bois avec l'Aube s'enfuit;
> Et seul, et seur, loin des chiens et du bruit,
> Or' sur un mont, or' dans une valée,
> Or' près d'une onde à l'escart recelée,
> Libre, folâtre où son pied le conduit;
> De rets ne d'arc sa liberté n'a crainte,
> Sinon alors que sa vie est atteinte
> D'un trait meurtrier empourpré de son sang;
> Ainsi j'allois, sans espoir de dommage,
> Le jour qu'un œil, sur l'avril de mon âge,
> Tira d'un coup mille traits dans mon flanc[2].

In the *Amours de Marie*, as the second book of the *Amours* is generally called, most of this Petrarchism is thrown aside, and, as we have seen, a less elevated and more natural style is purposely adopted, as more suited to the village beauty whom he is now addressing, and to the wholly mundane love with which she inspired him. There is consequently more warmth and more variety. One of the mos'

and comp. xix. (*ib.* 165):

> Je ne dy pas si Jane estoit prise de moy,
> Que bientost n'oubliasse et Marie et Cassandre.

[1] All this is admirably discussed in M. Piéri, *Pétrarque et Ronsard*, 1895. Cf. Mr Courthope on the Elizabethan sonneteers in *A History of English Poetry*, II. 298 ff. and III. 34 ff.

[2] *Œuvres*, I. 35; translated from the third sonnet of Bembo's *Le rime*. See Pasquier, *Recherches*, VII. viii.

La vie n'a point d'asseurance,
Et, pendant que nous desirons
La faveur des roys, nous mourons
Au milieu de nostre esperance.

L'homme, après son dernier trespas,
Plus ne boit ne mange là bas,
Et sa grange, qu'il a laissée
Pleine de blé devant sa fin,
Et sa cave pleine de vin,
Ne luy viennent plus en pensée.

Hé! quel gain apporte l'esmoy?
Va, Corydon, appreste-moy
Un lict de roses espanchées.
Il me plaist, pour me défascher,
A la renverse me coucher
Entre les pots et les jonchées.

Fay-moy venir Daurat icy;
Fais-y venir Jodelle aussi,
Et toute la musine troupe.
Depuis le soir jusqu'au matin
Je veux leur donner un festin
Et cent fois leur pendre la coupe.

Verse donc et reverse encor
Dedans ceste grand' coupe d'or:
Je vay boire à Henry Estienne,
Qui des enfers nous a rendu
Du vieil Anacreon perdu
La douce lyre teïenne.

A toy, gentil Anacreon,
Doit son plaisir le biberon,
Et Bacchus te doit ses bouteilles;
Amour son compagnon te doit
Venus, et Silène, qui boit
L'esté dessous l'ombre des treilles[1].

The consoling side of mortality, that it is the lot of rich and poor, great and small, alike, is represented in a striking little poem of sombre grandeur:

Pourquoy, chetif laboureur,
Trembles tu d'un empereur
Qui doit bien tost, legere ombre,
Des morts accroistre le nombre?

[1] *Œuvres*, II. 352.

Ne sçais-tu qu'à tout chacun
Le port d'enfer est commun,
Et qu'une ame imperiale
Aussi tost là bas devale
Dans le bateau de Charon
Que l'ame d'un bucheron?
  Courage, coupeur de terre !
Ces grands foudres de la guerre
Non plus que toy n'iront pas
Armez d'un plastron là bas
Comme ils alloient aux batailles :
Autant leur vaudront leurs mailles,
Leurs lances et leur estoc,
Comme à toy vaudra ton soc.
  Car le juge Rhadamante,
Asseuré, ne s'espouvante
Non plus de voir un harnois
Là bas qu'un levier de bois,
Ou voir une souquenie
Qu'une cape bien garnie,
Ou qu'un riche accoustrement
D'un roy mort pompeusement[1].

That must end my selection from the odes, but there are several others of hardly inferior merit, such as *Bel aubespin verdissant* (iv. 19), the one called *De l'élection de son sepulchre* (iv. 4), the one to his page (ii. 10) and the one to Cassandre beginning *Ma petite colombelle* (ii. 16)[2].

It must now be evident that Ronsard is at his best in the region of tender and reflective emotion. In other words he is before all things an elegiac poet. It is only therefore natural that we should find in his elegies his most evenly meritorious work. In the 1560 edition of his works there were only about half-a-dozen of the poems which he classified later as elegies ; the majority and some of the best were not written till after this date. These are not all, strictly speaking, elegies, for Ronsard is not always happy in his classification. Thus the twentieth and the twenty-fourth are pure narrative, but while the twentieth is a merely prosaic account of his early life[3], the

---

[1] *Œuvres*, II. 269. Compare Shirley's 'The glories of our blood and state.'

[2] *ib.* 275; 249; 149; 160.

[3] See *ante*, p. 308 n. 1.

twenty-fourth, *à Genèvre*, is a graceful love-story told in poetical language. The same story had already been told at greater length, and in a more truly elegiac form in the fourth elegy, entitled *Discours amoureux de Genèvre*, which contains the following beautiful lines:

> Or, Adieu, je m'en-vois aux rives amoureuses,
> Compagnon du troupeau des ames bien-heureuses,
> Dessous la grand' forest des myrtes ombrageux,
> Que l'orage cruel ny les vents outrageux
> N'effueillerent jamais, où sans cesse souspire,
> Par les vermeilles fleurs le gracieux Zephyre.
> Là portant sur le chef des roses en tout temps,
> Et dedans mon giron les moissons du Printemps,
> Couché sous le bocage à la fraischeur de l'ombre,
> J'iray pour augmenter des Amoureux le nombre;
> Comme bien asseuré que les gentils esprits
> Qui jadis ont aimé ne m'auront à mespris;
> Pres d'eux me feront place, et si pense, Madame,
> Qu'ils n'auront point là bas une plus gentille ame[1].

The second elegy, addressed to Desportes, is remarkable for its pessimistic tone:

> Nous devons à la Mort et nous et nos ouvrages......
> Chacun de son labeur doit en ce Monde attendre
> L'usufruit seulement, que present il doit prendre
> Sans se paistre d'attente et d'une· eternité,
> Qui n'est rien que fumée et pure vanité[2].

In complete contrast with this is the twelfth, in which Ronsard exhorts his friend Hurault to enjoy the May-season in verses which read like an expansion of Tennyson's

> In the spring a young man's fancy.

The opening lines are most beautiful:

> Voicy le temps, Hurault, qui joyeux nous convie
> Par l'amour, par le vin, d'esbatre notre vie.
> L'an reprend sa jeunesse, et nous montre comment
> Il faut ainsi que luy rajeunir doucement.
> Ne vois-tu pas, Hurault, ces jeunes Arondelles,
> Ces pigeons tremoussans et du bec et des ailes,
> Se baiser goulument et de nuict et de jour
> Sur le haut d'une tour se soulasser d'amour?

[1] *Œuvres*, IV. 232.
[2] IV. 218; first published in the posthumous edition of 1587.

Ne vois-tu pas comment ces Vignes enlassées
Serrent des grands Ormeaux les branches embrassées?
Regarde ce bocage, et voy d'une autre part
Les bras longs et tortus du Lierre grimpart
En serpent se virer à l'entour de l'escorce
De ce chesne aux longs bras, et le baiser à force.
N'ois-tu le Rossignol, chantre Cecropien,
Qui se plaint toute nuict du forfait ancien
Du mal-heureux Terée, et d'une langue habile
Gringote par les bois la mort de son Ityle?
Il reprend, il retient, il recoupe le son
Tantost haut, tantost bas, de sa longue chanson,
Apprise sans nul maistre, et d'une forte haleine
Raconte de sa sœur les larmes et la peine[1].

This and many other passages shew that Ronsard had to the full the feeling for nature which characterises so many elegiac poets. Naturally we must not expect to find in him the close observation, passing indeed sometimes beyond the domain of poetry into that of science, of modern poets, but we do not need the assurance of his biographer to learn that he had a genuine love of the country and a considerable knowledge of country life. Thus his inspiration moved him to his truest note when he had nature for a background. How far superior he is in description to narrative may be seen by contrasting the opening lines of the *Muses deslogées*[2] with the rest of the poem. And it is important to bear in mind—for this is what stamps him as beyond all question a true poet and not merely an admirable virtuoso—that his treatment of nature is not merely descriptive, but that it is really imaginative.

It is true that his imagination is not of the highest kind, that it does not penetrate to the depths; but whenever he is moved by emotion, whenever he is really himself, and is not merely putting into words the thoughts and emotions of others, his imagination never deserts him. It is imagination as well as the flawless quality of the workmanship which makes his famous sonnet to Hélène de Surgères the most perfect poem that had yet been produced in France :

[1] *Œuvres*, IV. 272; first published in 1584.   [2] III. 306 ff.

Quand vous serez bien vieille, au soir, à la chandelle,
Assise auprès du feu, devidant et filant,
Direz, chantant mes vers, et vous esmerveillant :
Ronsard me celebroit du temps que j'estois belle.
  Lors vous n'aurez servante oyant telle nouvelle,
Desja sous le labeur à demy sommeillant,
Qui, au bruit de Ronsard, ne s'aille réveillant,
Benissant vostre nom de louange immortelle.
  Je seray sous la terre, et, fantosme sans os,
Par les ombres myrteux je prendray mon repos ;
Vous serez au fouyer une vieille accroupie,
  Regrettant mon amour et vostre fier desdain.
Vivez, si m'en croyez, n'attendez à demain ;
Cueillez dès aujourd'huy les roses de la vie[1].

Of the inestimable service which the Pleiad rendered to French literature by the creation of a poetical style it will be more fitting to speak when I come to review the whole movement, but it should be pointed out here that the yeoman's share of the work was done by Ronsard. French poetry, when he began to write, was a poor and unworked soil; it needed not only deep cultivation, but a rich and generous treatment. It was Ronsard's innate feeling for style, stimulated no doubt by the teaching of Dorat, which led him to choose as his models the great masters of poetic style, Horace, Pindar, Virgil, Petrarch. As regards his own style, though it never sinks below a certain level, it is only in short pieces that it is flawless. His inspiration or draught of emotion is somewhat short-breathed, and conscientious and painstaking artist though he is, his power of self-criticism is not sufficiently rigorous to enable taste and artistic knowledge to supply its place. Considering however that he had no models to speak of in his own language, that he had to create a poetic style for himself, the wonder is that he maintains so high a level.

His services in the matter of metre and rhythm are even more incontestable[2]. It was not only that he added a large

---

[1] *Œuvres*, I. 340; translated by A. Lang, *op. cit.* p. 31.

[2] Ronsard's improvements in metre are fully and admirably discussed by M. Faguet, *Seizième siècle*, pp. 271 ff., and M. Piéri, *Pétrarque et Ronsard*, pp. 291 ff.

number of metres—M. Faguet has counted over a hundred[1]—
to the very small store which French poetry possessed at that
time, but he absolutely reformed the rhythm of the individual
line, giving it a dignity and a weight before unknown to it[2].
Moreover his accurate ear, his acute sense of harmony, enabled
him to utilise to the full all the resources which can be obtained
by the choice and combination of sounds, whether vowel or
consonantal, and which are all the more necessary in a language
which has to trust to them in a large measure for its more
subtle effects[3].

A special interest attaches to his use of Alexandrines. In
the first preface to the *Franciade* he says that he was the first
to bring them back to favour[4], a statement which need not
imply more than that he gave a general encouragement to
their use, and that he had employed them himself in unpublished verses. But as was his usual habit, he left it to
some younger or rasher member of the band to introduce
the novelty to the public. In this case it was Baïf, whose
Amours, published in December 1552, contain six sonnets
written in Alexandrines[5]. Jodelle also used them in some
of the scenes of his tragedy *Cléopatre*. But in a short time
Ronsard gave a more definite sanction to the practice by
printing in the year 1553 a fairly long poem in Alexandrines,
the *Harangue que fit le Duc de Guyse aux soldats de Metz*[6]. In
the *Bocage* and in the *Meslanges*, the printing of both of which
was finished in November 1554, he used the same metre
for several poems, including the Hymn to Bacchus and

---

[1] He has not, however, taken into account the metrical inventions of Margaret of Navarre (see *ante*, p. 119).

[2] 'It is the great glory of Ronsard that his reform started with the line.' G. Saintsbury, *French Literature* (5th ed.), p. 174.

[3] *Je veux t'advertir, lecteur, de prendre garde aux lettres, et feras jugement de celles qui ont plus de son, et de celles qui en ont le moins (Preface sur la Franciade, Œuvres*, III. 31).

[4] *Lesquels vers j'ay remis le premier en honeur (ib.* III. 11). Marot used them only once or twice by way of experiment, and Margaret of Navarre only in one fairly long poem (*ante*, p. 119). But Sibilet had used them freely in his translation of the *Iphigenia in Aulis* to represent the Greek trochaics.

[5] See Pasquier, *Recherches de la France*, VII. c. 7.

[6] *Œuvres*, VI. 28.

some odes and sonnets, and in the following year he
gave it still greater vogue by using it for nearly all the
sonnets in the *Amours de Marie*, and for nine out of the
twelve Hymns in the first book[1]. In the same year Baïf
published the *Amours de Francine*, in which there is as large
a proportion of sonnets written in Alexandrines as in the
Amours de Marie. Du Bellay's *Antiquités de Rome*, written
at the latest in 1555, though not published till 1558, shew the
same partial use of this form of sonnet, while in the later
Regrets it is used throughout. Again Peletier in his *Art
Poétique* of 1555 speaks of the Alexandrine as the true heroic
verse.

Yet Ronsard, who had handled the metre so effectively in
the Hymns, abandoned it in the *Franciade* for the decasyllabic
line. His explanation in the first preface is that long experience had taught him that Alexandrines were too prosaic
(*qu'ils sentent trop leur prose*), and that they should only be
used for tragedy[2], or for translations. But long before this,
in the *Abregé de l'art poétique* (1565) he had noted this
danger, and had pointed out that it could be avoided by the
use of choice and resonant words and of rich rhymes[3], and in
1573, the year after the publication of the *Franciade*, he added
a new paragraph to this section of the *Abregé*, in which he
says that he had abandoned the Alexandrine against his will,
to please those who had power to command him[4]. Possibly
this is the true explanation, for in the *Sonnets pour Hélène*
written in the following year 1574, and in the later *Les Muses
deslogées*, he returned to the use of the more stately metre.
Yet in the second preface to the *Franciade*, published after
his death, he gives the same explanation as in the first
preface.

According to M. Faguet, Ronsard's greatest achievement
(*sa vraie conquête*) in versification is the introduction of the
Alexandrine into lyrical verse; but he is wrong in supposing

[1] Five of these are headed *vers héroiques*.
[2] Jodelle in his *Didon*, played in 1558, uses it throughout.
[3] *Œuvres*, VII. 330.
[4] *ib.*; this passage was struck out in the posthumous editions.

that in the epitaph on Jean Bastier de la Péruse[1] Ronsard
invented the metre in which Malherbe wrote his celebrated
Consolation à M. du Perier. In this he had been anticipated
by Tahureau in his *De la vanité des hommes*[2]. Finally it must
be noted that both in his Alexandrines and in his verse
generally Ronsard allows himself much greater licence than
was permissible in French poetry after Malherbe had clipped
its wings. Having a musical and accurate ear he was a law
unto himself, and had not to submit to the laws of peda-
gogues who measure by the eye and not by the ear[3]. He is
the first great master of French metre. Victor Hugo may be
more brilliant, La Fontaine more sure, but Ronsard was the
first.

3. *Du Bellay.*

In the highest qualities of a poet, in poetic vision and in
poetic execution, Du Bellay is inferior to Ronsard. But he
has a finer perception and a more delicate, if more shallow,
sensibility. Thus his best work is rather a simple record
of passing emotions than an imaginative presentation of
deep passion. It took him several years of apprenticeship to
discover the true bent of his genius. The two volumes of
poetry which he published in the same year as the *Deffence*,
the *Olive* and the *Recueil*[4], are of little positive merit. The
sonnets of the *Olive*, like those of the Italian models from
which they are so largely borrowed, repel us by their cold and
artificial Petrarchism. But they have the elevation of thought
and style which was to be the characteristic of the new school.
A notable instance is the often-quoted sonnet :

[1] *Œuvres*, VII. 240. [2] See *post*, II. 17.

[3] Most of Ronsard's lyrics are written so that they can be set to music and a
large number were so set. See an interesting article by C. Comte and P. Laumonier in the *Rev. d'hist. litt.* VII. (1900) 341 ff.

Ronsard regarded as one test of a true ode that it was *propre à la lyre*, that is
to say capable of being set to music, and therefore rejected his earliest odes, in
which the stanzas were not identical or alternately identical in metre. These,
which he called *odes non mesurées*, form the *Bocage* of the 1550 edition. See his
épistre au lecteur (II. 10).

[4] See *ante*, p. 314.

Si nostre vie est moins qu'une journée
En l'eternel, si l'an qui fait le tour
Chasse nos jours sans espoir de retour,
Si perissable est toute chose née,
    Que songes-tu, mon ame emprisonnée?
Pourquoy te plaist l'obscur de nostre jour,
Si pour voler en un plus clair sejour
Tu as au dos l'aile bien empennée?
    Là est le bien que tout esprit desire,
Là le repos où tout le monde aspire,
Là est l'amour, là le plaisir encore.
    Là, ô mon ame, au plus haut ciel guidée,
Tu y pourras recognoistre l'idée
De la beauté qu'en ce monde j'adore[1].

The marked Neo-Platonism of this sonnet as well as the Petrarchism of the whole series is probably due to the influence of Maurice Scève. In spite of Du Bellay's acute criticism of Scève and Héroet in the *Deffence* his *Olive* recalls alike their merits and their defects. He is however less obscure than Scève and less prosaic than Héroet, while here and there we get touches of the tender grace which was to become so distinguishing a feature of his work. This is best shown in the following paraphrase of Catullus's *Ut flos in saeptis*:

Qui a peu voir la matinale rose
D'une liqueur celeste emmiellée,
Quand la rougeur de blanc entremeslée
Sur le naïf de sa branche repose :
    Il aura veu incliner toute chose
A sa faveur : le pied ne l'a foulée,
La main encor' ne l'a point violée
Et le trouppeau approcher d'elle n'ose.
    Mais si elle est de sa tige arrachée
De son beau tein la fraischeur desseichée
Perd la faveur des hommes et des dieux.
    Helas! on veut la mienne devorer
Et je ne puis, que de loin, l'adorer
Par humbles vers (sans fruict) ingenieux[2].

---

[1] No. cxiii. of the second edition; translated by A. Lang, *op. cit.* p. 18. M. Vianey points out that it is imitated from a sonnet by Bernardino Daniello (see *ante*, p. 317). The subject of spiritual love is also treated by Du Bellay in thirteen *sonnets de l'honneste amour* published in the volume of 1552.

[2] No. xcvii.

Nor must we forget to credit Du Bellay with the merit of having popularised the sonnet in France. It is true that Sibilet in his *Art Poétique* speaks of the sonnet as much in vogue (*fort usité*) but at that time (1548) few French sonnets had appeared in print[1], except possibly a translation of 196 sonnets of Petrarch by an obscure writer, Vasquin Philieul of Carpentras, which were published in that very year[2]. The claim of Pontus de Tyard, which Ronsard appeared at one time to recognise, is clearly disproved, for his *Erreurs Amoureuses* did not appear till November 1549, more than half a year after Du Bellay's *Olive*, and it was not till he published the third edition in 1555 that it occurred to him to put the date of 1548 to the epistle *A sa Dame* which precedes the first book[3].

The *Recueil de Poesie* dedicated to Margaret, sister of Henry II, which appeared towards the end of 1549, contains little that is of real merit. It consists largely of official pieces addressed to possible patrons, including an ode to Lancelot de Carle, the Bishop of Riez. There are also odes to the two representatives of the Marotic school, Saint-Gelais and Héroet, whom he had so recently attacked in the *Deffence*. The best piece in the volume is the ode, *Des conditions du vray poëte*, inspired by Horace's *Quem tu, Melpomene, semel.* Indeed at this period of Du Bellay's career it was only with the help of other men's ideas that he achieved real success. The mediocrity of the volume may, however, be partly accounted for by his state of health, for he had only recently recovered from a dangerous illness. In the following year he had a relapse which laid him up for two years and left him a victim to increasing deafness.

In 1552 he was sufficiently recovered to publish a new volume containing a translation of the fourth book of the *Æneid* and thirteen original pieces. The state of melancholy into which he had fallen owing to his long illness is reflected in the diffuse but sincere and pathetic *Complainte du désesperé*, and in the preface addressed to his friend Jean de Morel, in

---

[1] See *ante*, p. 152.	[2] Chamard, p. 169.
[3] *ib.* pp. 170 ff.

which he alleges his waning powers as an excuse for descending
to the work of translation, and speaks of the volume as 'the
last fruits of his garden.' So far, however, was he from having
closed his poetic career that he was on the eve of a change in
his outward circumstances which had the ultimate effect of
making him a really original poet instead of a mere versifier
of other men's ideas.

He left Paris with the Cardinal du Bellay towards the end
of April 1553, and having been delayed after crossing the
Alps by a touch of fever, joined him in Rome about the
middle of June[1]. His four years' residence in the eternal
city as the Cardinal's secretary and steward of his household
affected him in three ways. On the one hand the ruined
monuments, witnesses to its former grandeur, inspired him
with a still closer sympathy for classical antiquity. On the
other, the corruption of the Roman *curia*, which his relations
with the Cardinal gave him ample opportunity of studying,
and the laxity of Roman life in general, moved him to indignation. Finally the irksomeness of his dependent position
filled him with a regretful longing for his native land. It is
these states of feeling which are reflected in the two sonnet-
series written at Rome and published soon after his return
to France. The *Antiquités de Rome*, which were evidently
written first, represents the poetry of ruins, of the mutability
of human things. It consists of forty-seven sonnets, of which
the last fifteen are entitled *Songe ou Vision sur Rome*. As
Sainte-Beuve says, the intention of the work is far superior
to the execution, the sentiments to the style, and he might
have added that the sentiments are mostly borrowed[2]. Few of

---

[1] M. Chamard was the first person to determine accurately the duration of
Du Bellay's residence at Rome. The data are (1) that he was absent *quatre ans
et d'avantage* (*Regrets*, no. clxvi.), (2) that he arrived in Rome either with the
Cardinal in June 1553, or at any rate soon afterwards, (3) that he was still in
Rome in August 1557, but left apparently about the end of that month (Chamard,
p. 281 n. 3; p. 386 n. 5). M. Séché has made this more precise by showing
that an entry in the Geneva archives refers to the arrival of the Cardinal in that
city on May 6, and that the poet was delayed by an attack of fever (*Rev. de la Ren.*
I. 161).

[2] See Chamard, p. 295, and J. Vianey in *Rev. d'hist. litt.* VIII. (1901) 151 ff.

the sonnets are good throughout, the rhythm especially being often defective. The following paraphrase of a well-known passage of Lucan in praise of Pompey is one of the best:

> Qui a veu quelquefois un grand chesne asseiché,
> Qui pour son ornement quelque trophée porte,
> Lever encor au ciel sa vieille teste morte
> Dont le pied fermement n'est en terre fiché,
>   Mais qui dessus le champ, plus qu'à demi penché
> Monstre ses bras tous nuds et sa racine torte,
> Et sans feuille ombrageux, de son poids se supporte
> Sur son tronc nouailleux en cent lieux esbranché ;
>   Et bien qu'au premier vent il doive sa ruine,
> Et maint jeune à l'entour ait ferme la racine,
> Du devot populaire estre seul reveré :
>   Qui tel chesne a peu voir, qu'il imagine encores,
> Comme entre les cités, qui plus fleurissent ores,
> Ce vieil honneur poudreux est le plus honoré[1].

There are also fine passages in some of the others, such as:

> Pales esprits, et vous ombres poudreuses,
> Qui jouissant de la clarté du jour
> Fistes sortir cest orgueilleux sejour,
> Dont nous voyons les reliques cendreuses[2].

The *Regrets* belong to the latter half of Du Bellay's residence at Rome and were written under the influence of Ariosto and Berni[3]. In the first sonnet he gives us the keynote of the whole work:

> Je ne veulx point fouiller au sein de la nature,
> Je ne veulx point chercher l'esprit de l'univers,
> Je ne veulx point sonder les abysmes couvers,
> Ny dessigner du ciel la belle architecture.
>   Je ne peins mes tableaux de si riche peinture,
> Et si haults arguments ne recherche à mes vers :
> Mais suivant de ce lieu les accidents divers,
> Soit de bien, soit de mal, j'escris à l'adventure.
>   Je me plains à mes vers, si j'ay quelque regret,
> Je me ris avec eulx, je leur dy mon secret,

---

[1] No. xxviii., from the *Pharsalia* i. 137–143; the lines immediately follow *Stat magni nominis umbra*.

[2] No. xv.

[3] See J. Vianey, *Régnier*, pp. 61–65.

Comme estans de mon cœur les plus seurs secrétaires.
Aussi ne veulx-je tant les pigner et friser,
Et de plus braves noms ne les veulx desguiser,
Que de papiers journaulx, ou bien de commentaires.

It is to be an intimate journal, a journal not so much of
his doings as of his feelings. And it is to be written simply
and naturally, without any attempt to vie with Petrarch or
other masters of style:

Je me contenterai du simplement escrire.

At first the prevailing note is one of melancholy, and it is
in this elegiac portion of the work that the famous sonnet
occurs which is perhaps the finest of all Du Bellay's poems:

Heureux qui comme Ulysse, a fait un beau voyage,
Ou comme cestuy là qui conquit la toison,
Et puis est retourné, plein d'usage et raison,
Vivre entre ses parents le reste de son aage!
    Quand revoiray-je, hélas, de mon petit village
Fumer la cheminée, et en quelle saison
Revoiray-je le clos de ma pauvre maison,
Qui m'est une province, et beaucoup d'avantage?
    Plus me plaist le séjour qu'ont basty mes ayeux,
Que des palais Romains le front audacieux,
Plus que le marbre dur me plaist l'ardoise fine:
    Plus mon Loyre Gaulois, que le Tybre Latin,
Plus mon petit Lyré, que le mont Palatin,
Et plus que l'air marin la doulceur Angevine[1].

Then at the fifty-third sonnet, *Vivons, Gordes, vivons,* the
note changes to one of gaiety, which however soon passes
into one of satire:

Il fait bon voir (Paschal) un conclave serré,
Et l'une chambre à l'autre également voisine
D'antichambre servir, de salle, et de cuisine,
En un petit recoing de dix pieds en carré:
    Il fait bon voir autour le palais emmuré,
Et briguer là dedans ceste troppe divine,
L'un par ambition, l'autre par bonne mine,
Et par despit de l'un, estre l'autre adoré:
    Il fait bon voir dehors toute la ville en armes,
Crier, le Pape est fait, donner de faulx alarmes,

[1] No. xxxi.

Saccager un palais : mais plus que tout cela
  Fait bon voir, qui de l'un, qui de l'autre se vante,
  Qui met pour cestui-cy, qui met pour cestui-là,
  Et pour moins d'un escu dix Cardinaux en vente[1].

Marcher d'un grave pas, et d'un grave sourci,
  Et d'un grave soubriz, à chacun faire feste,
  Balancer tous ses mots, respondre de la teste,
  Avec un Messer non, ou bien un Messer si :
    Entremesler souvent un petit, Et cosi,
  Et d'un son Servitor' contrefaire l'honneste,
  Et comme si lon eust sa part en la conqueste,
  Discourir sur Florence, et sur Naples aussi :
    Seigneuriser chacun d'un baisement de main,
  Et suivant la façon du courtisan Romain,
  Cacher sa pauvreté d'une brave apparence :
    Voilà de ceste Court la plus grande vertu,
  Dont souvent mal monté, mal sain, et mal vestu,
  Sans barbe et sans argent on s'en retourne en France[2].

Il fait bon voir, Magny, ces coyons magnifiques,
  Leur superbe arsenal, leurs vaisseaux, leur abord,
  Leur Saint-Marc, leur palais, leur réalte, leur port,
  Leurs changes, leurs profits, leur banque et leurs trafiques.
  Il fait bon voir le bec de leurs chapprons antiques,
  Leurs robbes à grand'manche, et leurs bonnets sans bord,
  Leur parler tout grossier, leur gravité, leur port,
  Et leurs sages advis aux affaires publiques.
  Il fait bon voir de tout leur senat ballotter ;
  Il fait bon voir par tout leurs gondoles flotter,
  Leurs femmes, leurs festins, leur vivre solitaire :
    Mais ce que l'on en doit le meilleur estimer,
  C'est quand ces vieux cocus vont espouser la mer
  Dont ils sont les maris et le Turc l'adultere[3].

Noteworthy too are the lines in which he contrasts the
Pope Paul IV with Charles V. The same contrast was made
by Brantôme and in modern times by Stirling-Maxwell and
Motley, but in far less pregnant phrase :

Mais quoy? que dirons-nous de cet autre viellard,
  Lequel ayant passé son aage plus gaillard
  Au service de Dieu, ores César imite?

[1] No. lxxxi.   [2] No. lxxxvi.
          [3] No. cxxxiii.

Je ne sçay qui des deux est le moins abusé :
Mais je pense (Morel) qu'il est fort mal aisé,
Que l'un soit bon guerrier, ny l'autre bon hermite[1].

The *Regrets* certainly contain Du Bellay's strongest and most original work. Moreover they mark a new departure in French literature. Du Bellay had profited by the study of Ariosto and Berni : from Ariosto he had learnt the value of a sincere record of personal feelings and impressions, while Berni had taught him to draw satirical vignettes of contemporary life. Both alike had served as models for the lucid and pointed language, the natural and easy style (a style which the majority of Frenchmen appreciate as much in verse as in prose), in adopting which he broke entirely from the traditions of the Pleiad. Yet it is only in the general character of his work that he was indebted to his Italian masters ; the ideas and sentiments are no longer borrowed[2], and the use of the sonnet for poetry of this character is entirely novel. The *Regrets* evidently made a considerable impression upon his contemporaries, several of whom paid him the compliment of imitation, amongst others Claude Turrin of Dijon, and Nicolas Ellain, a Paris physician.

In the autumn of 1557 Du Bellay returned to France and after occupying himself with the Cardinal's affairs found time to publish early in 1558 the fruits of his residence in Rome. These included besides the *Antiquités* and the *Regrets*, to the latter of which he added fifty fresh sonnets, a volume of Latin poems[3], and a volume entitled *Divers jeux rustiques et autres œuvres poétiques*. The greater part of the Latin poems were inspired by a Roman lady whom he calls

---

[1] No. cxi. This is part of one of eight sonnets which were printed in only a few copies of the *Regrets*. The *Bib. Nat.* possesses the only one of these copies that is known to exist. The sonnets are printed in the editions of Marty-Laveaux and of Lizeux (II. 526 ff.), and by L. Séché in his *J. du Bellay*.

[2] The only exception seems to be no. xci., which is translated from Berni's well-known sonnet *Chiome d' argento fine* (Chamard, p. 376 n. 1).

[3] *I. Bellaii Poematum libri quatuor*. The privilege for the *Regrets* and the *Jeux Rustiques* is dated Jan. 17, 155⅞, that for the *Antiquités* and the Latin poems March 3 of the same year. Some of the Latin poems are printed in Gruter's *Deliciae Poetarum Gallorum*, I. 390–487.

Faustine. They shew how thoroughly Du Bellay had steeped
himself in Latin poetry, and how closely he could tread in the
footsteps of the most passionate and the most poetical of
Latin poets, Catullus[1]. The title *Jeux rustiques*, by which the
remaining Roman volume is generally known, belongs strictly
to twelve little poems translated or imitated from the *Lusus*
of Navagero. One of these is the well-known *D'un vanneur
de blé*, perhaps the best-known of all Du Bellay's poems:

> A vous troppe légère,
> Qui d'aile passagère
> Par le monde volez,
> Et d'un sifflant murmure
> L'ombrageuse verdure
> Doulcement esbranlez,
> J'offre ces violettes,
> Ces lis, et ces fleurettes,
> Et ces roses icy,
> Ces vermeillettes roses,
> Tout freschement écloses,
> Et ces œilletz aussi.
> De vostre doulce halaine
> Éventez ceste plaine,
> Éventez ce séjour :
> Ce pendant que j'ahanne
> A mon blé, que je vanne
> A la chaleur du jour[2].

Hardly less distinctive in its marvellous lightness of touch
is the following little poem to Venus :

> Ayant après long désir
> Pris de ma doulce ennemie
> Quelques arres du plaisir
> Que sa rigueur me dénie,
> Je t'offre ces beaux œillets,
> Vénus, je t'offre ces roses,
> Dont les boutons vermeillets,
> Imitent les lèvres closes,

---

[1] It may be said of Du Bellay as De Sanctis says of Ariosto, *I suoi amori in
italiano sono platonici, alla petrarchesca, in latino sono sensuali, all' oraziana*
(*Storia della letteratura italiana*, II. 3).

[2] Ed. Liseux, p. 12 ; translated by A. Lang, *op. cit.* p. 18.

Que j'ay baisé par trois fois,
Marchant tout beau dessoubs l'ombre
De ce buisson, que tu vois :
Et n'ay sceu passer ce nombre,
Pour ce que la mère estoit
Auprès de là, ce me semble,
Laquelle nous aguettoit :
De peur encores j'en tremble.
Or' je te donne des fleurs :
Mais si tu fais ma rebelle
Autant piteuse à mes pleurs,
Comme à mes yeux elle est belle,
Un Myrte je dédieray
Dessus les rives de Loyre,
Et sur l'écorse escriray
Ces quatre vers à ta gloire :
Thenot sur ce bord icy,
A Vénus sacre et ordonne
Ce myrte, et luy donne aussi
Ses troppeaux, et sa personne[1].

Imitations though these poems are, Du Bellay has contrived to invest them with originality. They are marked by that air of delicate distinction which is to be found in many productions of French genius, especially in Watteau's pictures.

But these rustic gems form only a small proportion of the whole volume. Many of the poems are of a satirical character, such as the *Épitaphe de l'abbé Bonnet*[2], part of which is evidently inspired by Marot's *ballade* of Frère Lubin, the *Hymne de la surdité*[3] addressed to Ronsard, in which Du Bellay humorously points out the many compensating advantages of the affliction from which he and his brother poet suffered, and especially the poem entitled *Contre les Pétrarquistes*[4]. In a poem addressed to Olivier de Magny, which immediately precedes[5] this, he had boasted of being the first to write Petrarchian sonnets in France :

Si est-ce pourtant que je puis
Me vanter qu'en France je suis

[1] *ib.* p. 19.   [2] *ib.* p. 97.   [3] *ib.* pp. 156 ff.
     [4] *ib.* pp. 61 ff.   [5] *ib.* pp. 50 ff.

Des premiers qui ont ozé dire
Leurs amours sur la Thusque lyre.
Et mon Olive (soit ce nom
D'Olive véritable, ou non)
Se peult vanter d'avoir première
Salué la douce lumière.

But now having learnt, as he says, to look at things in
their true light, he holds up to ridicule the worn-out machinery
of the Petrarchian sonnet, the roses and lilies, the corals and
pearls, the gold and ivory of the fair one's charms, the fountains of her lover's tears, the Etna of his heart, the frosty
Caucasus of hers; and he even scoffs at the whole doctrine
of spiritual love.

Nos bons Ayeulx, qui cest art démenoient,
Pour en parler, Pétrarque n'apprenoient,
Ains franchement leur Dame entretenoient
    Sans fard, ou couverture :
Mais aussi tost qu'Amour s'est faict sçavant,
Luy, qui estoit François au paravant,
Est devenu flatteur, et décevant,
    Et de Thusque nature[1].

Si toutefois Pétrarque vous plaist mieux,
Je reprendray mon chant mélodieux,
Et voleray jusqu'au séjour des Dieux
    D'une aile mieux guidée :
Là dans le sein de leurs divinitez
Je choisiray cent mille nouveautez,
Dont je peindray voz plus grandes beautez
    Sur la plus belle Idée[2].

But Du Bellay's chief satirical poem is *Le poëte courtisan,*
first published under a pseudonym at Poitiers in 1559[3].
It is, as Sainte-Beuve says, one of the first regular or
classical satires in the French language, preceding by a year
Ronsard's *Discours à Guillaume des Autels,* which after all
is only satirical in parts.   Du Bellay, as we have already
seen from the *Regrets,* has more capacity for pure satire than
Ronsard; he wields a rapier instead of a broad-sword, and

---

[1] *ib.* p. 66.   [2] *ib.* p. 68.

[3] *La nouvelle maniere de faire son profit des lettres traduitte de Latin en
François par* I. Quintil du Trounsay en Poictou.   *Ensemble le Poete Courtisan.*
Reproduced by E. Fournier in *Variétés hist. et litt.* x. pp. 131 ff.   See *Œuvres,* II.

keeping cooler gets his weapon more often home. No name
is mentioned in *Le poëte courtisan*, but it is manifestly aimed
at Saint-Gelais as the champion of the old school of poetry[1]:

> Car un petit sonnet qui n'a rien que le son,
> Un dizain à propos, ou bien une chanson,
> Un rondeau bien troussé, avec une ballade
> (Du temps qu'elle couroit), vaut mieux qu'une Iliade......
> Or si les grands seigneurs tu veux gratifier,
> Argumens à propos il te faut espier :
> Comme quelque victoire ou quelque ville prise,
> Quelque nopce et festin, ou bien quelque entreprise
> De masque ou de tournoy : avoir force desseins
> Desquels à ceste fin tes coffres seront pleins.

And later on there is a more palpable hit :

> Et, à la verité, la ruse coustumiere,
> Et la meilleure, c'est rien ne mettre en lumiere :
> Ains, jugeant librement des œuvres d'un chacun,
> Non se rendre sujét au jugement d'aucun,
> De peur que quelque fol te rende la pareille,
> S'il gaigne comme toy des grands princes l'oreille.

A poet's satire is perhaps more often prompted by envy
than by righteous indignation. This was certainly the case
with Du Bellay. The publication of the *Regrets* had greatly
incensed his patron the Cardinal, and made it difficult for
him to get preferment. It is true that hè already held
benefices, including a priory near Bordeaux, to the value of
3000 *livres*[2]; but this did not satisfy him, for it was apparently
his ambition at this time to abandon the Muses for a public
career. With this object in view he made every important
event an occasion for an appropriate poem. The capture of
Calais, the peace of Cateau-Cambresis, the impending marriage
of the King's sister with the Duke of Savoy, that source of
so many poems, were all celebrated by him in courtly verse.

---

[1] When Saint-Gelais died in October 1558, Du Bellay, who had addressed to
him during his lifetime several flattering poems, paid him further homage in a
sheaf of Latin verses. This new attack, which cannot, I am afraïd, be reconciled
with modern principles of honour, must probably, as M. Chamard suggests, be
regarded as a fresh protest of the new poetic school against the old. He conjectures that it was written after the death of Henry II with a view to securing the
favour of the new King and his advisers (*op. cit.* pp. 422 ff.).

[2] He was a canon of Notre-Dame from June 1555 to June 1556.

But the King's untimely death and the departure of Margaret, *le seul appuy et colonne de toute son esperance,* for Savoy left Du Bellay with little hope of realising his ambitions[1]. He was also much embittered by disputes with his first cousin, Eustache du Bellay, the bishop of Paris, for the Cardinal still retained the patronage of the see and had appointed Joachim his vicar-general. Add to this that the deafness from which he had suffered since 1552 was becoming increasingly troublesome. His melancholy found expression in the following touching sonnet addressed to Jacques Grévin :

> Comme celuy qui a de la course poudreuse
> Ou de la luyte huylée, ou du disque eslancé,
> Ou du ceste plombé de cuir entrelacé,
> Rapporté mainte palme en sa jeunesse heureuse,
> Regarde, en regrettant sa force vigoureuse,
> Les jeunes s'exercer, et jà vieil et cassé,
> Par un doux souvenir qu'il ha du temps passé,
> Resveille dans son cœur sa vertu genereuse :
> Ainsi voyant, Grévin, prochain de ma vieillesse
> Au pied de ton Olimpe exercer ta jeunesse,
> Je souspire le temps que d'un pareil esmoy
> Je chantay mon Olive, et resens en mon ame
> Je ne sçay quelle ardeur de ma premiere flâme
> Qui me fait souhaiter d'estre tel comme toy[2].

It was his swan-note, for before Grévin's volume, for which it was written, appeared Du Bellay was dead. On the evening of the first day of the year 1560 he was seized with an apoplectic fit, of which his deafness had been doubtless a symptom, and by midnight he was dead. His patron the Cardinal, with whom he had made his peace, survived him only two months.

Charming and sympathetic as is Pater's well-known study of Du Bellay, it hardly does him justice, especially on the side of his poetry[3]. He is considerably more than the poet

---

[1] See a pathetic letter written to his friend Jean de Morel in October 1559, first published at the end of the *Tumulus Henrici Secundi*, 1560. It is printed by Becq de Fouquières in his *Œuvres choisies*, p. 321.

[2] Printed at the head of Grévin's *Olimpe*, 1560.

[3] W. H. Pater, *Studies in the history of the Renaissance.*

of one poem (*D'un vanneur de blé*), and he has an interest
beyond the fact that he is a typical product of the Renaissance.
His tendency to melancholy, his oscillation between the joy
of living and the sense of the vanity of all things, his intense
humanistic sympathies, are true Renaissance characteristics,
but besides these he has a marked individuality of his own.
Almost alone of the poets of his school he had that quality
which the French call *esprit*, but which it is impossible to
render in English by a single word. It was this quality
which led him to follow in the footsteps of Ariosto and
Berni, to write about himself without being tedious or impertinent, to satirize his own imperfections as well as those
of his neighbours, to be natural in an artificial school. It
was this same quality, this mixture of good sense and
intelligence, which led him to take up an attitude of
partial detachment from his school, an attitude which somewhat resembles that of Alfred de Musset to the Romantic
school[1].

Indeed in more ways than one he recalls Alfred de Musset.
His sensibility like Musset's was stronger than his imagination.
His highly impressionable nature was easily moved by the
nearest influence, but his enthusiasm cooled as quickly as
it was aroused. He had not the strong imagination which
masters impressions instead of being mastered by them. He
was deficient in concentration and will-power, without which
this highest form of imagination is impossible. To the same
deficiency may be traced a certain weakness in his execution.
With a natural gift for expression[2] he lacked the true artist's
patient devotion to form. Though his later verse at any
rate is generally harmonious and the *Vanneur de blé* is a gem
of bewitching natural music, he never attained to Ronsard's
consummate mastery of sound and rhythm. Thus his work
by the side of his rival's has a somewhat amateurish air.
Like all his contemporaries, even beyond them, he has a
tendency to be diffuse. Inspiration came to him fitfully, but

---

[1] I find that the same idea has occurred to M. Lenient, *La poésie patriotique
en France dans les temps modernes*, I. 129.

[2] His brother poets applied both to him and Ovid the epithet of *doux-coulant*.

when once started he did not know when to stop. Enforced restraint was therefore good for him[1]; it is in his sonnets and his translations that we find his most perfect work. Yet in spite of these defects his grace, his melancholy, his delicate distinction are abiding charms, while his sincere rendering of his personal emotions makes him peculiarly attractive to the modern reader.

BIBLIOGRAPHY.

EDITIONS.

PIERRE DE RONSARD, *Les quatre premiers livres des Odes. Ensemble son Bocage*, 1550 (*Bib. Nat.* ; see Le Petit, p. 78 ; Picot, I. no. 671). *Les Amours, Ensemble le cinquiesme des Odes*, 1552. *Livret de Folastries*, 1553. *Les Amours...nouvellement augmentées par lui plus quelques Odes*, 1553 (Brit. Mus. ; *Bib. Nat.*). *Le cinquiesme des Odes, augmenté. Ensemble la Harangue que fit monseigneur le duc de Guise*, 1553 (*Bib. Nat.*). *Le Bocage*, 1554 (*Bib. Nat.*). *Les Meslanges*, 1555 (*Bib. Nat.*). *Continuation des Amours (Amours de Marie)*, 1555. *Les Hymnes*, 1555 (a copy in the library of Trinity College, Cambridge ; see Picot, I. no. 672). *Le second livre des Hymnes*, 1556. *Discours des misères de ce temps*, 1562. *Abrégé de l'art poétique françois*, 1565. *Elegies, Mascarades et Bergerie*, 1565. *Le Sixième et le Septième livre des Poèmes*, 1569. *Les quatre premiers livre[s] de la Franciade*, 1572. *Les Œuvres*, 4 vols. 1560 (I. *Amours*, II. *Odes*, III. *Poesmes*, IV. *Hymnes*) ; 6 vols. 1567--I–IV. as before, V. *Élégies*, VI. *Discours* (*Bib. de l'Arsenal* ; see Le Petit, p. 80 ; Picot, I. no. 667) ; 5 vols. 1578 (V. contains the *Franciade* ; this, the fifth corrected edition, contains 236 new poems ; it is very rare, and I have not seen a copy of it) ; 1 vol. fo. 1584 ; 5 vols. 1587 (the printing was finished Dec. 24, 1586) ; 1 vol. fo. 1609 (containing the poems which Ronsard had struck out of the preceding editions) ; 5 vols. 1617 (more complete than the preceding) ; 2 vols. fo. 1623, entirely revised by Claude Garnier (*Bib. de l'Arsenal*)[2] ; ed. P. Blanchemain in the *Bib. Elzévirienne*, 8 vols. 1857—1867 (based as far as possible on the

---

[1] Compare for instance the *Complainte du désespéré* with the sonnet to Grévin.

[2] Only the most important separate publications and collected editions are mentioned.

text of 1560) ; ed. Ch. Marty-Laveaux in *La Pléiade française*, 6 vols. 1887—1893 (based for vols. I–V. on the text of 1584 ; out of print and scarce). Neither of these editions indicates the date of publication of each piece, nor the changes introduced into the text by the author. It is therefore impossible to follow in them the growth of Ronsard's poetical developement. Meanwhile the materials for a really critical edition have been published by M. Paul Laumonier, as the result of long and patient research. See *Chronologie et variantes des poésies de P. de Ronsart* in *Rev. d'hist. litt.* IX. (1902) 29 ff., and X. (1903) 63 ff., 256 ff. (to be continued) ; *Tableau chronologique des œuvres de Ronsard* in *Annales fléchoises*, July, Aug. and Nov. 1903 ; *Rev. de la Ren.* II. 1902 ; *Rev. Universitaire* for Feb. 15, 1903. M. Laumonier has also discovered some unpublished matter ; see *Rev. d'hist. litt.* IX. (1902) 441 ff. and *Deux cent vingt vers inédits de Ronsard* in *Rev. de la Ren.* IV. 201 ff. A. Noël, *Choix de poésies*, 2 vols. 1862 ; *Poésies choisies*, ed. L. Becq de Fouquières, 1875 (the text is an arbitrary one).

JOACHIM DU BELLAY, *La Deffence et illustration de la langue Francoyse*, 1549. *Olive et quelques autres œuvres poëtiques*, 1549. *Recueil de Poësie*, 1549. *Le Quatriesme livre de l'Eneide...autres œuvres*, 155½. *Les Regrets*, 1558. *Divers Jeux rustiques et autres œuvres poëtiques*, 1558. *Le premier livre des Antiquites de Rome*, 1558. *Le poète courtisan*, 1559. Separate editions of the *Regrets* and the *Jeux rustiques* were published by Liseux in 1876 ; the best modern edition of the *Deffence* is that of E. Person, 2nd ed. 1892, but a new critical edition by H. Chamard will shortly be published. *Les œuvres françoises*, 2 vols. 1569 (a collected edition prepared by his friend Guillaume Aubert) ; ed. Ch. Marty-Laveaux in *La Pléiade française*, 2 vols. 1866–67 (based on the preceding). A new edition of his works, with an introduction and notes, is being prepared by L. Séché, and vol. I. containing *Olive* has appeared (1902). *Œuvres choisies*, ed. L. Becq de Fouquières, 1876 ; ed. L. Séché, 4to. 1894.

LIVES.

RONSARD—*Œuvres*, ed. Marty-Laveaux, VI. 1—cviii. This must be supplemented for the earlier part of it by P. Laumonier, *La Jeunesse de Pierre de Ronsart* in *Rev. de la Renaissance*, I. (1901), 96 ff. ; 169 ff ; II. (1902), 42 ff. ; 94 ff. ; 149 ff. ; 281 ff. See also A. de Rochambeau, *La famille de Ronsart (Bib. Elzévir.)*, 1868 ; P. Laumonier, *La Genèse du nom de Ronsard* in *Annales fléchoises*, May 1903.

DU BELLAY—*Œuvres*, ed. Marty-Laveaux, I. ix—xxxi ; H. Chamard, *Joachim du Bellay*, Lille, 1900 ; L. Séché, *J. du Bellay, Documents nouveaux et inédits*, 1880, and *Rev. de la Ren.* I. 56 ff. ; 74 ff. ; 128 ff. (life down to his arrival at Rome). M. Séché is preparing a complete life. See also P. de Nolhac, *Lettres de J. du Bellay*, 1883.

TO BE CONSULTED.

Estienne Pasquier, *Recherches de la France*, VIII. cc. 6—11 (of great importance for the history of the Pleiad). P. Bayle, *Dictionnaire, s.v.* Daurat and Ronsard. C.-A. Sainte-Beuve, *Tableau de la poésie française*, 1828. H. F. Cary, *Early French Poets*, 1846. E. Egger, *L'Hellénisme en France*, I. 230—410, 1869. E. Faguet, *Seizième siècle*, 1894. Ch. Lenient, *La poésie patriotique en France dans les temps modernes*, I. 117 ff., 1894. A. Rosenbauer, *Die poetischen Theorien der Plejade nach Ronsard und Dubellay*, Erlangen and Leipsic, 1895. Ch. Marty-Laveaux, *La langue de la Pléiade*, 2 vols. 1896-98. J. E. Spingarn, *A history of literary criticism in the Renaissance*, New York, 1899. F. Brunetière, *La Pléiade française* in *Rev. des deux mondes*, Dec. 15, 1900, Jan. 1 and Feb. 1, 1901. G. Saintsbury, *A history of criticism and literary taste in Europe*, II. 112—126, 1902.

C.-A. Sainte-Beuve, *Causeries du Lundi*, XII. 1855 (Ronsard). E. Gandar, *Ronsard considéré comme imitateur de Homère et de Pindare*, Metz, 1854. G. Chalandon, *Essai sur la vie et les œuvres de P. de Ronsard*, 1875. P. de Nolhac, *Le dernier amour de Ronsard*, 1880. Th. de Banville, *Petit traité de poésie française*, pp. 274 ff., 1881. L. Froger (L'abbé), *Les premières poésies de Ronsard*, Mamers, 1892. M. Piéri, *Pétrarque et Ronsard*, Marseilles, 1895. L. Mellerio, *Lexique de Ronsard, précédé d'une étude sur son vocabulaire, son orthographe et sa syntaxe* (*Bib. Elzévir.*), 1895. G. Bizos, *Ronsard* (*Classiques populaires*), 1897. P. Perdrizet, *Ronsard et la Réforme*, 1902. E. Stemplinger, *Ronsard und der Lyriker Horaz* in *Zeitschr. für franz. Spr.* XXVI. 70 ff., 1903.

C.-A. Sainte-Beuve, *Nouveaux Lundis*, XIII. 1867 (three articles on Du Bellay, of which only the last is important). E. Turquety, *Étude sur J. du Bellay* in *Bull. du Bib.* for 1864, 1125 ff. W. H. Pater, *Studies in the history of the Renaissance*, 1873 (*Works*, I. 155 ff.). G. Plötz, *Étude sur J. du Bellay*, Berlin, 1874.

For EU product safety concerns, contact us at Calle de José Abascal, 56–1°,
28003 Madrid, Spain or eugpsr@cambridge.org.

www.ingramcontent.com/pod-product-compliance
Ingram Content Group UK Ltd.
Pitfield, Milton Keynes, MK11 3LW, UK
UKHW010351140625
459647UK00010B/998